𝔚eb 𝔇evelopment

𝒥n

PHP, MySQL, JavaScript, HTML & CSS

Step-by-Step Web Project

RIAZ AHMED

Web Development in PHP, MySQL, JavaScript, HTML & CSS

Dedication

I dedicate this book to the two greatest personalities in my life - my parents - who taught me two brilliant arts: reading and writing.

CONTENTS

Preface

During my programming career, I developed many desktop applications all with the help of a single tool. With the advent of World Wide Web, I also dared to get my feet wet. But, to develop my first web application I had to put on many hats like HTML, CSS, Client and Server-side scripting languages and databases; scattered under individual titles. Just like my previous books, this one too shares my experience with the world and teaches the above mentioned technologies under one umbrella. This book is neither a comprehensive guide nor it can be treated as a manual on any of these comprehensive topics, but, it surely lays a solid foundation that helps building both static and dynamic websites.

With uncountable sites and freely available material, I wrote this book due to the following reasons:

- Assemble all scattered pieces in one place. This volume contains HTML/5, CSS/3, JavaScript, PHP and MySQL. Sequential instructions are provided to download and install all the required software and components to setup a complete development environment on your own pc.
- Focus on inspiring practical aspect of these web technologies.
- Last, but the most significant one - take the audience gradually right from creating an HTML file with a text editor, through learning HTML, CSS, JavaScript, PHP and MySQL all the way to creating a professional website.

It covers:
- Definitions and exercises of various HTML/5, CSS/3, JavaScript, PHP & MySQL components.
- The last part is the essence of this book where you will create a website for ABC Global Consulting - a fictitious company. In this part, you will apply almost all the techniques you went through in the book. The website project is divided into two parts: static and dynamic. In the static part, you'll create web pages that remain unchanged and deliver static content whenever they are accessed. In contrast, the dynamic part will teach you how to create pages that access fresh content from a database. This part comprises an E-Commerce module that allows visitors to purchase products online, a Newsletter subscription module to subscribe to company's newsletters, and Contact Form module which will be provided to interact with site visitors. The E-commerce application development is divided into two major parts: Admin and Member interfaces. In the Admin part you will undergo five tasks: Admin Login module, Manage Categories, Manage Products, Manager Orders, and Manage Admin Accounts. The Member part comprises eight tasks: Member Login module, Register New Member, Reset Password, My Account, Featured Products Catalog, Individual Product Details, Shopping Cart, and Checkout (confirm order). After accomplishing all the above tasks, you'll be guided on how to deploy the project on a host server.

From web introduction to hands-on examples and from website designing to its deployment, this book surely is a complete resource for those who know little or nothing about professional web development.

Download Book Code ➜ http://www.creating-website.com/TheWebBookCode.rar
URL ➜ http://www.creating-website.com

- Riaz Ahmed, Author
realtech@cyber.net.pk

CHAPTER 1

THE WORLD WIDE WEB

AN INTRODUCTION

▾

I am a great believer in luck, and I find that the harder I work, the more I have of it.

1.1   The Internet and the World Wide Web

The Internet is playing a vital role in our lives and has become a mainstay in personal, work and education fields. It can be defined as a global system of interconnected computer networks that serve billions of users worldwide. It consists of millions of public, private, business, academic, and government networks that are linked by a wide range of electronic, wireless, and optical network technologies. It provides a huge information resource such as the inter-linked hypertext documents of the World Wide Web (WWW) and renders infrastructure support service for electronic mails (E-mails). It enables you to read the latest news, to do research, to shop, to communicate, to listen to music, to play games, and to access a wide variety of information. It has provided new means of human interactions through messaging, forums, and social networking and has boomed businesses through online shopping.

1.1.1 Is Web & Internet the same?	1.1.2 What is Internet Backbone?
No. The two are not synonymous. The Internet connects millions of computers together globally to form a massive network in which these computers can communicate with each other. The World Wide Web, on the other hand, is a system of interlinked hypertext documents accessed via the Internet. It is an information-sharing model that is built on top of the Internet.	A collection of fiber-optic cables and telephone lines spread all over the world form the Internet's backbone. Data travels at the speed of light along this backbone enabling you to access data within seconds from any part of the world.

1.1.3 Who is Internet Service Provider?

The Internet cannot be accessed directly. Instead, you have to rent a connection from an Internet Service Provider (ISP). An ISP is a company that has direct access to the Internet backbone. You're provided with a modem or wireless router that you use to connect to your ISP, which then connects you to the Internet.

1.1.4 Types of Internet Connections

Dial-up Connection: In the past, the most widely used connection to access the Internet was through dial-up modems. These connections provide a speed of 28.8 kilobits per second and do not exceed a speed of 56 kbit/s downstream (towards the end user) and 34 or 48 kbit/s upstream (toward the global Internet). Although inexpensive, it is the slowest connection and people are, therefore, switching over to other available options.

Broadband Connection: This technology uses wires or fiber optic cables. Slightly more expensive than dial-up, broadband connections are extremely fast. They provide connection speed of 1 to several megabits per second. ISPs provide a high-speed modem to their subscribers to connect to the Internet. It commonly uses digital subscriber line (DSL) telephone service for the connection which uses existing 2-wire copper telephone line connected to the premise so service is delivered simultaneously with wired telephone service (it doesn't tie up your phone line as an analog dial-up connection does). The two main categories of DSL are called ADSL and SDSL. The data throughput of consumer DSL services typically ranges from 256 kbit/s to 20 Mbit/s in the direction to the customer (downstream), depending on DSL technology, line conditions, and service-level implementation. VDSL or VHDSL (very-high-bit-rate digital subscriber line) is a DSL standard that provides data rates up to 52 Mbit/s downstream and 16 Mbit/s upstream over copper wires and up to 85 Mbit/s down and upstream on coaxial cable. VDSL2 is an enhanced second-generation version of VDSL. It is able to provide data rates exceeding 100 Mbit/s simultaneously in both the upstream and downstream directions. Cable broadband internet is another connection that is designed to operate over cable TV lines. Because the coaxial cable used by cable TV provides much greater bandwidth than telephone lines, a cable connection can be used to achieve extremely fast access.

Wireless broadband: Wireless Internet or wireless broadband is one of the newest Internet connection types that provide high-speed wireless Internet access or computer networking access. Instead of using telephone or cable networks for Internet connection, it uses radio frequency bands. Wireless Internet can be accessed from anywhere — as long as you're within a geographically network coverage area. It includes Wi-Fi, WiMAX, Satellite broadband, and Mobile broadband.

1.1.5 Security Consideration	1.1.6 The World Wide Web
After connecting to the Internet, it is very much possible that your computer gets infected through viruses or other malicious attacks. You must draw your first line of defense before connecting to the Internet by setting Windows Firewall. Turn this option on to prevent intruders from accessing your computer over the Internet.	The World Wide Web, or simply the Web, is a massive storehouse of information that resides on computers, called Web servers, located all over the world.

1.1.7 What a Web Page is?

The web provides information on almost every imaginable topic through billions of web pages. A webpage is a document, typically written in plain text with formatting instructions of Hypertext Markup Language (HTML, XHTML). Web pages are accessed and transported with the Hypertext Transfer Protocol (HTTP), which may optionally employ encryption (HTTPS - HTTP Secure) to provide security and privacy for the user of the webpage content. The pages of a website can usually be accessed from a simple Uniform Resource Locator (URL) called the web address. When you seek some information, it is returned by a web server - that holds that information - to your computer using a web browser, such as Firefox or Internet Explorer. A web page can carry text, images, sounds, and videos on any subject.

1.1.8 What is a Website?

A website is a set of related web pages associated with a particular person, business, government, school, or organization containing content such as text, images, video, audio, etc. A website is hosted on at least one web server, accessible via a network such as the Internet or a private local area network through an Internet address known as a Uniform Resource Locator (URL).

1.1.9 What is a Web Server?

Web server can either be the hardware (the powerful computer capable of handling thousands of site visitors at a time) or the software (the computer application) that delivers Web content through the Internet. It is the primary function of web servers to deliver HTML documents and other content such as images, style sheets and scripts in shape of web pages to the requesting clients. Besides entertaining client requests, web servers also receive content from them through web forms and uploaded files. A large website is often run by hundreds of servers which is referred to as server farms in web terminology.

1.1.10 What is a Web Browser?

A web browser can be defined as an application software designed to enable users to access, retrieve and view documents and other resources on the Internet or a program designed to download and display web pages. The primary purpose of a web browser is to bring information resources to the users, allow them to view the information, and then access other information through navigational links.

Although browsers are primarily intended to use the World Wide Web, they can also be used to access information provided by web servers in private networks or files in file systems. The major web browsers are Chrome, Firefox, Internet Explorer, Opera, and Safari.

All major web browsers allow the user to open multiple information resources at the same time, either in different browser windows or in different tabs of the same window. Major browsers also include pop-up blockers to prevent unwanted windows from "popping up" without the user's consent. Most web browsers can display a list of web pages that the user has bookmarked (called "Favorites" in Internet Explorer) so that the user can quickly return to them.

1.1.11 What are Hyperlinks?

In computing, a hyperlink (or link) is a cross-reference to data that the reader can directly follow, or that is followed automatically. It takes visitors to another page on the same site or to a page on another Web site. A hyperlink points to a whole document or to a specific element within a document. A web browser usually displays a hyperlink in some distinguishing way, e.g. in a different color, font or style. The behavior and style of links can be specified using the Cascading Style Sheets (CSS) language. A link can also appear as an image. When you click a link the page loads in a new browser window or in a new tab in the existing window.

1.1.12 What is a Web Address or URL?

Every site and page on the web is identified by its own unique address which is also called Uniform Resource Locator (URL). Visitors usually access a website by clicking a link found on another site. They can also access a site or a page within a site by typing its URL in the address bar of their web browsers. The URL of a website carries four pieces of information: 1-the transfer protocol (http or https), 2-the domain name, 3-directory and 4-filename:

Each domain name ends with a suffix that defines the type of organization. For example, any commercial enterprise or corporation that has a Web site will have a domain suffix of .com, which means it is a commercial entity. The domain suffix provides you with a clue about the purpose or audience of a website. The domain suffix might also give you a clue about the geographic origin of a website. Many sites from the United Kingdom will have a domain suffix of .uk. Here follows a list of the most common domain suffixes and the types of organizations that would use them.

Domain suffixes		Country domain suffixes	
.com	Commercial site	.au	Australia
.edu	Educational institution	.ca	Canada
.gov	Government	.fr	France
.org	Non-profit organization	.it	Italy
.mil	Military	.mx	Mexico
.net	Network	.uk	United Kingdom

1.1.13 What is a Search Engine?

You can use free search engines on the web to find information on a specific subject. A search engine is a web-based tool that helps you locate information on the World Wide Web. Google, bing, and Yahoo! Search are the top ranking search engines. Search engines utilize automated software applications (referred to as robots, bots, or spiders) that travel along the Web, following links from page to page, site to site. The information gathered by the spiders is used to create a searchable index of the Web. You can either go to these search engine sites to find the required information or you can use search feature provided with your browser.

1.1.14 How do Search Engines work?

Every search engine uses different complex mathematical formulas to generate search results. The results for a specific query are then displayed on the search engine results page (SERP). Search engine algorithms take the key elements of a web page, including the page title, content and keyword density, and come up with a ranking for where to place the results on the pages. Each search engine's algorithm is unique, so a top ranking on Yahoo! does not guarantee a prominent ranking on Google, and vice versa. To make things more complicated, the algorithms used by search engines are not only closely guarded secrets, they are also constantly undergoing modification and revision. This means that the criteria to best optimize a site with must be surmised through observation, as well as trial and error — and not just once, but continuously.

Search engines only "see" the text on web pages, and use the underlying HTML structure to determine relevance. Large photos, or dynamic Flash animation mean nothing to search engines, but the actual text on your pages does. It is difficult to build a Flash site that is as friendly to search engines; as a result, Flash sites will tend not to rank as high as sites developed with well coded HTML and CSS (Cascading Style Sheets — a complex mechanism for adding styles to website pages above and beyond regular HTML). It will be very difficult for your website to yield high placement in the SERPs if the terms you want to be found but do not appear in the text of your website.

1.1.15 What are Web Logs or Blogs?

A Web log, or blog, is a discussion or informational site published on the World Wide Web consisting of frequently updated, reverse-chronological entries (the most recent post appears first) on a particular topic. Many blogs provide commentary on a particular subject; some function as more personal online diaries; others function more as online brand advertising of a particular individual or company. A typical blog combines text, images, and links to other blogs, Web pages, and other media related to its topic. The ability of readers to leave comments in an interactive format is an important contribution to the popularity of many blogs. Most blogs are primarily textual, although some focus on art (art blogs), photographs (photoblogs), videos (video blogs or "vlogs"), music (MP3 blogs), and audio (podcasts). Microblogging (such as twitter) is another type of blogging, featuring very short posts. In education, blogs can be used as instructional resources. These blogs are referred to as edublogs.

1.1.16 What is a Web Portal?

A web portal is a web site that gathers information from hundreds or even thousands of online sources in a uniform way. Usually, each information source gets its dedicated area on the page for displaying information (a portlet); often, the user can configure which ones to display. Apart from the standard search engines feature, web portals offer other services such as e-mail, news, stock prices, information, databases and entertainment. Examples of public web portals are AOL, Excite, iGoogle, MSN, Naver, India.com and Yahoo!

1.1.17 What is Web Syndication?

Rather than surfing the web from one site to another to get the desired information, you can have the information set to you. Web syndication is a form of syndication in which website material is made available to multiple other sites. Most commonly, web syndication refers to making web feeds available from a site in order to provide other people with a summary or update of the website's recently added content (for example, the latest news or forum posts). Today, many sites use syndication by enabling an aggregator (Real Simple Syndication - RSS) to show the syndicated content. Latest versions of Firefox, IE, and Safari have built in aggregators.

1.1.18 What is E-Commerce?

Electronic Commerce, often referred to as simply ecommerce (or e-commerce), is a phrase used to describe business that is conducted over the Internet using any of the applications that rely on the Internet, such as e-mail, instant messaging, shopping carts, Web services, UDDI, FTP, and EDI, among others. Electronic commerce can be between two businesses transmitting funds, goods, services and/or data or between a business and a customer. It is the buying and selling of product or service over electronic systems such as the Internet and other computer networks and draws on such technologies as mobile commerce, electronic funds transfer, supply chain management, Internet marketing, online transaction processing, electronic data interchange (EDI), inventory management systems, and automated data collection systems. You can use Web-based stores to purchase books, theater tickets, and even cars. You can also create your own virtual store at http://smallbusiness.yahoo.com. There are also many sites that enable you to sell or auction your products or household items. Sites like eBay (www.ebay.com) allow you to put your products online for auction.

Thousands of Web sites are devoted to online shopping. Some focus on one product or service, while others, such as Amazon.com offer a wide range of goods. When you shop at an e-commerce site, you usually add the items that you want to purchase to a virtual shopping cart — also called a shopping basket — that keeps track of these items and the quantity. Most sites have a View Cart link that enables you to view the contents of your shopping cart. The cart usually has a Proceed to Checkout link that leads you to a page where you provide your address and payment information. Payments on the web are usually made by credit cards. You are required to provide the credit card number, cvv number and expiry date. To ensure the security of this sensitive data, you must provide this information only on secured sites which are prefixed with https rather than http.

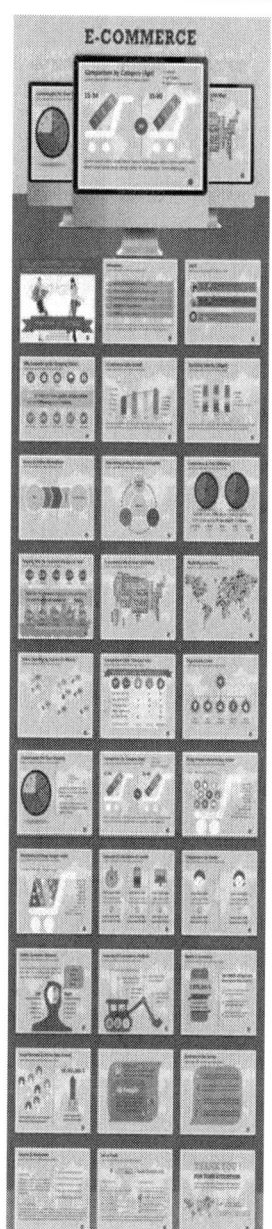

1.2 Launching a Website

The initial step in this process is to create web pages that constitute a website. To do so, you need a simple text editor such as Notepad or some special web page designing software such as Microsoft Expression Web or Adobe Dreamweaver. After creating your site, the next step is to acquire a domain name (www.abcglobal.com) and setup an account with a web-hosting company. Web hosting providers offer different packages (including free domain registration) to store your web pages on their servers from where the world can access your website. For further instructions, see section 6.25 - Website Deployment.

1.3 Choosing the right Hosting Company

There are thousands of Web Hosting Companies out there and counting. How do you choose the ideal plan for your Web Site? The key here is to understand what your Web Site needs are. Once you know what is required, you can eliminate many options. These are the most important points that you need to focus on:

- How much storage space does your Web Site require?

- How much Monthly Transfer (Bandwidth) do you need?

- How many e-mail accounts do you need?

- What type of database is required for your site?

- What Scripting Languages does your web site use?

- Does your site need Server-side scripting language?

- If so, What Servlet Technology does your web site use?

- What Operating System should you go for?

- Should you use SHARED hosting or DEDICATED hosting?

1.3.1 Storage Space

Storage space refers to the amount of disk space allotted on the hosting Web server to store your website files. If you have a 100MB limit, then you cannot store more than 100MB worth of files on the server. HTML files are not big, but if your website holds files such as images, videos, audio etc., you need to watch your limit.

1.3.2 Bandwidth

Bandwidth is a measure of how much of your data the server sends out. For example, if you have a page that is 10KB, including images, and 10 people access the page (either at the same time or over a period of time), the total bandwidth is 100KB. Most hosts give you a bandwidth limit (or cap), which is usually a specified number of megabytes or gigabytes per month.

1.3.3 Domain Name

A domain name is a general Internet address, such as microsoft.com or cyber.net. Domain names are formed by the rules and procedures of the Domain Name System (DNS). DNS is the most recognized system for assigning addresses to Internet web servers. Somewhat like international phone numbers, the domain name system helps to give every Internet server a memorable and easy-to-spell address. Simultaneously, the domain names keep the really technical IP address invisible from end users. The registration of domain names is usually administered by domain name registrars who sell their services to the public. A domain name registrar is an organization or commercial entity that manages the reservation of Internet domain names. Some hosting providers supply free domain name registration service with their packages.

1.4 What E-mail is and how it works?

Electronic mail, commonly referred to as email or e-mail, is a method of exchanging digital messages from an author to one or more recipients anywhere in the world. Modern email operates across the Internet or other computer networks. Today's email systems are based on a store-and-forward model. Email servers accept, forward, deliver and store messages. When you send an e-mail message, it travels along your Internet connection and then through your ISP's outgoing mail server. This server routes the messages to the recipient's incoming mail server, which then stores the message in his or her mailbox. The next time the recipient check for messages, your message is moved from the recipient's server to the recipient's computer.

To use e-mail, you have to have an e-mail account. There are three ways to get an e-mail account: through ISP, through your hosting plan, and through free services such as Hotmail and Yahoo. An e-mail address is a set of characters that uniquely identifies the location of your Internet mailbox. A message sent to your address is delivered to you and no one else.

Example: admin@abcglobal.com

Each e-mail address, as shown above, carries three pieces of information:

Username: The username is the name of the person's account with the ISP or within an organization. This is often the person's first name, last name, or a combination of the two, but it could also be a nickname or some other text. No two people using the same ISP or within the same organization, can have the same username.

@ Symbol: The "@" sign separates the username from the domain name in an e-mail address.

Domain Name: The domain name is the Internet name of the company that provides the person's e-mail account. This is usually the domain name of the ISP, an organization, or a Web e-mail service.

E-mail Client Software

An email client is a computer program used to access and manage emails. There are two basic categories of email client:

Local Clients: These email clients are installed locally on a PC and include Microsoft Outlook, Mozilla's Thunderbird, IBM Lotus Notes, Pegasus Mail, and Apple Inc.'s Mail.

Web-Based Clients: A web application that provides message management, composition, and reception functions is commonly referred to as webmail. Examples of web-based clients are Gmail, Yahoo! Mail, and Hotmail.

1.5 Scripting Languages

A scripting language or script language is a programming language that supports the writing of scripts, programs written for a software environment that automate the execution of tasks which could alternatively be executed one-by-one by a human operator.

Scripts are invisible to the visitor's eye but their availability within the code of a website defines how the website behaves in response to certain click requests sent by the user. Apart from the World Wide Web, scripts are also used for the automation of processes on a local computer. All in all, scripts have contributed a lot to making the web such a usable and flexibility driven environment as we are used to seeing it today.

Each script represents a text document containing a list of instructions that need to be executed by a certain program or scripting manager so that the desired automated action could be achieved. This will prevent users from having to go through many complicated steps in order to reach certain results while browsing a website or working on their personal computers. The text nature of the scripts allows them to be opened and edited with the help of a basic text editor.

1.5.1 Client-Side Scripting

Client-side scripting generally refers to the class of computer programs on the web that are executed client-side, by the user's web browser, instead of server-side (on the web server). This type of computer programming is an important part of the Dynamic HTML (DHTML) concept, enabling web pages to be scripted.

Client-side scripts are often embedded within an HTML or XHTML document (hence known as an "embedded or internal script"), but they may also be contained in a separate file, which is referenced by the document (or documents) that use it (hence known as an "external script"). Upon request, the necessary files are sent to the user's computer by the web server (or servers) where they reside. The user's web browser executes the script, and then displays the document, including any visible output from the script. Client-side scripts may also contain instructions for the browser to follow in response to certain user actions, (e.g., clicking a button).

1.5.2 Server-Side Scripting

Server-side scripting is usually used to provide an interface and to limit client access to proprietary databases or other data sources. These scripts may assemble client characteristics for use in customizing the response based on those characteristics, the user's requirements, access rights, etc. Server-side scripting also enables the website owner to reduce user access to the source code of server-side scripts which may be proprietary and valuable in itself.

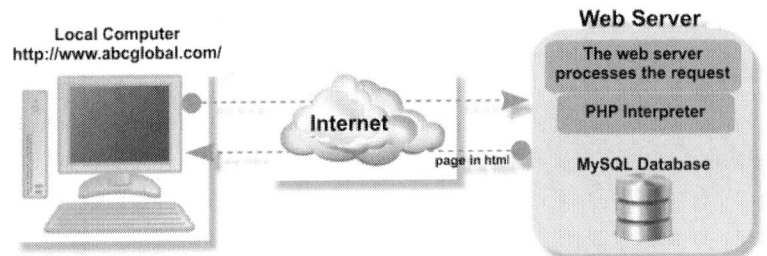

Figure 1-1 Server-side scripting (PHP and MySQL)

The server-side scripts are interpreted by the web server. Most server-side scripting languages usually embed their scripting components within a HTML file. So, when the web server reads them from the file system to serve a request from a browser, it interprets the script and generates the appropriate HTML to be returned to the browser. This contrasts with ordinary web pages where the server fetches an HTML-only static page directly from the file system and passes it onto the browser without any interpretation. The script interpretation might not actually be done by the web server but by a special software called CGI interpreter in the case of CGI scripts. For example, if the script language used is PHP, then it is PHP interpreter.

Server-side Scripting Languages

- PHP (*.php)
- Python via Django (*.py)
- Ruby (*.rb, *.rbw)
- SMX (*.smx)
- Lasso (*.lasso)
- WebDNA (*.dna,*.tpl)
- C via CGI (*.c, *.csp)
- ColdFusion (*.cfm)
- JavaServer Pages (*.jsp)
- Lua (*.lp *.op)
- Perl CGI (*.cgi, *.ipl, *.pl)

Some Interesting Facts

- The world # 1 video site YouTube is written in Python.
- Amazon.com & Slashdot run on Perl.
- NBC broadcast center runs 24x7 on TCL.
- Flight simulator systems used to train commercial and military pilots are written in Perl.

1.5.3 Client-Side vs. Server-side Scripting

- Server side scripting, (ex. ASP.Net, ASP, JSP, PHP, Ruby, or others), is executed by the server (Web Server), and the page that is sent to the browser is produced by the serve-side scripting.
- So when a server sends out a page, it executes server-side scripts, but does not execute client-side scripts. Once the browser receives the page, it executes the client-side scripts.
- Server side scripting can connect to databases that reside on the web server or another server reachable from web server. Client side scripting cannot do that.
- Server side scripting can access the file system that reside at the web server, client side cannot.
- Server side scripting can access settings belonging to Web server while client side cannot.
- The server may do things like database lookup, reading/writing files and user authentication that would be either impossible or very insecure to do in a browser.

- Client side scripting is a script, (ex. JavaScript, VB script), that is executed by the browser (i.e. Firefox, Internet Explorer, Safari, Opera, etc.) that resides at the user computer.
- Client side scripting consumes cycles from user's computer not web server one, while server side scripting consumes cycles form web server one.
- Client side scripting can access files and settings that are local at the user computer.
- Client-side scripts have greater access to the information and functions available on the user's browser, whereas server-side scripts have greater access to the information and functions available on the server.
- Client side script such as JavaScript runs primarily in the browser, which server side languages like PHP, JSP, Ruby on Rails etc. cannot do.

Client-Side vs. Server-side Scripting (Continued)

- Server-side scripts require that their language's interpreter be installed on the server, and produce the same output regardless of the client's browser, operating system, or other system details. Client-side scripts do not require additional software on the server (making them popular with authors who lack administrative access to their servers); however, they do require that the user's web browser understands the scripting language in which they are written. It is therefore impractical for an author to write scripts in a language that is not supported by popular web browsers.

- There are also a couple of tasks that are commonly done both places, like form validation - on the client to give quick feedback. This validation can also be done on the server to ensure that what is submitted is actually safe and valid. Note that an attacker could easily skip any browser validation and submit illegal values.

- About Markup Languages

- All basic elements & attributes in HTML required to build a website such as divisions, headings, paragraphs, text formatting, and more.

- How to add web, email links, and bookmarks to a web page?

- Incorporate images, lists, and tables

- Forms and related controls such as Radio buttons, Checkbox, Dropdown list, File input and Submit buttons

- Play videos on a web page and

- What's new in HTML5?

CHAPTER 2

HYPERTEXT MARKUP LANGUAGE

<HTML>

Your aspirations are your possibilities.

2.1 About Markup Languages

HTML stands for HyperText Markup Language. It is a markup language for structuring and presenting content in a web browser for the World Wide Web, and is a core technology of the Internet. HTML is written in the form of HTML elements consisting of tags enclosed in angle brackets (like <html>), within the web page content. HTML tags most commonly come in pairs like <h1> and </h1>, although some tags, known as empty elements, are unpaired, for example <img>. The first tag in a pair is the start tag, the second tag is the end tag (they are also called opening tags and closing tags). In between these tags web designers can add text, tags, comments and other types of text-based content.

HTML documents are read in a web browser (Chrome, Internet Explorer, Firefox etc.) which is responsible to organize these documents into visible or audible web pages. The browser uses the HTML tags to interpret the content of the page. Web browsers can also refer to Cascading Style Sheets (CSS) to define the appearance and layout of text and other material.

HTML elements form the building blocks of all websites. HTML allows images and objects to be embedded and can be used to create interactive forms. It provides a resource to create structured documents by denoting structural semantics for text such as headings, paragraphs, lists, links, quotes and other items. It can embed scripts in languages such as JavaScript which affect the behavior of HTML web pages.

XHTML is a separate language that began as a reformulation of HTML 4.01 using XML 1.0. XML (eXtensible Markup Language) was published in 1998. HTML4 was reformulated to follow the rules of XML and hence the term XHTML (eXtensible Hypertext Markup Language) evolved. The emergence of XHTML set some new and stricter rules for developers to write markup. For example, a mandatory closing tag (except empty elements such as <img>), use of lowercase for attribute names, mandatory attribute value in double quotes etc. The three versions of XHTML are Strict XHTML 1.0, Transitional XHTML 1.0, and XHTML 1.0 Frameset.

HTML5 is the fifth revision of the HTML standard and is focused in this book. Its core aims have been to improve the language with support for the latest multimedia while keeping it easily readable by humans and consistently understood by computers and devices. HTML5 is intended to subsume not only HTML 4, but XHTML 1 and DOM Level 2 HTML as well.

HTML5 is an attempt to define a single markup language that can be written in either HTML or XHTML syntax. It includes detailed processing models to encourage more interoperable implementations and introduces markup and application programming interfaces (APIs) for complex web applications. For the same reasons, HTML5 is also a potential candidate for cross- platform mobile applications.

Many features of HTML5 have been built with the consideration of being able to run on low-powered devices such as smartphones and tablets. In particular, HTML5 adds many new syntactical features. These include the new <video>, <audio> and <canvas> elements, as well as the integration of scalable vector graphics (SVG) content that replaces the uses of generic <object> tags and MathML for mathematical formulas. These features are designed to make it easy to include and handle multimedia and graphical content on the web without having to resort to proprietary plugins and APIs. Other new elements, such as <section>, <article>, <header>, <footer> and <nav>, are designed to enrich the semantic content of documents.

New attributes have been introduced for the same purpose, while some elements and attributes have been removed. Some elements, such as <a>, <cite> and <menu> have been changed, redefined or standardized. The APIs and document object model (DOM) are no longer afterthoughts, but are fundamental parts of the HTML5 specification. HTML5 also defines in some detail the required processing for invalid documents so that syntax errors will be treated uniformly by all conforming browsers and other user agents.

DOCTYPE DECLARATION

Each web page begins with a DOCTYPE declaration which informs the browser about the HTML version the page is using. Although this declaration is not mandatory, it helps browsers to correctly render a page. Due to various flavors of HTML, this declaration also varies as shown in the following table.

HTML Version	DOCTYPE Declaration
HTML 4	<!DOCTYPE html PUBLIC "-//W3C//DTD HTML 4.01 Transitional//EN" "http://www.w3.org/TR/html4/loose.dtd">
XML	<?xml version="1.0" ?>
Strict XHTML 1.0	<!DOCTYPE html PUBLIC "-//W3C//DTD XHTML 1.0 Strict//EN" "http://www.w3.org/TR/xhtml1/DTD/xhtml1-strict.dtd">
Transitional XHTML 1.0	<!DOCTYPE html PUBLIC "-//W3C//DTD HTML 4.01 Transitional//EN" "http://www.w3.org/TR/html4/loose.dtd">
HTML 5	<!DOCTYPE html>

2.2 Your First HTML Web Page

Open Notepad or any text editor and type the following code:

MyWebPage.html

```
<!DOCTYPE html>
<html>
  <head>
    <title>My First HTML Page</title>
    <meta name="description" content="How to create an HTML page" />
    <meta name="keywords" content="HTML, CSS, JavaScript" />
    <meta name="robots" content="nofollow" />
    <meta name="author" content="Riaz Ahmed" />
  </head>
  <body>
    <h1>This is the heading of my web page</h1>
    <p>This is a paragraph.</p>
  </body>
</html>
```

CODING BY HAND

Throughout this book, you'll be writing out documents (html, css, php, etc.) by hand using a text editor, such as Notepad. In the future, you may choose a web-authoring tool such as Dreamweaver or Microsoft Expression Web, but there is no better way to understand how things works then typing them out. This approach will make you understand the code and will allow you to use your tool more efficiently and much more easily.

Save the file as **MyWebPage.html** on your desktop or any other location you prefer. The icon of the saved file would change to the icon of your default browser. Double click the file to see your first web page in the browser as shown in the following figure.

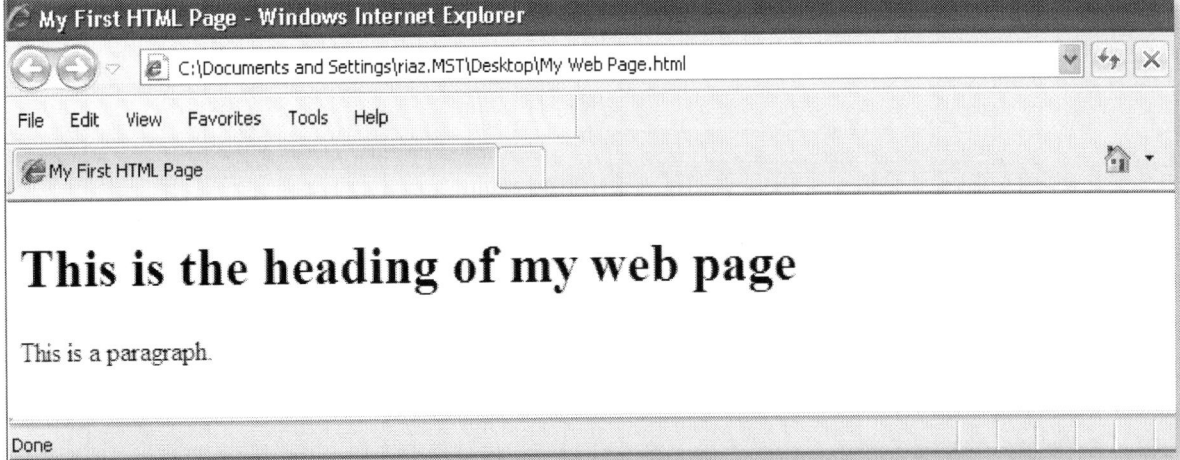

Figure 2-1

Let's see what the above code did for us.

2.3 Elements in HTML

Elements define an HTML document. Elements are usually made up of two tags: an opening tag (start tag) and a closing tag (end tag). Some HTML elements, such as <br>, are called empty elements. These elements are without a closing tag and are closed in the start tag. The first line in this example <!DOCTYPE html> defines the document type and is a declaration for the latest HTML5 generation. The text between <html> and </html> describes the web page. The <body></body> tags hold the visible page content. Page heading is enclosed in the <h1></h1> tags whereas a paragraph is displayed within the <p></p> tags.

Opening Tag	Element Content	Closing Tag
<p>	This is a paragraph.	</p>
<h1>	This is the heading of my web page	</h1>
<body>	<h1>This is the heading of my web page</h1> <p>This is a paragraph.</p>	</body>
<html>	**<head>** <title>My First HTML Page</title> <meta name="description"... /> ... **</head>** **<body>** <h1>This is the heading of my web page</h1> <p>This is a paragraph.</p> **</body>**	</html>

Your first page has the following HTML elements:

The <html> element: It defines the whole HTML document. It has a start tag <html> and an end tag </html>. Each HTML element contains some content that sits between its opening and closing tags and tells the browser something about the information. This one contains two other HTML elements - <head> and <body>.

The <head> element: The <head> element is a container for all the head elements. The <head> element must include a title for the document, and can include scripts, styles, meta information, and more.

The following elements can go inside the <head> element:

<title> It defines a title for your HTML document and is a required element in the head section. When defined, the page title is shown in the browser's title bar and displayed in search engine results.

<style> It specifies how HTML elements will be rendered in a browser. The required type attribute defines the content of the <style> element. The only possible value is "text/css".

<link> Links to an external style sheet. See section 3.5 about external style sheets.

<meta> Describe metadata within an HTML document. Metadata is data (information) about data. It provides metadata about the HTML document. Metadata is not displayed on the page. Meta elements are typically used to specify page description, keywords, author of the document, last modified, and other relevant information. The metadata can be used by browsers (how to display content or reload page), by search engines for keywords, or by other web services.

<script> It is used to define a client-side script, such as a JavaScript. The <script> element either contains scripting statements, or it points to an external script file through the src attribute. Common uses for JavaScript are image manipulation, form validation, and dynamic changes of content. See Chapter 4 to learn how scripts are added to a web page.

<noscript> It provides an alternate content for users who have disabled scripts in their browser or have a browser that doesn't support client-side scripting.

The <body> element: This element defines the body of the HTML document. It starts with the tag <body> and ends with </body>. In the above example, it is holding two other HTML elements – a heading <h1> element and a paragraph <p> element.

The <h1> element: You can use <h1> to <h6> tags to define HTML headings where <h1> is the most important heading and <h6> is the least one. Its content in the above example is: *This is the heading of my web page*.

The <p> element: Paragraphs in an HTML document are defined using the <p> element which has a start tag <p> and an end tag </p>. The element's content in the above example is: *This is a paragraph*.

Usage Recommendations

Keep the following recommendations in mind while using elements in HTML documents:

- Always put the end tags to avoid unexpected results and/or errors.
- Although HTML tags are not case sensitive, it is recommended to use lowercase.

2.4 Attributes in HTML

HTML elements can have attributes. Web page customization begins with HTML attributes. Attributes are responsible for customizing HTML elements and provide additional information about the contents of an element. While processing an HTML tag, the web browser looks to these attributes as guides for the construction of web elements. Without any attribute values specified, the browser will render the element using the default settings.

Attributes are always specified in the start tag of the element and are made up of two parts - Name and Value - separated by an equals sign as shown in the following example for the <a> element.

Figure 2-2

Usage Recommendations

- Attribute values should always be enclosed in quotes. Double style quotes are the most common, but single style quotes are also allowed.
- Attribute names and attribute values are case-insensitive. However, recommended way is to use lowercase.

2.5 Headings in HTML

Headings and subheadings in a document are used to present information in a hierarchical format. For instance, a document usually starts with a big heading before the main introduction of a topic, followed by relevant subheadings.

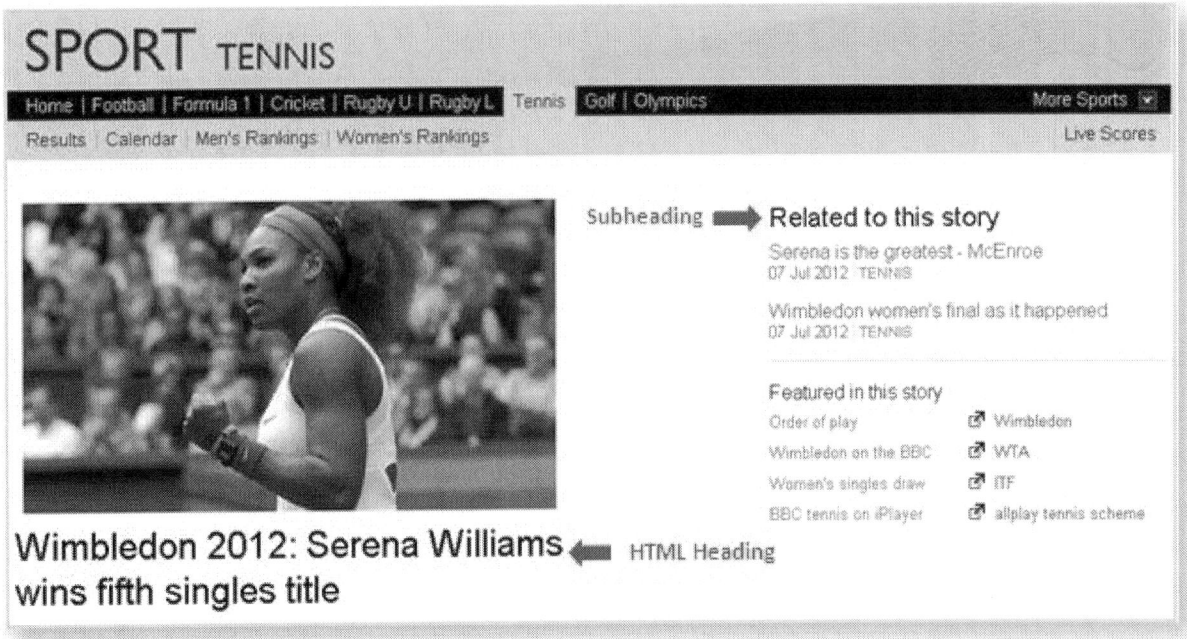

Figure 2-3

You can use <h1> to <h6> tags to define headings in your website where <h1> defines the most important heading while <h6> defines the least important one. Headings are displayed in different sizes by the browser. The content enclosed in <h1> is the largest, and that in <h6> is the smallest. You will learn how to set the size of content, its color, and font in the second part of this book where you'll be taught about Cascading Style Sheets (CSS).

Heading Example

```html
<!DOCTYPE html>
<html>
  <body>
    <h1>This is heading 1</h1>
    <h2>This is heading 2</h2>
    <h3>This is heading 3</h3>
    <h4>This is heading 4</h4>
    <h5>This is heading 5</h5>
    <h6>This is heading 6</h6>
  </body>
</html>
```

Output

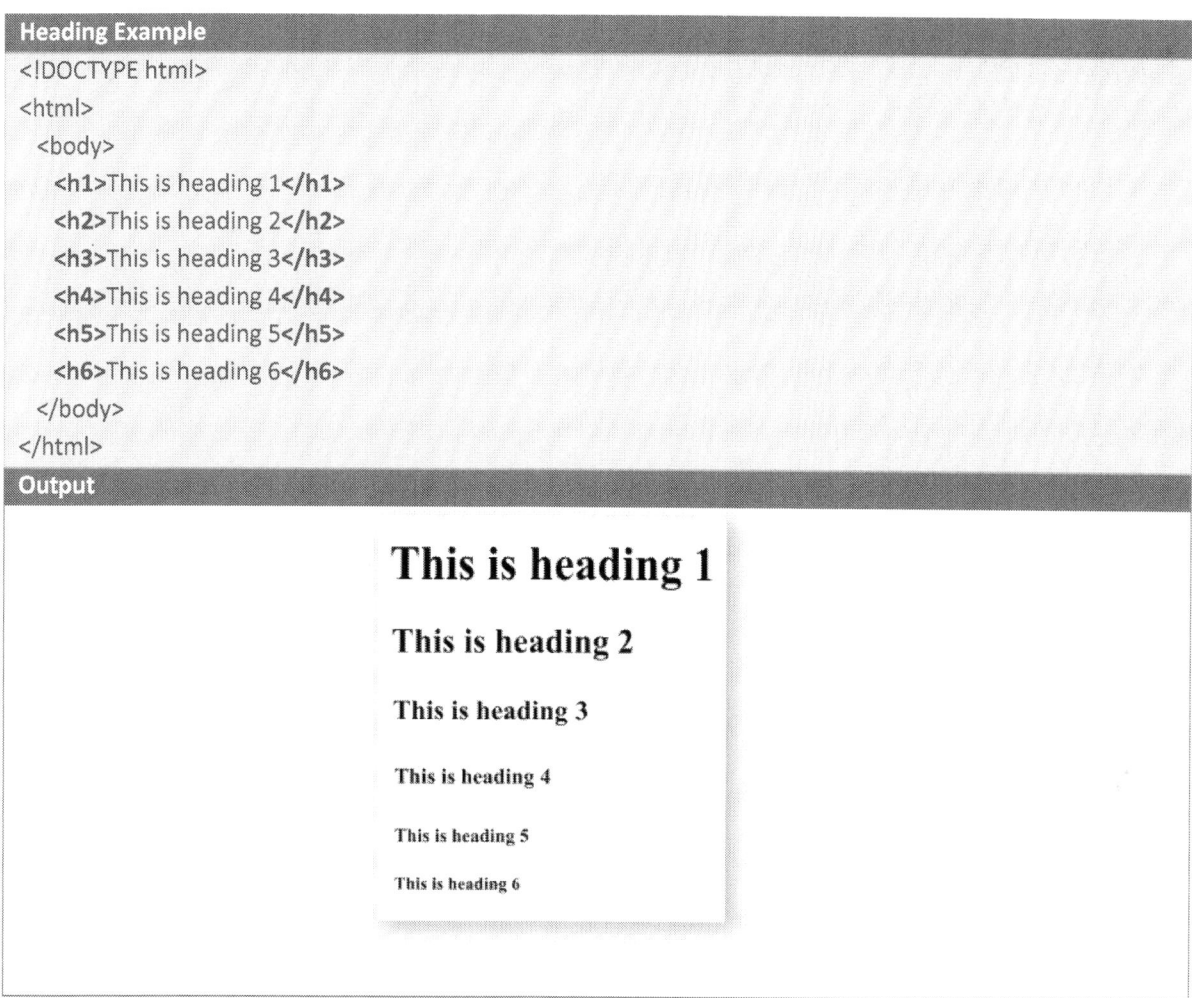

Usage Recommendations

Here are some tips on how to properly utilize these tags to improve your page structure for search engine ranking purposes.

- Don't use headings to make text bold.
- Header tag (h1, h2, h3 etc.) gives a specified amount of importance to the surrounding text on a page. So you can have as many h1 tags as necessary as long as you have the same amount of important sections on your page.
- Usually one h1 tag is enough for the search engine to see what the page is about.
- Multiple h1 tags on a website can trigger a penalty if you have other spamming techniques on your page.

2.6 Paragraphs in HTML

A paragraph is the composition of one or more sentences. Each paragraph is indicated by a new line. In HTML you use the paragraph tag <p> when you want to break up two streams of information into separate thoughts. Most browsers display paragraphs with one blank line between them. Here is an example of paragraph in HTML:

Paragraph Example

```
<!DOCTYPE html>
<html>
<body>
   <p>Book's Overview: The book "Create Rapid Web Applications Using Oracle Application Express" is full of practical stuff. In this book, I am sharing my personal APEX learning experience that I got by developing a clone of the sample application provided with Oracle Application Express.</p>
   <p>This book will walk you through to create a professional looking web-based database application. A great starting point for novice and equally beneficial for intermediate users, this book will allow users to practically explore Oracle Application Express (APEX) themselves. </p>
   <p>Besides creation of individual application pages, this book will demonstrate many professional techniques, summarized at the end of each chapter, to apply them to your own projects.</p>
</body>
</html>
```

Output

Book's Overview: The book "Create Rapid Web Applications Using Oracle Application Express" is full of practical stuff. In this book, I am sharing my personal APEX learning experience that I got by developing a clone of the sample application provided with Oracle Application Express.

This book will walk you through to create a professional looking web-based database application. A great starting point for novice and equally beneficial for intermediate users, this book will allow users to practically explore Oracle Application Express (APEX) themselves.

Besides creation of individual application pages, this book will demonstrate many professional techniques, summarized at the end of each chapter, to apply them to your own projects.

2.7 Lines and Breaks in HTML

In the previous example, you saw how browser automatically shows a new paragraph on a new line. Suppose you have a situation where you need to add a line break inside the middle of a paragraph. In such a case you can use the line break tag <br> as shown under. The <hr> (horizontal rule) tag is used to create a line between sections to separate content of your web page.

Line & Line Break Example

```
<!DOCTYPE html>
<html>
<body>
  <p>Book's Overview: <br><br>The book "Create Rapid Web Applications Using Oracle
      Application Express"...</p>
  <hr>
  <p>This book will walk you through to create a professional looking web-based database
      application.  A great starting point for novice and... </p>
  <hr>
  <p>Besides creation of individual application pages, this book will demonstrate many professional
      techniques, summarized at the end of each chapter, to apply them to your own projects.</p>
</body>
</html>
```

Output

Book's Overview:

The book "Create Rapid Web Applications Using Oracle Application Express" is full of practical stuff. In this book, I am sharing my personal APEX learning experience that I got by developing a clone of the sample application provided with Oracle Application Express.

This book will walk you through to create a professional looking web-based database application. A great starting point for novice and equally beneficial for intermediate users, this book will allow users to practically explore Oracle Application Express (APEX) themselves.

Besides creation of individual application pages, this book will demonstrate many professional techniques, summarized at the end of each chapter, to apply them to your own projects.

2.8 Comments In HTML

Web developers usually add comments to HTML to understand what the code is expected to do. The markup *<!-- Some comments -->* is used for this purpose as demonstrated in the example hereunder. Comments are ignored and are not displayed by the browser.

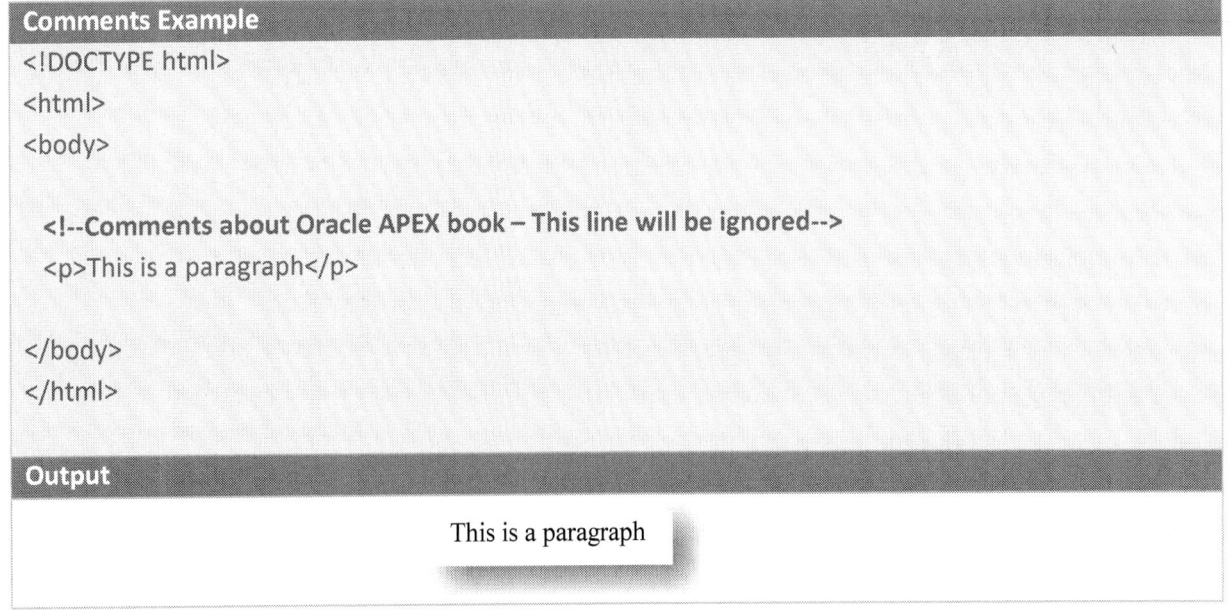

Comments Example

```
<!DOCTYPE html>
<html>
<body>

  <!--Comments about Oracle APEX book – This line will be ignored-->
  <p>This is a paragraph</p>

</body>
</html>
```

Output

This is a paragraph

2.9 Formatting Text In HTML

To make text bold within a paragraph you can use the **<b></b>** tags. Similarly, enclose words in the **<i></i>** tags to present them in italic. HTML also provides elements to superscript or subscript characters using **** and **** tags respectively.

Text Formatting Example

```
<!DOCTYPE html>
<html>
<body>
  A <b>mathematical square</b> expression 3<sup>2</sup> = 9 and 4<sup>2</sup> = 16 written
  using <i>superscript</i>.
  <br>
  A <b>chemical formula</b> H<sub>2</sub>O written using <i>subscript</i>.
</body>
</html>
```

Output

A **mathematical square** expression $3^2 = 9$ and $4^2 = 16$ written using *superscript*.

A **chemical formula** H_2O written using *subscript*.

You might have seen old and the new discounted prices of a product side by side on the internet. This is done using the **<s>** tag which specifies text that is no longer correct, accurate or relevant. This tag is redefined in HTML5.

Text Formatting Example

```
<!DOCTYPE html>
<html>
<body>


<p>New Inspiron All-in-One PC <br>
Price: <s>$599.99</s> $499.99</p>


</body>
</html>
```

Output

New Inspiron All-in-One PC
Price: ~~$599.99~~ $499.99

2.10 White Space In HTML

Spaces, tabs, and newlines are called whitespace characters. HTML treats whitespace characters including newlines or a sequence of whitespace characters as a single space and eliminates leading/trailing whitespaces. This is known as 'collapsing whitespace'. Web developers often use this technique to indent their code to make it easier to read.

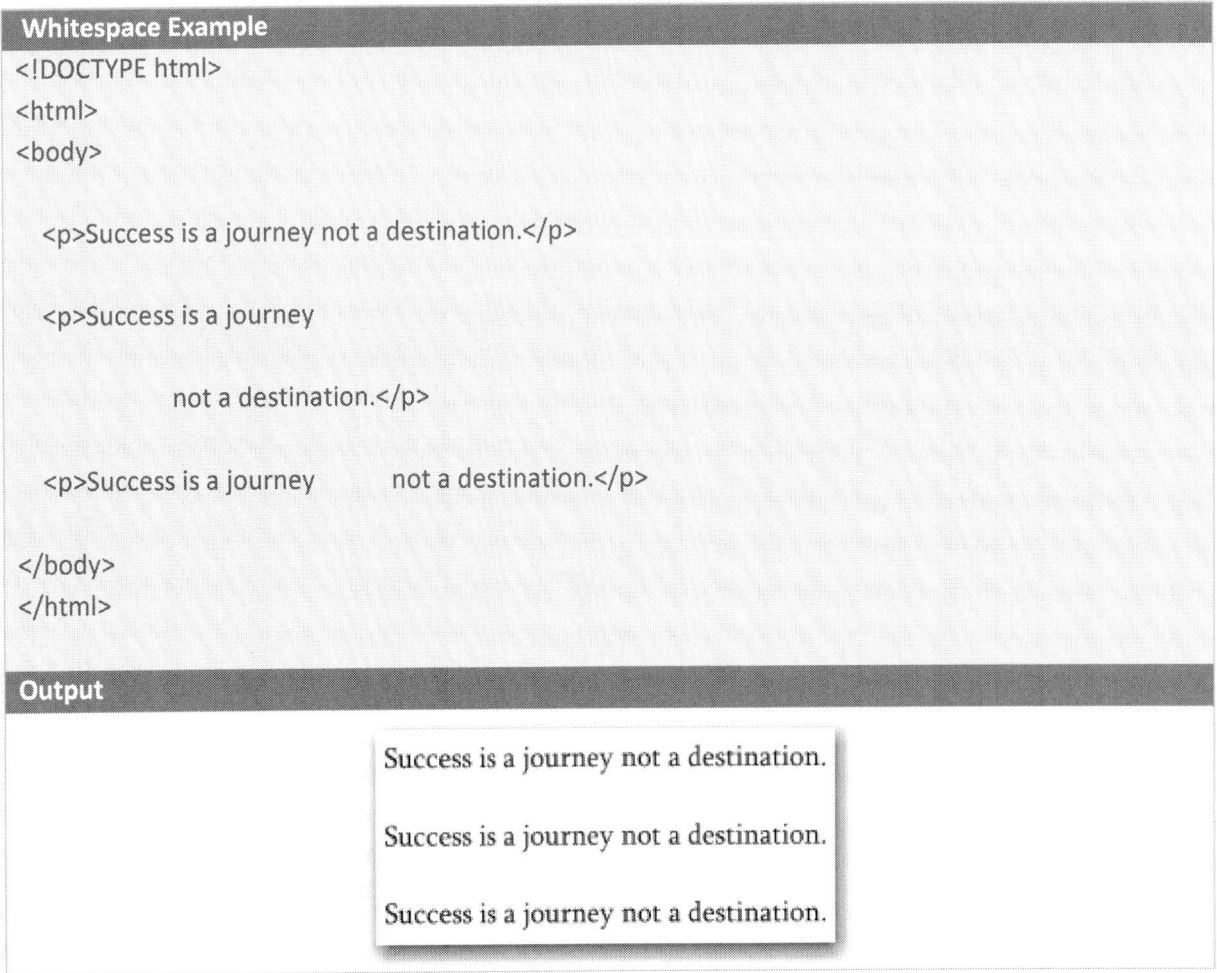

Whitespace Example

```
<!DOCTYPE html>
<html>
<body>

   <p>Success is a journey not a destination.</p>

   <p>Success is a journey

           not a destination.</p>

   <p>Success is a journey        not a destination.</p>

</body>
</html>
```

Output

Success is a journey not a destination.

Success is a journey not a destination.

Success is a journey not a destination.

On the contrary if you do want to preserve line breaks and spaces, HTML offers you a tag to control the appearance of your code. The <pre> tag is used to define preformatted text and is used to display text with unusual formatting, or computer program code.

Preformatted Text Example

```
<!DOCTYPE html>
<html>
<body>
  <pre>
    An example of preformatted text.
    It preserves     both spaces
    and line breaks.
  </pre>

  <p>Usually applied to display computer program code:</p>

  <pre>
    if a = 1
       c=c+1
    end if
  </pre>
</body>
</html>
```

Output

```
An example of preformatted text.
It preserves      both spaces
and line breaks.

Usually applied to display computer program code:

if a = 1
  c=c+1
endif
```

2.11 Abbreviations & Acronyms In HTML

Abbreviations & Acronyms Example

```
<!DOCTYPE html>
<html>
<body>

  <p>The <abbr title="Fourth-Generation Programming Language">4GL</abbr> is a
     programming language for commercial business software.</p>

  <p>An <acronym title="Application Program Interface">API</acronym> is a description of
     the way one piece of software asks another program to perform a service.</p>

  <p><b>Hold the mouse pointer over the acronym or abbreviation to see the spelled-out
     version that is displayed by the TITLE attribute.</b></p>

</body>
</html>
```

Output

The 4GL is a programming language for commercial business software.

Fourth-Generation Programming Language

An API is a description of the way one piece of software asks another program
to perfo Application Program Interface

**Hold the mouse pointer over the acronym or abbreviation to see the
spelled-out version that is displayed by the TITLE attribute.**

2.12 Long and Short Quotations In HTML

Quotes are used to emphasize excerpts of text. According to HTML specifications, there are three elements which are supposed to semantically mark up quotations, namely <blockquote>, <q> and <cite>. Although all intended to markup quotes, they should be used in different contexts.

In HTML long quotation are defined by the tag <blockquote>. Blockquote are set off from the main text as a distinct paragraph or block. However, they refer to some external citation which isn't already mentioned in the article. This element can also have an optional attribute cite that specifies the location (in the form of a URL) where the quote has come from. The browser inserts white space before and after a blockquote element. It also inserts margins.

Short quotation is defined by the tag <q>. The browser inserts quotation marks around the short quotation. In practice, usually only blockquote and q are used.

Long and Short Quotations Example

```
<!DOCTYPE html>
<html>
<body>
    Example of long quotation:
    <blockquote>
        The Giant Eye is a telescope placed on Mount Palomar in Southern California...
    </blockquote>
    Example of short quotation:
    <q>This is a short quotation</q>
</body>
</html>
```

Output

Example of long quotation:

The Giant Eye is a telescope placed on Mount Palomar in Southern California. By far, it is the largest telescope ever built. Its most important feature is its lens which weighs 20 tons and measures 200 inches across. It was designed with fantastic care. Twenty highly skilled men worked for around 11 years to polish the mirror of the largest telescope to such a perfect finish that the most powerful magnifying glass could not find out a single flaw in it.

Example of short quotation: "This is a short quotation"

2.13 Web Links In HTML

The word Surfing is often used while discussing the internet which means moving from one web page to another. You can surf on the web using Links. Links are created using the HTML anchor tag **<a>**. An anchor is used in the following ways:

- Create links to access other pages on the same website
- Create a link to another website or page
- Create a link to send email
- Create a bookmark inside a web page

You define the link destination in the href attribute of the <a> element. The **target** attribute with the value **_blank** is used in the following example to open Amazon's website in a new window.

Text Links Example

```
<!DOCTYPE html>
<html>
<body>
  <p>Link to other pages within a website:
    <a href="index.html">Home</a>
    <a href="services.html">Services</a>
    <a href="about-us.html">About</a>
    <a href="contact.html">Contact</a>
  </p>
  <p>Link to another website:
    Buy from <a href="http://www.amazon.com/" target="_blank">Amazon!</a>.
  </p>
</body>
</html>
```

Output

Link to other pages within a website: Home Services About Contact

Link to another website: Buy from Amazon!

Using a shorthand known as relative URL, you can link to other pages within the same website and do not need to specify the domain name. The first four links in the above example demonstrate relative URL.

When you link to a different website, the value of the href attribute will have the full web address for the site, which is known as an absolute URL as shown in the last link.

You can also create an image link in addition to text link.

Image Link Example

```
<!DOCTYPE html>
<html>
<body>
  <p>
    <a href="http://www.amazon.com/"><img src="amazon.jpg" alt="Amazon!" height="20"/></a>
  </p>
</body>
</html>
```

2.14 E-mail Links In HTML

The <a> element along with the href attribute can also be used to send email. You prefix mailto: to the email address of the recipient after the href attribute. When you click the email link, the default email program opens a new message displaying the recipient's address in the To: box. Optionally, you can also add a subject line as shown in the following example. Spaces between words should be replaced by %20 to ensure that the browser will display the text properly.

Email Link Example

Please <u>Contact us</u> through email.

```
<!DOCTYPE html>
<html>
<body>
  <p>
    Please <a href="mailto:someone@abc.com?Subject=Ticket%20Inquiry">Contact us</a> through email.
  </p>
</body>
</html>
```

2.15 Bookmarking In HTML

In your website, you have a long page with several sections. To make this page user-friendly, you use the bookmark feature in HTML by creating a list at the top of the page and link it to corresponding sections. Likewise, to save users from having to scroll back to the top, you also add a link at the bottom or at the end of each section which instantly takes the user to the top.

You can achieve this task by using the **id** attribute which can be used with every HTML element. First you need to identify the points in the page the link will go to and mark them with the **id** attribute. Next, you link to these points using the # symbol followed by the value of the id attribute in the href attribute of the created list. To test the following example, make your browser's window smaller so that you could see the jumping effect.

Bookmarking Example

```
<!DOCTYPE html>
<html>
<body>
  <!--The top link at the bottom will bring you here-->
  <h1 id="top">Books Review</h1>
  <!--List of books that points to corresponding section-->
  <a href="#obiee">Implement Oracle Business Intelligence</a><br>
  <a href="#apex">Create Rapid Web Applications Using Oracle APEX</a><br>
  <a href="#web">The Web Book</a><br><br>
  <!-- The first marked point with the id "obiee"-->
  <h2 id="obiee">Implement Oracle Business Intelligence</h2>
  <p>This book is aimed at giving you insights into running your organization in a more intelligent
     fashion. It not  only presents the BI concepts, but also guides you to implement Oracle Business
     Intelligence using real world scenarios.</p>
  <!--The second marked point with the id "apex"-->
  <h2 id="apex">Create Rapid Web Applications Using Oracle APEX</h2>
  <p>This book will walk you through to create a professional looking web-based database
     application.</p>
  <!--The third marked point book with the id "web"-->
  <h2 id="web">The Web Book</h2>
  <p>This book teaches how to create professional looking websites using HTML, CSS, and
     JavaScript.</p>
  <!--The top link which takes you to the main heading-->
  <p><a href="#top">Top</a></p>
</body>
</html>
```

Output

Books Review

Implement Oracle Business Intelligence
Create Rapid Web Applications Using Oracle Application Express
The Web Book

Implement Oracle Business Intelligence

This book is aimed at giving you insights into running your organization in a more intelligent fashion. It not only presents the BI concepts, but also guides you to implement Oracle Business Intelligence using real world scenarios.

Create Rapid Web Applications Using Oracle APEX

This book will walk you through to create a professional looking web-based database application.

The Web Book

This book teaches how to create professional looking websites using HTML, CSS, and JavaScript.

Top

2.16 Images In HTML

The adage *"A picture is worth a thousand words"* refers to the notion that a complex idea can be conveyed with just a single still image. This fits more in the world of web than any other place. A web site having great images is more engaging than a dull text-based one.

You add images to your web page to display:

- Company logo
- Photographs
- Diagram, chart or illustration

Images are defined using the <img> tag in HTML which is an empty tag since it doesn't have an associated end tag. Some common attributes of <img> tag are src, alt, width, and height. The src attribute, which stands for source, is used to display images on a web page. Its value holds the location of the image. The alt attribute contains an alternate text that is displayed if the image cannot be displayed. The height and width attributes specify the image size (by default in pixels).

Image Example
```
<!DOCTYPE html>
<html>
<body>

  <h1>Tour de France</h1>
  <p>Race leader Alberto Contador (Astana) had guests on the podium: <br>
      Cameron Diaz and Tom Cruise, in town for the Bordeaux premiere of their latest film, Knight
      and Day.
  </p>
  <img border="0" src="tomcruise.jpg" alt="Tom Curise" width="500" height="250" />

</body>
</html>
```

Output

Tour de France

Race leader Alberto Contador (Astana) had guests on the podium:
Cameron Diaz and Tom Cruise, in town for the Bordeaux premiere of their latest
film, Knight and Day.

2.17 Lists In HTML

HTML lists are great for calling your reader's attention to specific information. It has been a popular tool even when writing business and technical documents. Lists draw attention to important information. Readers like them because they are visually appealing and make it easy to quickly find pertinent information. In HTML you can use three types of lists:

Ordered List: This list has items marked with numbers. It is defined using the tag <ol> and each item starts with the tag <li>.

Unordered List: Items in this list are marked with bullets. It is defined with the tag <ul>. Each list item is enclosed in the <li> tag.

Definition List: This list contains description of each item and is defined with the <dl> tag in conjunction with <dt> and <dd> to define list items and corresponding descriptions respectively.

Lists Example

```
<!DOCTYPE html>
<html>
<body>
  <h4>Ordered List with numbers:</h4>
  <ol>
    <li>Go to <b>Shared Components</b> page</li>
    <li>Click <b>Lists</b> under Navigation Section</li>
    <li>Click the <b>Create</b> button</li>
  </ol>
  <h4> Unordered List with numbers:</h4>
  <ul>
    <li>APEX introduction</li>
   <li>Create a professional looking web-based database application</li>
    <li>Advanced Reporting</li>
  </ul>
  <h4>Definition List:</h4>
  <dl>
   <dt>- Coffee</dt>
     <dd>Black hot drink</dd>
   <dt>- Milk</dt>
     <dd>White cold drink</dd>
  </dl>
</body>
</html>
```

Ordered List with numbers:
1. Go to **Shared Components** page
2. Click **Lists** under Navigation Section
3. Click the **Create** button

Unordered List with numbers:
- APEX introduction
- Create a professional looking web-based database application
- Advanced Reporting

Definition List:
- Coffee
    Black hot drink
- Milk
    White cold drink

You can use different Ordered and Unordered list on your web page by applying the following TYPE attributes:

Ordered List		Unordered List	
List	Type	List	Type
Uppercase letters	<ol type="A">	Disc bullets	<ul type="disc">
Lowercase letters	<ol type="a">	Circle bullets	<ul type="circle">
Roman numbers	<ol type="I">	Square bullets	<ul type="square">
Lowercase Roman numbers	<ol type="i">		

You can also create nested listing as demonstrated below by putting a second list inside the existing one.

Nested List Example	Output

<pre><!DOCTYPE html>
<html>
<body>
<h4>A nested List:</h4>
<ul>
 <li>Personal Computers</li>
 <li>Laptops
  <ul>
  <li>HP</li>
  <li>Dell
   <ul>
    <li>Inspiron 15R</li>
    <li>Inspiron 17R</li>
   </ul>
  </li>
  </ul>
 </li>
 <li>All-in-One</li>
</ul>
</body>
</html></pre>
	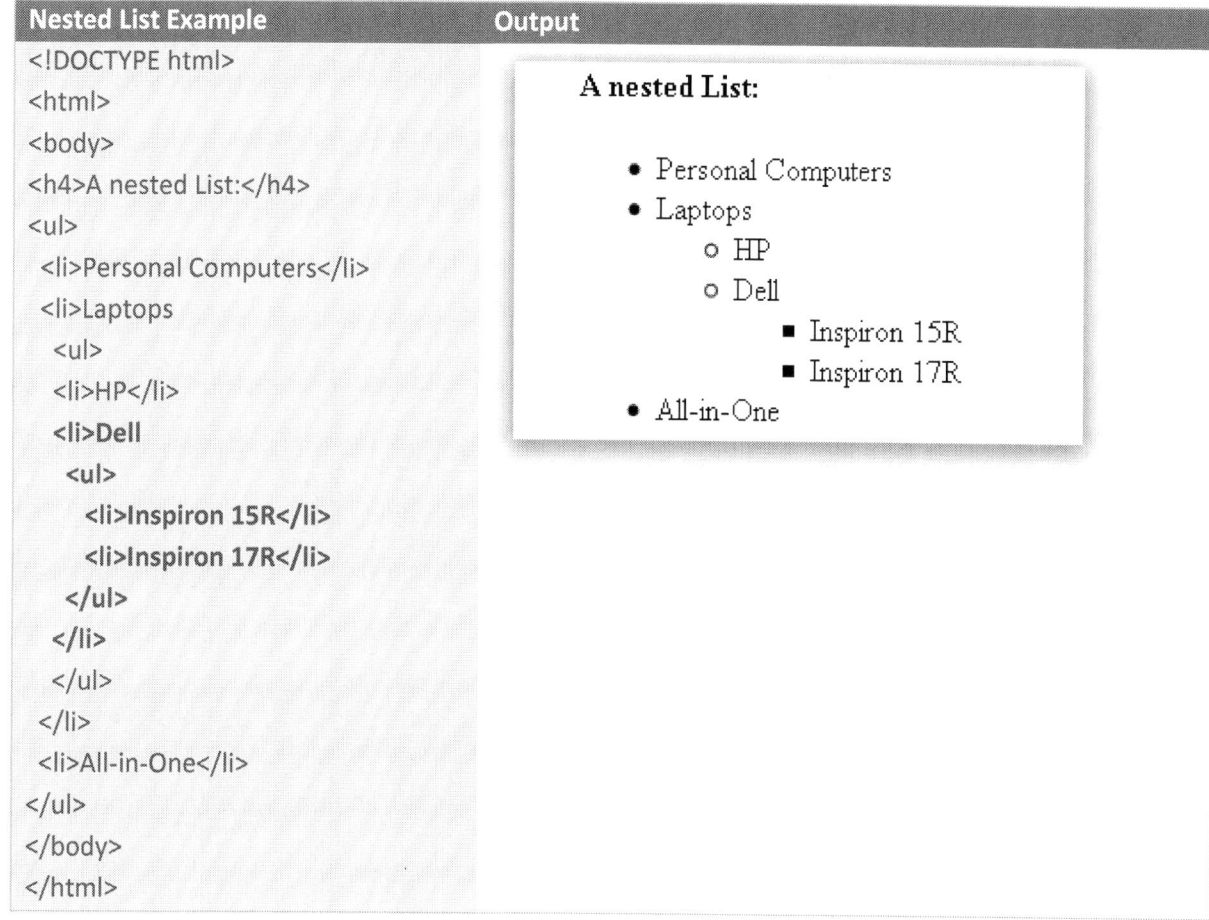

2.18 Tables In HTML

A table is a set of data elements (values) that is organized using a model of vertical columns and horizontal rows, the cell being the unit where a row and column intersect. In HTML you use the following elements while defining a table:

Element	Description
Table <table>	Defines the table itself
Table Rows <tr>	Rows in a table
Table Data <td>	Table cell that holds data
Header Cell <th>	Column heading
Table Heading <thead>	To group header content
Table Body <tbody>	To group body content
Table Footer <tfoot>	To group footer content

Horizontal Table Example	Output

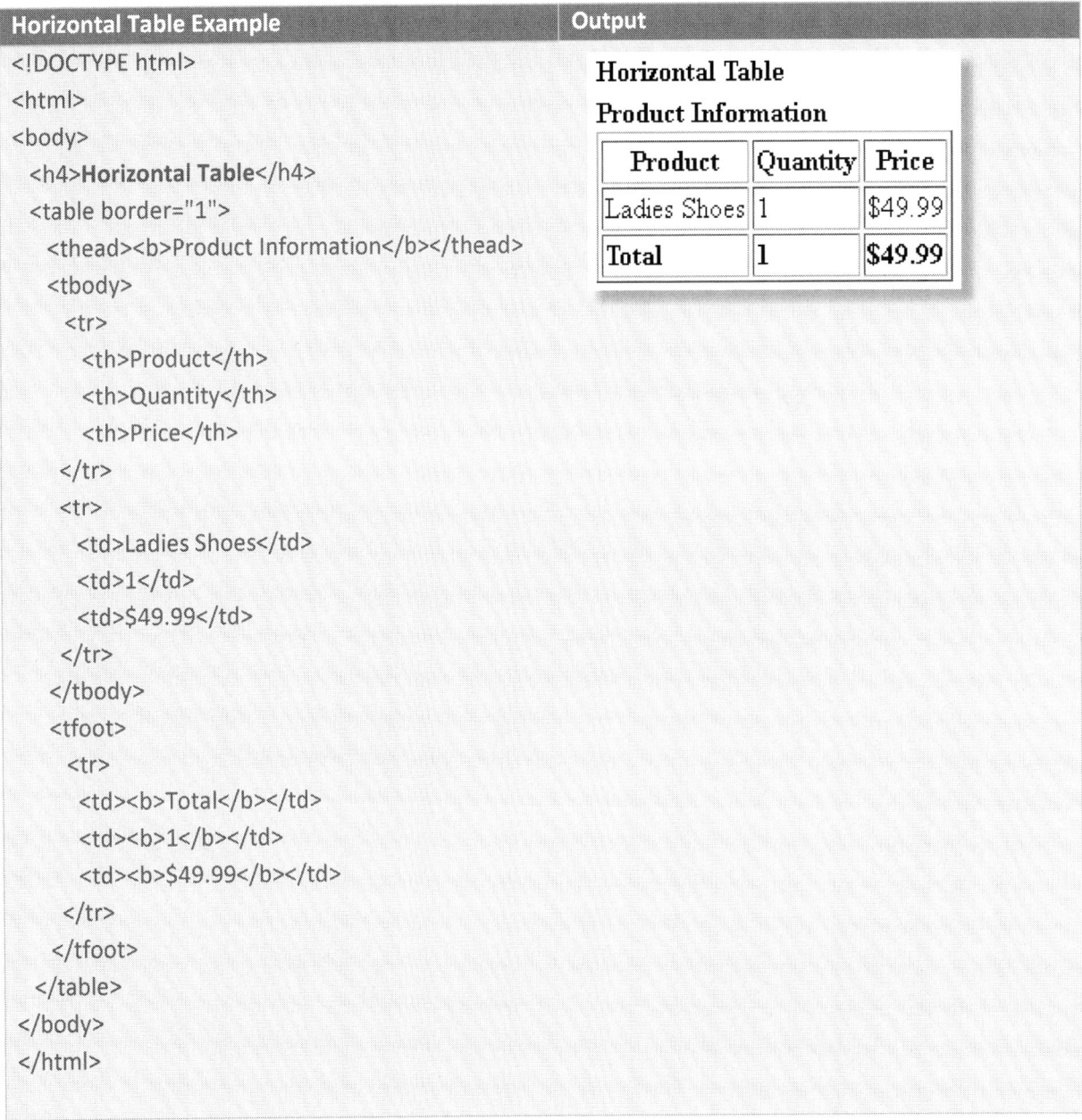

```
<!DOCTYPE html>
<html>
<body>
  <h4>Horizontal Table</h4>
  <table border="1">
    <thead><b>Product Information</b></thead>
    <tbody>
      <tr>
        <th>Product</th>
        <th>Quantity</th>
        <th>Price</th>
      </tr>
      <tr>
        <td>Ladies Shoes</td>
        <td>1</td>
        <td>$49.99</td>
      </tr>
    </tbody>
    <tfoot>
      <tr>
        <td><b>Total</b></td>
        <td><b>1</b></td>
        <td><b>$49.99</b></td>
      </tr>
    </tfoot>
  </table>
</body>
</html>
```

Output:

Horizontal Table

Product Information

Product	Quantity	Price
Ladies Shoes	1	$49.99
Total	1	**$49.99**

Vertical Table Example	Output

```
<!DOCTYPE html>
<html>
<body>
<h4>Vertical Table</h4>
<table border="1">
  <tbody>
    <tr>
      <th>Product</th>
      <td>Men's Shirt</td>
      <td><b>Total</b></td>
    </tr>
    <tr>
      <th>Quantity</th>
      <td>1</td>
      <td><b>1</b></td>
    </tr>
    <tr>
      <th>Price</th>
      <td>$30.00</td>
      <td><b>$30.00</b></td>
    </tr>
  </tbody>
</table>
</body>
</html>
```

2.19 Divisions/Sections In HTML

The <div> tag defines a division or a section in an HTML document. It is used to group block-elements to format them with styles and is often used together with CSS to layout a web page. For example, you might create a <div> element to group header objects (such as logo and navigation links), a second one to group main content of the page, and the last one to group footer objects (links or copyright text). The code *&copy* displays the copyright symbol © while "id" attribute references css rules to style a single element. For further details, see chapter 3 section 3.7 CSS ID and Class.

Division Example

```
<!DOCTYPE html>
<html>
<body>

<div id="header">
  <img src="logo.png" alt="ABC Global Consulting" />
  <ul>
    <li><a href="company.html">Home</a></li>
    <li><a href="products.html">Products</a></li>
    <li><a href="services.html">Services</a></li>
    <li><a href="contact.html">Contact</a></li>
  </ul>
</div><!-- end of header -->

<div id="content">
  <h3>WELCOME</h3>
  <p>ABC Global Consulting, a provider of scalable business solutions.</p>
</div><!-- end of content -->

<div id="footer">
  <p>&copy; ABC Global Consulting</p>
</div><!-- end of footer -->

</body>
</html>
```

Output

ID:Header

- Home
- Products
- Services
- Contact

WELCOME   ID:Content

ABC Global Consulting, a provider of scalable business solutions.

© ABC Global Consulting   ID:Footer

2.20   Forms In HTML

Forms are everywhere on the web. You might have interacted with HTML forms on web sites like Amazon, eBay, Yahoo!, and Google. The use of form on a page is a higher level phase of Web development to collect information from visitors. Whether it's through registration forms, mailing lists, site searches, or online ordering, forms facilitate interaction between organizations/individuals with their clients or end users.

Let's take Amazon as an example. You visit Amazon's website as a buyer and don't verbally tell Amazon to find an item. Instead, you interact with a form containing form controls in the shape of a search text box and a Search button. You enter your search criteria into the text box, click the Search button, and get the results in a clean list format that you can quickly browse through.

From a seller's perspective, the process is slightly more complex, but again, involves forms and form controls. When you want to sell an item on Amazon's Web site, the first step is to register as a seller. During the registration process, you'll see a form with numerous form controls that collect different types of information from you.

In HTML you use the <form> tag to create a form; all form controls reside inside this tag. Every <form> tag requires an action attribute which specifies where to send the form-data when a form is submitted. You also use form's *method* attribute to send or retrieve data to or from server. This attribute can have either a GET or a POST value. The GET method is the default and is used when you want to retrieve something from the server, while the POST method is used to manipulate information on the server.

As per functionality both GET and POST methods are same with the following differences:

- GET method shows the information to the users as it is sent appended to the URL. But in the case of POST method information will not be visible as it is sent encapsulated within the HTTP request body.

- GET method has limitation in the size of data transmitted, but POST method hasn't.

- Web browser can usually cache the response pages for GET requests, because they do not change. POST requests, however, cannot be cached, and the server is re-contacted each time the page is displayed.

- GET requests should be used for pure queries that don't affect anything on the server. POST requests are most suitable for queries where the response page will change over time – like a shopping cart. For more information on these two methods, see Chapter 5 - section 5.12.2.

The controls you can use in your web form include the following:

- Text and password fields
- Text area
- Radio buttons
- Checkbox
- Drop-down list box
- Button
- File input to upload a file
- Group box
- Label

Let's go through these form elements with some practical examples.

2.21 Text & Password Elements

These are the most commonly used input fields defined with the <input> tag. This <input> tag is an empty tag without a closing tag and contains a TYPE attribute which determines what kind of input is being created. The <input type="text" /> defines a one-line input field that a user can enter text into whereas, <input type="password" /> creates a password field. The characters in a password field are masked - shown as asterisks or circles. The following table shows some more attributes associated with the <input> tag:

Attribute	Description
name	Each form control should have a name to identify it on the server
maxlength	To limit the number of input characters

Text & Password Example

```
<!DOCTYPE html>
<html>
<body>

<form action="http://www.abc.com/login.php">
 <p>Username:
 <input type="text" name="username" maxlength="30"/>
 </p>
 <p>Password:
 <input type="password" name="password" maxlength="30"/>
 </p>
</form>

</body>
</html>
```

Output

Username:	Riaz Ahmed
Password:	****************

2.22 Text Area Element

If you're acquainted with blogs, you must have seen a large text box under a blog post where users provide their comments. This box is a multi-line input control and is defined using its own tag called <textarea>. It can hold an unlimited number of characters and is specified by cols and rows attributes. The cols attribute, measured in numbers of characters, sets the width of the text area. The rows attribute indicates the height of the text area. The browser automatically adds a scroll bar when the text crosses the row attribute limit.

Text Area Example

```
<!DOCTYPE html>
<html>
<body>

<form action="http://www.abc.com/comments.php">
 <p>Comments:</p>
 <textarea name="comments" cols="50" rows="10">Please enter your comments...</textarea>
</form>

</body>
</html>
```

Output

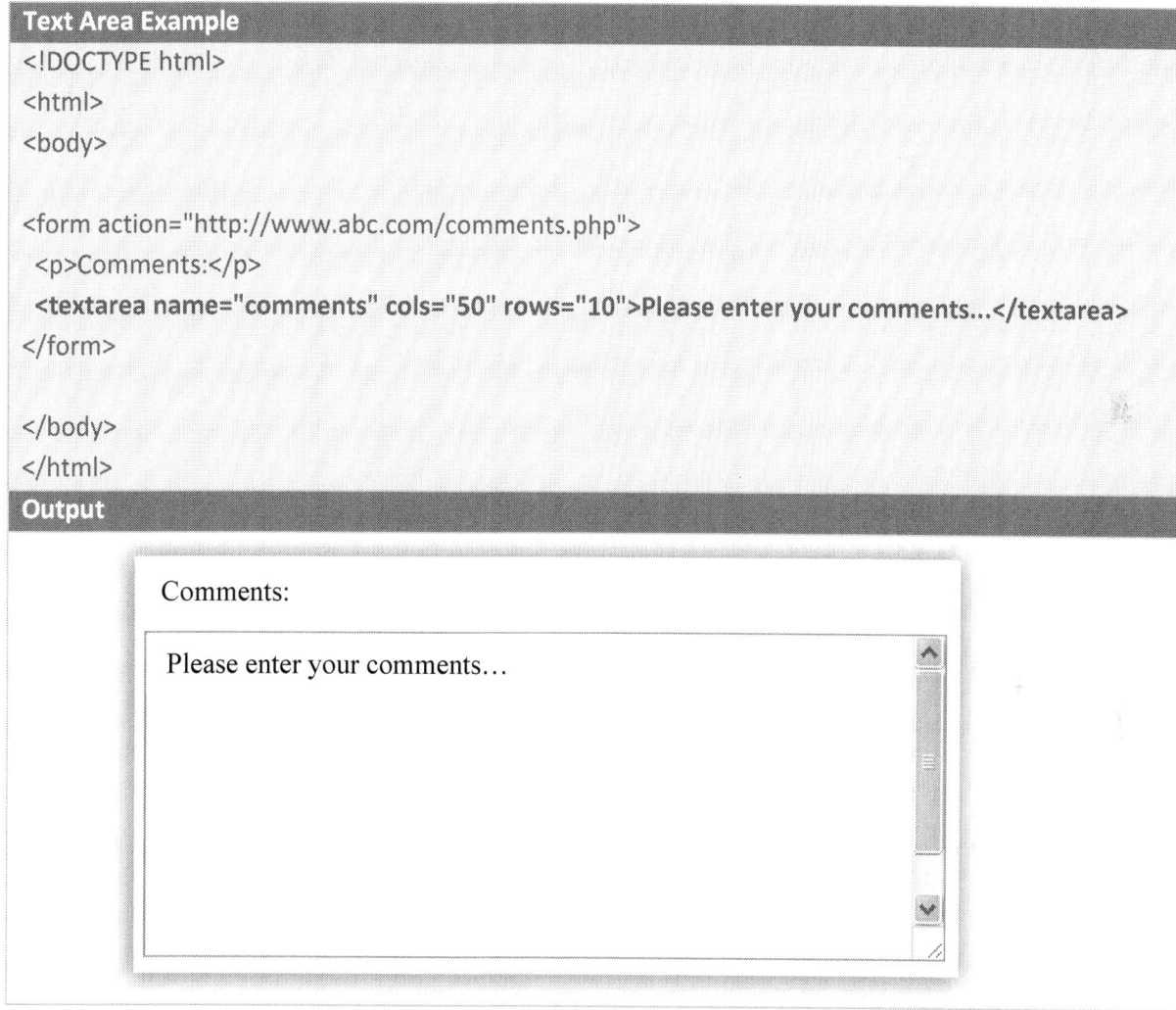

2.23 Radio Button Element

Radio buttons let a user select ONLY ONE of a limited number of choices. It is defined as <input type="radio" /> and has three main attributes - name, value, and checked. The name is sent along with the selected value to the server. The value attribute is the value passed to a script or a CGI program to indicate which button is selected. Be sure you assign a different value to each button. The checked attribute sets a default value when the page loads into the browser and is used with only one radio button in a group.

The entire group of radio buttons shares a single name and a single object. To access the individual buttons, you treat the radio object as an array. The buttons are indexed, starting with 0. You use the checked property of a radio button to check its current state. The following statement checks the first radio button in the ctype group on the contact form:

document.contact.ctype[0].checked == true;

Radio Button Example

```
<!DOCTYPE html>
<html>
<body>

<form action="http://www.abc.com/submit.php">
 <p><b>Customer Type:</b>
 <input type="radio" name="ctype" value="Corporate"  checked="checked" /> Corporate
 <input type="radio" name="ctype" value="Home User" /> Home User
</p>
</form>


</body>
</html>
```

> **NOTE**
>
> *See Chapter 6 - Task 1 for a complete example on Radio button element.*

Output

Customer Type: ⦿ Corporate ◯ Home User

2.24 Checkbox Element

Defined using the tag <input type="checkbox"/>, checkboxes let a user select or de-select ONE or MORE options from the available choices. It has same attributes as radio buttons. It also has a single event, onClick, which occurs whenever the check box is clicked. This event examines the checked property to see whether the box was turned on or off.

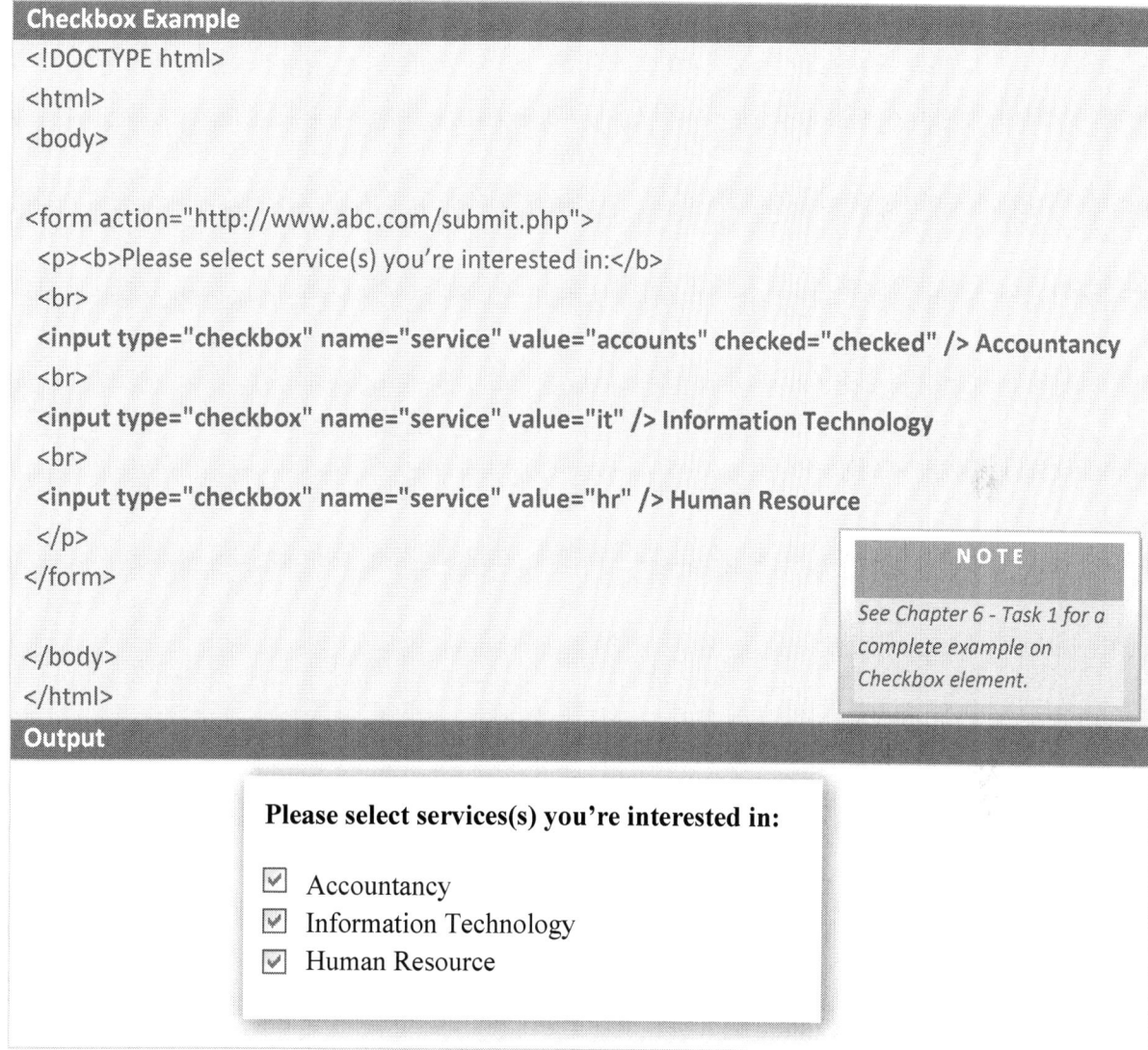

Checkbox Example

```html
<!DOCTYPE html>
<html>
<body>

<form action="http://www.abc.com/submit.php">
 <p><b>Please select service(s) you're interested in:</b>
 <br>
 <input type="checkbox" name="service" value="accounts" checked="checked" /> Accountancy
 <br>
 <input type="checkbox" name="service" value="it" /> Information Technology
 <br>
 <input type="checkbox" name="service" value="hr" /> Human Resource
 </p>
</form>

</body>
</html>
```

> **NOTE**
>
> *See Chapter 6 - Task 1 for a complete example on Checkbox element.*

Output

Please select services(s) you're interested in:

☑ Accountancy
☑ Information Technology
☑ Human Resource

2.25 Dropdown List Box Element

Similar to radio buttons, a drop down list box also allows you to select a single option from the provided list. Usage depends on the scenario. For example, if the list has few options, use the radio buttons and to display a long list of products you must choose a drop down list box.

In HTML a dropdown list box is defined with the \<select\> tag in conjunction with two or more \<option\> elements. The \<option\> tags inside the \<select\> element define the available options in the list. An attribute called *selected* can be added to an option to mark it as the default selected option when the page loads.

Reading the value of a selected item is a two-step process. You first use the selectedIndex property, and then use the value property to find the value of the selected choice. Here's an example:

> *nIdx = document.contactform.category.selectedIndex;*
> *sCat = document.contactform.category.options[nIdx].value;*

This uses the nIdx variable to store the selected index, and then assigns the value of the selected choice to the sCat variable. Things are a bit more complicated with a multiple selection where you need to test each option's selected attribute separately.

Dropdown List Box Example

```
<!DOCTYPE html>
<html>
<body>

<form action="http://www.abc.com/submit.php">
 <p><b>Services - Sub-category</b></p>
 <select name="category">
  <option value="sw">Software</option>
  <option selected="selected" value="hw">Hardware</option>
  <option value="nw">Network</option>
 </select>
</form>

</body>
</html>
```

> **NOTE**
>
> *See Chapter 6 - Task 1 for a complete example on Dropdown List Box element.*

Output

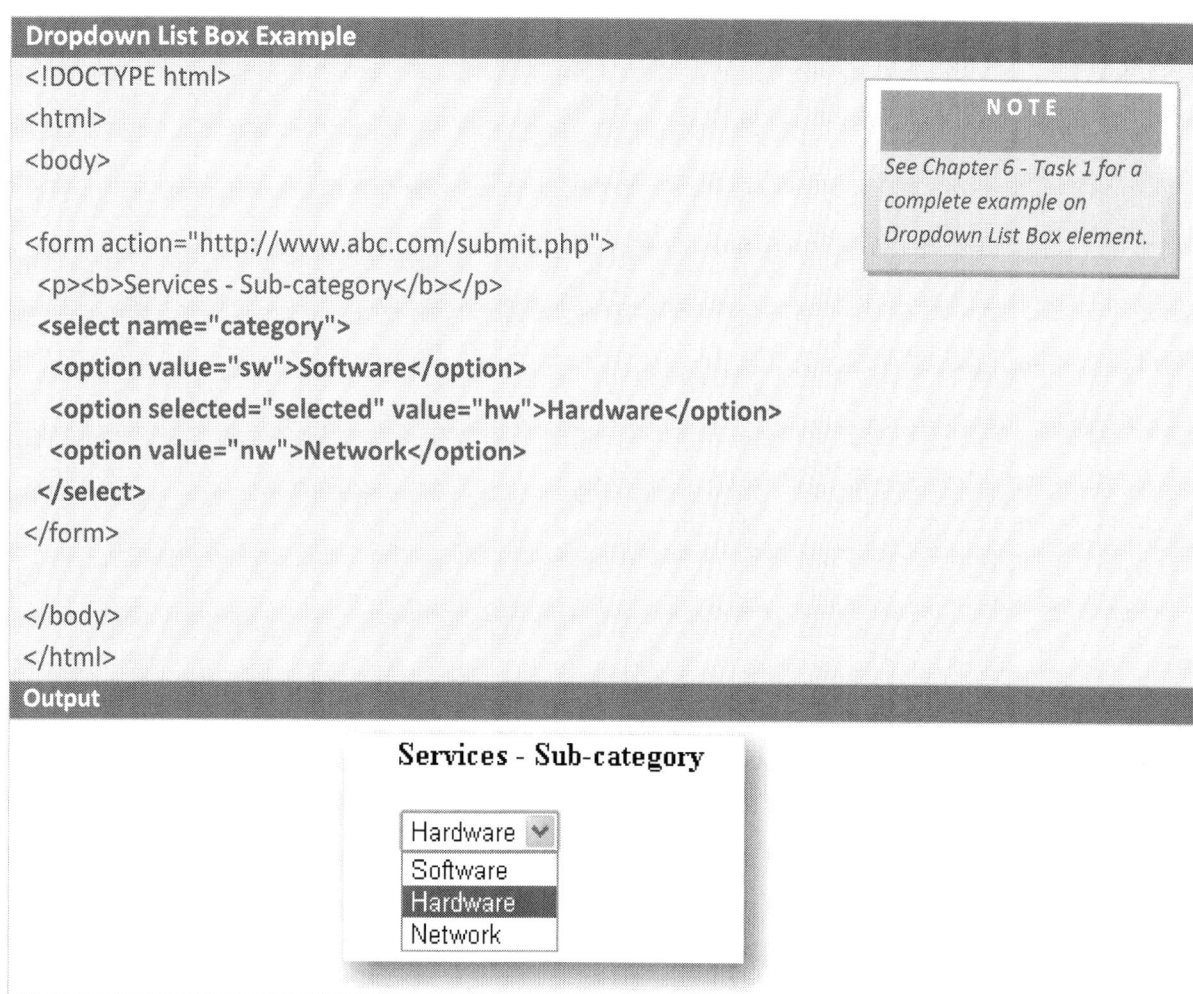

2.26 Submit Button Element

After completing a web form you need something to inform the browser to send the information to the server. A submit button is used to accomplish this task and is the recommended way to submit HTML forms. It is defined using the tag <input type="submit" /> and its value attribute acts as the button's label. After clicking this button, the data is sent to the page specified in the form's action attribute which performs some actions with the received input. In the following exercise, the information is sent to a page "xyz.php" on the server. The server processes the input and returns the answer as shown in the output pane. For this purpose, we used the GET method which retrieves the inputted information from the server. Server processing is an advanced topic and will be discussed in Chapter 5 and Chapter 6. At this stage, if you click the submit button after running the example code, you'll get an error indicating that the browser could not find the file 'submit.php'.

Besides SUBMIT you can use two other types, RESET and BUTTON. The RESET button sets all the form fields back to their default value, or blank. The BUTTON performs an action associated with a JavaScript event handler. If the user presses a Submit or a Reset button, you can detect it with the onSubmit or onReset event handlers. For generic buttons, you can use an onClick event handler.

Submit Button Example

```
<!DOCTYPE html>
<html>
<body>

<form name="input" action="xyz.php" method="get">
 <input type="checkbox" name="service" value="accounts" /> Accountancy <br>
 <input type="checkbox" name="service" value="it" /> Information Technology <br>
 <input type="checkbox" name="service" value="hr" /> Human Resource  <br><br>
 <input type="submit" value="Submit" />
 <input type="reset" value="Reset" />
</form>

<p>Click the Submit button to get the form-data from a page xyz.php</p>

</body>
</html>
```

> **NOTE**
>
> *For further details on the usage of Submit button, see the following sections:*
>
> *Chapter 6 - Task 1*
> *Chapter 5 - Section 5.12.2*
> *Chapter 6 - Section 6.4*

Output

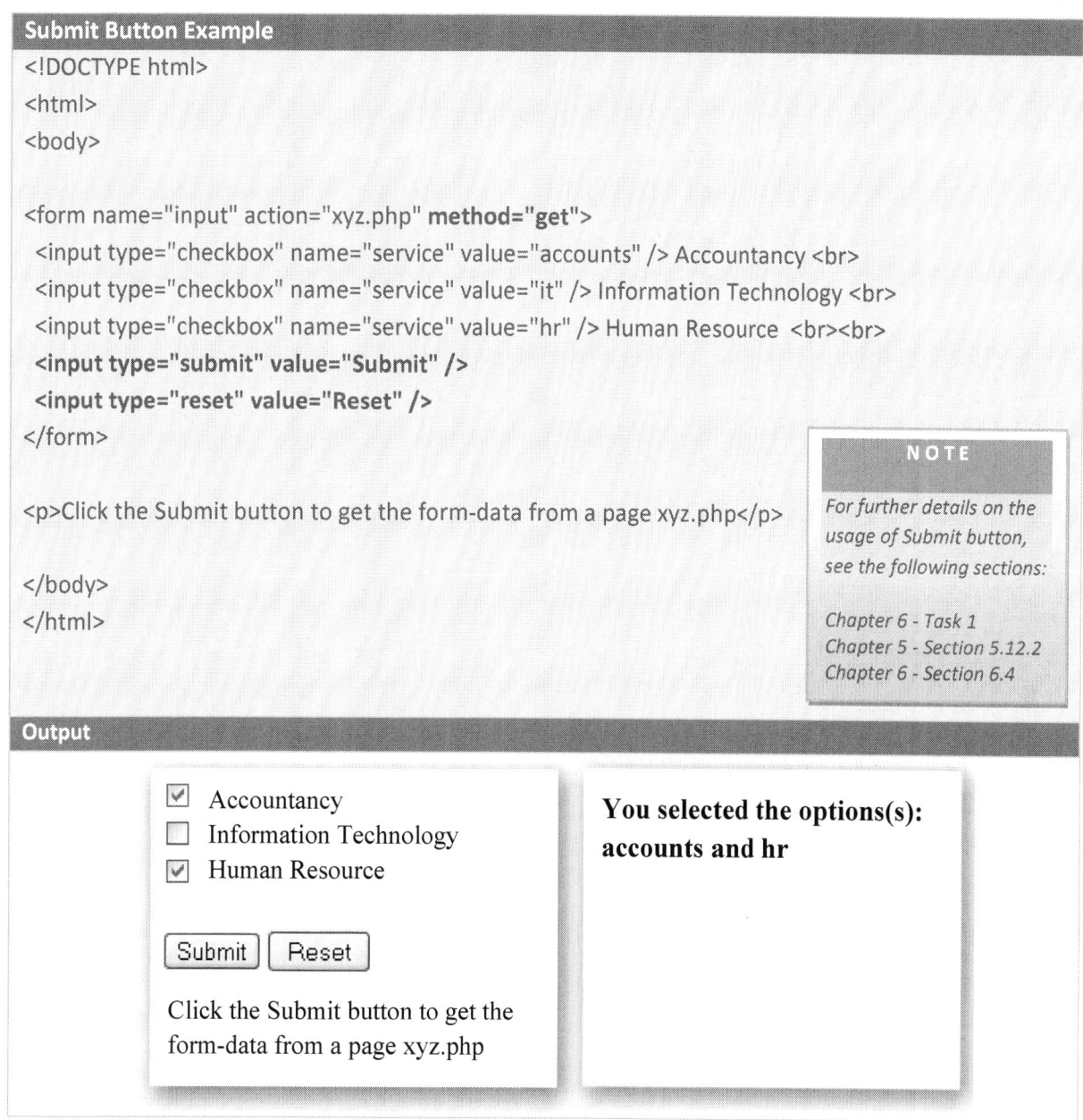

Besides a usual button, you can also use an image by replacing the code with the following one. Here, submit.jpg is a JPEG file located in the images folder. You'll use this input type extensively in the last project in Chapter 6.

<input type="image" src="images/submit.jpg" width="70" height="20"/>

2.27 Button Element

Just like desktop application forms, you can create a push button on a web form as well using the markup <button type="button">text/image</button>. The main difference between this element and buttons created with the <input> element is that you can add text or image inside a button element which provides you more control over button's appearance. It is recommended to always specify the *type* attribute for this element because browsers use different types for it. In addition, due to variation in browsers' way of submission, use the <input> element to create buttons in an HTML form.

Button Example

```
<!DOCTYPE html>
<html>
<body>
<form action="http://www.abc.com/add.php">
  <button><img src="images/add.gif" alt="add" width="10" height="10" /> Add</button>
</form>
</body>
</html>
```

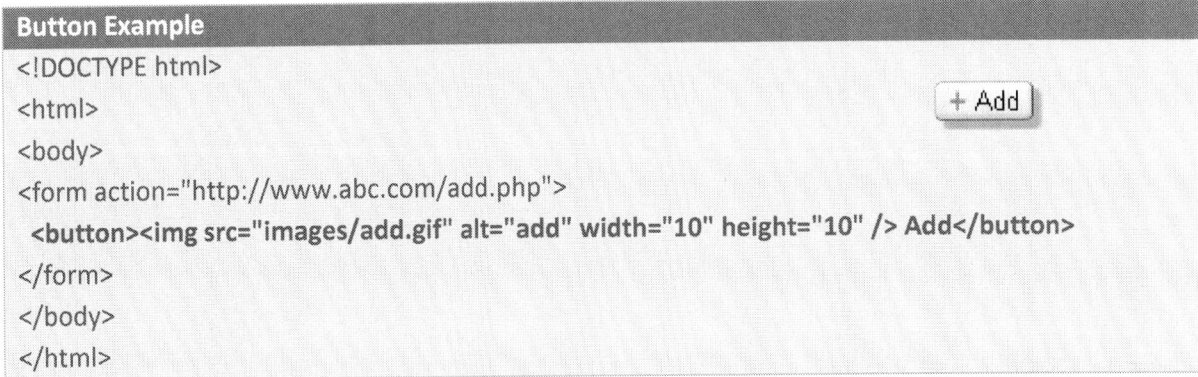

2.28 File Input Element

To allow users to upload their documents, images, videos or other files to your web server you again use the <input> element with type="file" attribute. In such situations, you must set the method attribute value to POST. The accept attribute specifies the types of files that the server accepts. To specify more than one value, separate the values with a comma e.g. accept="audio/*,video/*,image/*".

File Input Example

```
<!DOCTYPE html>
<html>
<body>
  <form action="http://www.abc.com/upload.php" method="post">
    <p>Upload your image in GIF format:</p>
    <input type="file" name="pic" accept="image/gif" />
    <input type="submit" value="Upload" />
  </form>
</body>
</html>
```

NOTE

See Chapter 6 - Section 6.13.5 on how to use this input type.

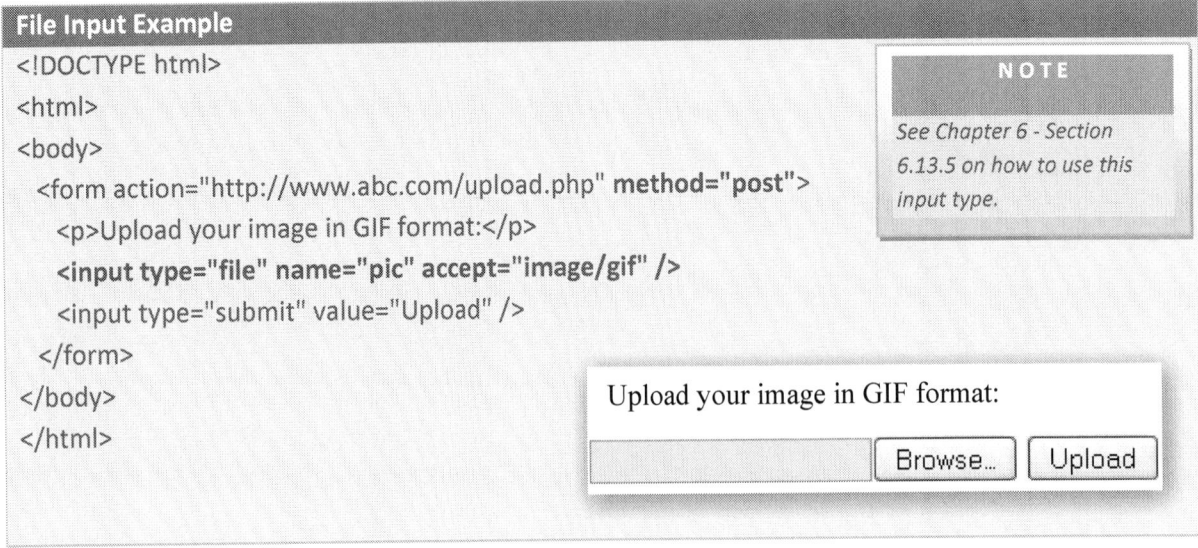

2.29 Grouping Form Elements

If your form has different sections, you can separate them using the <fieldset> element which draws a box around the related form controls to group them. You add the <legend> tag immediately after the opening <fieldset> tag to define a caption that informs the purpose of that section.

Form Controls Grouping Example

```
<!DOCTYPE html>
<html>
<body>
  <form>
    <fieldset>
      <legend>Contact Information</legend>
      <label>Name:<br>
      <input type="text" name="name" /></label><br>
      <label>Email:<br>
      <input type="text" name="email" /></label><br>
      <label>Mobile:<br>
      <input type="text" name="mobile" /></label>
    </fieldset>
  </form>
</body>
</html>
```

> **NOTE**
>
> See Chapter 4 - Section 4.2.1 for a more comprehensive example.

Output

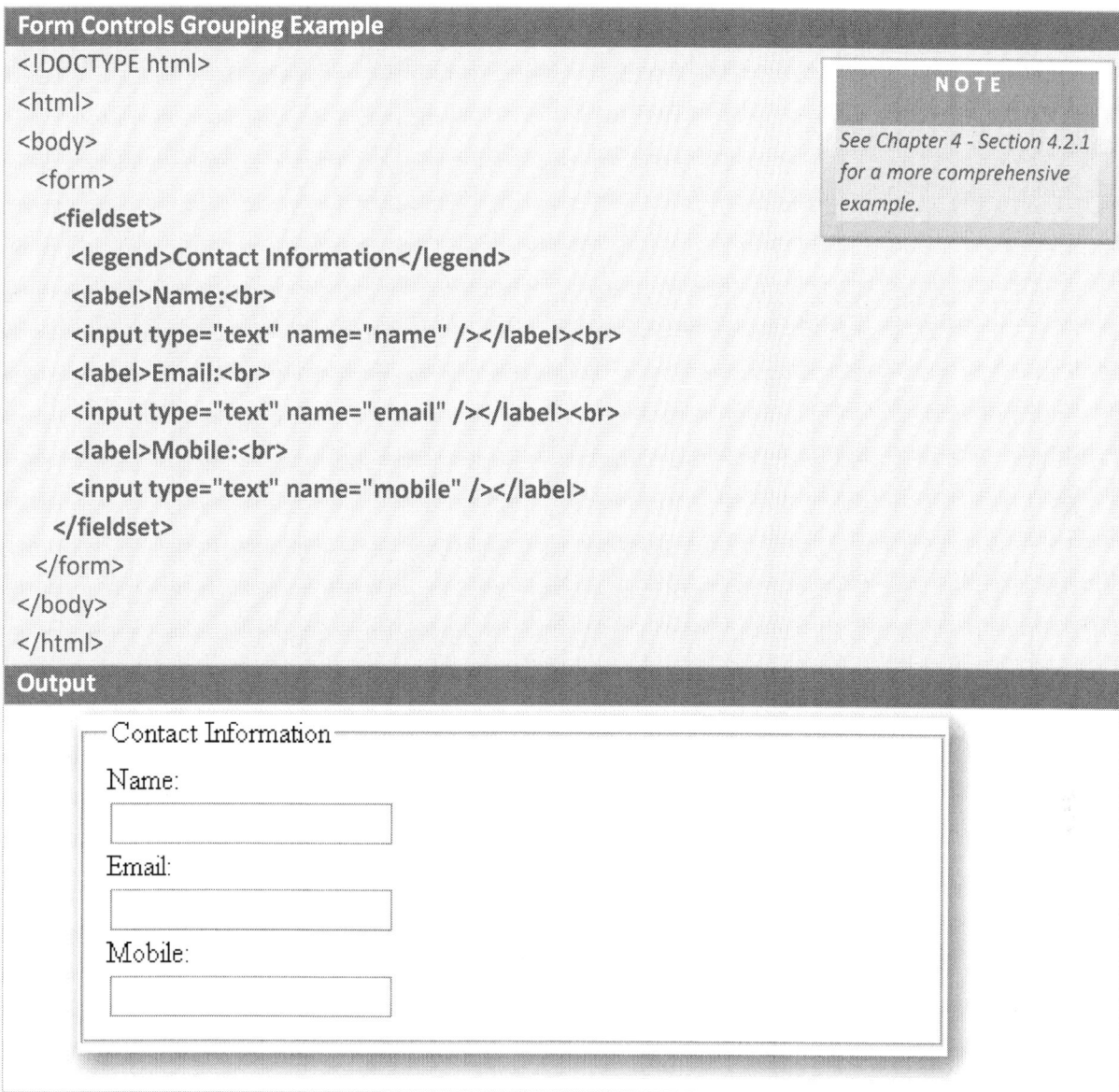

2.30   iFrames in HTML

Use an iframe to display another web page within a web page. It stands for inline frame and its content is defined using the src attribute. Use width and height attributes to set the frame size. You can show a page either from your own website or any other on the web.

iFrame Example

```
<!DOCTYPE html>
<html>
<body>
  <iframe src="http://www.oracle.com" width="450" height="380"></iframe>
</body>
</html>
```

Output

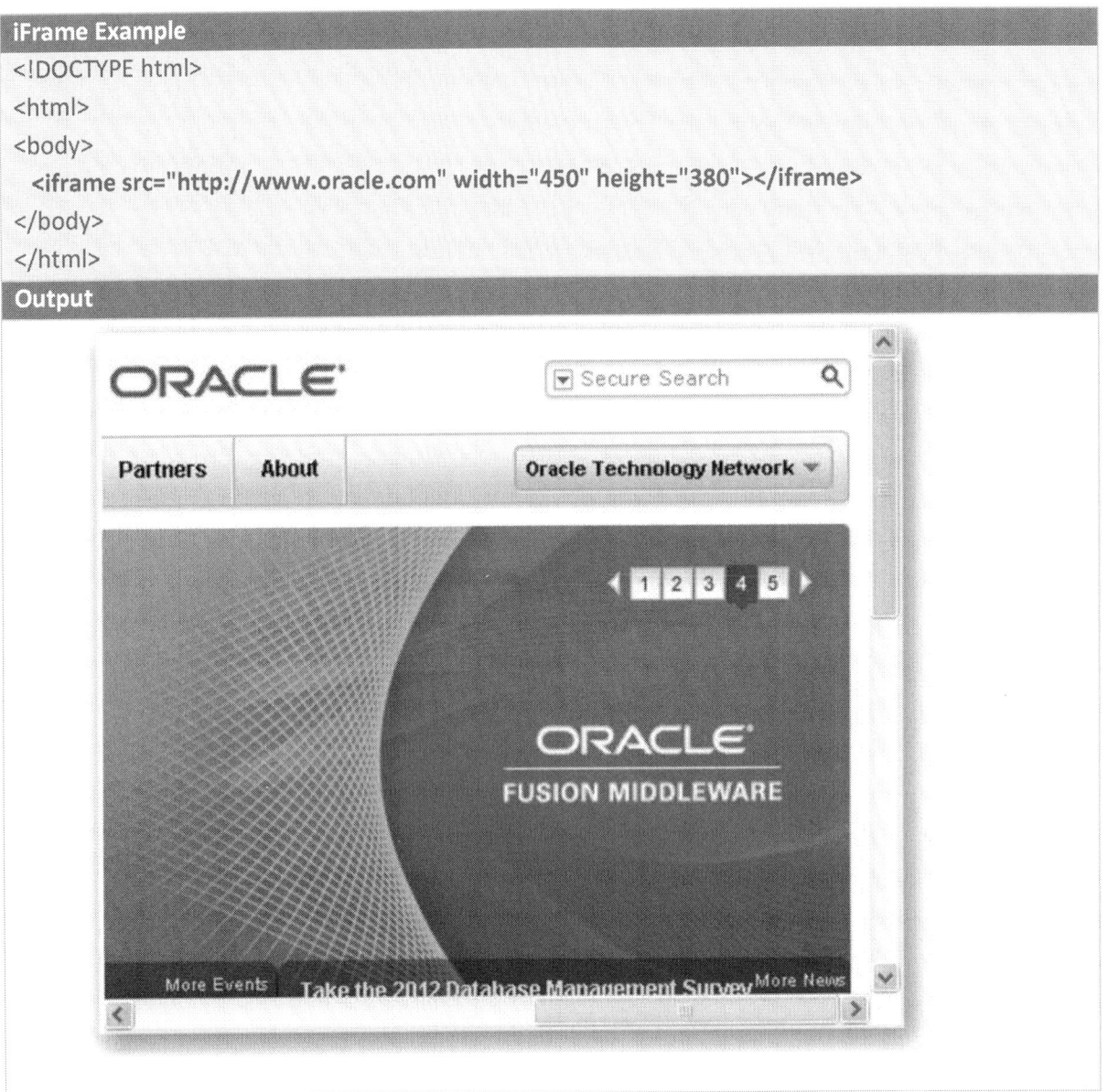

2.31 What's New in HTML5

In previous sections you saw many examples of <input> HTML element. The new flavor of this markup language, HTML5, has introduced some new attribute values that are discussed in the next few sections.

Structural Element	Description
<article>	Defines an article such as a blog post or main content on a web page
<aside>	Defines content aside from the page content like blog archives or events list
<figure>	Contains content like illustrations, diagrams, photos, code listings, etc.
<figcaption>	Defines a caption for a <figure> element
<footer>	Defines a footer for a document or section
<header>	Defines a header for a document or section
<hgroup>	Groups a set of <h1> to <h6> elements when a heading has multiple levels
<nav>	Defines navigation links
<section>	Defines a section in a document

Media Element	Description
<audio>	Defines sound content
<video>	Defines a video or movie
<source>	Defines multiple media resources for <video> and <audio>

HTML5 has several new input types for forms. These new features allow better input control and validation.

HTML5 New Input Types		
color	datetime-local	number
date	email	range
datetime	month	search
tel	time	url
week		

NOTE

Not supported under the older browsers, the examples in this section should be executed in a latest browsers.

2.31.1 Calendar Element

In HTML5, a new date value is added to the type attribute which displays a calendar control on your web page from which users can select a desired date as demonstrated in the following example.

Calendar Control Example

```
<!DOCTYPE html>
<html>
<body>
<form action="http://www.abc.com/info/" method="post">
  <label for="username">Date of birth:</label>
  <input type="date" name="dob" />
  <input type="submit" value="Submit" />
</form>
</body>
</html>
```

> **NOTE**
> *Supported only by Safari, Chrome, and Opera browsers at the time of this writing.*

Output

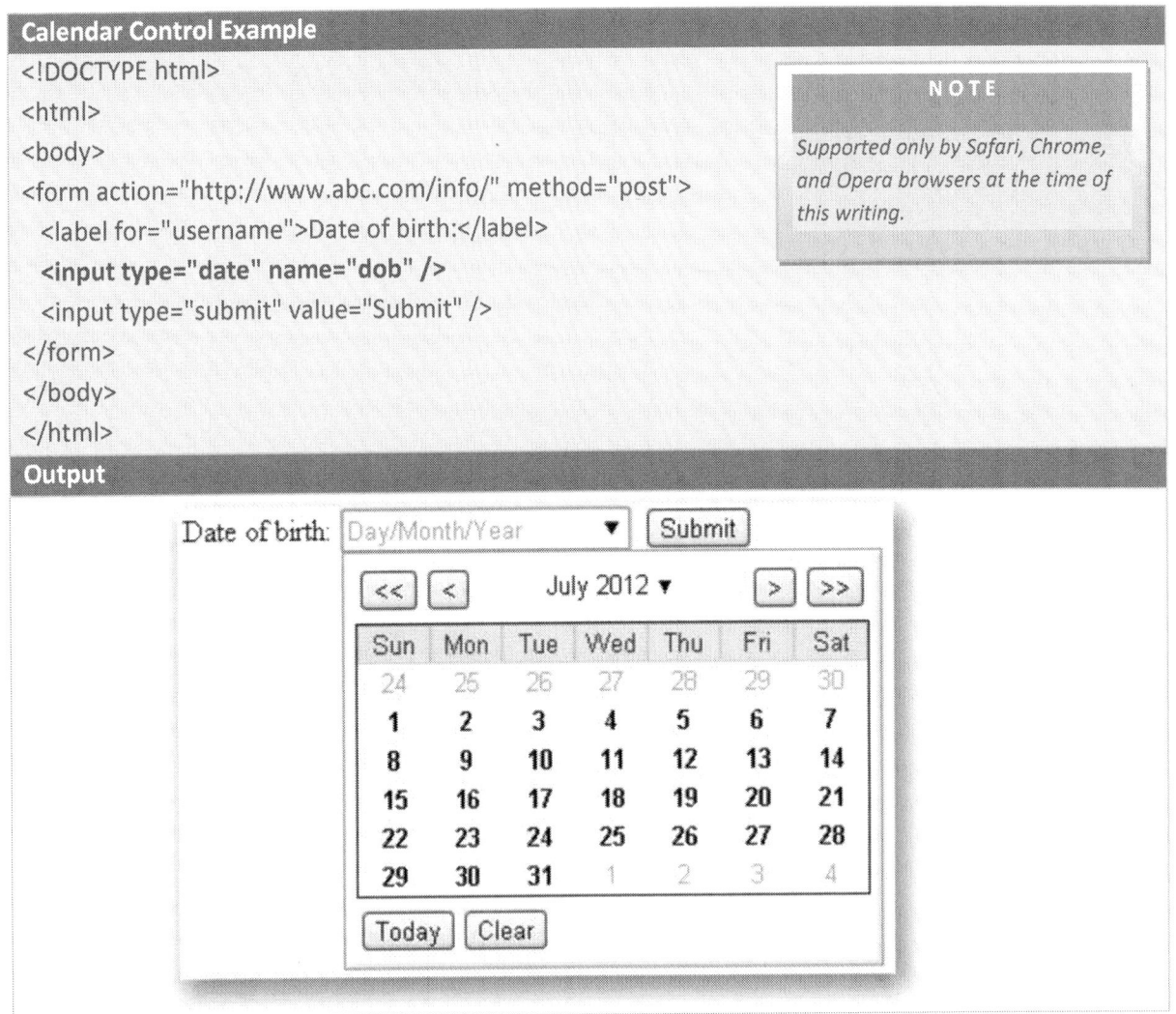

2.31.2 Form Validation

There are some mandatory fields in a form that must not be left blank e.g. User ID, Password etc. Users are alerted to provide such information if they omit them. This process is called form validation. Usually, a scripting language (such as JavaScript - discussed in Part III of this book) is used by developers to validate a form on client machines prior to posting data to the server. But now, HTML5 is introducing client side validation to quickly identify problems in a form. Some of these are listed below with examples.

2.31.2-i Required & Placeholder Attributes

The required attribute applies to all input fields, and specifies that an input field must be filled out before submitting the form. It is defined as <input required="required" />. The placeholder attribute specifies a short hint that describes the expected value of an input field (e.g. a sample e-mail address in the expected format). The hint is displayed in the input field when it is empty, and disappears when the field gets focus.

Required Attribute Example

```
<!DOCTYPE html>
<html>
<body>
<form action="abc.php">
   User ID: <input type="text" name="userid" required="vital" placeholder="me@example.com"/>
   Password: <input type="password" name="password" required="vital" />
   <input type="submit" value="Submit" />
</form>
</body>
</html>
```

Output

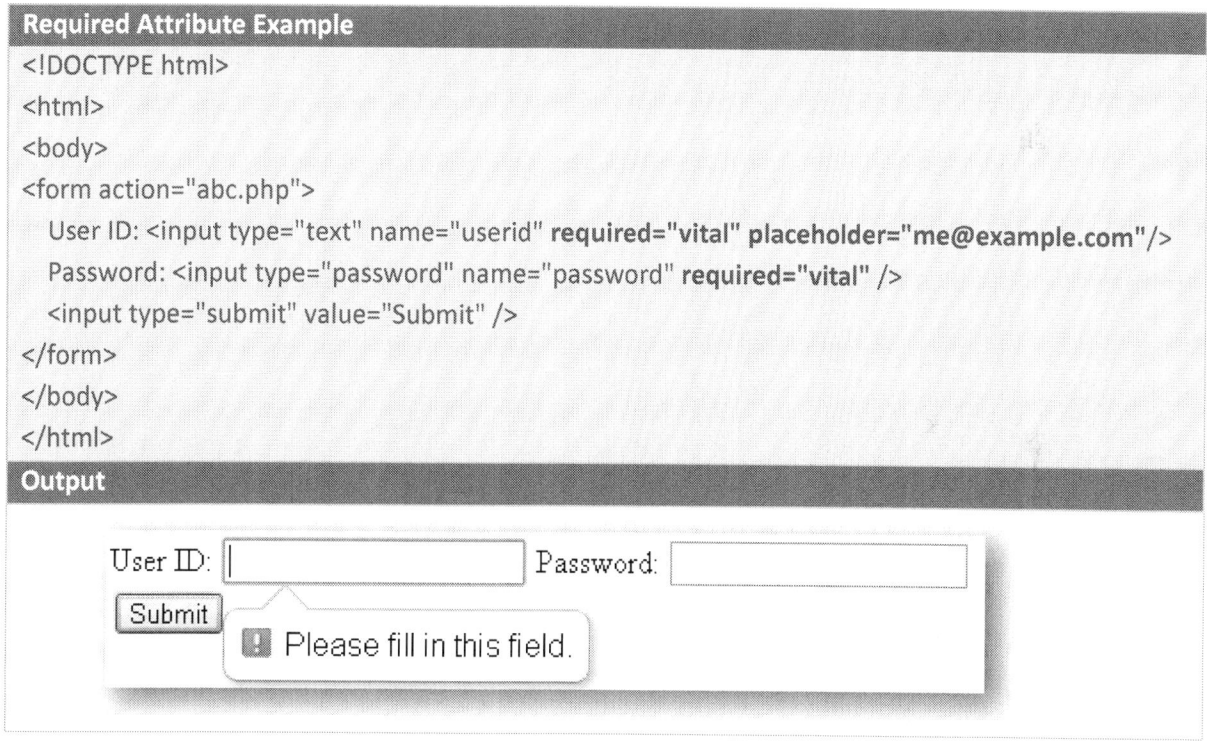

2.31.2-ii Validate E-mail and URL

If your form has mandatory email and url fields, you can validate them using the new input type values as shown in the following examples. Browsers supporting HTML5 will check and validate the correct format.

```
<input type="email" name="email" />
<input type="url" name="website" />
```

NOTE

You'll use the email input type in Newsletter Subscription, Admin & Member login, and Reset Password modules in the final project.

31.3 Add Search Box to a Web Page

Like every good website you could add search capabilities to your site. A search box allows users to search content that is not apparently visible to them. HTML5 has provided a new input type called search to address search queries. Once again, the following code sends the search criteria to a page (abc.php) on the server to process the request.

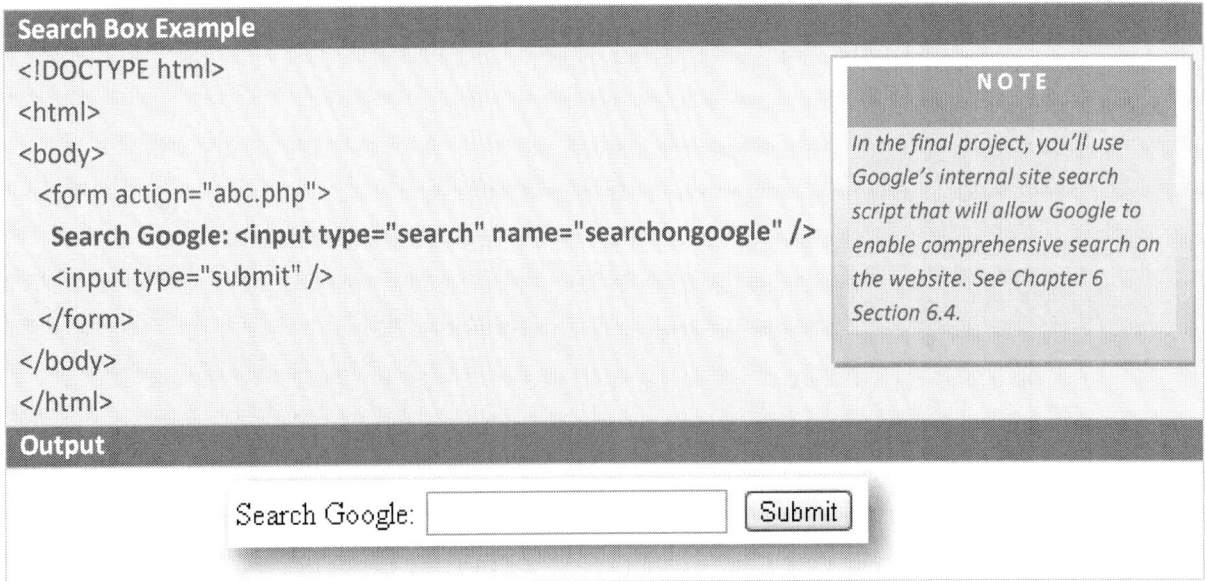

Search Box Example

```
<!DOCTYPE html>
<html>
<body>
  <form action="abc.php">
    Search Google: <input type="search" name="searchongoogle" />
    <input type="submit" />
  </form>
</body>
</html>
```

> **NOTE**
>
> *In the final project, you'll use Google's internal site search script that will allow Google to enable comprehensive search on the website. See Chapter 6 Section 6.4.*

Output

Search Google: [   ] [Submit]

31.4 Play Videos on a Web Page

In HTML5 you can play movie clip and other video streams using the new <video> tag. The src attribute specifies the URL of the video file. The controls attribute displays video controls which include:

- Play
- Pause
- Seeking
- Volume
- Fullscreen toggle
- Captions/Subtitles (when available)
- Track (when available)

Internet Explorer 8 and earlier versions do not support the <video> tag. In order for users viewing your video through older or latest browsers you need to upload the video in at least two different formats as did in the example below. The <source> element inside the <video> element is used to run this video on all supported browsers. You specify alternative video/audio files which the browser may choose from, based on its media type or codec support. Use the <audio> tag to play audio files in HTML5.

Video Example	Output

``html
<!DOCTYPE html>
<html>
<body>
 	
<video width="320" height="240"
controls="controls">
  <source src="tennis.mp4" type="video/mp4" />
  <source src="tennis.webm" type="video/webm" />
  Your browser does not support the video tag.
</video>
 	
</body>
</html>
``
	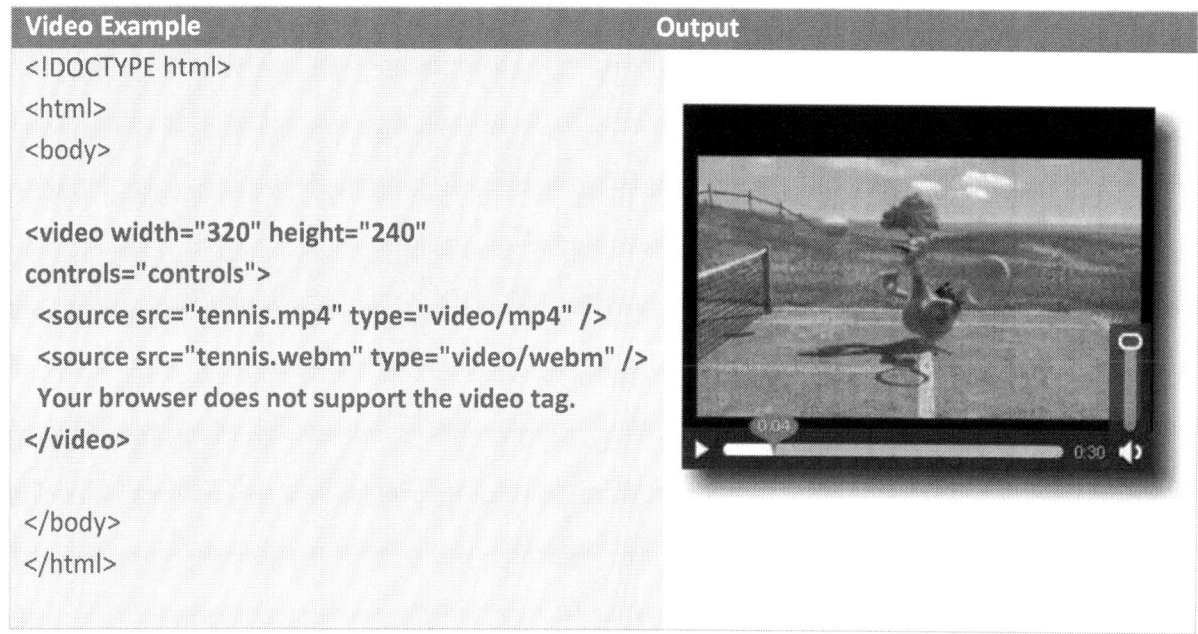

31.5 New HTML5 Layout

HTML5 introduces a new set of elements (depicted in the illustration below) that help web page authors describe the structure of the page. The names of these elements indicate the kind of content they carry. For example, the header sits inside a new <header> element, the navigation in a <nav> element, and the articles are in individual <article> elements. With this structure, screen reader software might allow users to ignore headers and footers and get straight to the content. Similarly, search engines might place more weight on the content in an <article> element than that in the <header> or <footer> elements. You'll see this layout throughout the final project in Chapter 6.

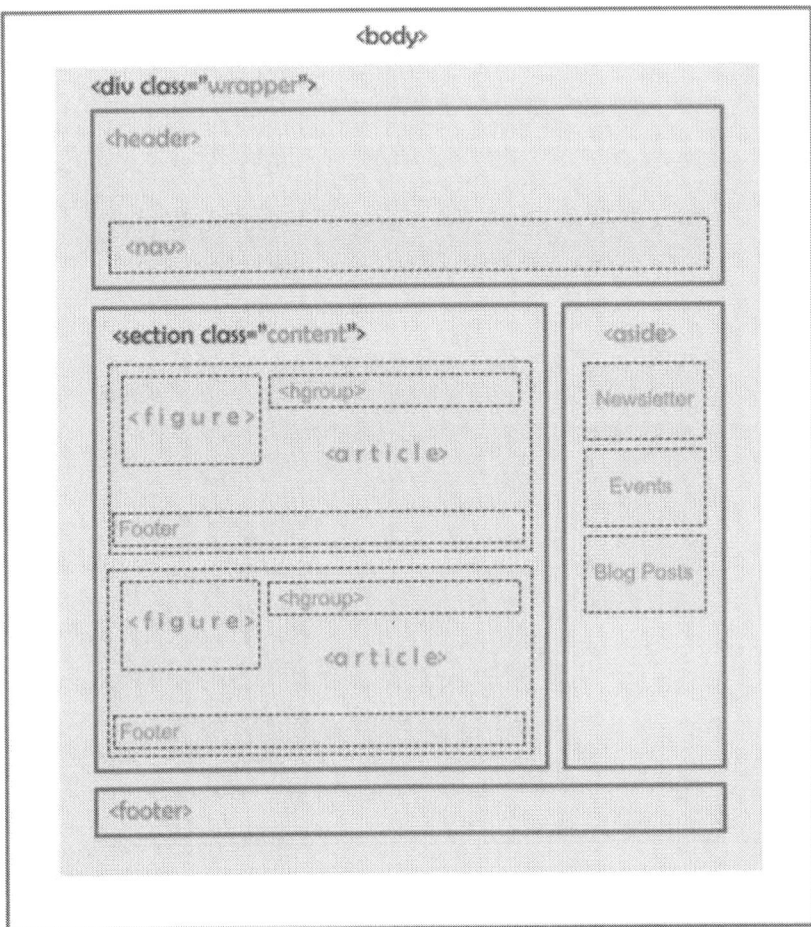

Figure 2-4

- What is CSS?

- Why use CSS?

- What are different types of cascading style sheets and how CSS rules are defined using its syntax?

- Add CSS color, font, text alignment, size, borders, spacing and more to make your website professional

- How to add animation?

CHAPTER 3

CASCADING STYLE SHEETS

{CSS}

A winner never quits and a quitter never wins.

3.1 About Cascading Style Sheets

Having gone through the previous part, you might have observed that HTML is very restrictive with respect to web page formatting. This is because it was designed to format and send documents over sparse networks in a fastest possible way. Due to this limitation of HTML, the need for a styling language surfaced and caused the basis for the emergence of Cascading Style Sheet (CSS).

CSS is a style sheet language used for describing the presentation semantics of a document written in a markup language. Its most common application is to style web pages written in HTML and XHTML, but the language can also be applied to any kind of XML document, including plain XML, SVG and XUL. CSS is designed primarily to enable the separation of document content from document presentation, including elements such as the layout, colors, and fonts.

Prior to CSS, nearly all of the presentational attributes of HTML documents were contained within the HTML markup; all font colors, background styles, element alignments, borders and sizes had to be explicitly described, often repeatedly, within the HTML. This made documents more complex, larger, and more difficult to maintain. CSS allows authors to move much of that information to another file, the style sheet, resulting in considerably simpler HTML. CSS can define color, font, text alignment, size, borders, spacing, layout and many other typographic characteristics, and can do so independently for on-screen and printed views.

Style sheets are usually contained within an external CSS file (but they don't have to be) and are linked in to every web page that you are working with using the <link> tag. Therefore, any or all styles from that CSS file can be applied to the web pages that you are working with, ultimately providing you with the flexibility to quickly and easily modify one CSS file that propagates changes to all web pages that share the CSS file in your Web site. You can refer multiple style sheet files in your web page. For instance, use one file to control the presentation (such as fonts and colors) and use another to control the layout. Due to these capabilities of CSS, the use of all presentational HTML markups has been deprecated.

STYLE SHEET RULES

A style sheet is a collection of one or more styling instructions called rules that define how an element or a group of elements should appear on the web page. The initial step to learn CSS is to understand the parts of a rule - briefed in section 3.4.

3.2 CSS Benefits

A consulting firm - ABC Global Consulting - created a web site with more than a hundres pages. To provide a consistent look, they used the same font face, size, and color on all pages. After some time, they decided to change the font from Times to Arial, and the font color from gray to black for their whole site. Just imagine how frustrating it would be to apply these changes to the whole bunch of pages individually. This is where CSS comes in to resolve the issue. It allows you to create just one file which holds all style rules that dictate how the text within your web site should look. Had ABC Global Consulting used CSS, they would have made changes just to a single style sheet file to instantly change the style and layout of the entire web site all at once.

3.3 What is CSS3?

CSS3 is the latest standard for CSS. It is completely backward compatible, so you will not have to change existing designs. Browsers will always support CSS2. CSS3 is split up into "modules". The old specification has been split into smaller pieces, and new ones are also added.

Some of the most important CSS3 modules are:

- Selectors
- Box Model
- Backgrounds and Borders
- Text Effects
- 2D/3D Transformations
- Animations
- Multiple Column Layout
- User Interface

3.4 CSS Rules and Syntax

A CSS file consists of various rules that enhance the look of your web pages. These rules are associated with HTML elements and format the content of specified elements such as font properties, positioning properties, border properties, and much more. A CSS rule has two main parts: a selector, and one or more declarations (separated by a semi-colon):

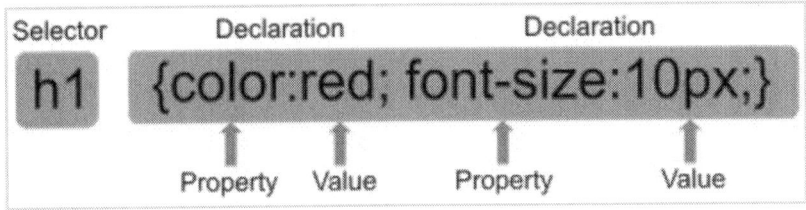

Figure 3-1

The selector is normally the HTML element you want to style. Selectors are case sensitive, so they must exactly match element names and attribute values. Declarations sit inside curly brackets. Each declaration consists of a property and a value. The property is the style attribute you want to change with an associated value. You can specify multiple selectors in a single rule as well as multiple alternative values for a single property like:

h1, h2 {font-family: Arial, Verdana, sans-serif;}

You create generic rules in a style sheet that apply to most elements and then override individual element properties that you need to display differently with inline styling.

3.5 Creating Style Sheets

Usually, the following three methods are used to add style to your web pages:

External CSS: The most popular and time-efficient way to create style sheet is using an external CSS file. It is ideal when the style is applied to many pages. An external style sheet can be created in any text editor, should not contain any html tags, and must be saved with a .css extension. After creating an external style sheet file, you link each page to it using the <link> tag, which goes inside the <head> section. The href attribute holds name and path of the style sheet (.css file).

```
<head>
  <link rel="stylesheet" type="text/css" href="style.css" />
</head>
```

> **NOTE**
>
> *To take full advantage of this technology, you'll use an external css file named style.css in the final project.*

Later, when the time comes to make changes to the appearance or structure of your web site, you make modifications on the one CSS file, and all of the pages of your web site will instantly change to reflect the changes made within the CSS file.

Internal CSS: An internal style sheet, also known as document-wide style sheet, should be used when a single document (web page) is to be provided a unique style. It is defined in the <head> section of an HTML page using the <style> tag.

```
<head>
  <style type="text/css">
    hr {color:gray;}
    p {margin-left:10px;}
    body {background-image:url("images/bg.png");}
  </style>
</head>
```

Inline CSS: In this method a style attribute is directly added to the relevant element resulting in loss of advantages of a style sheet. It is not a recommended method and should be used sparingly. In the following example a text box is created and styled with a beveled border:

```
<input type="text" style="border-style:groove" />
```

> **NOTE**
>
> *For inline style usage, see Section 6.13.4 - Update Product and 6.13.5 - Image Manager modules in the final project.*

3.6 Understand the Cascade

As mentioned in a preceding section, you can reference multiple style sheets in a single web page. In a situation like this, if you've set some properties for the same selector in different style sheets, the values are taken and applied from the more specific style sheet. A question arises here: What is a specific style sheet? Looking at the scenario, you must first understand the cascading order prior to going through a practical example.

When you apply a style to an HTML element through multiple style sheets, all styles cascade into a new virtual style sheet using the following order of priority rules:

1. Inline style
2. Internal style sheet
3. External style sheet
4. Browser default

The above rule says that an inline style, specified within an HTML element, has the highest priority and will override a style defined in an internal style sheet, defined inside the <head> section, or in an external style sheet, or in a browser. Moreover, if an external style sheet link is placed after the internal style sheet in HTML <head> tag, the external style sheet will override the internal style sheet.

Let's try to understand the cascading concept through an example. You created an **external style sheet** that contains three declarations for the h3 selector:

```
h3
{
  color:blue;
  text-align:left;
  font-size:10pt;
}
```

You also set two properties in an **internal style sheet** for the same h3 selector:

```
h3
{
  text-align:right;
  font-size:20pt;
}
```

The properties for h3 selector will cascade into a new virtual style sheet as follows:

```
color:blue;
text-align:right;
font-size:20pt;
```

The color is taken from the external style sheet because this property is defined only in the external style sheet. Since the internal style sheet is more specific to the page and has higher priority, the text alignment and the font size are inherited from it.

One more concept relevant to the current scenario is the *!important* property. It is a way to make your CSS cascade but also have the rules you feel are most crucial always be applied. A rule that has the *!important* property will always be applied no matter where that rule appears in the CSS document. To make sure that a property always applied, you would add the *!important* property to the tag. So, to make the paragraph text always red, you would write:

```
p { color: #ff0000 !important; }
```

3.7 CSS ID and Class

Besides setting styles for HTML elements, CSS allows you to specify your own selectors called "id" and "class".

The id Selector is used to specify a style for a single, unique element. It uses the id attribute of the HTML element, and is defined with a "#" identifier.

N O T E

Note: In order to evaluate the following examples, create an external style sheet file named "styles.css" in a text editor, such as Notepad, using the code provided in the CSS Code section below. Place the files styles.css and html together so that the browser could access the style sheet.

HTML Code

```
<!DOCTYPE html>
<html>
<head>
  <link rel="stylesheet" type="text/css" href="styles.css" />
</head>
<body>
  <p id="para1">A paragraph styled with id selector</p>
  <p>This paragraph is not affected by the style.</p>
</body>
</html>
```

CSS Code

```
#para1
  {
  text-align:center;
  color:red;
  }
```

Output

A paragraph styled with id selector

This paragraph is not affected by the style.

The class selector is used to specify a style for a group of elements. This means you can set a particular style for many HTML elements with the same class. It uses the HTML class attribute, and is defined with a "." identifier.

HTML Code - Class Selector Example

```
<!DOCTYPE html>
<html>
<head>
  <link rel="stylesheet" type="text/css" href="styles.css" />
</head>
<body>
  <h1 class="center">Heading aligned centrally using class selector</h1>
  <p class="center">Paragraph aligned centrally using the same class selector.</p>
</body>
</html>
```

CSS Code

```
.center
 {
   text-align:center;
 }
```

Output

Heading aligned centrally using class selector

Paragraph aligned centrally using the same class selector.

3.8 Comments in CSS

Developers add comments to explain their code. Comments also help them assess the source code at a later date. In CSS comments are enclosed in /* and */ pair and are ignored by browsers. You'll see use of comments in the next example.

3.9 CSS Color Property

Powerful and important communication tool, colors are the life of modern websites. Without effective colors it is nearly impossible to design a winning site. In CSS, color and background-color properties are used to set foreground and background colors respectively and are specified by:

- **HEX value** - Hex values represent values for red, green, and blue in hexadecimal code like "#ff0000".
- **Color name** - Colors are represented by predefined names like red, blue, green etc. There are 147 color names defined in the HTML and CSS color specification.
- **RGB value** - Values for red, green, and blue are expressed as numbers between 0 and 255 like "rgb(255,0,0)".
- **RGBA colors** - Supported in latest browsers, these color values are an extension of RGB and are specified as: rgba(red,green,blue,alpha) where the alpha parameter is a number between 0.0 and 1.0. The lowest value is used for full transparency whereas the highest number is used for full opaque.
- **HSL colors** - An HSL color value is specified with: hsl(hue, saturation, lightness). Hue is a degree on the color wheel (from 0 to 360) - 0 (or 360) is red, 120 is green, 240 is blue. Saturation is a percentage value; 0% means a shade of gray and 100% is the full color. Lightness is also a percentage; 0% is black, 100% is white. Example: *background-color:hsl(120,65%,75%);*
- **HSLA colors** - An HSLA color value is specified with: hsla(hue, saturation, lightness, alpha), where the alpha parameter defines the opacity. The alpha parameter is a number between 0.0 (fully transparent) and 1.0 (fully opaque). Example: *background-color:hsla(120,65%,75%,0.3);*

HTML Code with Internal CSS to demonstrate CSS Comment and CSS Color

```html
<!DOCTYPE html>
<html>
<head>
<style type="text/css">
  /* Body background color set using a HEX code */
  body {background-color: #A66600;}

  /* Main heading font and background colors set using names */
  h1 {color:white;}
  h1 {background-color:orange;}

  /* Used RGB values for paragraph with a class */
  p.ex {color:rgb(255,201,115);}
  p.ex {background-color:rgb(255,140,0);}
</style>
</head>

<body>
  <h1>ABC Global Consulting</h1>
  <p class="ex">This is a paragraph with class="ex".</p>
  <p>This is an ordinary paragraph without any color applied through CSS.</p>
</body>
</html>
```

Output

ABC Global Consulting

This is a paragraph with class="ex".

This is an ordinary paragraph without any color applied through CSS.

3.10 CSS Font

CSS font properties define the font family, boldness, size, and the style of a text.

Font Family

The font-family property allows you to specify the typeface that is applied to a text inside the element using a CSS rule. The font-family property should hold several font names as a "fallback" system. If the browser does not support the first font, it tries the next font. If the name of a font family is more than one word, it must be in quotation marks.

Examples:

body {font-family: Georgia, Times, serif;}
h1, h2 {font-family: Arial, Verdana, sans-serif;}
.fclass {font-family: "Courier New", Courier, monospace;}

Font Style

This property has three values:

normal - The text is shown normally

italic - The text is shown in italics

oblique - The text is leaning similar to italic, but less supported

Example:

.fclass {font-style: italic;}

Font Size

To set the size of a text you use the font-size property. You can specify font size using Pixels (px), Percentages (%) or em. Setting font size in pixels is the best way to ensure that the type appears at the size you intended.

Examples:

body {font-family: Arial, Verdana, sans-serif; font-size: 12px;}
h1 {font-size: 200%;}
h2 {font-size: 1.3em;}

Font Weight

This property takes two values - normal and bold. The normal value displays text in normal weight, bold makes the text bold.

Example:

.fclass {font-weight: bold;}

FONT SYNTAX

- *All font names, except generic font families, must be capitalized. For example, use "Arial" instead of "arial".*

- *Use commas to separate multiple font name.*

- *Font names that contain a character space (such as Courier New in the third example) must be placed within quotation marks.*

WHY USE MULTIPLE FONTS?

In CSS you can use a list of back-up fonts (font stack) if your first choice is not available. In the absence of the first specified font, the browser tries the next one, and down through the list until it finds one that works. For instance, in the first Font-Family example, if the browser does not find Georgia, it will use Times, and if Times is not available, it will substitute a generic serif font.

serif Examples: *Times, Times New Roman, Georgia*
sans-serif Examples: *Arial, Arial Black, Verdana, Trebuchet MS, Helvetica, Geneva*
monospaceExamples: *Courier, Courier New, and Andale Mono*

3.11 CSS Text

Described below are some common text properties that developers usually apply through CSS:

Text Transformation

Text-transform property is used to turn everything into uppercase or lowercase letters, or capitalize the first letter of each word.

Text Decoration

Text-decoration property is used to set or remove decorations from text. It is mostly used to remove underlines from links.

Text Alignment

Text-align property is used to set the horizontal alignment of a text. Text can be centered, or aligned to the left or right, or justified.

Text Indentation

Text-indent property is used to specify the indentation of the first line of a text.

Letter Spacing

The letter-spacing property increases or decreases the space between characters in a text.

Word Spacing

The word-spacing property increases or decreases the white space between words.

First Letter

The :first-letter selector is used to add a style to the first letter of the specified selector.

First Line

The :first-line selector is used to add a style to the first line of the specified selector.

A comprehensive example is presented on the next page to demonstrate CSS Fonts and CSS Text.

3.12 Style Links with Pseudo-Classes

CSS pseudo-classes are used to add special effects to some selectors. For example, you can set different styles to links that have or have not been visited.

:link - It is used to style links that have not been visited.

:visited - Sets styles for links that have been clicked.

:hover - Changes the appearance of an element when a pointing device such as a mouse is moved over it.

:active - It is applied when a button or a link is being clicked.

These classes should be used in the following order:

1. :link
2. :visited
3. :hover
4. :active

See an example on the four Pseudo-Classes in section 3.18.

CSS Font, Text, and Pseudo Class Example using Internal CSS Style

```
<!DOCTYPE html>
<html>
<head>
<style type="text/css">
    h1{text-align: center; text-transform: uppercase; color: #A7C942;}
    p {text-indent: 50px; text-align:justify; letter-spacing:3px;}
    p.c1{font-weight: bold;}
    p.c2:first-letter{color:#ff0000; font-size: 40px;}
    p.c2:first-line{color:#ff0000; font-variant:small-caps;}
    .c3{font-style: italic; text-align: right;}
    a{text-decoration:none;}
    a:hover {text-decoration: underline;}
</style>
</head>
<body>
    <h1>formatting text in css</h1>
    <p class="c1">A paragraph styled with class selector</p>
    <p class="c2">This text is styled with some of the text formatting properties. The heading uses the
            text-align, text-transform, and color properties. The paragraph is indented, aligned, space
            between characters is specified, first character of the paragraph is capitalized with a larger
            font size, and the first line is displayed in red color with all letters in small-caps. The
            underline is removed from the   <a target="_blank"
            href="http://www.abc.com/index.html">Visit our website</a> link but appears when
            mouse moves over it.</p>
    <p class="c3">by ABC</p>
</body>
</html>
```

Output

FORMATTING TEXT IN CSS

A paragraph styled with class selector

This text is styled with some of the text formatting properties. The heading uses the text-align, text-transform, and color properties. The paragraph is indented, aligned, space between characters is specified, first character of the paragraph is capitalized with a larger font size, and the first line is displayed in red color with all letters in small-caps. The underline is removed from the Visit our website link but appears when mouse moves over it.

by ABC

3.13 Styling Lists

In chapter 2 section 2.17 you saw three types of HTML lists: Ordered, Unordered, and Definition. Browsers automatically insert bullets before unordered list items and numbers before items in ordered lists. For the most part, the rendering of these markers is determined by the browser. In CSS, you can further style these lists and add images to act as list item marker instead of traditional bullet points.

CSS provides the following properties that allow you to choose the type and position of the marker, or turn them off entirely.

Property	Value
list-style-type	none
	disc
	circle
	square
	decimal
	decimal-leading-zero
	lower-alpha
	upper-alpha
	lower-latin
	upper-latin
	lower-roman
	upper-roman
	lower-greek
list-style-image	none
	url
list-style-position	Inside
	outside

list-style-type: With this property you can use various shapes and styles of markers. For example, you can use disc, circle, or square with unordered lists and decimal with leading-zero, lower/upper alpha, lower/upper roman etc. with ordered lists.

Example list-style-type

```
<!DOCTYPE html>
<html>
<head>
<style type="text/css">
  ul.c1 {list-style-type:circle;}
  ul.c2 {list-style-type:square;}
  ol.c3 {list-style-type:upper-roman;}
  ol.c4 {list-style-type:lower-alpha;}
</style>
</head>
<body>
  <h3>Examples of list-style-type property</h3>
  <p><b>Unordered Lists:</b></p>
  <ul class="c1">
   <li>Accountancy</li>
   <li>Software</li>
   <li>Human Resource</li>
  </ul>
  <ul class="c2">
   <li>Accountancy</li>
   <li>Software</li>
   <li>Human Resource</li>
  </ul>
  <p><b>Ordered Lists:</b></p>
  <ol class="c3">
   <li>Accountancy</li>
   <li>Software</li>
   <li>Human Resource</li>
  </ol>
  <ol class="c4">
   <li>Accountancy</li>
   <li>Software</li>
   <li>Human Resource</li>
  </ol>
</body>
</html>
```

Examples of list-style-type property

Unordered Lists:
- ○ Accountancy
- ○ Software
- ○ Human Resource

- ■ Accountancy
- ■ Software
- ■ Human Resource

Ordered Lists:
- I. Accountancy
- II. Software
- III. Human Resource

- a. Accountancy
- b. Software
- c. Human Resource

list-style-image: This property lets you specify an image as the list-item marker in a list. The example below uses an external style sheet. It also has margin property that is applied to set vertical space of 15 pixels among list items.

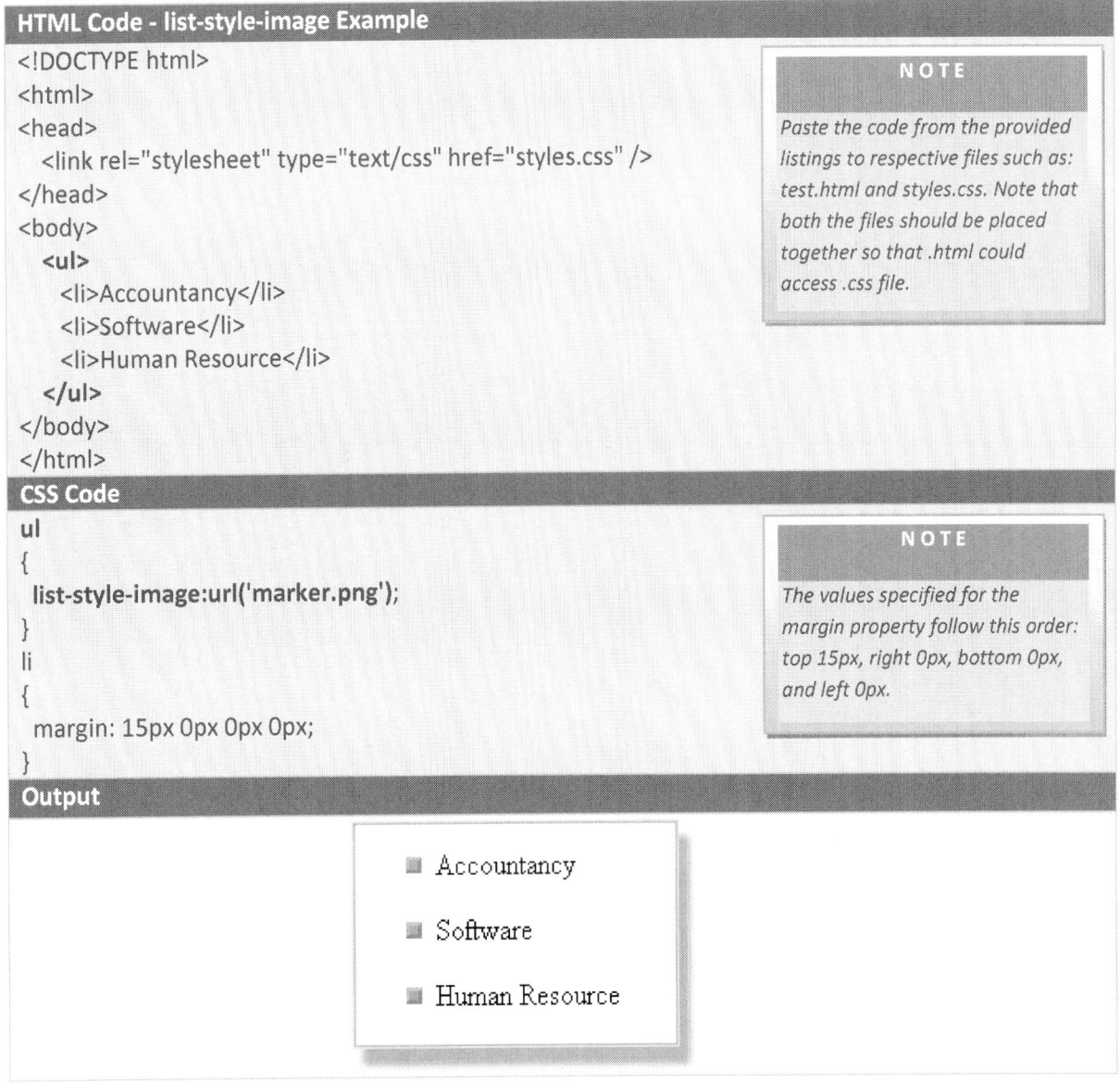

HTML Code - list-style-image Example

```
<!DOCTYPE html>
<html>
<head>
  <link rel="stylesheet" type="text/css" href="styles.css" />
</head>
<body>
  <ul>
    <li>Accountancy</li>
    <li>Software</li>
    <li>Human Resource</li>
  </ul>
</body>
</html>
```

NOTE

Paste the code from the provided listings to respective files such as: test.html and styles.css. Note that both the files should be placed together so that .html could access .css file.

CSS Code

```
ul
{
  list-style-image:url('marker.png');
}
li
{
  margin: 15px 0px 0px 0px;
}
```

NOTE

The values specified for the margin property follow this order: top 15px, right 0px, bottom 0px, and left 0px.

Output

- Accountancy
- Software
- Human Resource

list-style-position: Use this property to place markers inside or outside the content flow.

HTML Code - list-style-position Example

```
<!DOCTYPE html>
<html>
<head>
   <link rel="stylesheet" type="text/css" href="styles.css" />
</head>

<body>
   <ul class="c1">
      <li>Accountancy: ABC Global Consulting provides accountancy services...</li>
      <li>Software: We design tailor-cut desktop and web-based solutions to...</li>
   </ul>

   <ul class="c2">
      <li>Accountancy: ABC Global Consulting provides accountancy services...</li>
      <li>Software: We design tailor-cut desktop and web-based solutions to...</li>
   </ul>

</body>
</html>
```

CSS Code

```
ul
{
   width: 250px;
}
ul.c1
{
   list-style-position:
outside;
}
ul.c2
{
   list-style-position: inside;
}
```

Outside Position

- Accountancy: ABC Global Consulting provides accountancy services to its clients at very economical rates.

- Software: We design tailor-cut desktop and web-based solutions to cater your needs.

Inside Position

- Accountancy: ABC Global Consulting provides accountancy services to its clients at very economical rates.

- Software: We design tailor-cut desktop and web-based solutions to cater your needs.

A SHORTHAND PROPERTY

list-style: Use this shorthand property to set all the list properties in one declaration in the order: list-style-type, list-style-position, and list-style-image. **Example: list-style:circle inside;**

3.14 Styling Tables

You can also improve the look of a table through CSS as done in the following example.

HTML Code

```
<!DOCTYPE html>
<html>
<head>
<style type="text/css">
  /*Rule 1*/
  table, td, th {border-spacing: 0px;}
  /*Rule 2*/
  th {background-color:#0066cc; color:white;}
  /*Rule 3*/
  table {width:100%;}
  /*Rule 4*/
  tr.head th:first-child {-webkit-border-top-left-radius: 5px;-moz-border-radius-topleft: 5px;
  border-top-left-radius: 5px;}
  /*Rule 5*/
  tr.head th:last-child {-webkit-border-top-right-radius: 5px;-moz-border-radius-topright: 5px;
  border-top-right-radius: 5px;}
  /*Rule 6*/
  tr.even {background-color: #e0e9f0;}
  /*Rule 7*/
  td {border-top: 1px solid #f1f8fe; border-bottom: 1px solid #cbd2d8; border-right: 1px solid
  #cbd2d8;}
  /*Rule 8*/
  th {height:30px;}
  /*Rule 9*/
  .c1 {text-align:right;}
</style>
</head>
```

Continued ➜

```
<body>
<table>
  <tr class="head">
    <th>Firstname</th>
    <th>Lastname</th>
    <th>Salary</th>
  </tr>
  <tr>
    <td>Peter</td>
    <td>Griffin</td>
    <td class="c1">$100</td>
  </tr>
  <tr class="even">
    <td>Lois</td>
    <td>Griffin</td>
    <td class="c1">$150</td>
  </tr>
  <tr>
    <td>Joe</td>
    <td>Swanson</td>
    <td class="c1">$300</td>
  </tr>
  <tr class="even">
    <td>Cleveland</td>
    <td>Brown</td>
    <td class="c1">$250</td>
  </tr>
</table>
</body>
</html>
```

CSS RULES EXPLAINED

Rule 1: Zero pixel border-spacing is set at once for table, table data, and table heading. This is called selector grouping.

Rule 2: Table header background color is set to #006cc and font color to white.

Rule 3: Table's width is set to 100% to use the whole browser's width.

Rule 4: Adds a rounded border to the top-left corner of the table. Firefox requires the prefix -moz- while Chrome and Safari requires the prefix -webkit-.

Rule 5: Adds a rounded border to the top-right corner of the table.

Rule 6: Sets a different color for even rows; odd rows will have the default white.

Rule 7: Added top, bottom, and right borders to data cells.

Rule 8: Set heading height to 30 pixels.

Rule 9: Right-aligned salary data.

Output

Firstname	Lastname	Salary
Peter	Griffin	$100
Lois	Griffin	$150
Joe	Swanson	$300
Cleveland	Brown	$250

3.15 Understanding the Box Model

In order to set the width and height of an element correctly in all browsers, CSS presents a box model. In this model each HTML element is wrapped in a box that has multiple layers as indicated in the following illustration:

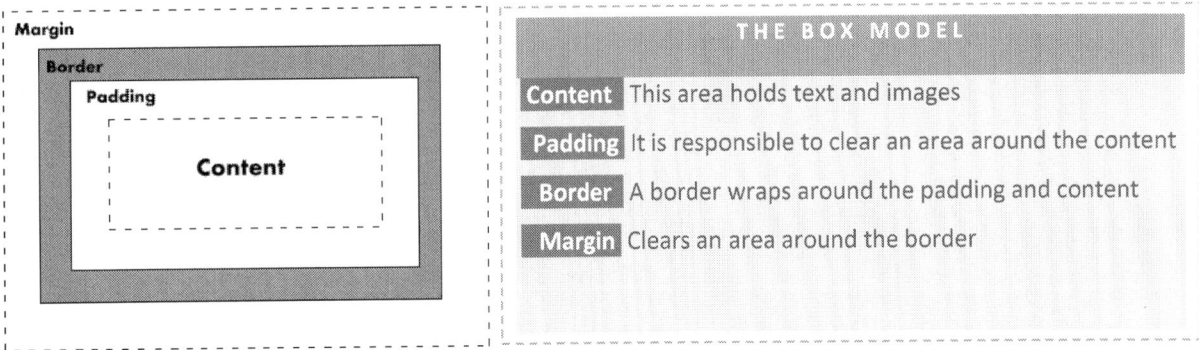

Figure 3-2

Let's do some practical exercise to understand this model. In the following example, you're shown how a 250px space is used.

HTML Code

```
<!DOCTYPE html>
<html>
<head>
<style type="text/css">
   div.c1 {width:240px; border:5px solid gray; border-color:#ff0000  #0000ff;}
   div.c2 {width:240px; padding:0px; border:5px solid gray; margin:0px;}
</style>
</head>

<body>
  <div class="c1"></div>
  <br>
  <div class="c2">The line above is 250px wide (width+left and right borders).<br>
    The total width of this element is also 250px (width+borders).</div>
</body>
</html>
```

> **NOTE**
>
> *The first CSS rule **div.c1{}** applies to **<div class="c1"></div>** which draws a red line to act as a guage.*

Output

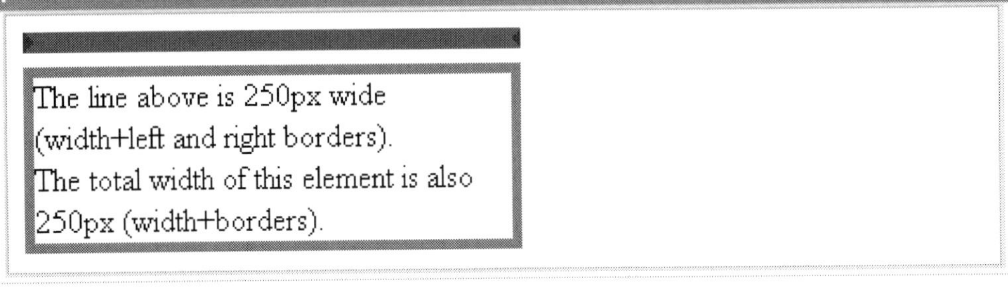

The line above is 250px wide (width+left and right borders).
The total width of this element is also 250px (width+borders).

The total width of an element is calculated like this:

Total element width = width + left padding + right padding + left border + right border + left margin + right margin

The total height of an element is calculated like this:

Total element height = height + top padding + bottom padding + top border + bottom border + top margin + bottom margin

So, as per the first equation, the width of the above element is calculated as under:

240px (width)+ 0px (left and right padding)+ 10px (left and right border)+ 0px (left and right margin) = 250px

This is how you control content within the specified limits. Now, change the value of padding to 10px. This change adds a space of 10px (between content and surrounding border) on all four sides of the content resulting in expansion of width from the allowed 250px space, as shown in the illustration below.

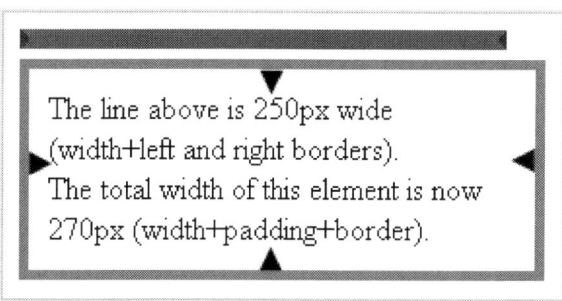

Figure 3-3

Considering the equation mentioned above, the browser calculated the width of the element like this:

240px (width)+ 20px (left and right padding)+ 10px (left and right border) = 270px

The above example demonstrated that you must also consider the padding, borders and margins to calculate the full size of an element.

3.16 Control Element Positioning

CSS has the following positioning schemes that allow you to control the layout of a page:

- Static
- Fixed
- Relative
- Absolute

These positioning properties allow you to position an element. Besides placing an element behind another, you can also handle large content with them. You position elements using the top, bottom, left, and right properties. However, these properties require that you set the position scheme first. You specify the positioning scheme using the position property in CSS. Let's go through these positioning methods using some examples.

Static Positioning: By default, all HTML elements have static positions, which mean that such elements are always positioned according to the normal flow of the page. Every element appears on a new line, causing each new item to appear under the previous one. No two elements sit side-by-side even if there is space. These elements do not take effect of top, bottom, left, and right properties. The following example shows that <h1> and all <p> elements appear on a new line.

Static Positioning Example

```
<!DOCTYPE html>
<html>
<body>
  <h1>About Us</h1>

  <p>Many small and medium sized companies have grown and reached greater profitability by
     adopting the strategic solutions we deliver for today's business.</p>

  <p>We provide better decision making tools to business owners and specialize in improving
     processes and systems. We provide specific customer focused solutions to our clients to
     enhance their profitability.</p>

  <p>We have the mission to increase the success of our clients and be an innovative and valuable
     resource to them.</p>

</body>
</html>
```

Output

About Us

Many small and medium sized companies have grown and reached greater profitability by adopting the strategic solutions we deliver for today's business.

We provide better decision making tools to business owners and specialize in improving processes and systems. We provide specific customer focused solutions to our clients to enhance their profitability.

We have the mission to increase the success of our clients and be an innovative and valuable resource to them.

Fixed Positioning: In this scheme, an element is positioned relative to the browser window and doesn't move when the user scrolls up or down the page. In the following example, <h1> element is marked with fixed position. After adding few more paragraphs, the About Us heading remains fixed and doesn't move when you scroll through the page.

Fixed Positioning Example

```
<!DOCTYPE html>
<html>
<head>
<style type="text/css">
   h1.fixed {position:fixed; background-color: #efefef;}
</style>
</head>
<body>
   <h1 class="fixed">About Us</h1>
   <p>Many small and medium sized companies have grown and reached greater profitability....</p>
   <p>We provide better decision making tools to business owners and specialize in improving ...</p>
   <p>We have the mission to increase the success of our clients and be an innovative and ...</p>
   <p>New paragraph</p>
   ...
</body>
</html>
```

Output

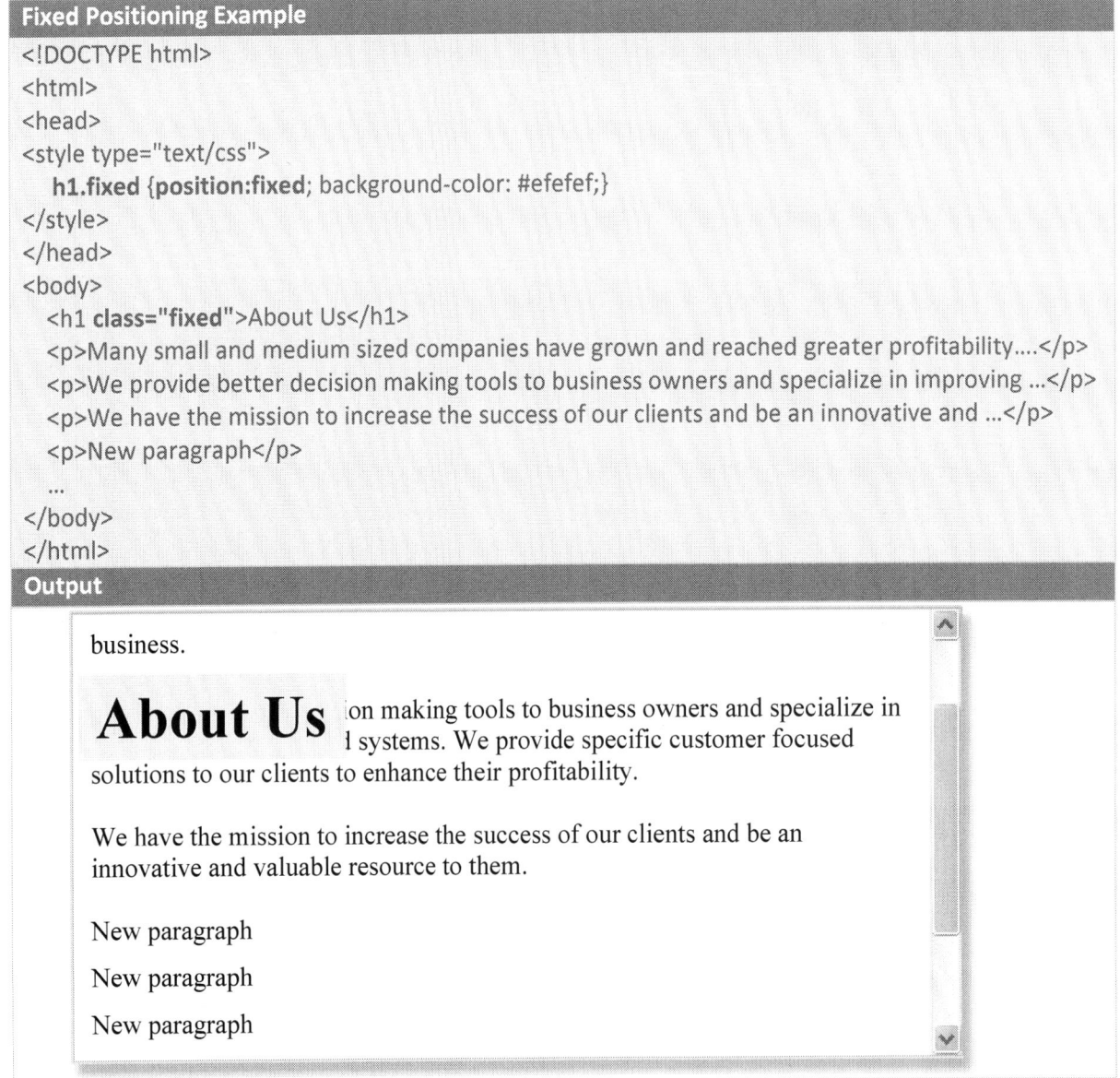

Relative Positioning: Set the value of position property to relative to move an element relative to its normal position. This scheme moves an element in relation to where it would have been in normal flow. You use top, bottom, left, or right properties to indicate how far to move the element from where it would have been in normal flow. In the following example, you moved the second paragraph 10 pixels from the top and 50 pixels from the left. If you increase the top value to 40 pixels, the second paragraph will overlap the third one.

Relative Positioning Example

```html
<!DOCTYPE html>
<html>
<head>
<style type="text/css">
   p.relative {position:relative; top: 10px; left: 50px;}
</style>
</head>
<body>
   <h1>About Us</h1>

   <p>Many small and medium sized companies have grown and reached greater profitability...</p>
   <p class="relative">We provide better decision making tools to business owners and specialize in improving processes and systems. We provide specific customer focused solutions to our clients to enhance their profitability.</p>

   <p>We have the mission to increase the success of our clients and be an innovative...</p>
</body>
</html>
```

Output

About Us

Many small and medium sized companies have grown and reached greater profitability by adopting the strategic solutions we deliver for today's business.

   We provide better decision making tools to business owners and specialize in improving processes and systems. We provide specific customer focused solutions to our clients to enhance their profitability.

We have the mission to increase the success of our clients and be an innovative and valuable resource to them.

Absolute Positioning: With absolute positioning, an element can be placed anywhere on a page. The heading below is placed 170px from the left of the page and 0px from the top of the page. If you change the value of the top property to 90px, the heading is pushed below the paragraph.

Absolute Positioning Example

```
<!DOCTYPE html>
<html>
<head>
<style type="text/css">
   h1 {position:absolute; left:170px; top:0px;}
</style>
</head>

<body>
   <h1>About Us</h1>
   <br><br>
   <p>Many small and medium sized companies have grown and reached greater profitability by adopting the strategic solutions we deliver for today's business.</p>
</body>

</html>
```

Output

About Us

Many small and medium sized companies have grown and reached greater profitability by adopting the strategic solutions we deliver for today's business.

Overlapping Elements: When you use relative, fixed, or absolute positioning, boxes can overlap. In such case, the element that appears later in the HTML code sits on top of those that are earlier in the page. If you want to control which element sits on top, you can use the z-index property. Its value is a number, and the higher the number the closer that element is to the front. For example, an element with a z-index of 10 will appear over the top of one with a z-index of 5.

Overlapping Elements Example

```
<!DOCTYPE html>
<html>
<head>
<style type="text/css">
    Img {position:absolute; left:0px; top:0px; z-index:-1;}
</style>
</head>

<body>
    <h1>ABC Global Consulting</h1>
    <img src="logo.png" width="80" height="80" />
    <p>The image has a z-index of -1 therefore it is placed behind the text.</p>
</body>
</html>
```

Output

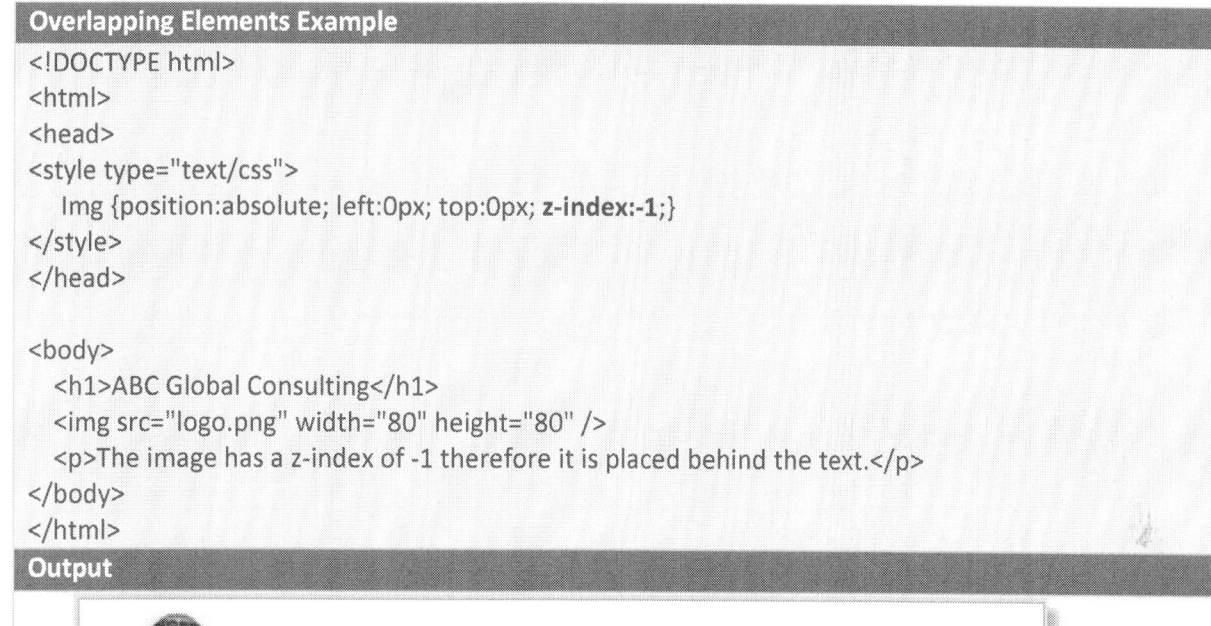

3.17 Floating Elements

In situations where elements are to be placed side-by-side, CSS provides a property called float. Elements are floated horizontally, which means that an element can either be pushed to the left or right. Elements before the floating elements are not affected, but, those that follow will flow around it. The float property takes one of the five values: left, right, none, or inherit. The inherit value specifies that the value of the float property should be inherited from the parent element. In the first example below, an image is added with a style *float:left*. The result is that the image will float to the left in the paragraph.

HTML Code

```
<!DOCTYPE html>
<html>
<head>
<style type="text/css">
   img {float:left;}
   p {width:500px; font-family: Verdana, Arial, sans-serif; font-size: 12px;}
</style>
</head>
<body>
  <p>
    <img src="product2.jpg" width="100" height="100" />
    Successful importers utilize technology to better manage the movement of cargo, create
    accurate Documentation, and execute financial transactions. We have designed an imports
    software, The Import Manager, to provide the innovative technology you need to operate your
    import entries more efficiently, profitably and competitively. It is designed to address
    importers' unique requirements, accelerate the entire import process from end-to-end.
    Automates critical import activities such as duty management, compliance, landed cost
    calculations, customs clearance etc. Close management of these functions results in reduced
    shipment delays, taxes, fees and fines.
  </p>
</body>
</html>
```

Output

Successful importers utilize technology to better manage the movement of cargo, create accurate Documentation, and execute financial transactions. We have designed an imports software, The Import Manager, to provide the innovative technology you need to operate your import entries more efficiently, profitably and competitively. It is designed to address importers' unique requirements, accelerate the entire import process from end-to- end. Automates critical import activities such as duty management, compliance, landed cost calculations, customs clearance etc. Close management of these functions results in reduced shipment delays, taxes, fees and fines.

Multiple floating elements float next to each other if there is room as demonstrated in the following example. Make your browser's window small and see that the images scroll down when there in not enough room.

Multiple Floating Elements Example

```html
<!DOCTYPE html>
<html>
<head>
<style type="text/css">
   img {float:left; width:100px; height:140px; margin:5px;}
</style>
</head>

<body>
  <h3>Products</h3>
  <img src="product1.jpg">
  <img src="product2.jpg">
  <img src="product3.jpg">
  <img src="product4.jpg">
</body>
</html>
```

Output

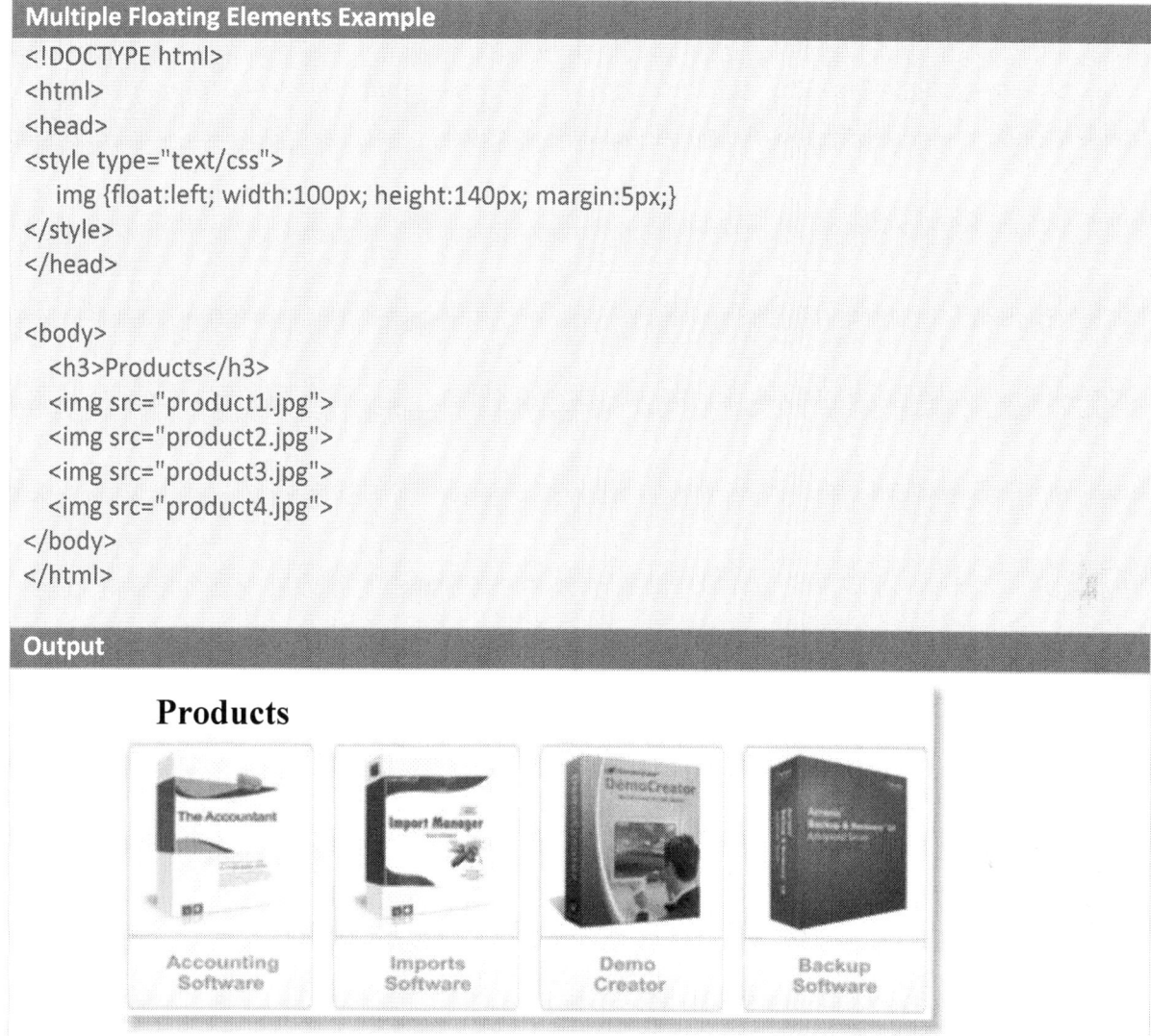

The Clear Property: As mentioned earlier, elements defined after the floating element flow around it. CSS provides a property named clear to avoid this situation. It specifies which sides of an element other floating elements should not be allowed. In the following example we have two sections: Products and Services. We have to keep them apart. First use the code as is with the clear property set to *both* which means no floating elements are allowed on both sides, and then, test it by setting the value to *none*.

```
CSS Clear Property Example
<!DOCTYPE html>
<html>
<head>
<style type="text/css">
    .images {float:left; width:100px; height:140px; margin:5px;}
    .services {clear:both; margin-bottom:2px;}
</style>
</head>
<body>
  <h3>Products</h3>
  <img class="images" src="Product1.jpg">
  <img class="images" src="Product2.jpg">
  <h3 class="services">Services</h3>
  <img class="images" src="service1.jpg">
  <img class="images" src="service2.jpg">
</body>
</html>
```

Output with clear:both

Output with clear:none

3.18 Navigation

Every website has an important section on each page that allows visitors to surf. This is called a navigation bar and is created using a list of links with <ul> and <li> elements. CSS allows you to create fancy navigation bars like the one presented below. The *list-style-type* CSS property specifies appearance of a list item element and sets the type of bullet or numbering to a list. Here, we set it to none which mean no item marker are shown. See section 3.13 for more information on styling list.

HTML Code

```html
<!DOCTYPE html>
<html>
<head>
<style type="text/css">
  ul {list-style-type:none; margin:0; padding:0;}
  li {float:left;}
  a:link {display:block; width:120px; font-weight:bold; color:#FFFFFF; background-color:orange;
        text-align:center; padding:4px; text-decoration:none; text-transform:uppercase;}
  a:visited {color:black;}
  a:hover {background-color:darkorange;}
  a:active {color:green;}
</style>
</head>
<body>
  <ul>
    <li><a href="#home">Home</a></li>
    <li><a href="#services">Services</a></li>
    <li><a href="#products">Products</a></li>
    <li><a href="#support">Support</a></li>
  </ul>
</body>
</html>
```

> **NOTE**
>
> *For further details, see page 212
> Step 3 - Create Main Naviation Bar.*

Output

HOME   SERVICES   PRODUCTS   SUPPORT

We also added special effects to these links using the four pseudo classes that we went through in section 3.12. When you press and hold the left mouse button, the *:active* pseudo class activates and displays the link in green. Releasing the button would turn the link color to black through the *:visited* class. By default, the *:link* class presents the links in white color whereas, the *:hover* changes the background color to dark orange when you just move the mouse over these links.

3.19 Opacity and Transparency

To make pictures or other elements transparent, CSS provides a property called opacity. It takes a value from 0.0 - 1.0. The lower value makes the element more transparent. We used the hover pseudo class to show actual picture by setting the opacity to 1.0 when the user hovers over it. When the mouse pointer moves away from the image, the image will be transparent again.

HTML Code

```
<!DOCTYPE html>
<html>
<head>
<style type="text/css">
  .images {float:left; width:100px; height:140px; margin:5px;}
  img {opacity:0.5;filter:alpha(opacity=40); }
  img:hover {opacity:1.0;filter:alpha(opacity=100);}
</style>
</head>

<body>
  <h3>Products</h3>
  <img class="images" src="Product1.jpg">
  <img class="images" src="Product2.jpg">
</body>
</html>
```

Output

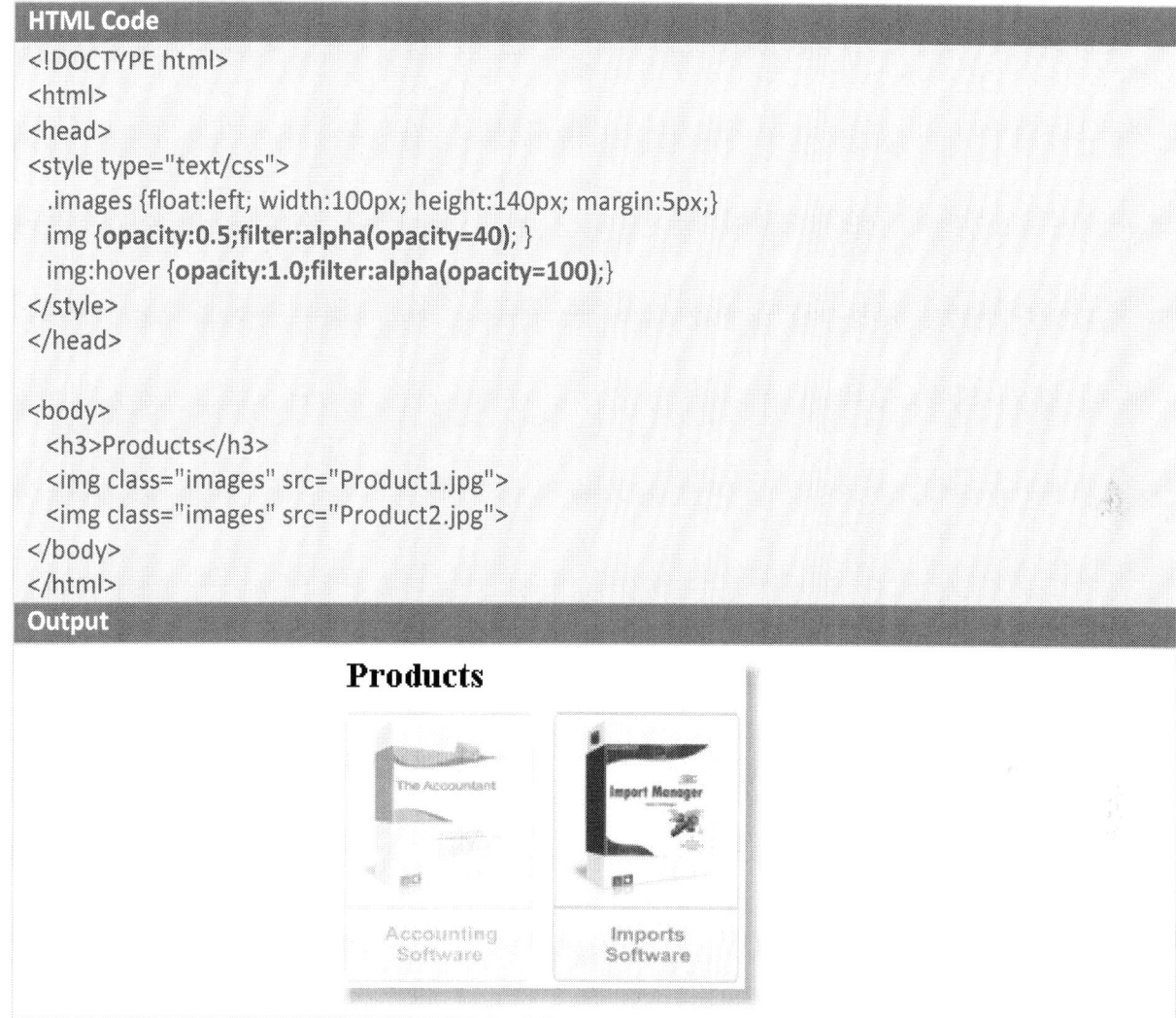

3.20 CSS3 Borders

In CSS3 you can create borders using the following three new properties.

border-radius: This property allows you to create rounded borders
box-shadow: Add shadow to boxes
border-image: Create a border using an image

For specific browser support, use the following prefix:

-moz- for Firefox
-webkit- for Chrome and Safari
-o- for Opera

HTML Code

```
<!DOCTYPE html>
<html>
<head>
<style type="text/css">
  div
  {
    color: white;
    background:orange;
    width:300px;
    padding:10px 40px;
    border-radius:50px;
    box-shadow: 10px 10px 5px #888888;
    -moz-border-radius:50px;
    -moz-box-shadow: 10px 10px 5px #888888;
  }
</style>
</head>
<body>

<div>The border-radius property allows you to add rounded corners to elements.</div>

</body>
</html>
```

The border-radius property allows you to add rounded corners to elements.

3.21 CSS3 Fonts

Before CSS3, you had to use fonts that were already installed on the user's computer. But now, with CSS3, you can use any font you want. You've to get the desired font and upload the font file to your web server so that it is downloaded with your web page. To use your own font you must add *@font-face* rule to your style sheet. Within this rule you have to define a name for the font (e.g. myFont), and then specify the path to the font. In the rule that you set for HTML element, refer this name (myFont) through the font-family property. In the following example we're using a custom font named Redressed.ttf.

HTML Code

```
<!DOCTYPE html>
<html>
<head>
<style type="text/css">
  @font-face {font-family: myFont; src: url('Redressed.ttf'); }
  h2 {font-family:myFont; font-size:40px; color: Orange;}
</style>
</head>
<body>
  <h2>ABC Global Consulting</h2>
</body>
</html>
```

NOTE

You can download and test different fonts from:
http://www.fonts2u.com
http://fontzone.net

Output

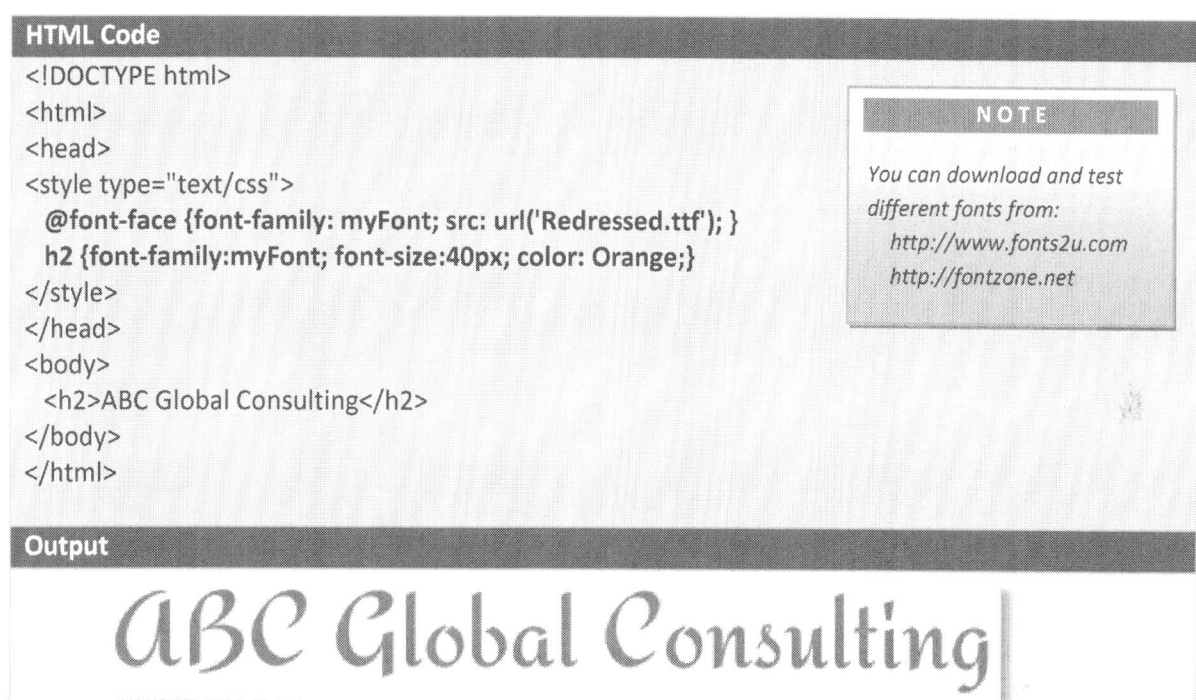

3.22 CSS3 Animation

Animation is another great feature included in CSS3; it is an effect that lets an element gradually change from one style to another. You can use CSS3 animations in place of animated images, Flash animations, and JavaScript. The rule @keyframes is added to the style sheet to achieve this objective.

HTML Code

```
<!DOCTYPE html>
<html>
<head>
<style type="text/css">
/* Point # 1*/
  @-moz-keyframes myAnimation {
     0% {opacity:1;}
     50% {opacity:0;}
     100% {opacity:1;}
  }
/* Point # 2*/
  #f1 img {position:absolute;}
/* Point # 3*/
  #f1 img {
     -moz-animation-name: myAnimation;
     -moz-animation-timing-function: ease-in-out;
     -moz-animation-iteration-count: infinite;
     -moz-animation-duration: 10s;
  }
/* Point # 4*/
  #f1 img:nth-of-type(1) {-moz-animation-delay: 5s;}
  #f1 img:nth-of-type(2) {-moz-animation-delay: 0s;}
</style>
</head>
<body>
/* Point # 5*/
  <div id="f1">
     <img src="Frame1.png" width="300" height="200" />
     <img src="Frame2.png" width="300" height="200" />
  </div>
</body>
</html>
```

> **BROWSER PREFIX**
>
> *You have to set appropriate prefix according to your browser. This example is prefixed with -moz- and will run on Firefox, for Chrome and Safari set prefix to -webkit-, and for Opera set it to -o-.*

In this example, we're using two images that will cross fade infinitely one after the other.

Point # 1:

Created a keyframe rule for Firefox and named it myAnimation. Specified when the change will happen in percent, which ranges from 0% to 100%. Initially, we will display actual picture by setting the opacity to 1. When the animation is at 50%, it will become transparent (opacity:0), and again to actual when the animation is 100% complete. This rule will be applied to all images defined in Point 5.

Point # 2:

In this rule we provided absolute position to images. If you omit this rule, both pictures will appear relatively (side-by-side).

Point # 3:

The animation-name property specifies the name of the keyframe you want to bind to the selector. Here, you have provided the name myAnimation to the keyframe and bound it to #f1 selector that has <img> elements.

The animation-timing-function property describes how the animation will progress over one cycle of its duration. We set it to ease-in-out which means that the animation has both a slow start and a slow end.

The animation-iteration-count property specifies the number of times an animation is played. The infinite value is set to play the animation forever.

The animation-duration property specifies how many seconds or milliseconds an animation takes to complete one cycle. We set the value to ten seconds (5 seconds for each picture).

Point # 4:

The :nth-of-type pseudo-class matches elements based on their position within the parent element's list of child elements of the same type. This pseudo-class accepts an argument (N) which can be a number, keyword, or expression. In our example we're referencing the two images defined in Point#5.

The animation-delay property defines when the animation will start.
The total duration of this animation is 10s (Point#3). The animation will start with the second image (Frame2.png) and will last for 5 seconds. Then the first image (Frame1.png) will appear and it too will last for 5 seconds.

Point # 5:

We defined two images in a <div> element. These images will act as a source for the animation and will appear and fade in a cycle.

Calculate Keyframe Points:

For proper animation, you need to set appropriate points (in percentage) while defining the keyframe rule. This section explains how to calculate these points. There are two factors that help in evaluating the proper range: number of images and display time of each image. In our example, there are two images and each one will be displayed for 5 seconds. We also know that an animation cycle starts with 0% and finishes at 100%. The first calculation that you will perform is to divide the value of 100 with the number of images to get the change point. In our scenario the answer is 50 (100/2). Based on this calculation, we added a new point as 50% and set the opacity to 0. We set total animation duration to 10s in Point 3 and, in Point 4, equally divided this duration between the two images.

Let's do some more experiments to further evaluate this theory:

1. Add another picture (Frame3.png) to Point 5
2. Set animation-duration property in Point 3 to 15s (5 seconds x 3 images)
3. Add another rule to Point 4 with nth-of-type(3), and set animation delay as under:
   - nth-of-type(1) delay 10s
   - nth-of-type(2) delay 5s
   - nth-of-type(3) delay 0s
4. Add another point to keyframes in Point 1 using the 100/3 formula. The keyframe should now hold four points:
   - 0% {opacity:1;}
   - 33% {opacity:0;}
   - 66% {opacity:0;}
   - 100% {opacity:1;}
5. Run the animation and see smooth transition of images

> **NOTE**
>
> *You'll use this technique in the final project. See Section 6.4 Step 4.*

The following table contains parameters (for six pictures) that you can use and follow if you want to add more images to your animation.

Property	2 Images	3 Images	4 Images	5 Images	6 Images
Duration (seconds)	10	15	20	25	30
Delay (seconds)	0/5	0/5/10	0/5/10/15	0/5/10/15/20	0/5/10/15/20/25
Keyframes (%)	0/50/100	0/33/66/100	0/25/50/75/100	0/20/40/60/80/100	0/17/34/51/68/85/100
Opacity	1/0/1	1/0/0/1	1/0/0/0/1	1/0/0/0/0/1	1/0/0/0/0/0/1

YOU WILL LEARN

- Integrate HTML & JavaScript

- Variables & Operators in JavaScript

- Evaluate Conditions

- Iterative Statements

- Objects in JavaScript

- JavaScript Events

- JavaScript & HTML Forms

CHAPTER 4

JAVASCRIPT

<SCRIPT>

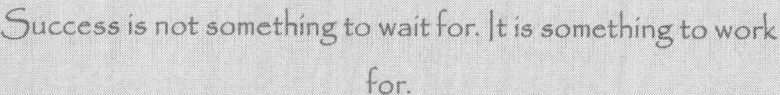

Success is not something to wait for. It is something to work for.

4.1　About JavaScript

HTML is a simple text markup language, it can't respond to the user, make decisions, or automate repetitive tasks. Interactive tasks such as these require a more sophisticated language: a programming language, or a scripting language.

Although many programming languages are complex, scripting languages are generally simple. They have a simple syntax, can perform tasks with a minimum of commands, and are easy to learn. Web scripting languages enable you to combine scripting with HTML to create interactive web pages.

JavaScript is one of the most popular and widely used scripting language of the web and is used in billions of Web pages to add functionality, validate forms, communicate with the server, and much more. It is primarily a client-side scripting language for use in Web browsers. Its main focus is to help developers interact with Web pages and the Web browser window itself. Because it is embedded in all modern browsers, it has an extraordinary wide distribution.

One of the most powerful features of the language is its flexibility. As a JavaScript programmer, you can make your programs as simple or as complex as you wish them to be. The language also allows several different programming styles. You can write your code in the functional style or in the slightly more complex object-oriented style. It also lets you write relatively complex programs without knowing anything at all about functional or object-oriented programming; you can be productive in this language just by writing simple functions. It allows programmers to accomplish useful tasks with a very small, easy-to-learn subset of the language.

JavaScript is almost as easy to learn as HTML, and it can be included directly in HTML documents. Here are the few things you can do with JavaScript:

- Display messages to the user as part of a web page, in the browser's status line, or in alert boxes.
- Validate the contents of a form and make calculations (for example, an order form can automatically display a running total as you enter item quantities).
- Animate images or create images that change when you move the mouse over them.
- Create ad banners that interact with the user, rather than simply displaying a graphic
- Detect the browser in use or its features and perform advanced functions only on browsers that support them.
- Detect installed plug-ins and notify the user if a plug-in is required.
- Modify all or part of a web page without requiring the user to reload it.
- Display or interact with data retrieved from a remote server.

You can do all this and more with JavaScript, including creating entire applications. A JavaScript is added to an HTML document using the *<script>* tag with *type="text/javascript"*. It is typically used to manipulate existing HTML elements using the *id* attribute of those elements. To access these elements JavaScript provides a method called *document.getElementById()*. Within the parenthesis of this method you specify the id of the element you're trying to access.

Let's go through a simple example to embed JavaScript in an HTML document. In this example a JavaScript is used to manipulate text of a paragraph using the paragraph's id p1. The *innerHTML* property returns the inner HTML of an element.

Embed JavaScript in HTML

```
<!DOCTYPE html>
<html>
<body>
<h2>JavaScript Example</h2>
<p id="p1">This text will be replaced with the text in the following JavaScript.</p>
<script type="text/javascript">
   document.getElementById("p1").innerHTML="Welcome to the exciting world of JavaScript!";
</script>
</body>
</html>
```

Output

JavaScript Example

Welcome to the exciting world of JavaScript!

4.2 Comments in JavaScript

Like HTML and CSS, JavaScript too allows you to add comments to your code. You do this for two purposes:

- To explain your code
- To prevent its execution

Here as well, browsers ignore JS comments. Comments in JavaScript are added using the following two methods:

Single Line Comments: In this method you add two forward slashes before your comment or before a JS statement, for example:

// Added elements to JS
//document.write("<h1>Added h1 element to JS</h1><p>Added p HTML element to JS</p>");

The first line above is used to provide an explanation whereas the second one is a JS statement that is prevented from being executed.

Multi Line Comments: Use the symbols /* and */ to add comments that span multiple lines.

/*
The write() method does not add a new line
The writeln() method adds a new line
*/

> **NOTE**
>
> *PHP also uses the same set of characters for single and multi line comments.*

/*
document.writeln("The Writeln() method");
document.writeln("Added a new line");
*/

You can also add comments at the end of each statement to describe its functionality:

document.writeln("The Writeln() method");   *//writeln() method adds a new line*
document.writeln("Added a new line");

4.3 Few Points To Remember

- JavaScript code is a sequence of JavaScript statements. Each statement is executed by the browser in the sequence they are written. For example:

  document.write("JavaScript Example");

  document.getElementById("p1").innerHTML="Welcome to the exciting world of JavaScript!";

- Statements that execute together in a block are enclosed in curly brackets {} and are known as JavaScript functions.

  function jsFunction()

  {

  document.write("<h1>Added h1 element to JS</h1><p>Added p HTML element to JS</p>");

  document.write("The write() method does not add a new line");

  }

- JavaScripts are placed in the <head> and in the <body> sections.

- JavaScripts can be added both to the body and the head sections at the same time. Usually, all scripts are placed in one place either in the head section, or at the bottom of the page. If you're referencing elements in the script, place the script at the bottom to make sure it is not executed before the element.

- There is no limit to the number of scripts in a document; we added two scripts in the next example.

- To use the same JavaScript code in multiple web pages, you have to create an external file with a .js extension. Such external scripts are referenced through the src attribute of the <script> tag such as: *<script type="text/javascript" src="External.js"></script>*

- Unlike HTML, JavaScript is case sensitive - therefore pay close attention to alphabets' case when you write JavaScript statements, create or call variables, objects and functions.

- Add a semicolon at the end of each executable JS statement. Although it is optional, the use of semicolon allows you to write multiple statements on one line.

4.4 Using HTML Elements in JavaScript

You can also add HTML elements to JS code using *write()* and *writeln()* methods. Methods define functions performed by an object. Making a reference to an object method is similar to referencing its property. Thus, *document.write();* calls the *write()* method of the document object. Methods are always followed by a pair of parenthesis. There is a little difference between the *write()* and the *writeln()* methods. The *write()* method does not add a new line while *writeln()* adds a new line after each statement.

Using HTML Elements in JavaScript

```html
<!DOCTYPE html>
<html>
<body>
<pre>
<script type="text/javascript">
  document.write("<h1>Added h1 element to JS</h1><p>Added p HTML element to JS</p>");
  document.write("The write() method ");
  document.write("does not add a new line");
</script>
</pre>
<pre>
<script type="text/javascript">
  document.writeln("The Writeln() method");
  document.writeln("Added a new line");
</script>
</pre>

</body>
</html>
```

Output

Added h1 element to JS

Added p HTML element to JS

The write() method does not add a new line

The Writeln() method
Added a new line

4.5 Variables in JavaScript

A variable is a storage location and an associated symbolic name which contains some known or unknown quantity or information. Every variable has a name, called the variable name, and a value. For example, in the expression x=10, x is the variable name and it holds the value 10. A variable can have a short name, like x, or a more descriptive name, like VtotalAmount.

Variables can represent numeric values, characters, character strings, or memory addresses. They can hold values or expressions, such as n=x+y. The opposite of a variable is a constant. Constants are values that never change.

4.6 Types of Variables

In JavaScript variables are of two types:

Local Variables: These variables are declared within a JavaScript function and are specific to that function. You can access these variables in the function you created them. Since these variables have a local scope, you can use same variable name in different functions. Local variables are destroyed upon completion of the function.

Global Variables: Contrary to local variables, these variables are declared outside a function and can be accessed by all scripts and functions within a web page. If you declare a new variable that does not already exist, and assign a value to it, such variable automatically becomes a global variable. These variables are wiped out when the page is closed.

You must consider the following rules while declaring a variable in JavaScript:

- JavaScript is case-sensitive therefore variable names are also case sensitive - a and A are two different variable names
- Start variable names with a letter, underscore, or $ character
- Use the var keyword to declare JavaScript variables (e.g. var Vtotalamount;)
- Use the (=) operator to assign a value to a variable (e.g. Vtotalamount=1000; or Vservice="Accountancy";)
- Enclose text values in quotes and do not put quotes around numeric values. Numeric values enclosed in quotes are treated as text.

Variable Example

```
<!DOCTYPE html>
<html>
<body>
  <p>Click the button to create and display two variables.</p>
  <button onclick="myVariables()">Click Me</button>
  <p id="number"></p>
  <p id="text"></p>
  <script type="text/javascript">
    function myVariables()
    {
      var Vtotalamount=1000;
      var Vservice="Accountancy";
      document.getElementById("number").innerHTML="Amount: "+Vtotalamount;
      document.getElementById("text").innerHTML="Service: "+Vservice;
    }
  </script>
</body>
</html>
```

Output

Click the button to create and display two variables.

Click Me

Amount: 1000

Service: Accountancy

The example above contains a JavaScript function named myVariables (you will learn more about functions soon). The function holds two variables: a numeric variable Vtotalamount with a value of 1000 and a string variable Vservice having the value Accountancy. The last two lines in the script concatenate variable values with appropriate labels.

4.7 Assignment & Arithmetic Operators in JavaScript

The Assignment Operators are used to assign values to JavaScript variables and Arithmetic operators are used to perform mathematical calculations between variables and/or values. We used couple of these operators in the preceding example in the function myVariables.

Examples of Arithmetic Operators

The following table explains the use of arithmetic operators in JavaScript assuming that z=5.

Operator	Symbol	Formula	Description	Value of a	Value of z
Addition	+	a=z+2	Add 2 to the value of z	7	5
Subtraction	-	a=z-2	Subtract 2 from the value of z	3	5
Multiplication	*	a=z*2	Multiply z and 2	10	5
Division	/	a=z/2	Divide z by 2	2.5	5
Increment	++	a=++z	Increment z by 1 and assign new value to a	6	6
		a=z++	Assign old value to a and then increment z by 1	5	6
Decrement	--	a=--z	Decrease z by 1 and assign new value to a	4	4
		a=z--	Assign old value to a and then decrease z by 1	5	4

Examples of Assignment Operators

Assuming that the value of a=10 and z=5, the following table demonstrates the use of assignment operators in JavaScript:

Operator	Formula	Description	Output	Equivalent
=	a=z	a is equal to z	a=5	
-=	a-=z	subtract z from a	a=5	a=a-z
+=	a+=z	add a to z	a=15	a=a+z
/=	a/=z	divide a by z	a=2	a=a/z
*=	a*=z	multiply a and z	a=50	a=a*z

You can also join string variables with the help of + operator and can also add a space like this:

```
fname="Riaz";
lname="Ahmed";
fullname=fname+" "+lname;
```

4.8 Comparison Operators in JavaScript

In computer programming, comparison of two data items is affected by the comparison operators mentioned in the table below. These operators produce the logical value true or false, depending on the result of the comparison. For example, in the pseudo-code

if a > 1 then ...

the statements following *then* are executed only if the value of the variable "a" is greater than 1 (i.e. when the logical value of a > 1 is true).

Assuming that the value of a=5, the following table demonstrates the comparison operators:

Operator	Symbol	Compare	Return & Reason
Is greater than	>	a>8	False – The value of a is 5 and is less than 8
Is less than	<	a<8	True – 5 is less than 8
Greater than or equal to	>=	a>=8	False – 5 is not greater than or equal to 8
Less than or equal to	<=	a<=8	True – One condition is true i.e. 5 is less than 8
Is equal to	==	a==8	False – 5 is not equal to 8
		a==5	True – 5 is equal to 5
Is exactly equal to (both value and type)	===	a==="5"	False – Cannot compare number to string
		a===5	True – Both value and type are same
Is not equal	!=	a!=8	True – 5 is not equal to 8
Is not equal neither value or type	!==	a!=="5"	True – types are not same
		a!==5	False – values are equal

4.9 Logical Operators in JavaScript

The logical operators compare expressions and return a Boolean result (true or false).

The NOT operator: It performs logical negation on an expression. It yields the opposite of the expression it evaluates. If the expression evaluates to True, Not yields False; if the expression evaluates to False, Not yields True.

The And operator: It performs logical conjunction on two expressions. That is, if both expressions evaluate to True, then the And operator returns True. If both expressions evaluate to False, And returns False.

The Or operator: It performs logical disjunction on two expressions. If either expression evaluates to True, it returns True. If neither expression evaluates to True, it returns False.

The following table describes logical operators through examples. Here the value of a=6 and z=3.

Operator	Symbol	Expression	Return & Reason
not	!	!(a==z)	True – a and z are not equal
and	&&	(a < 10 && z > 1)	True – Both expressions are true
		(a > 10 && z > 1)	False – First expression a>10 is false
or	||	(a==5 || z==5)	False – Both expressions evaluate to false
		(a==6 || z== 6)	True – First expression meets the criteria

4.10 Conditional Operators

JavaScript provides a special conditional operator that assigns a value to a variable based on some condition.

Syntax

variablename=(condition) ?value1:value2

Example

reorder=(stock<10)?"Low":"High";

In the above example, if the value of variable *stock* is less than 10, move *Low* to reorder level, otherwise set the value of reorder to *High*.

4.11 The IF Conditional Statement

In computer science, conditional statements are features of a programming language which perform different computations or actions depending on whether a programmer-specified condition evaluates to true or false. In other words, conditional statements are used to perform different actions based on different conditions.

For example, x > 0 means "the variable x contains a number that is greater than zero". The computer evaluates this condition. If the condition is true, the statements within the braces are executed. Otherwise, the execution continues in the following branch – either in the else block (which is usually optional), or if there is no else branch, then after the closing brace. After either branch has been executed, control returns to the point after the ending brace.

You can also combine several conditions using "else if". Only the statements following the first condition that is found to be true will be executed. All other statements will be skipped.

IF Condition Example

```html
<!DOCTYPE html>
<html>
<body>
  <h3>Check the stock level</h3>
  <button onclick="StockLevel()">Click Me</button>
  <p id="stock"></p>
  <script type="text/javascript">
    function StockLevel()
    {
      var stock=5;
      var reorder=10;
      if (stock<reorder) {Alert="Low";}
      else if (stock<100){Alert="Good";}
      else{Alert="High";}
      document.getElementById("stock").innerHTML=Alert;
    }
  </script>
</body>
</html>
```

Output

Check the stock level

Click Me

Low

Example Explained:

The onclick event of the button calls the function StockLevel. Two variables (stock and reorder) are declared with respective values on the first two lines of this function. Initially, with stock value equal to 5, the first condition stock<reorder will evaluate to true and the alert Low will be displayed. If you change the stock value to 99, the else if condition will be triggered to show the Good alert. Finally, if you set the stock to 100 or more, the else condition will come into action and will throw the High alert. Using this technique you can check different conditions and perform some actions based on the evaluation.

4.12 The Switch Statement

Typically, nested if-else statements are used in the program's logic where there isn't only one condition to evaluate. A switch statement, on the other hand, evaluates only one variable and starts to work there. You can think of a switch statement as a simplified (and stripped-down) version of an if-else block.

```
switch(x) {
case 1: // do this
case 2: // do this
case 3: // do this
// etc
}
```

The nested if-else statement's power comes from the fact that it is able to evaluate more than one condition at once, and/or use lots of different conditions in one logical structure.

```
if(x == 0) {
// do this
} else if(y == 1) {
// do this
} else if(x == 1 && y == 0) {
// do this
}
```

If you're going to evaluate only one variable in the condition statement, you're better off going with a switch statement, since it looks a lot neater than nested ifs. The following example evaluates a product's price based on a single variable (jacketColor). Change color in the variable declaration from Black to Brown or Green and see display of relevant price. We used break to prevent the code from running into the next case and added the default keyword to specify what to do if there is no match.

Switch Statement Example

```
<!DOCTYPE html>
<html>
<body>
  <h3>Price Checker</h3>
  <button onclick="myFunction()">Click Me</button>
  <p id="test"></p>
  <script type="text/javascript">
  function myFunction()
  {
    var jacketColor = "Black";
    var result;
    switch (jacketColor) {
     case "Black":
      result = "Price $300";
      break;
     case "Brown":
      result = "Price $200";
      break;
     case "Green":
      result = "Price $100";
      break;
     default:
      result = "No color selected";
    }
    document.getElementById("test").innerHTML=jacketColor+" Jacket: "+result;
  }
  </script>
</body>
</html>
```

Output

Price Checker

Click Me

Black Jacket: Price $300

4.13 Alert Box

It is a small box that appears on the display screen to give you some information. For example, it might alert you to provide the mandatory email address that you left blank in the subscription form. Unlike dialog boxes, alert boxes do not require any user input. However, you need to acknowledge the alert box by pressing the Enter key or clicking the OK button to make it go away. Alert boxes are also called message boxes.

Alert Box Example

```html
<!DOCTYPE html>
<html>
<head>
   <script type="text/javascript">
   function testAlert()
   {
      alert("Please enter a valid email address");
   }
   </script>
</head>
<body>
   <input type="button" onclick="testAlert()" value="Click Me" />
</body>
</html>
```

Output

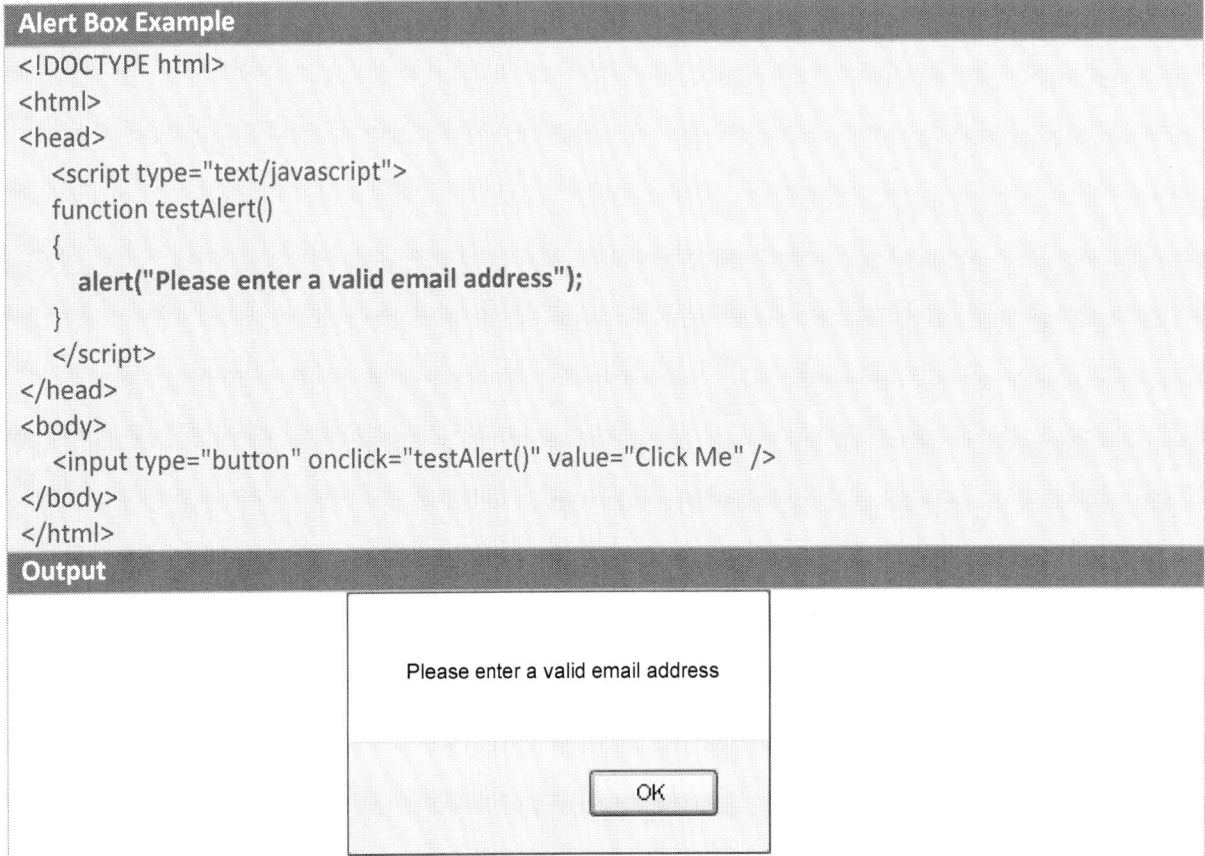

4.14 Confirm Box

You use a confirm box to verify some information or ask the user to accept something. This box has two buttons: OK and Cancel. The box return true if the user clicks OK, and returns false if Cancel is selected.

Confirm Box Example

```html
<!DOCTYPE html>
<html>
<body>
  <button onclick="cbox()">Click me to display a confirm box</button>
  <p id="p1"></p>
  <script type="text/javascript">
  function cbox()
  {
    var x;
    var r=confirm("Click on a button!");
    if (r==true)
    {
      x="You clicked OK!";
    }
    else
    {
      x="You clicked Cancel!";
    }
    document.getElementById("p1").innerHTML=x;
  }
  </script>
</body>
</html>
```

Output

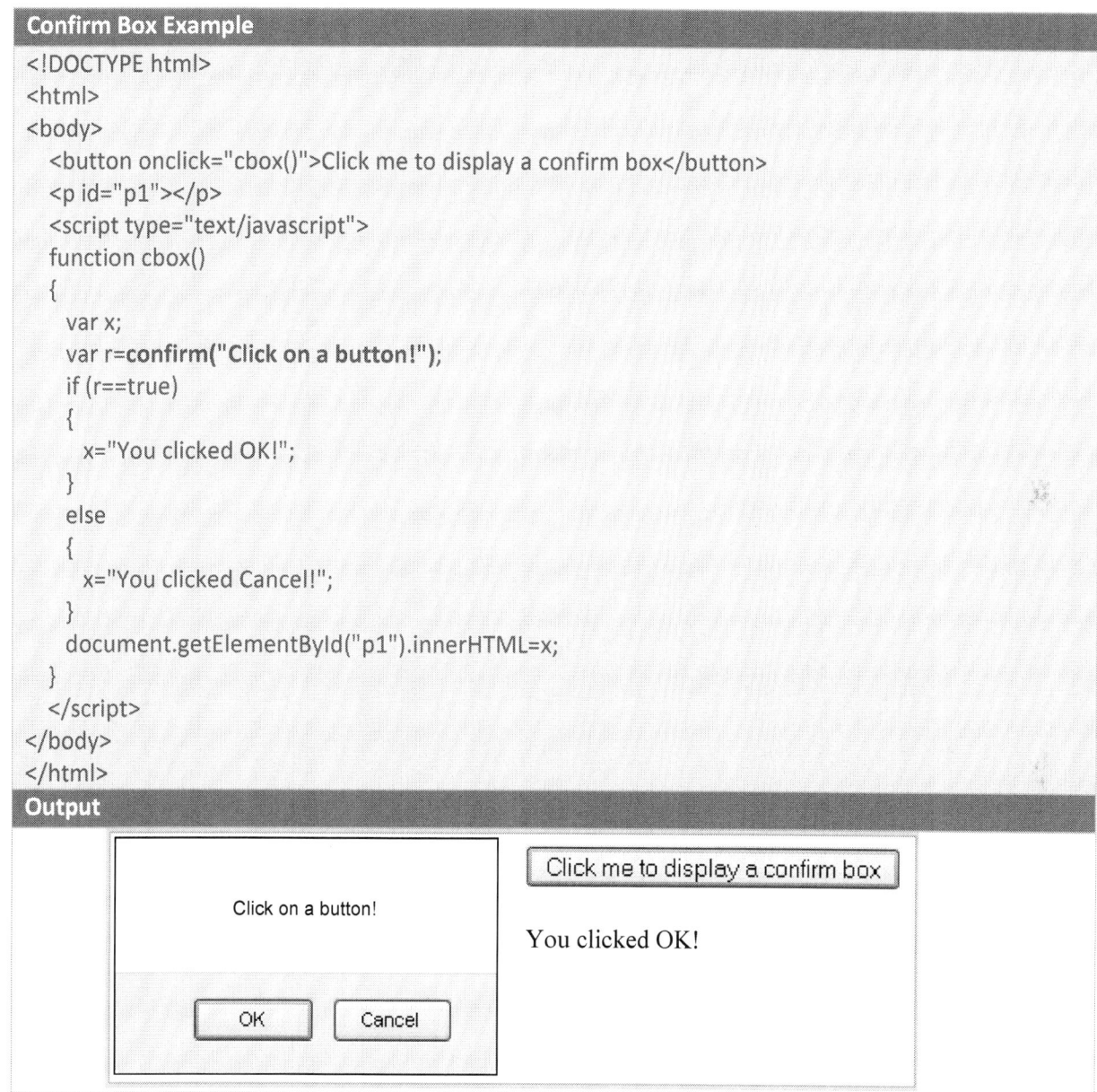

4.15 Prompt Box

A prompt box is used to accept a value from the user before proceeding to the desired page. This box also presents two buttons to move ahead or stay on the same page. The OK button returns the input value while clicking the Cancel button gives null.

Prompt Box Example

```html
<!DOCTYPE html>
<html>
<body>
  <button onclick="pBox()">Click me to bring up a Prompt Box</button>
  <p id="p1"></p>
  <script type="text/javascript">
  function pBox()
  {
    var msg;
    var name=prompt("What is your name? ","Riaz Ahmed");
    if (name!=null)
    {
      msg="Hello " + name + "! Welcome to the world of JS";
      document.getElementById("p1").innerHTML=msg;
    }
  }
  </script>
</body>
</html>
```

Output

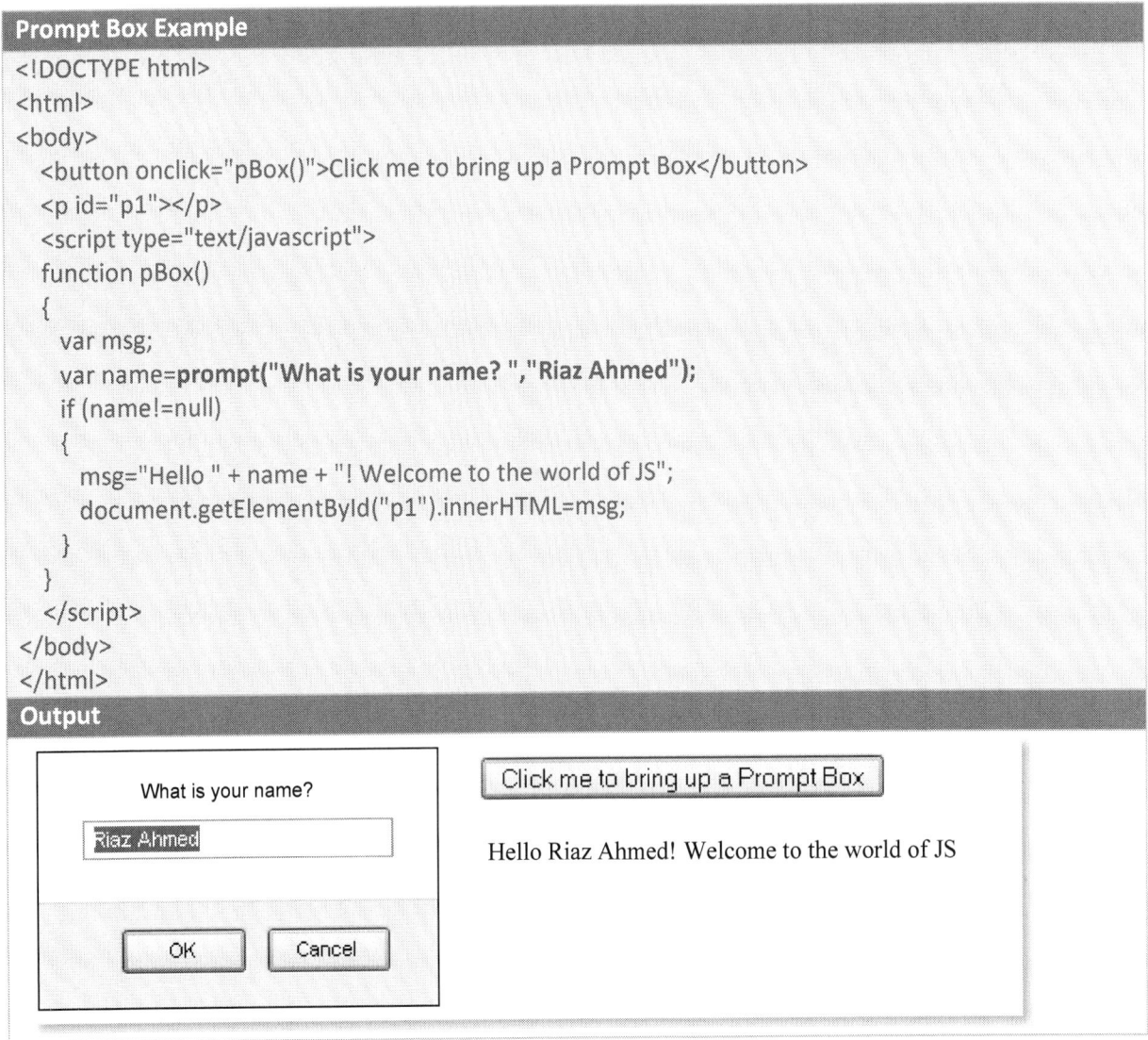

4.16 Using Functions in JavaScript

A function is a collection of statements that executes when:

- An event occurs (such as a button is clicked)
- Called from a script
- Called from another function

Functions are declared with the keyword *function*, followed by a set of arguments, and finally by the code to execute enclosed in braces. The basic syntax is:

```
function functionName(var1, var2,..., varN) {
   statements
}
```

Remember the following points associated with functions:

- Functions can be placed both in the <head> and in the <body> section of a document.
- The keyword *function* must be written in lowercase letters.
- You must call a function with the exact same capitals as in the function name.
- You can pass some values, called parameters, when you call a function.
- You can specify any number of parameters, separated by commas.
- Functions receive parameters as variables in the expected order i.e. the first variable receive the value of the first passed parameter and so on.
- A function can return a value (which is optional) back to where the call was made using the *return* statement.
- When the *return* statement in encountered, the function stops executing and returns the value, if any.
- Any code that comes after a *return* statement is not executed.
- The *return* statement stops only the function, not the whole JavaScript.
- The *return* statement can also be used to exit a function.
- All variables declared within a function are destroyed when you exit the function.

Example 1:

```
function Greeting(sName, sMessage){
    alert("Hello " + name + ", " + sMessage);
}
```

The above function will be called like this:

Greeting ('Riaz', 'welcome to the world of JS');

In the above calling statement, we are passing two parameters enclosed in parentheses to the function named Greeting. The function will receive these parameters in the two variables, sName and sMessage, respectively and will show the alert illustrated in the output section below.

Example 2 – Code after a return statement is not executed:

```
function sum(iNum1, iNum2) {
    return iNum1 + iNum2;
    alert(iNum1 + iNum2);  // this line will not execute
}
```

Example 3 – Function with multiple return statements based on some condition:

```
function diff(iNum1, iNum2) {
    if (iNum1 > iNum2)
    {
        return iNum1 – iNum2;
    }
    else
    {
        return iNum2 – iNum1;
    }
}
```

Example 4 – Exit a function without a return value:

```
function Greeting(sMessage) {
    if (sMessage == " ")
    {
        return;
    }
    alert(sMessage);
}
```

Example 1 - Passing String Values

```
<!DOCTYPE html>
<html>
<body>
  <button onclick="Greeting('Riaz', 'welcome to the world of JS')">Click Me</button>
  <script type="text/javascript">
  function Greeting(sName, sMessage){
    alert("Hello " + sName + ", " + sMessage);
  }
  </script>
</body>
</html>
```

> Hello Riaz, welcome to the world of JS
>
> OK

Example 2 - Passing Numeric Values

```
<!DOCTYPE html>
<html>
<body>
  <p>Call a function to perform mathematical operation</p>
  <p id="p1"></p>
  <script type="text/javascript">
  function Add(x,y)
  {
    return x+y;
  }
  document.getElementById("p1").innerHTML="Sum of 10 and 3 is: "+Add(10,3);
  </script>
</body>
</html>
```

> Call a function to perform mathematical operation
>
> Sum of 10 and 3 is: 13

4.17   Iterative Statements

Iterative statements, also called loop statements, specify certain commands to be executed repeatedly until some condition is met.

4.17.1   The FOR loop

This loop iterates through a block of code a specified number of times and is used when the number of iteration is known. Its syntax is:

for (initialization; expression; post-loop-expression) {block of code}

The following example creates a loop to generate a sequence of number from 1-9. The variable i is initialized with 1 (i=1) and is incremented by 1 on each iteration (i++). The loop terminates when the value of i reaches 10.

FOR Loop Example

```
<!DOCTYPE html>
<html>
<body>
  <button onclick="fLoop()">Click Me</button>
  <p id="p1"></p>
  <script type="text/javascript">
  function fLoop()
  {
    var a="",i;
    for (i=1;i<10;i++)
    {
      a=a + "The number is " + i + "<br>";
    }
    document.getElementById("p1").innerHTML=a;
  }
  </script>
</body>
</html>
```

Click Me

The number is 1
The number is 2
The number is 3
The number is 4
The number is 5
The number is 6
The number is 7
The number is 8
The number is 9

4.17.2 The WHILE Loop

This loop executes a block of code while a specified condition is true. It has two variants while and do...while. While loops are conditional loops where a condition is checked at the starting of the loop and if the condition is true then the statements inside the loop are executed.

WHILE Loop Example

```
<!DOCTYPE html>
<html>
<body>
  <button onclick="wLoop()">Click Me</button>
  <p id="p1"></p>
  <script type="text/javascript">
  function wLoop()
  {
    var a="",i=1,c=true;
    while (c==true)
    {
      a=a + "This is loop number " + i + "<br>";
      i++;
      if(i == 10){
        c=false;
      }
    }
    document.getElementById("p1").innerHTML=a;
  }
  </script>
</body>
</html>
```

Click Me

This is loop number 1
This is loop number 2
This is loop number 3
This is loop number 4
This is loop number 5
This is loop number 6
This is loop number 7
This is loop number 8
This is loop number 9

4.17.3 The DO...WHILE Loop

Do...While loop is little different than while loop. Here the condition is checked at the end of the loop. Statements inside the loop will be executed at least once even if the expression is FALSE. This is the basic difference between do while loop and while loop.

DO...WHILE Loop Example

```
<!DOCTYPE html>
<html>
<body>
  <button onclick="dwLoop()">Click Me</button>
  <p id="p1"></p>
  <script type="text/javascript">
  function dwLoop()
  {
    var a="",i=1,c=false;
    do
    {
      a=a + "This is loop number " + i + "<br>";
      i++;
      if(i == 10){
        c=false;
      }
    }
    while (c==true)
    document.getElementById("p1").innerHTML=a;
  }
  </script>
</body>
</html>
```

Output

Click Me

This is loop number 1

4.18 Break & Continue Statements

Break leaves a loop, continue skips the current iteration and jumps to the next iteration. Break is used in *switch, for, while, and do-while* statements continue is used in *for, while, and do-while* loop. Continue means, whatever code that follows the continue statement WITHIN the loop code block will not be executed and the program will go to the next iteration, in the following example, when the program reaches i=5 it checks the condition in the if statement and executes *continue*, everything after continue will not be executed and the control will be transferred to the beginning of the loop.

Break statement will just stop execution of the loop and go to the next statement after the loop if any. In this case when i=8 the program will jump out of the loop. Meaning, it will not continue to show 8, 9 and 10. The following example demonstrates the use of these two statements. The code will print 1 to 7 except 5.

HTML Code - Break & Continue Example

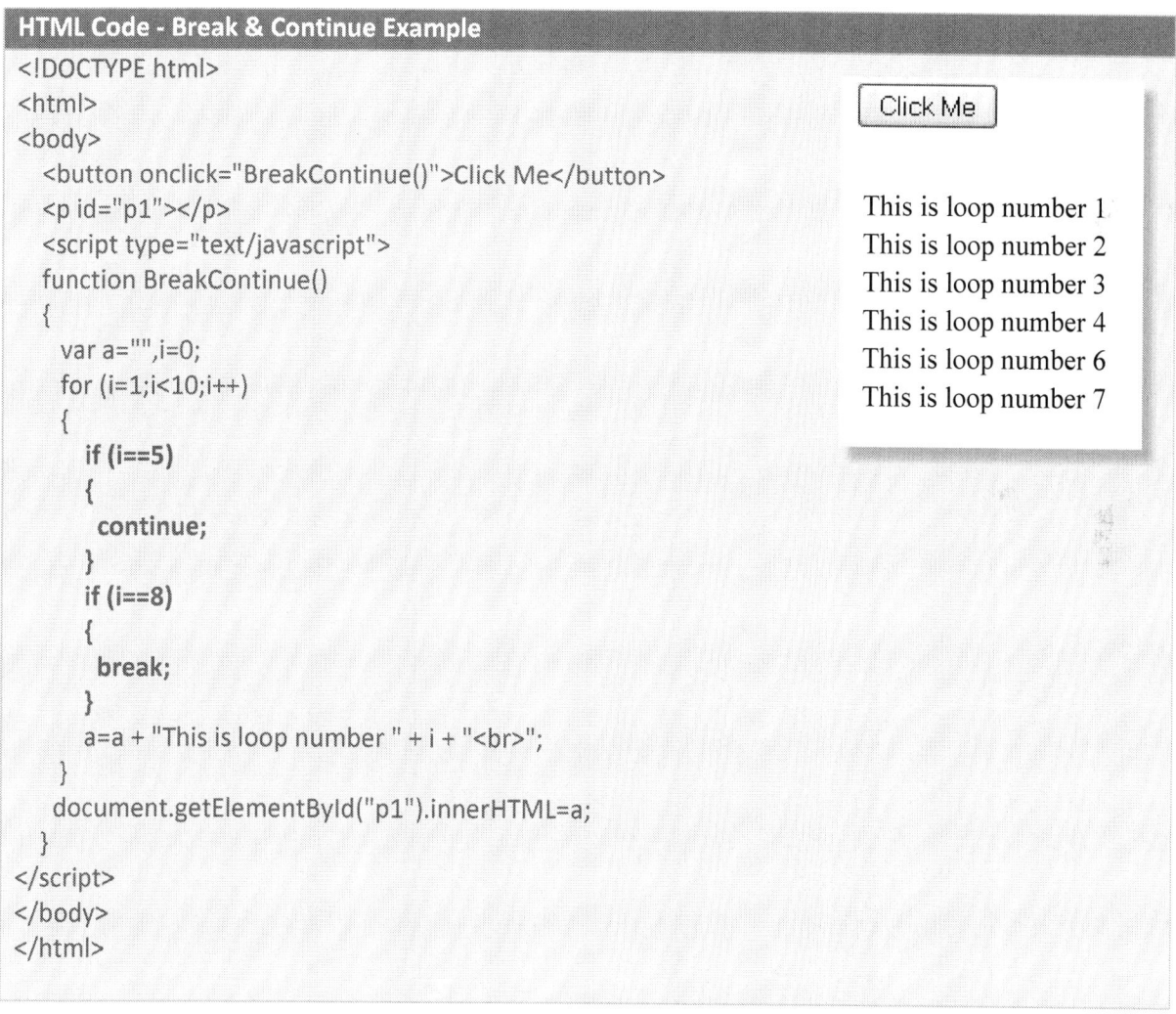

```
<!DOCTYPE html>
<html>
<body>
  <button onclick="BreakContinue()">Click Me</button>
  <p id="p1"></p>
  <script type="text/javascript">
  function BreakContinue()
  {
    var a="",i=0;
    for (i=1;i<10;i++)
    {
      if (i==5)
      {
        continue;
      }
      if (i==8)
      {
        break;
      }
      a=a + "This is loop number " + i + "<br>";
    }
    document.getElementById("p1").innerHTML=a;
  }
</script>
</body>
</html>
```

Click Me

This is loop number 1
This is loop number 2
This is loop number 3
This is loop number 4
This is loop number 6
This is loop number 7

4.19 Objects in JavaScript

An object can be defined as a special kind of data that comprises properties and methods.

Properties are the values associated with the object. For example, a car is an object. Its properties include model, color, doors, speed, etc. All cars have these properties, but the values vary from car to car. Property values can be a number, a string or a Boolean. When you call them, like *object.property*, you get (or set) this value. For example, to get and set the *innerWidth* property of the window object you use *window.innerWidth* and *window.innerWidth=pixels* respectively.

Methods are the actions that can be performed on objects. Some of the car methods are start(), gearshift(), stop, etc. When you call them, like *object.method()*, something happens. For example, if you write *document.write('Hello World!')* you execute the pre-defined *write()* method of the document object.

As properties basically hold values associated with the object, the methods provide the definitions of how the object can be acted on which can include changing the values of the properties (for example the gearshift() method of a car would update the speed property to indicate which speed the car is now running at).

In JavaScript, you have two types of Objects: built-in and user defined. We will start by looking at the user defined objects that you create yourself, and will explain the built-in objects later.

4.19.1 Declaring an Object

Objects are created by using the *new* keyword followed by the name of the class you wish to instantiate:

```
var oCar = new Object();
var oStringObject = new String();
```

The first line creates a new instance of Object and stores it in the variable oCar; the second line creates a new instance of String and stores it in the variable oStringObject. The parentheses aren't required when the constructor doesn't require arguments, so these two lines could be rewritten as follows:

```
var oCar = new Object;
var oStringObject = new String;
```

4.19.2   Add Properties to Objects

Properties are added to an object by simply giving them values like this:

```
oCar=new Object();
oCar.model="VTI";
oCar.color="Red";
oCar.door=4;
oCar.speed=250;
```

To get the color property of this object, the following code will be used:

```
document.write(oCar.color);
```

This code will render "Red" as the output.

4.19.3   Why Use Objects?

In JavaScript you use variables and arrays to store data, but there are situations that are more complicated and where you need another mechanism to act differently. For instance, you want to access and display a list of software along with title, price, and description on your web page from a database table.

To deal with a situation like this, you create objects. In the following section, we will try to understand objects and their utilization through the scenario mentioned above. First, you need to define an object named oSWList, add properties (title, price, description), and finally create methods to work with the information.

4.19.4　Creating Objects and Defining Properties

You create a function to make the new oSWList objects. This function is called the constructor for an object. The constructor is a simple function that accepts parameters to initialize a new object and assigns them to the corresponding properties. The function below accepts several parameters from the statement that calls the function, and then treats them as objects' properties. Because the function is called oSWList, the object is the oSWList object. The "this" keyword is referring to the current object that is being created by the function. The last line is referencing a method, mSoftware() that is created in the next section, to make the method part of the function definition for oSWList objects.

```
function oSWList(title,price,description) {
    this.title = title;
    this.price = price;
    this.description = description;
    this.mSoftware = mSoftware;
}
```

4.19.5　Creating a Method

After defining the object oSWList, you create a method named mSoftware() to work with it. Note that all oSWList objects will have the same properties. The mSoftware() function is created to act as a method for oSWList objects, so you do not have to ask for the parameters. Again, you will use the "this" keyword to refer to the current object's properties.

```
function mSoftware() {
    sTitle = "Title: "+ this.title + "<br>\n";
    nPrice = "Price: "+ this.price + "<br>\n";
    sDescription = "Description: "+ this.description + "<br>\n";
    document.write(sTitle, nPrice, sDescription);
}
```

This function simply reads the properties from the current object (this), displays each one with a label, and skips to a new line. To officially make mSoftware() part of the oSWList object, you already added a line while defining the object above.

4.19.6 Creating an Object Instance

To use an object definition, you create an instance of that object with the *new* keyword. The following statement creates a new oSWList object instance called *accounts*:

> *accounts = new oSWList("The Millennium Accountant", 100, "A handy software to manage finance of an organization");*

The above statement creates an instance (accounts - to hold accounting software information), and calls the oSWList function (the object definition) and passes it the required attributes in the defined order. This is called an instance of the oSWList object. In JavaScript, you can define several instances of an object.

After creating an instance of an object, you can use the mSoftware() method to show the information. For example, this statement displays the properties of the accounts software:

> *accounts.mSoftware();*

4.19.7 Testing the Objects

After scratching the basics, let's see the complete example of the subject scenario. This section demonstrates how to use objects in a web page to display software information. The first step is to create a test.js file having mSoftware(), oSWList, and three software records as shown below. Finally, create an HTML file (test.html) that calls the JavaScript file and displays the result in a browser. Save both .js and .html files in the same folder and run test.html.

HTML Code - JavaScript Objects Example

```html
<html>
<head>
<title>Software Products</title>
</head>
<body>
  <h1>Software Products</h1>
  <p></p><hr>
  <script language="JavaScript" type="text/javascript" src="test.js">
  </script>
</body>
</html>
```

JavaScript Code

```javascript
// This is the method
function mSoftware() {
   sTitle = "<b>Title: </b>" + this.title + "<br>\n";
   nPrice = "<b>Price: </b>" + this.price + "<br>\n";
   sDescription = "<b>Description: </b>" + this.description + "<br>\n<hr>";
   document.write(sTitle, nPrice, sDescription);
}
// The object function
function oSWList(title,price,description) {
   this.title = title;
   this.price = "$"+price;
   this.description = description;
   this.mSoftware = mSoftware;
}
// Create instance of the objects
accounts = new oSWList("The Millennium Accountant", 100, "A handy software to manage finance of
an organization");

imports = new oSWList("The Import Manager", 200, "A software to manage your import processes");

demo = new oSWList("Demo Creator", 300, "Create professional videos of your products");

// And print them
accounts.mSoftware();
imports.mSoftware();
demo.mSoftware();
```

Software Products

Title: The Millennium Accountant
Price: $100
Description: A handy software to manage finance of an organization

Title: The Import Manager
Price: $200
Description: A software to manage your import processes

Title: Demo Creator
Price: $300
Description: Create professional videos of your products

For demonstration purpose, we manually added three software records. However, in real-world you'll definitely fetch this information from a back end database and an object like this could be used to hold database records retrieved from a database with thousands of records.

4.20 JavaScript Events

Events are actions that happen when a button is clicked on a web page, the mouse pointer is moved, key is pressed on a keyboard, or a web page or image load from the server. JavaScript programs detect events and react to them. This reaction makes web documents interactive. The script that you use to detect and respond to an event is called an event handler.

Each event has a name. For instance, the onMouseOver event occurs when the mouse pointer moves over an object on the page. An event handler attribute can be added to an individual HTML tag as:

<a href="http://www.cnn.com/" onMouseOver="window.alert('You are over the link');">Click Me</a>

The above statement shows an alert when the mouse moves over the link. It is recommended to use a function in case of multiple statements. Function is defined in the header of the document, and is called as the event handler like this:

<a href="#tlink" onMouseOver="GoTop();">Hover over this link</a>

This example calls a function called GoTop() when the mouse is moved over the link.

4.20.1   Common Events

onMouseOver: This handler is called when the mouse pointer moves over an object on a web page. For example, change an image when the mouse moves over the image.

onMouseOut: Opposite to onMouseOver, this handler is called when the pointer leaves the object's border. It is used to reverse the action taken with onMouseOver handler such as, changing an image back to its previous status.

onClick: This event handler comes into action when the mouse button is clicked on an object. For example, the following statement displays an alert when the link is clicked:

<a href="http://www.cnn.com/" onClick="alert('You will be taken to CNN site');">Go to CNN.com</a>

The statement below displays a confirmation box and returns a value. If the user clicks Cancel, false is returned and prevents the link from being followed.

<a href="http://www.cnn.com/" onClick="return(window.confirm('Are you sure?"));">Click Here</a>

onMouseDown: It is used when the user presses the mouse button.

onMouseUp: This handler is used when the user releases the mouse button.

onLoad: This event is triggered when the current page finishes loading from the server.

<body onLoad="alert('Loading complete.');">

onUnload: It happens when another page is loaded or when the browser window is closed.

4.21 Using JavaScript with HTML Forms

We went through HTML forms in section 2.20 earlier in this book and exercised various aspect of it using different form controls. In this section, you will learn how to make a form interactive with JavaScript. In JavaScript, each form is represented as an object with the same name as the NAME attribute mentioned in the <form> tag.

4.21.1 Form Attributes

name: Using this attribute, you provide a name to your form in the <form> tag. You assign a name to a form to recognize it in JavaScript.

method: It has two values, GET and POST. You send data to the server using these methods. For further details on these two method, see Chapter 2 - section 2.20.

action: Using this attribute you send form's data either through a CGI script or through email to the desired destination.

4.21.2 Form Methods

The form object has two methods, submit() and reset(). The former one lets you submit the form's data whereas the later one clears the form.

4.21.3 Form Events

You can use two event handlers for a form object in JavaScript, onSubmit and onReset. The onSubmit event is called before the data is submitted to the CGI script. If the statement or function returns true, the data is submitted. This submission can be prevented by returning a value of false for the event handler. Similarly, the functionality of a Reset button can be prevented with the onReset event handler.

4.21.4 Referring Form Elements

You can refer to a form element either by its name or by its index. For example, the two expressions below correspond to the first element in the contact form, the fname text field.

document.contactform.elements[0]
document.contactform.fname

To find a form object you use the *document.getElementById()* method. The following statement finds a text field called fname and stores it in the sFname variable:

sFname = document.getElementById("fname");

Display Form Data

```
<!DOCTYPE html>
<html>
<head>
<title>Using JavaScript with HTML Form</title>
<script language="JavaScript" type="text/javascript">
  function showData() {
    oPopWin = window.open('','Window1','toolbar=no,status=no,width=300,height=100')
    message = "<ul><li><b>Name: </b>" + document.contactform.name.value;
    message += "<li><b>E-mail: </b>" + document.contactform.email.value;
    message += "<li><b>Mobile: </b>" + document.contactform.mobile.value + "</ul>";
    oPopWin.document.write(message);
  }
</script>
</head>


<body>
<form name="contactform">
  <fieldset>
    <legend>Contact Information</legend>
    <label>Name:<br>
    <input type="text" name="name" /></label><br>
    <label>Email:<br>
    <input type="text" name="email" /></label><br>
    <label>Mobile:<br>
    <input type="text" name="mobile" /></label>
  </fieldset>
  <p><input type="BUTTON" value="Show Data" onClick="showData();"></p>
</form>


</body>
</html>
```

> This example is an extension to the one we went through in section 2.29. We added JavaScript to it which displays data from the form in a pop-up window through a function named showData.

Output

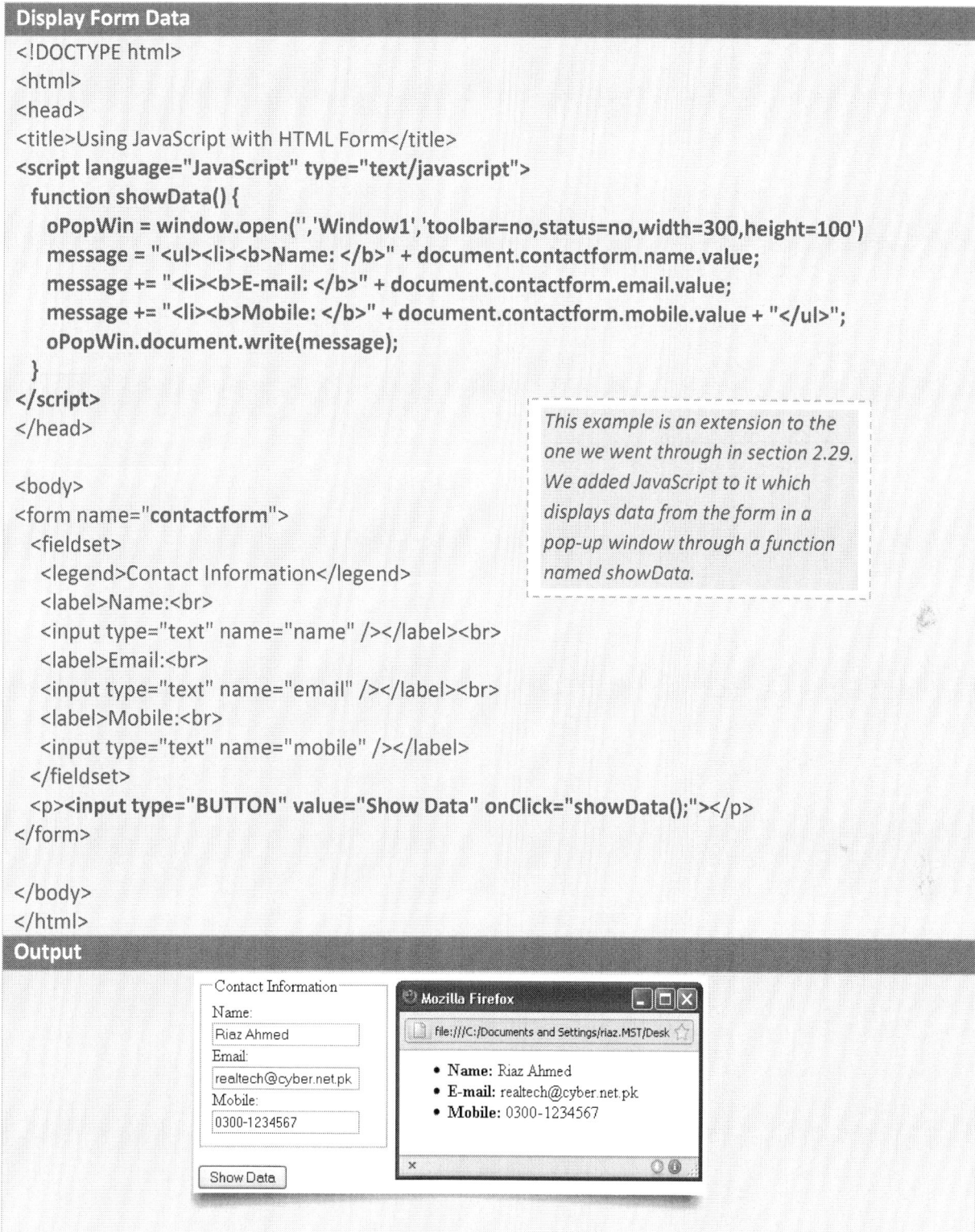

4.21.5 Validating Form's Data

You saw how JavaScript is used in HTML forms, but its most significant use is to validate data entered in these forms. For example, you can check that the form's mandatory fields are not left blank or, if entered, they are in the correct format. Data in the previous form could be validated as shown in the following example. The checkData() JavaScript function is used to check data in the name field through the field's length. If you leave the field blank and hit the submit button, the submission is stopped and an alert message comes up with relevant information.

We used *document.contactform.name.focus()* statement to place the cursor on the field where the error occurred. The function checkData() is called using the onSubmit event handler in the <form> tag. The value returned by the checkData() function is determined by the *return* keyword to assess whether to submit the form. You can use the onChange event handler in each form field to validate data individually prior to submission.

Data Validation Example

```
<!DOCTYPE html>
<html>
<head>
<title>JavaScript in HTML Form</title>
<script language="JavaScript" type="text/javascript">
  function checkData() {
     if (document.contactform.name.value.length < 1) {
       alert ("Please enter your name");
          document.contactform.name.focus();
       return false;
     }
  }
  return true;
</script>
</head>
<body>
  <form name="contactform" onSubmit="return checkData();">
    <fieldset>
      <legend>Contact Information</legend>
      <label>Name:<br>
      <input type="text" name="name" /></label><br>
      <label>Email:<br>
      <input type="text" name="email" /></label><br>
      <label>Mobile:<br>
      <input type="text" name="mobile" /></label>
    </fieldset>
    <p><input type="SUBMIT" value="Submit"></p>
  </form>
</body>
</html>
```

Output

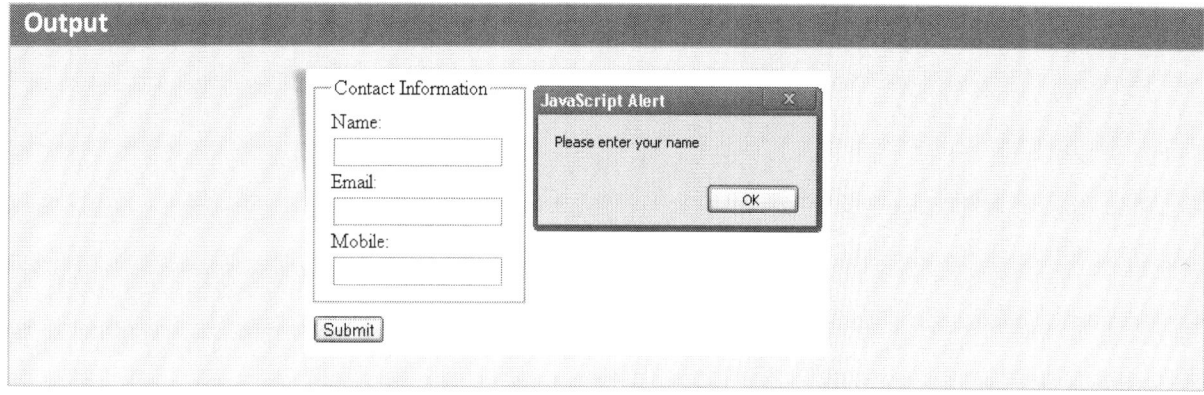

At this point, we have seen how to handle different aspects of HTML Forms using client side scripting to avoid server round trips. Forms are designed to receive input from users and then to store this input into a database. This functionality lacks in client side scripting languages, and this is where server-side scripting comes into action. In the next part, you will learn how to validate and store HTML Form data on the server using PHP and MySQL.

JavaScript & PHP

Although PHP offers plenty of power for creating dynamically generated Web pages, it is strictly a server-side language. There's a common category of Web site tasks that perhaps don't require all the processing power of a server and would best be done quickly—for instance, changing the look of a button on mouseover. JavaScript, a purely client-side language (there's a server-side version, but we're assuming you've already chosen PHP on that end), can be easily integrated into PHP to fill in many of these gaps.

Client-side JavaScript (aka Javascript, JScript,ECMAScript) itself has many limitations. For example, because it can't communicate directly with a database, JavaScript cannot update itself with fresh data depending on the page. Even worse, it's impossible to depend on client-side technologies, because they may not be present in a visitor's browser or may be disabled. PHP can help to mitigate the effects of client-side indeterminacy.

Where to use JavaScript

Some places you should definitely consider replacing or enhancing PHP with JavaScript include:
- Simple arithmetic in forms and calculators (such as shopping cart running total, mortgage calculator etc.)
- Simple form validation (such as making sure e-mail addresses have @ symbols)
- Site navigation (such as pull-down navigation menus)
- Pop-ups (alerts, search boxes)
- Browser events (mouseover, onClick)

Where to use PHP

Server-side scripting languages such as PHP perfectly serve most of the truly useful aspects of the Web, as such as the items in this list:

- Content sites (both production and display)
- Community features (forums, bulletin boards, Groupware, and so on)
- E-mail (Web mail, mail forwarding, and sending mail from a Web application)
- Customer-support and technical-support systems
- Web-based business applications
- Surveys, polls, and tests
- Filling out and submitting forms online
- Catalog, brochure, and informational sites
- Games (for example, chess) with lots of logic but simple/static graphics
- Any other application that needs to connect a backend server

- Introduction to PHP and MySQL database

- Setup Environment for Server-Side Scripting - Download and install PHP and MySQL database and configure all the required components

- An overview of SQL, database, datatypes, and tables

- Variables and Functions in PHP

- Dealing with Forms - connecting to database and performing insert, update, and delete operations

- PHP Data Objects (PDO)

- Sessions, Arrays, FOREACH Loop, and Include & Require Statements in PHP

- Send E-mail from PHP

CHAPTER 5

PHP & MySQL

The highest result of education is tolerance.

5.1 Introduction to PHP and MySQL Database

In this part, you will be introduced to PHP, MySQL, and the interaction of the two.

PHP	MySQL
PHP stands for *PHP: Hypertext Preprocessor*. It is a server-side scripting language, which can be embedded in HTML or used as a standalone binary (although the former use is much more common). PHP is a powerful tool for making dynamic and interactive Web pages and is the widely-used, free, and efficient alternative to competitors such as Microsoft's ASP. Below are some basic general facts about PHP: <ul><li>PHP is a server-side scripting language and its scripts are executed on the server.</li><li>PHP is an open source software and is free to download and use.</li><li>PHP files have extensions ".php", ".php3", or ".phtml". These files can hold text, HTML tags and scripts.</li><li>PHP files are returned to the browser as plain HTML.</li><li>PHP supports many databases (MySQL, Oracle, PostgreSQL, Sybase, Informix, Solid, Generic ODBC, etc.)</li><li>PHP is easy to learn, compared to the other ways to achieve similar functionality. Unlike Java Server Pages or C-based CGI, PHP doesn't require you to gain a deep understanding of a major programming language before you can make a trivial database or remote-server call. Unlike Perl, which has been called a "write-only language," PHP has a syntax that is quite easy to parse and human-friendly. And unlike ASP.NET, PHP is stable and ready to solve your problems today.</li></ul>	MySQL (pronounced My Ess Q El) is an open source, SQL Relational Database Management System (RDBMS) that is free for many uses. It is used to store data. Data in MySQL is stored in objects called tables. For example, a database of a company can have the following tables: <ul><li>Customers</li><li>Vendors</li><li>Products</li><li>Orders</li><li>Contact</li></ul>

A table consists of rows and columns and holds related records. For instance, the Contact table holds feedback data from customers as shown below:

ID	Name	Email	Age	Message
1	Riaz Ahmed	realtech@cyber.net.pk	30	This is feedback message # 1
2	Daniel Clarke	daniel@gmail.com	25	This is feedback message # 2
3	Michael Peter	mpeter@yahoo.com	40	This is feedback message # 3
4	Michael Jackson	mjackson@hotmail.com	55	This is feedback message # 4

This table (Contact) consists of five columns (ID, Name, Email, Age, and Message) and contains four records (rows 1 through 4). Each row holds same type of record with unique IDs and different values.

Here are some basic facts about MySQL:

- MySQL is free for most uses and relatively inexpensive for other uses.
- MySQL is one of the fastest relational databases.
- MySQL is easy to install and use.
- MySQL runs on Windows, Unix, Solaris, and OS/2 operating systems.
- MySQL supports SQL, which is the standard language for working with data stored in relational databases.
- MySQL provides access to data via intranet and the Internet.
- MySQL supports access from multiple clients from a variety of interfaces and programming languages including Java, C, Perl, Python, and of course PHP.
- MySQL allows you to implement high security to protect your data from unauthorized access.
- MySQL supports referential integrity and transaction processing offered by some big names such as Oracle Database and Microsoft SQL Server.

Looking at the above advantages, we will be using PHP and MySQL to provide server-side scripting functionality to our final project - web site for ABC Global Consulting. In the next sections you will be guided to setup PHP and MySQL on your computer.

5.2   Setup Environment for Server-Side Scripting

To make things simple, this installation assumes that you have Windows XP SP3 (32 bit) or higher operating system and are intending to use IIS 5.1 or higher as your web server. In this section, you will perform the following tasks:

- Install Internet Information Services (IIS 5.1) on Windows XP SP3
- Download and configure PHP
- Set Environment Variable for PHP
- Configure IIS to process PHP requests
- Test PHP installation
- Download and install MySQL prerequisites
- Download and setup MySQL database
- Test MySQL installation

5.2.1   Install Internet Information Services (IIS)

To make your web site visible to the world, you'll have to store it on a web server. Your own PC can act as a web server if you install Internet Information Services (IIS). IIS is easy to install and ideal for developing and testing web applications.

IIS is a web server application and set of feature extension modules created by Microsoft for use with Microsoft Windows. IIS 7.5, the latest version, supports HTTP, HTTPS, FTP, FTPS, SMTP and NNTP. It is an integral part of the Windows Server family of products, as well as certain editions of Windows XP, Windows Vista, Windows 7 and Windows 8. IIS is Microsoft's entry to compete in the Internet server market that is also addressed by Apache, Sun Microsystems, O'Reilly, and others.

In this section, you will install IIS on your computer to locally run your web site. When you create a local IIS Web Site, the pages and folders for your site are stored in a folder under the default IIS folder (Inetpub\wwwroot).

IIS is not turned on by default when Windows is installed; follow to steps mentioned below to turn it on.

1. Click **Start | Control Panel**
2. Double click **Add Remove Programs** and click **Add/Remove Windows Components**
3. Under Components, select **Internet Information Services** ☑ 🗐 Internet Information Services (IIS)
4. Click **Next**. You might be asked to provide Windows XP CD.
5. Once the installation completes, click **Start | Run |** type **inetmgr** and click **OK**.
6. In the Internet Information Services console, expand all nodes to your left till you see the node **Default Web Site**.
7. Right click this node and select **Browse** from the context menu. This should open a Windows XP web page saying your web service is now running.

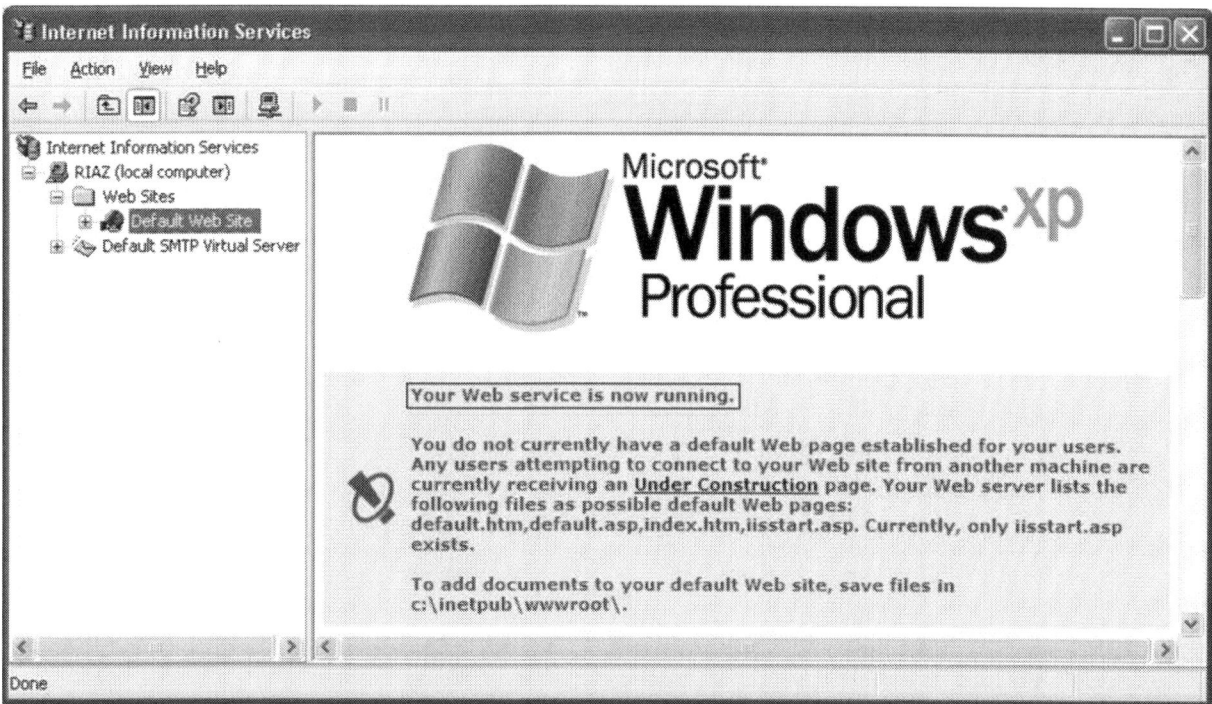

Figure 5-1

5.2.2 Add Default Documents to IIS

If a client accesses your Web site or Web application without specifying a document name (for example, requesting http://www.abcglobal.com/ instead of http://www.abcglobal.com/index.html), you can configure IIS to serve a default document, such as index.html. If you list more than one default document, IIS reviews the default document list (in order) until it finds a match in the directory and then serves the file to the client.

When both default documents and directory browsing are disabled and the request too doesn't include a document name, client browsers receive a *404—File Not Found* error because the Web server cannot determine which file to serve and cannot return a directory listing. However, if default documents are disabled but directory browsing is enabled, client browsers receive a directory listing instead of a *404—File Not Found* error.

The Default Document feature must be enabled to add file names to the default document list and to serve default documents to client browsers. In the following steps you'll add two default documents (index.php and index.html) to deliver dynamic and static pages respectively.

1. In the Internet Information Services console, right-click **Default Web Site** and select **Properties**
2. Click on the **Documents** tab
3. Click the **Add...** button
4. Type **index.php** in Default Document Name box and click **OK**
5. Click the **Add** button again
6. Type **index.html** in Default Document Name box and click OK
7. Click **Apply** and then **OK** to dismiss all open dialogs

5.2.3 Download and Configure PHP

PHP is available in different flavors. The latest versions of PHP are only being distributed in VC9 form. The sub categories include Thread Safe and Non Thread Safe versions. A Thread Safe version should be used if you install PHP as an Apache module. The Non Thread Safe version should be used if you install PHP as a CGI binary. The non thread safe binaries allow you to configure IIS (and other Windows based web servers) to use PHP as a standard CGI interface with increased performance.

1. The VC9 versions require you to have the Microsoft 2008 C++ Runtime (x86) (vcredist_x86.exe) which you can download from: **http://www.microsoft.com/en-us/download/details.aspx?id=29** Launch the vcredist_x86.exe file to install the runtime.
2. Download PHP from **http://www.php.net/downloads.php**
3. Click the link **Windows 5.4.6 binaries and source** under PHP 5.4.6 section
4. Click the **Zip** link under VC9 x86 Non Thread Safe section under PHP 5.4 (5.4.6)

Figure 5-2

5. Create a folder on your C drive (**C:\PHP**) and unpack the content of the php-5.4.6-nts-Win32-VC9-x86.zip archive into this directory
6. Rename file php.ini-production to **php.ini** (if you can't see the file extension, follow these step):
   a. On your desktop, open **My Computer**. If you don't see My Computer, then open any folder.
   b. Select the **Tools** menu, and then select **Folder Options**.
   c. In the Folder Options windows, click on the **View** tab.
   d. Uncheck the box next to **Hide file extensions for known file types**
   e. Rename php.ini-production to **php.ini**
   f. Click **Yes** to change the name

Figure 5-3

7. Open **php.ini** in Notepad, press **ctrl+f**, search **extension_dir** directive, **uncomment** it, i.e., delete the prefixed semi-colon ";". Add the path so that it looks like **extension_dir = "C:\PHP\ext"**. Set few more directives as shown below. Don't forget to remove the ";".

   a. log_errors = On

   b. error_log = "C:\inetpub\php-errors.log"

   c. cgi.force_redirect = 0

   d. cgi.fix_pathinfo = 1

   e. fastcgi.impersonate = 1

   f. fastcgi.logging = 0

   g. Remove ";" from extension=php_mysql.dll to uncomment this line

   h. Remove ";" from extension=php_mysqli.dll to uncomment this line

   i. Remove ";" from extension=php_pdo_mysql.dll to uncomment this line

   j. Set the timezone directive as date.timezone = "America/Chicago" and uncomment this line. Check this site for other zones: http://www.php.net/manual/en/timezones.php

   k. Enable GD library by removing ";" from extension=php_gd2.dll. GD library is an image processing library that lets you to work with most image types including GIF, JPEG, and PNG. You'll see this library in action is section 6.13.5 - Image Manager.

8. **Save** the file.

PHP is now setup on your system. The next steps are: set the environment variables, choose a web server, and enable it to run PHP.

5.2.4 Add PHP directory to the PATH on Windows

Environment variables are a set of dynamic named values that can affect the way running processes will behave on a computer. They can be said in some sense to create the operating environment in which a process runs. System path variables refer to locations of critical operating system resources, and as such generally are not user-dependent.

The path to a file is basically its address on the computer. It tells programs how to find a file. It is the drive plus any directories and sub-directories where the file is located. The PATH environment variable specifies the command search path. Typically, this is a group of directories where executable files that are repeatedly used are to be found. When the user types a command without providing the full path, this list is checked if it contains a path that leads to the command.

1. Right click **My Computer** and select **Properties**.
2. Click the **Advanced** tab | Click the **Environment Variables** button | select the **variable Path** in System Variable section and click the **Edit** button under this section.
3. BE CAREFUL HERE. You do not want to delete anything in Variable value. Simply find the end of the line and add a semi-colon (;) if there is not one already. After the semi-colon, type: **C:\PHP;C:\php\ext;**

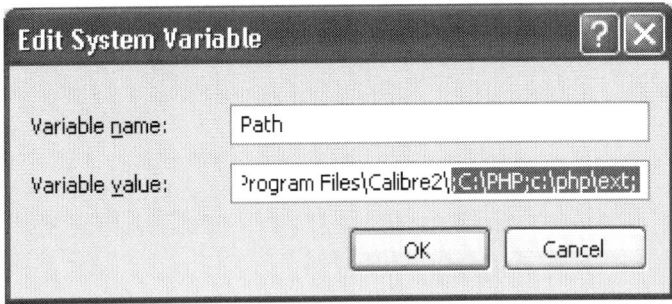

Figure 5-4

4. Click **OK** to close all dialogs.
5. Restart your computer to take effect of environment variables.

5.2.5 Configuring IIS to Process PHP Requests

FastCGI for IIS enables popular application frameworks that support the FastCGI protocol to be hosted on the IIS web server in a high-performance and reliable way. FastCGI provides a high-performance alternative to the Common Gateway Interface (CGI), a standard way of interfacing external applications with Web servers that has been supported as part of the IIS feature-set.

1. Download and install the Microsoft FastCGI Extension for IIS 5.1 from **http://www.iis.net/download/fastcgi**. The extension is available for 32-bit and 64-bit platforms - Click the **x86** download link for this exercise.

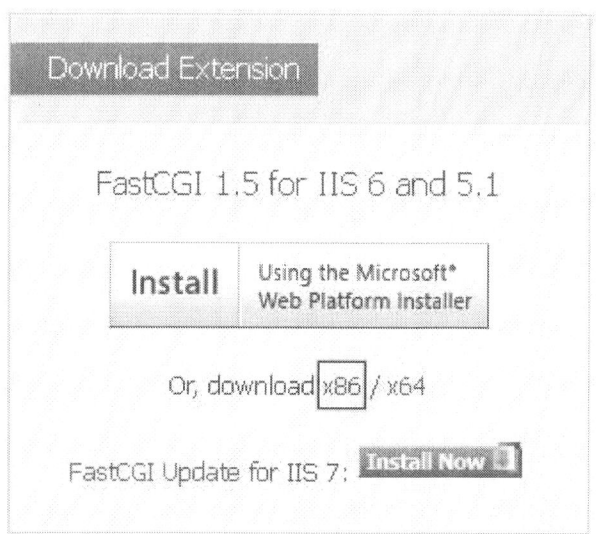

Figure 5-5

2. After downloading, launch **fcgisetup_1.5_rtw_x86**.
3. Configure the FastCGI extension to handle PHP-specific requests by running the command shown below on a command prompt (**Start** | **Run** | type **cmd** in the Open box and hit **OK**). This command will create an IIS script mapping for *.php file extension, which will result in all URLs that end with .php being handled by FastCGI extension. Also, it will configure FastCGI extension to use the executable php-cgi.exe to process the PHP requests.

```
cscript %windir%\system32\inetsrv\fcgiconfig.js -add -section:"PHP" -extension:php -
path:"C:\PHP\php-cgi.exe"
```

After execution, the script should end up with the message "INI successfully written".

5.2.6   Test PHP

The PHP environment is set on your computer. Let's give it a try by running a small .php file.

1. Open Notepad and type the following code in it:

```
<html>
  <head>
   <title>PHP Test</title>
  </head>
  <body>
   <?php echo '<p>Hello World</p>'; ?>
  </body>
</html>
```

2. Select **All Files** from *Save as type* and save the file as **Hello.php** in C:\Inetpub\wwwroot folder
3. Open a browser session and type **http://localhost/hello.php** to see the text "Hello World" in the browser.

We will dig further PHP details in an upcoming sections; but first, you must explore basics of MySQL database.

5.2.7   Download and Install MySQL Database

In our final project to design a web site for ABC Global Consulting, we will create dynamic web pages that will take users' input through HTML forms and will store that data in MySQL database. This section provides the sequence to download and install MySQL database on your PC to fulfill the data storage requirement.

Prerequisites:

MySQL Installer for Windows needs the following components prior to installing the database:

- Microsoft .NET Framework 4 (dotNetFx40_Full_setup.exe). Get it from http://www.microsoft.com/en-us/download/details.aspx?id=17851
- Microsoft Visual C++ 2010 Redistributable Package (x86) (vcredist_x86.exe) http://www.microsoft.com/en-us/download/details.aspx?id=5555

Install the above components after downloading.

Download MySQL Database:

1. Open a browser session and type **http://www.mysql.com/downloads/**
2. Click the banner to start the proceedings

Figure 5-6

3. On the next page click the **download** button next to Windows (x86, 32-bit), MSI Installer
4. Click the link **» No thanks, just start my download!**
5. Click the **Save file** button to start downloading
6. After completion, launch **mysql-installer-community-5.5.27.2.msi** and follow on-screen instructions.

> **NOTE**
>
> *During the database installation, you will be prompted to provide password for the **root** user. I set it to **gemini** and will use it in subsequent sections.*

5.2.8   Test MySQL

After installation, you will see a new program group named MySQL in your Windows Start | All Program group. You are given two options to work with MySQL database; either graphically, using *MySQL Workbench*, or through a command prompt using *MySQL Command Line Client*. We're going to use the later approach to get familiar with different SQL statements.

Before you start, make a small change to the Target line of MYSQL Command Line Client program item.

1. Under **Start | All Programs | MySQL | MySQL Server 5.5**, right click **MySQL 5.5 Command Line Client** and select **Properties** from the context menu.
2. On the shortcut tab, set .ini file to *my-huge.ini* in the Target line as shown below:
   "C:\Program Files\MySQL\MySQL Server 5.5\bin\mysql.exe" "--defaults-file=C:\Program Files\MySQL\MySQL Server 5.5**my-huge.ini**" "-uroot" "-p"
3. Click **OK**

After setting the appropriate ini file, let's move ahead in sequence to test MySQL.

1. Click **Start | All Programs | MySQL | MySQL Server 5.5 | MySQL 5.5 Command Line Client**. This should open a command prompt asking for password.
2. Enter the password you set for the "root" user during the installation process and hit the Enter key. I set it to gemini. The mysql prompt appears ready to take commands.
3. On the command prompt, type **use sakila** to open sakila database that comes with MySQL. Hit Enter. A message *Database changed* should appear.
4. Type **select database();** - put the terminating semicolon. This would give the name of the currently selected database i.e. sakila.
5. Type **show tables;** to get a list of tables in the sakila database.
6. Type **describe store;** to get column information from the store table.
7. Type **exit** and press Enter.

In this exercise, we tested the MySQL database setup by passing various statements to interact with the database. In the next section, you will be guided on how to create a new database and tables using SQL DDL statements and how to manipulate data in tables with DML statements.

5.3 Structured Query Language (SQL)

A discussion about database is meaningless without mentioning SQL. SQL is the language of relational databases. It is the common vocabulary and syntax that enables you to interact with numerous databases including Oracle, SQL Server, MySQL etc. Instructions that you pass to these databases through SQL are called statements. SQL statements are broadly categorized as: DML, DCL, and DDL.

Data Definition Language (DDL) is the part of SQL that you use to CREATE, ALTER, and DROP database objects (database, tables, users and so on).

Data Control Language (DCL) statements are used to control database access such as GRANT and REVOKE statements which you use to grant and revoke privileges on database objects to users.

Data Manipulation Language (DML) statements let users move data into and out of a database. The four basic data-manipulation statements supported by essentially all SQL databases are: SELECT, INSERT, UPDATE, and DELETE. SELECT gets data out of the database, INSERT puts in a new entry, UPDATE edits pieces of the entry in place, and DELETE gets rid of an entry.

5.4 Handling A Database

A new database is created using the DDL syntax: CREATE DATABASE. Follow the procedure outlined below to create a database named TESTDB:

1. Connect to MySQL (as mentioned in Test MySQL section 5.2.8 above)
2. On mysql prompt, type the following statement and press Enter (do not forget to put the terminating ";" semi-colon):

Example

CREATE DATABASE testdb;

A message, "Query OK, 1 row affected (0.13 sec)", should be displayed after you hit the Enter key.

3. To display the newly created database along with others, type **SHOW DATABASES;**

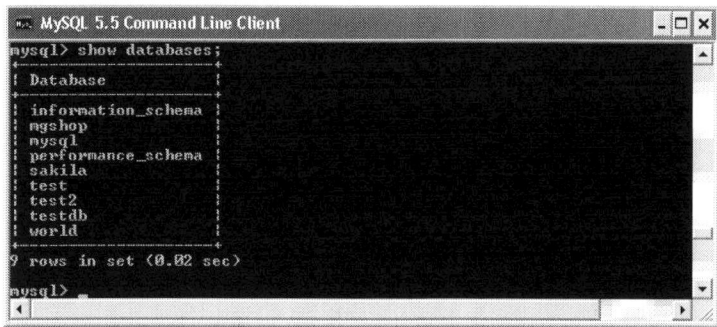

Figure 5-7

4. To connect to the MYSQL database, type **USE MYSQL** and hit Enter.
5. Type **SHOW TABLES;** to get a list of tables from the currently selected database i.e. MYSQL.

Figure 5-8

5.5   MySQL Datatypes

All RDBMS require the user to specify the data type of each column in a table. The available data types vary from one programming language to another, and from one database application to another, but the following usually exist in one form or another:

- Character (text): Readable text
- Integer : An integer is a whole number; a number that has no fractional part.
- Floating-point : A number with a decimal point. For example, 3 is an integer, but 3.5 is a floating-point number.

In MySQL data types are divided into three main categories: text, number, and Date/Time.

Text Types:

Type	Description
CHAR(size)	Stores string (letters, numbers, and special characters) of fixed length up to 255 characters
VARCHAR(size)	Values in VARCHAR columns are variable-length strings. The length can be specified as a value from 0 to 255 before MySQL 5.0.3, and 0 to 65,535 in 5.0.3 and later versions.
BLOB	A BLOB is a binary large object that can hold a variable amount of data such as images. The four BLOB types are TINYBLOB, BLOB, MEDIUMBLOB, and LONGBLOB.
TEXT	TEXT values are treated as nonbinary strings (character strings). The four TEXT types are TINYTEXT, TEXT, MEDIUMTEXT, and LONGTEXT.

Number Types:

Type	Description
INT(size)	An integer is what is more commonly known as a whole number. It may be positive, negative, or the number zero. MySQL supports the SQL standard integer types including INTEGER or (INT), SMALLINT, TINYINT, MEDIUMINT, and BIGINT.
Fixed-Point Types	The DECIMAL and NUMERIC types store exact numeric data values. These types are used when it is important to preserve exact precision, for example with monetary data. In MySQL, NUMERIC is implemented as DECIMAL. In a DECIMAL column declaration, the precision and scale can be (and usually is) specified; for example: *salary DECIMAL(5,2)* In this example, 5 is the precision and 2 is the scale. The precision represents the number of significant digits that are stored for values, and the scale represents the number of digits that can be stored following the decimal point.

Date Type:

Type	Description
DATE()	The DATE type is used for values with a date part but no time part. MySQL retrieves and displays DATE values in 'YYYY-MM-DD' format. The supported range is '1000-01-01' to '9999-12-31'.
DATETIME()	The DATETIME type is used for values that contain both date and time parts. MySQL retrieves and displays DATETIME values in 'YYYY-MM-DD HH:MM:SS' format. The supported range is '1000-01-01 00:00:00' to '9999-12-31 23:59:59'.
TIMESTAMP()	The TIMESTAMP data type is used for values that contain both date and time parts. TIMESTAMP has a range of '1970-01-01 00:00:01' UTC to '2038-01-19 03:14:07' UTC.
YEAR()	The YEAR type is a type used to represent year values. It can be declared as YEAR(4) or YEAR(2) to specify a display width of four or two characters. The default is four characters if no width is given.
TIME()	MySQL retrieves and displays TIME values in 'HH:MM:SS' format (or 'HHH:MM:SS' format for large hours values). TIME values may range from '-838:59:59' to '838:59:59'. The hours part may be so large because the TIME type can be used not only to represent a time of day (which must be less than 24 hours), but also elapsed time or a time interval between two events (which may be much greater than 24 hours, or even negative).

5.6 Creating Table

After creating an empty database and understanding different data types, you can now add tables to your database to hold data. Tables are created using the DDL syntax: CREATE TABLE.

> *CREATE TABLE table_name*
>
> *(*
> *column_name1 data_type,*
> *column_name2 data_type,*
> *column_name3 data_type,*
>
> *....*
> *)*

Let's create the Contact table, you saw earlier in section 5.1, in our new database: TESTDB.

1. On mysql prompt, type **use testdb** and hit Enter to connect to the newly created database. The *Database Changed* message should be displayed.
2. Type the statement mentioned below and hit Enter:

> **Example**
> CREATE TABLE contact (id int, name varchar(50), email varchar(100), age int(3), message varchar(2000));

Query OK, 0 rows affected (0.55 sec) message should appear

3. Type **describe contact;** to see the Contact table's structure

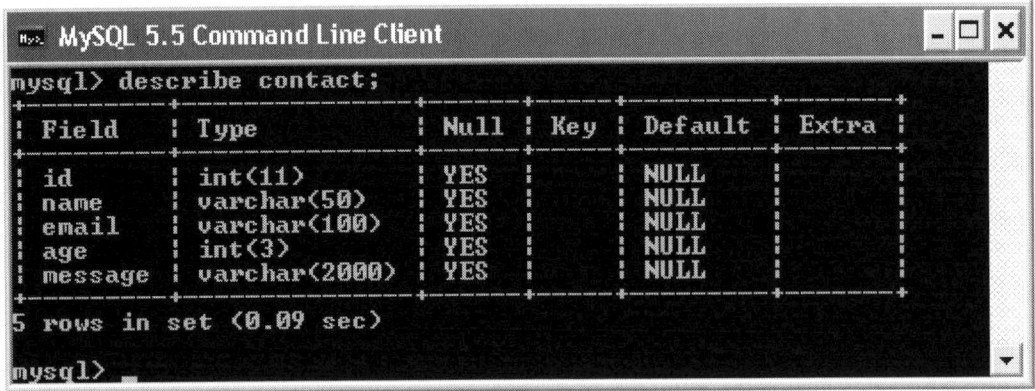

Figure 5-9

5.6.1 Adding Data

The INSERT INTO statement is used to insert new records in a table. This statement has the following two forms:

INSERT INTO table_name VALUES (value1, value2, value3,...)

Use this syntax (without mentioning column names) if you want to populate all columns in a table with some data.

INSERT INTO table_name (column1, column3, column5,...) VALUES (value1, value2, value3,...)

If you wish to add values to specific columns in a table, use this syntax specifying column names. For example, you want to skip column2 and column4 and just want to insert values in column 1, 3, and 5.

1. Type the following statement and hit Enter to add the first record. This statement will populate all table columns with relevant information.

Examples

Insert into contact values (1, 'Riaz Ahmed', 'realtech@cyber.net.pk', 30, 'Feedback message');

Insert into contact values (2, 'Daniel Clarke', 'daniel@gmail.com', 25, 'This is a comment');

The two statements would execute displaying *Query OK, 1 row affected (0.08 sec)*.

2. Add another record by using the second syntax:

Example

Insert into contact (id, email, message) values (99, 'abc@abc.com', 'This is a message');

The above statement will insert values only in id, email, and message columns, leaving name and age columns blank.

5.6.2 Querying Data

You now have three records in your Contact table. To query this data you will use the SELECT statement. Its syntax is:

SELECT column_name(s) FROM table_name

1. Type the following statement to retrieve all the rows from the Contact table:

Example
SELECT id, name, email, age, message FROM Contact;

The result should resemble as shown in the following figure.

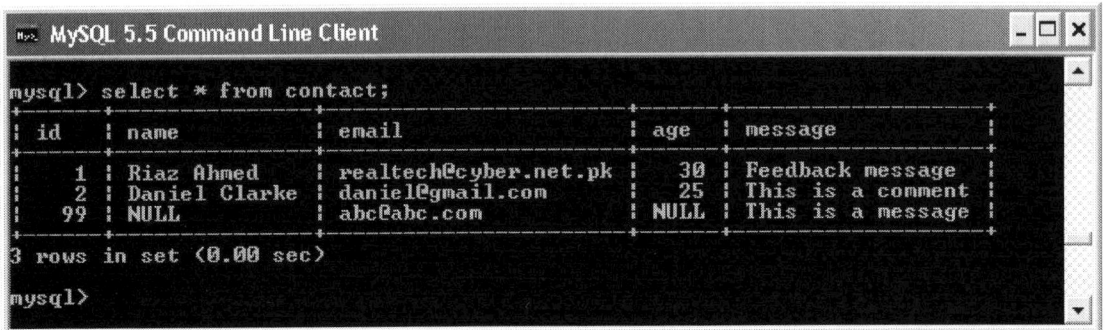

Figure 5-10

2. To select all columns at once, you can use the asterisk (*) character instead of individual column names like this:

Example
SELECT * FROM Contact;

This statement will provide the same output as shown in Figure 5-10.

3. Use the WHERE clause to get only those records that satisfy a specified criterion. The syntax is:

SELECT column_name(s) FROM table_name WHERE column_name operator value

Example
SELECT * FROM Contact where Name = 'Riaz Ahmed';

This statement fetches only one record; the one having value Riaz Ahmed in the Name column. You can use the following operators in the WHERE clause:

Operator	Description	Example
=	Equal	SELECT * FROM Contact where Name = 'Riaz Ahmed'; *Returns record # 1*
<> or !=	Not Equal	SELECT * FROM Contact where Name <> 'Riaz Ahmed'; *Returns record # 2*
>	Greater than	SELECT * FROM Contact where Age > 25; *Returns record # 1*
>=	Greater than or equal	SELECT * FROM Contact where Age >= 25; *Returns record # 1 and 2*
<	Less than	SELECT * FROM Contact where Id < 2; *Returns record # 1*
<=	Less than or equal	SELECT * FROM Contact where Id <= 2; *Returns record # 1 and 2*
BETWEEN	Data range between two values	SELECT * FROM Contact where Id BETWEEN 2 AND 100; *Returns record # 2and 99*
LIKE	Matches a pattern	SELECT * FROM Contact where message like '%feed%'; *Returns record # 1*
IN	Search multiple values	SELECT * FROM Contact where name IN ('Riaz Ahmed', 'Daniel Clarke'); *Returns record # 1 and 2*
AND & OR	Filter records	SELECT * FROM Contact where name='Riaz Ahmed' AND age=30; *Returns record # 1* SELECT * FROM Contact where name='Riaz Ahmed' AND age=25; *Returns record # 1 and 2* SELECT * FROM Contact where name='Riaz Ahmed' AND (age=25 or age=30 or age=99); *Returns record # 1*

5.6.3 Updating Data

We inserted record number 99 with some missing values that we wish to populate now. The process of updating existing records in a table is accomplished through the UPDATE statement whose syntax is:

> UPDATE table_name SET column1=value, column2=value2,...
> WHERE some_column=some_value

1. Type the following statement to update record number 99:

Example

UPDATE Contact SET name='ABC', age=99 WHERE id=99;   *(press Enter)*

Type the following statements to check the updated row:

SELECT * FROM Contact;

Here is the output.

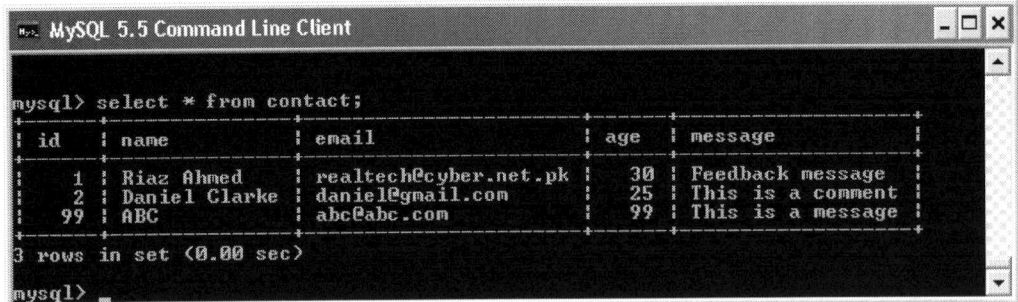

Figure 5-11

WARNING

It is important to use the WHERE clause specifying conditions while updating table records. The WHERE clause states which record or records that should be updated. If you omit the WHERE clause, all records will be updated!

5.6.4 Removing Data

In this exercise you will remove record number 99 from the table using the DELETE statement. Syntax for the DELETE statement is:

DELETE FROM table_name WHERE some_column=some_value

1. Type any of the following statement to remove record number 99:

> **Example**
>
> DELETE FROM Contact WHERE id=99;
>
> Alternatively, you can use a string condition in the WHERE clause like this:
>
> DELETE FROM Contact WHERE name='ABC';

Both the above statements will delete record number 99. Again, you must use the WHERE clause, if you omit, all records will be deleted!

Database and SQL are huge topics that require dedicated books. In this section, I merely scratched the surface to give you some basic knowledge about database and how to interact with it using SQL. You'll need this information in the last part of this book where you will create a database to store data received from your website visitors. The next section, which discusses PHP, will tell you how to connect to your database and insert users' feedback in a table.

5.7 PHP: Hypertext Preprocessor

We discussed the significance of PHP earlier in this chapter. Now, we're going to dig deeper to evaluate this robust server-side technology to fulfill the purpose of our project – taking users' feedback, newsletter subscription, and e-commerce modules. Following is the basic syntax of PHP script that starts with *<?php* and ends with *?>*:

```
<?php
    ...
    ...
    ...
?>
```

Basic Information:

- A PHP script can be placed anywhere in the document.
- It is executed on the server, and the result is sent back to the browser in plain HTML.
- It usually has a .php extension and carries HTML tags besides PHP scripting code as we saw in section 5.2.6 while testing PHP installation.
- Each PHP code line terminates with a semicolon to separate a set of instructions from another.

5.8 Variables in PHP

Variables are temporary containers for storing information. Consider the following points while declaring variables in PHP.

- In PHP, variables start with a $ sign, followed by a name e.g. $s_Phone1.
- Variable name should not contain spaces.
- Variable name must start with a letter or the underscore character and can contain alphabets (A-z), numbers (0-9) and the underscore (_).
- Variable names are case sensitive e.g. $s_Phone1 is different from $s_phone1.
- Variables in PHP are created when you assign value to them like:
    ```
    $s_Phone1="800-235-4365";
    $n_Age=30;
    $d_Today = date("d/m/Y");
    $b_Married = false;
    ```
- To concatenate two string variables together, use the concatenation operator (.):
    ```
    $s_Address1 = "301 S. Prospect Rd.";
    $s_Address2 = "Bloomington, IL 61704";
    echo "Address: " . $s_Address1 . " " . $s_Address2;
    ```
- Local variables can only be accessed within the function they are declared in.
- Global variables, declared using the *global* keyword, can be accessed from any part of the script.

PHP Code - Variables Example

```
<html>
<head>
 <title>PHP Variable Examples</title>
</head>
<body>
 <?php
  // String Variable – The "echo" language construct is used to output one or more strings

  $s_Address1 = "301 S. Prospect Rd.";
  $s_Address2 = "Bloomington, IL 61704";
  echo "Address: ".$s_Address1 . " " . $s_Address2;
  echo ("<br>");
  // Numeric Variable
  $n_Age = 30;
  echo "Your age is ".$n_Age;
  echo ("<br>");
  // Store and display system date
  $d_today = date("d/m/Y");
  echo "The date today is ".$d_today;
  echo ("<br>");
  // Boolean Example
  $b_Married = false;
  if($b_Married == true)
  {
    echo "You're married";
  }
  else
  {
    echo "You're unmarried";
  }
 ?>
</body>
</html>
```

NOTE

Just like JavaScript, PHP too uses // for single line and /* */ combination for multi line comments. For further details, see chapter 4 section 4.2 Comments in JavaScript.

Address: 301 S. Prospect Rd. Bloomington, IL 61704
Your age is 30
The date today is 01/01/2013
You're unmarried

5.9 Arrays in PHP

In PHP arrays are used to store data. It can be defined as a super-variable containing a collection of variables called elements. Each element has three components: index, datatype, and value. An element's value can be accessed through its corresponding index. By default, PHP uses integer indices starting with 0. Indices can be either strings or numbers, and are presented in square brackets. For example, the expression $categories[0] refers to the first value stored in $categories array.

Syntax:

Create an array: *$array_name = array(value1,value2,...)*

Access value in an element: *$array_name[index];*

Example:

$categories = array('Software','Hardware','Network');

Alternate method:

$categories = array();
$categories[0] = 'Software';
$categories[1] = 'Hardware';
$categories[2] = 'Network';

Besides the default numeric indices, you can also define strings index values. This type of array is called associative array. The indices in an associative array are called keys. Instead of element values separated by commas, you supply key-value pairs separated by commas, where the key and value are separated by the special symbol =>.

Syntax:

array('key' => value ...)

Example:

$product = array('PRODUCT' => 'The Import Manager', 'PRICE' => 99.99);

Many PHP built-in environment variables are in the form of arrays. For instance $_SESSION, which carries all the variable names, types, and values and propagates this data from one page to the other via PHP's session mechanism.

5.10 PHP Session

Sessions and cookies are closely allied concepts in PHP and in Web programming more generally, largely because the best way to actually implement sessions is by using cookies. PHP uses cookies to work with sessions and only works when cookies are enabled in client browsers. For clients who have cookies disabled, PHP presents an alternative called URL encoding.

What's a Session?

In Web terminology, a session is a period of time during which a person visits a number of different Web sites using his or her browser. A session ends when the visitor quits the browser. From the perspective of a single website, the session runs from that person's first download of a page from the site through the last. Session tracking is a term that refers to keeping track of users as they move around a website.

Why Track Session?

Web applications use HTTP by which browsers talk to Web servers. Since HTTP doesn't maintain state, it is known as a stateless protocol. Here, your Web server reacts independently to each individual request it receives and has no way to link requests together even if it is logging requests. For example, a client browser requests a page from a web server. After rendering the page, the server closes the connection. When a subsequent request is forwarded from the same client, the web server doesn't know how to associate the current request with the previous one.

Session Tracking in PHP

PHP provides a strong session tracking mechanism to cope with a situation like the one mentioned above. When a client sends a request, PHP evaluates whether the request has a PHP session ID. If not, it creates a new session on the server and assigns it a unique ID. This ID is sent back to the client browser as a cookie. The client includes this session ID with all subsequent requests. PHP uses this ID to access the session data stored on the web server and thus links requests sent against individual sessions.

> **NOTE**
>
> *After starting a session, you can store data in session variables with the help of a global array called $_SESSION. To remove an element from this array, you use the UNSET() function. Similarly, by setting it to an empty array you can remove its contents. A session ends when the browser is closed, or specified amount of time elapses without a request, or when a function such as session_destroy() is called. You'll be using this array extensively throughout the e-commerce module.*

Starting a Session

In PHP, you can start a new session or resume a previously defined session by calling the *SESSION_START()* built-in function. It prompts PHP to check for session ID in the sent request and to create a new session ID and cookie if one doesn't already exist. It returns true on success and false otherwise. Since it sets a cookie, it must be called before the page sends any HTML output to an application. PHP stores session ID in the client browser using the default per-session cookie mechanism. This type of session ends when the users closes the browser. You can use *session_set_cookie_params()* function to create a session cookie that persists longer.

5.11 Creating a PHP Function

Like JavaScript, you can create your functions in PHP. A function created in PHP is executed by a call to it from anywhere within a page. Functions in PHP are created using the following syntax:

```
function functionName($para1,$para2,...)
{
  function code;
}
```

Guidelines:

- Start the function name with a letter or underscore
- Give function a meaningful name to reflect its purpose
- You can add parameters (arguments) to your functions
- Use the return statement to get back a value from a function

The first example on the next page demonstrates a simple function named Greeting which doesn't pass or receive any values. In this code the text *Hello* is displayed and just after that, the function Greeting() is called which in turn displays the text *Riaz Ahmed* next to the word *Hello*.

The second example passes two numeric values to the function named sum - *sum(5,10)*. On line 4 the function receives these values in two variables *($a,$z)*, adds them up on the next line, and returns the result through the variable *$n_Sum* using the keyword *return*.

PHP Code (Simple Function)

```
<html>
<body>

<?php
  function Greeting()
  {
    echo "Riaz Ahmed";
  }
  echo "Hello ";
  Greeting();
?>


</body>
</html>
```

Output

Hello Riaz Ahmed

PHP Code (Parameterized Function)

```
<html>
<body>

<?php
  function sum($a,$z)
  {
    $n_Sum=$a+$z;
    return $n_Sum;
  }
  echo "The sum of 5 + 10 is: " . sum(5,10);
?>


</body>
</html>
```

Output

The sum of 5 + 10 is: 15

5.12 Dealing With Forms

In chapter 2 section 2.20, you saw how to create a form in HTML and made that form interactive with JavaScript in chapter 4 section 4.21. In this part of the book, you are going to use PHP and SQL's DML statements to insert information in MySQL database provided by users. But initially, you will learn how to connect to the MySQL database and fetch records from the Contact table that you manually entered in the previous section.

5.12.1 Connect to MySQL Database and Query Records

Before you can access data in a database, you must create a connection to the database. In PHP, this is done through:

- MySQL extension
- MySQLi extension
- PHP Data Objects (PDO)

> **NOTE**
>
> *We enabled these extensions in php.ini file in section 5.2.3 - points g,h, and i.*

In MySQL extension, you access the database with the mysql_connect() function. Its syntax is:

mysql_connect(servername,username,password);

servername: This parameter specifies the server running your database. Since we have the database on the same machine, we'll set this parameter to *localhost*. In computer networking, localhost (meaning this computer) is the standard hostname given to the address of the loopback network interface. This mechanism is useful for programmers to test their software during development.

username: A default user, *root*, was created during MySQL database installation. Right now, we are going to connect the database through that user's credentials.

password: We set password for the user root to *gemini* during installation. So we'll pass it over to the function: mysql_connect().

To close the database connection, you'll use mysql_close() function.

The initial example presented on the next page is named SELECT.PHP to demonstrate the use of SELECT statement after connecting to the database.

Line	Select.php - SELECT Statement Example
1	`<html>`
2	`<head>`
3	`<title>PHP Test</title>`
4	`</head>`
5	`<body>`
6	`<?php`
7	`Print "Connecting..."; // Like echo Print is also used to output string`
8	`echo " ";`
9	`$con = mysql_connect("localhost","root","gemini");`
10	`if (!$con)`
11	`{`
12	`die('Could not connect: ' . mysql_error());`
13	`}`
14	`mysql_select_db("testdb", $con);`
15	`$result = mysql_query("SELECT * FROM Contact");`
16	`while($row = mysql_fetch_array($result))`
17	`{`
18	`echo $row['name'] . " - " . $row['email'] . " - " . $row['age'];`
19	`echo " ";`
20	`}`
21	`mysql_close($con);`
22	`?>`
23	`</body>`
24	`</html>`

Connecting…
Riaz Ahmed - realtech@cyber.net.pk - 30
Daniel Clarke - daniel@gmail.com - 25

- Code on line # 9 stores the connection string in a variable *$con*.
- The statement *if(!$con)* (line 10) evaluates whether the connection failed. The symbol (!) represents the NOT operator. In case of failure, the PHP die() function is called (line 12) that prints a message and exits the current script. The PHP function, *mysql_error()*, returns the error description of the last MySQL operation.
- On line # 14, another PHP function named mysql_select_db() is called to set the active MySQL database i.e. testdb. We also specified to use $con for connection. The function mysql_select_db() returns TRUE on success, or FALSE on failure.
- The *mysql_query()* function (line 15) executes a query on the database. In this scenario, we asked to fetch all rows from the Contact table and then store the result set in the *$result* variable.
- Next, we used the *mysql_fetch_array()* function to return the first row from the recordset as an array. Each call to *mysql_fetch_array()* returns the next row in the recordset. The *while* loop iterates through all the records in the recordset. To print the values from each row, we used the PHP *$row* variable *($row['column name'])*. The code, echo "<br>", displays each record on a new line.
- Finally, we closed the connection through mysql_close($con) function.
- Save this file as *select.php* in the C:\inetpub\wwwroot folder. If you created this file in Notepad, make sure that you select *All Files* in Save as type dropdown list before clicking the Save button.
- Open a browser and type *http://localhost/select.php* in the address bar and hit Enter to see the output as shown above.

5.12.2   Insert Form's Data in MySQL Database

As you already know, HTML and JavaScript are unable to process form data on the server. A scripting language such as PHP must be used with HTML forms to process data captured by HTML form elements. HTML form elements rely on action and method attributes to identify where to send the form data for processing (action) and how to process the data (method).

An HTML form has one required attribute, ACTION, specifying the URL of a CGI script which processes the form and sends back feedback. The URL to a document may be on the same server (for example, a shared CGI folder that has various form-processing scripts), or even a page or script on an entirely separate server.

There are two methods to send form data to a server. GET, the default, will send the form input in a URL, whereas POST sends it in the body of the submission. The latter method means you can send larger amounts of data, and that the URL of the form results doesn't show the encoded form. For further details see Chapter 2 - section 2.20.

Upon receipt, PHP stores form values in $_GET array that it receives through the form GET method. For example, the following portion of the URL requests a page named member.php and passes two values to it using the default GET method:

member.php?fName=Riaz&lName=Ahmed

Here, the question mark indicates that there is some data following the symbol. Each data item carries the name of the form element, an equals sign, and a corresponding value. The ampersand symbol (&) is used to separate the items. In the above example, the URL carries data from two form text boxes named *fName* and *lName* along with respective values *Riaz* and *Ahmed*. After receiving these values, PHP creates the $_GET array as shown in the following illustration.

⊟◇ $_GET	array[2]	
◇ [fName]	string	"Riaz"
◇ [lName]	string	"Ahmed"

Later on, to retrieve the values from the $_GET array and store it in a PHP variable; you use the following code:

$first_name = $_GET['fName'];
$last_name = $_GET['lName'];

The above code will create two PHP variable $first_name and $last_name to get values from fName and lName array elements.

The HTTP POST method works just like the GET method without appending the parameters to the URL. Values passed to PHP using the POST method are held under another built-in array called $_POST that you'll see shortly.

In the previous example you fetched existing records from the database using the SELECT statement and used PHP code in conjunction with HTML in a .php file. In this exercise, you will use an html file with form action attribute to call a server-side script (.php) to INSERT form's data into the database. To accomplish this task follow the steps listed below:

1. Open Notepad, add code listed in the HTML Code section on the next page, and save the file as *insert.html* in c:\inetpub\wwwroot folder. You must save all the files created in this part to wwwroot folder.

2. Create another file named *insert.php* in Notepad as shown in the PHP Code section, also listed on the next page, and save it in the same folder.

3. Open a browser session and type *http://localhost/insert.html* to see the form illustrated on the next page.

4. Fill in the form and click the *Submit Query* button. If everything went well, you will see a message *"1 record added"*.

5. Type *select * from contact* on mysql prompt to check the new record.

HTML Code (insert.html) - Insert Form Data

```
<html>
<body>
<form action="insert.php" method="post">
  <fieldset>
    <legend>Contact Us</legend>
    <label>Name:<br>
    <input type="text" name="s_Name" />
    </label><br>
    <label>Email:<br>
    <input type="text" name="s_Email" />
    </label><br>
    <label>Age:<br>
    <input type="text" name="n_Age" />
    </label><br><br>
    <textarea name="s_Message" cols="50" rows="10">Please enter your comments...</textarea>
    <br>
    <input type="submit" />
  </fieldset>
</form>
</body>
</html>
```

Contact Us

Name:
Michael Peter

Email:
mpeter@yahoo.com

Age:
40

This is a feedback message

[Submit Query]

Line	PHP Code (insert.php)
1	`<?php`
2	`$con = mysql_connect("localhost","root","gemini");`
3	`if (!$con)`
4	`{`
5	`  die('Could not connect: ' . mysql_error($con));`
6	`}`
7	`mysql_select_db("testdb", $con);`
8	`//Move form values to local PHP variables`
9	`$s_Name = $_POST['s_Name'];`
10	`$s_Email = $_POST['s_Email'];`
11	`// Assess $_POST['n_Age'] as a valid integer, or move 0 to $n_Age`
12	`$n_Age = (is_numeric($_POST['n_Age']) ? (int)$_POST['n_Age'] : 0);`
13	`$s_Message = $_POST['s_Message'];`
14	`//Insert record using PHP variable values`
15	`$sql="INSERT INTO Contact VALUES (3,'$s_Name','$s_Email',$n_Age,'$s_Message')";`
16	`if (!mysql_query($sql,$con))`
17	`{`
18	`  die('Error: ' . mysql_error($con));`
19	`}`
20	`echo "1 record added";`
21	`mysql_close($con);`
22	`?>`

Example Explained:

- The html code (insert.html) uses <fieldset> to group form control. See Grouping Form Controls in section 2.29.
- The form's ACTION attribute in the html code calls insert.php file using the POST method. This file is called when the *Submit Query* button is clicked.
- In the php file, the database connection method is similar to the one you saw in the previous example.
- In PHP, the predefined $_POST array is used to collect values - *$_POST['s_Name']* - from a form sent with *method="post"*. These values are then stored in corresponding local variables: *$s_Name, $s_Email* etc.
- The code *$n_Age = (is_numeric($_POST['n_Age']) ? (int)$_POST['n_Age'] : 0)* evaluates the $_POST['n_Age'] to be a number, if not, 0 is inserted in the Age column. The is_numeric() function is used to check whether a variable is numeric or not.
- All the values are written to the database table using INSERT INTO statement (line 15). Note that we used a static value 3 for the ID column. In our final project, we will use the AUTO_INCREMENT attribute of MySQL to automatically generate a unique number when a new record is inserted in a table.

5.12.3 Update Form's Data in MySQL Database

In the previous two exercises, we used MySQL functions (mysql_connect, mysql_error, mysql_select_db, mysql_query, and mysql_fetch_array) to interact with the database. The next couple of exercises uses MySQLi.

The MySQLi Extension (MySQL Improved) is a relational database driver used in the PHP programming language to provide an interface with MySQL databases. MySQLi is an improved version of the older PHP MySQL driver, offering various benefits. The developers of the PHP programming language recommend using MySQLi when dealing with MySQL server versions 4.1.3 and newer. If the MySQL database you are connecting to is less than or equal to 4.1.3, use mysql_connect.

Run this example in a browser by typing *http://localhost/update.php* in the address bar.

PHP Code (Update.php)

```html
<html>
 <head>
  <title>PHP Test</title>
 </head>
 <body>

<?php
 $con = mysqli_connect("localhost","root","gemini","testdb") or die("Error connecting to MYSQL server.");

 $sql="UPDATE contact SET Age=35 WHERE name like 'Michael%' and id=3";

 mysqli_query($con,$sql) or die('Error: ' . mysqli_error($con));

 echo "<br>";

 printf ("Updated records: %d\n", mysqli_affected_rows($con));

 mysqli_close($con);
?>

 </body>
</html>
```

Example Explained:

- The mysqli_connect() function adds a fourth parameter allowing you to select a database, testdb, in the same function you used to connect. A function with the name mysqli_select_db() also exists to select a database, but you'll need it only if you want to use multiple databases on the same connection. The die() function is also used on this line.
- The UPDATE statement is used to modify the record of Michael Peter having id=3 to change his age from 40 to 35.
- The printf() function outputs a formatted string to display number of rows affected.
- The mysqli_affected_rows() gets number of affected rows in the last MySQL Insert, Update or Delete operation.

5.12.4 Deleting Form's Data from MySQL Database

Create a new feedback record in the Contact table. I created one with id=9 and mentioned it in the WHERE clause in the DELETE statement. The IF condition is used in conjunction with mysqli_affected_rows() function to evaluate number of deleted rows. If the number returned by this function is greater than zero, the message *Deleted records:* is printed with the number.

PHP Code (Delete.php)

```php
<html>
 <head>
  <title>PHP Test</title>
 </head>
 <body>

<?php
 $con = mysqli_connect("localhost","root","gemini","testdb") or die("Error connecting to MYSQL server.");

 $sql="DELETE FROM Contact WHERE id = 9";

 mysqli_query($con,$sql) or die('Error: ' . mysqli_error($con));

 echo "<br>";

 if (mysqli_affected_rows($con) > 0)
 {
   printf ("Deleted records: %d\n", mysqli_affected_rows($con));
 }
 else
 {
   printf ("No records deleted");
 }

 mysqli_close($con);
?>

 </body>
</html>
```

5.13 PHP Data Objects (PDO)

The previous section demonstrated couple of older techniques to interact with MySQL database (using MySQL and MySQLi extensions). This topic shows you how to use PDO (PHP Data Objects) to work with a database. PDO is relatively new to PHP, and it supports most popular databases. It defines a consistent interface for accessing databases and uses the same PHP code with more than one type of database. PDO doesn't work with earlier versions of PHP. To maintain legacy code, you have to use techniques mentioned in the previous section. For new development, though, PDO is recommended.

5.13.1 Connect to MySQL Database through PDO

```
$con = 'mysql:host=localhost; dbname=testdb';
$username = 'root';
$password = 'gemini';
$db = new PDO($con, $username, $password);
```

The first line assigns a DSN (Data Source Name) to the variable *$con*. This code specifies a MySQL database named *testdb* that is running on the same computer (localhost) as the PHP. Then, the *$username* and *$password* variables are assigned values, as we did in former sections. Finally, these variables are used as the arguments for creating a new PDO object that is assigned to the variable named *$db*. Alternatively, you can write it as under:

```
$con = new PDO('mysql:host=localhost; dbname=testdb', 'root', 'gemini');
```

Execute the SELECT Statement

```
$query = 'SELECT * FROM contact';
$rs = $con->query($query);          // $rs contains the result set
```

Here, *$con* is an object and query is a method. To call a method from any object, you define the name of the object (*$con*), followed by a special symbol (->) and then by the name of the method (*query*). Within the method parentheses, you provide the argument (*$query*).

In the next example, you are using "query" method of the PDO object to execute a SELECT statement. It requires just one argument, which is the SELECT statement. This argument can be a variable (*$query*) that contains the SELECT statement, as we used above, or the statement itself.

5.13.2 Execute a SELECT Statement

PHP Code (SelectPDO.php)

```
<html>
  <head>
    <title>Test PDO</title>
  </head>
  <body>
    <?php
    $con = new PDO('mysql:host=localhost; dbname=testdb', 'root', 'gemini');
    $rs = $con->query('SELECT * FROM contact');
    echo '<br><br>';
    $count = 0;
    // Fetch() is for getting current row from result set
    while ($row = $rs->fetch())
    {
      print "ID:{$row[0]} Name:{$row[1]} Email:{$row[2]} Age:{$row[3]} Message:{$row[4]}";
      $count++;
      echo '<br>';
    }
    echo '<br>';
    print "Number of rows in result set: ". $count;
    ?>
  </body>
</html>
```

Output

ID:1 Name:Riaz Ahmed Email:realtech@cyber.net.pk Age:30 Message: Feedback message
ID:2 Name:Daniel Clarke Email:Daniel@gmail.com Age:25 Message: This is a comment
ID:3 Name:Michael Peter Email:mpeter@yahoo.com Age:35 Message: This is a feedback

Number of rows in result set: 3

Example Explained:

- Fetch() is used to get current row from the result set.
- By default, PDO returns each row as an array indexed by column name and 0-indexed column position in the row. For example, $row[0] returns data from column number 1, $row[1] gives column 2 and so on.
- We used $count++ as a record counter to evaluate number of records in the result set.

5.13.3 Execute an INSERT Statement

For INSERT, UPDATE, and DELETE statements the *exec* method of the PDO object is used with the SQL statement as the argument. The variables $rec_insert, $rec_update, and $rec_delete store the number of rows affected by each statement.

HTML Code (InsertPDO.html)

```html
<html>
<body>
<form action="insertPDO.php" method="post">
  <fieldset>
    <legend>Contact Us</legend>
    <label>Name:*<br>
    <input type="text" name="s_Name" />
    </label><br>
    <label>Email:*<br>
    <input type="text" name="s_Email" />
    </label><br>
    <label>Age:<br>
    <input type="text" name="n_Age" />
    </label><br><br>
    <textarea name="s_Message" cols="50" rows="10">Please enter your  comments...</textarea>
    <br>
    <input type="submit" />
  </fieldset>
</form>
</body>
</html>
```

PHP Code (InsertPDO.php)

```php
<?php
 $con = new PDO('mysql:host=localhost; dbname=testdb', 'root', 'gemini');
 $s_Name = $_POST['s_Name'];
 $s_Email = $_POST['s_Email'];
 // Assess $_POST['n_Age'] as a valid integer, or move 0 to $n_Age
 $n_Age = (is_numeric($_POST['n_Age']) ? (int)$_POST['n_Age'] : 0);
 $s_Message = $_POST['s_Message'];

 // Validate inputs
 if (empty ($s_Name) || empty ($s_Email))
 {
   Print "Invalid data. Click the back button and enter all fields.";
 }
 else
 {
   $query = "INSERT INTO Contact VALUES (4,'$s_Name','$s_Email',$n_Age,'$s_Message')";
   $rec_insert = $con->exec($query);
 }
 echo '<br>';
 print "Number of records added: ".$rec_insert;
?>
```

5.13.4 Execute an UPDATE Statement

```php
$n_Id = 4;
$n_Age = 29;
$query = "UPDATE Contact SET age = $n_Age WHERE id = $n_Id";
$rec_update = $db->exec($query);
```

5.13.5 Execute a DELETE Statement

```php
$n_Id = 4;
$query = "DELETE FROM Contact WHERE id = $n_Id";
$rec_delete = $db->exec($query);
```

5.14 Using FOREACH Loop

In section 5.12, we saw how to loop through database records using the While statement. In this exercise, we're going to use FOREACH for the same purpose. Please note that FOREACH works only on arrays and objects, and will issue an error when you try to use it on a variable with a different data type or an uninitialized variable. It has two syntaxes:

> *foreach (array_expression as $value)*
>   *statement*

> *foreach (array_expression as $key => $value)*
>   *statement*

The first form loops over the array given by *array_expression*. On each iteration, the value of the current element is assigned to *$value* and the internal array pointer is advanced by one and the next iteration gives the next element.

The second form will additionally assign the current element's key to the *$key* variable on each iteration. The symbol => is the separator for associative arrays. In the following example, the keys (Riaz/Daniel) of the array ($users) is assigned to *$user* and the values (mypassword123/Dc5649) to *$password*.

Example:

```php
$users = array(
   'Riaz' => 'mypassword123',
   'Daniel' => 'Dc5649'
);

foreach ($users as $user => $password) {
   echo "{$user}'s password is: {$password}\n";
}
```

Prints:

```
Riaz's password is: mypassword123
Daniel's password is: Dc5649
```

You can also use this symbol for numerically indexed arrays.

Example:

```php
$vehicles = array('airplane', 'bus', 'train', 'car', 'bike');
foreach ($vehicles as $idx => $vtype) {
   echo "{$idx}: {$vtype}\n";
}
```

Prints:

```
0: airplane
1: bus
2: train
3: car
4: bike
```

PHP Code (foreach.php)

```php
<html>
<head>
 <title>Test FOREACH Loop</title>
</head>
<body>

  <?php
  $con = new PDO('mysql:host=localhost; dbname=testdb', 'root', 'gemini');
  $rs = $con->query('SELECT * FROM contact');

  foreach ($rs as $currentrow)
  {
   echo $currentrow['id'];
   echo ' - ';
   echo $currentrow['name'];
   echo '<br>';
  }

?>
 </body>
</html>
```

```
1 - Riaz Ahmed
2 - Daniel Clarke
3 - Michael Peter
4 - Michael Jackson
```

5.15 Include and Require Statements

One of the great benefits of dynamic Web page generation over static HTML is the opportunity to fight redundancy. It's very common to use the same set of functions across a set of Web site pages. PHP makes it very easy to drop anything into your scripts, from one character to a whole separate program, by using the *include* or *require* statements.

These statements import the contents of some other file into the file being executed. Using either one of these forms is vastly preferable and saves a lot of work. You can create a standard header, footer, or menu file for all your web pages. When you want to modify your website functions or appearance, you will have to do it only once. For example, when the header needs to be updated on all web pages, you only need to update the included header file.

Both require and include are identical except upon failure require produces a fatal E_COMPILE_ERROR. In other words, it will halt the script; whereas, include only emits a warning (E_WARNING) which allows the script to continue. So, if you want the execution to go on and show users the output, even if the included file is missing, use "include". Otherwise, always use require to add in a key file to the flow of execution. This will help avoid compromising your application's security and integrity. You can use the "include" and "require" functions to pass control to another web page. When that page finishes, control returns to the statement after the "include" or "require" function.

To better understand the functionality, let's see a simple example. This example has two file: Testinclude.html and bio.php. The first four PHP statements in the html file do not show name and age values. After adding bio.php (*include 'bio.php'*), the values are fetched from the file and included in the text.

TestInclude.php

```
<html>
<head>
 <title>Test PHP Include Statement</title>
</head>
<body>

  <?php
    echo "My name is $s_Name"; // Displays My name is
    echo "<br>";
    echo "My age is $n_Age";   // Displays My age is
    echo "<br>";
    include 'bio.php';
    echo "My name is $s_Name, I'm aged $n_Age"; // Displays My name is Riaz Ahmed, I'm aged 30
  ?>

</body>
</html>
```

My name is
My age is
My name is Riaz Ahmed, I'm aged 30

Bio.php

```
<?php
  $s_Name = 'Riaz Ahmed';
  $n_Age = 30;
?>
```

5.16 Send Mail from PHP

The simplest way to send an email with PHP is to use its mail() function inside a script. But the PHP mail() function lacks flexibility. Most importantly and frustratingly, it does not usually allow you to use the SMTP server of your choice, and it does not support SMTP authentication, required by many mail servers today, at all.

Fortunately, overcoming PHP's built-in shortcomings need not be difficult, complicated or painful either. For most email uses, the free PEAR Mail package offers all the power and flexibility needed, and it authenticates with your desired outgoing mail server, too. For enhanced security, secure SSL connections are supported.

PEAR stands for *PHP Extension and Application Repository*, which is a collection of PHP reusable classes. Using PEAR can save you great amount of time to code something that other people have already coded, tested, and used. For example, if you need a HTML form validation routine, PEAR has it in its Validate Package.

Installing PEAR on Windows is a confusing task if you use the PEAR Installer. In this section, we're going to manually install PEAR and it will give you great control, flexibility, and opportunity to not only install it with a breeze, but also learn a bunch of knowledge about PHP, especially how to set up PHP include path.

What you need to install is actually PEAR Base System (a core package) which is called PEAR. All other packages use the core package to extend their functionalities. In this section, you are going to install and use a package named Mail that is not available in the core package. Please read the following recommendations before proceeding:

- Use a direct internet connection. Although you can use a proxy server, it is feasible to use internet connected directly to your pc. You'll have to consider some other things like DNS, Firewall etc. if you're behind a proxy.
- Obtain SMTP address from your Internet Service Provider.
- You must have two email addresses to complete this exercise. You can create free account on Gmail, Hotmail, and Yahoo.

Step # 1 — Download and Setup PEAR Core Package

1.1. Open your browser and type **http://pear.php.net/package/PEAR/download**

1.2. Click the link **1.9.4** under the Download section. The file I downloaded was PEAR-1.9.4.tgz. Yours may be newer.

1.3. Create a folder named **TEMP** and extract the downloaded package in it. You can use WinRAR utility to extract the archive.

1.4. After extracting, open the TEMP folder. You should have a folder: PEAR-1.9.4. Double click this folder. You will see three sub-folders (OS, Scripts, and PEAR) and some files in it. Move PEAR5.php and PEAR.php files to the PEAR sub-folder. Leave this folder open.

1.5. Create a new folder named **PEAR** under C:\PHP (c:\php\pear).

1.6. Move contents of the PEAR sub-folder (step 1.4) to C:\PHP\PEAR (using ctrl+A and ctrl+c). The PHP folder now contains four sub-folders (dev, ext, extras and PEAR). The PEAR folder contains all the core classes we need.

Step # 2 — Set Include Path for PEAR

To use all the classes provided by PEAR library, we need to set up an include path that can be used by PHP to easily call any PEAR class we want.

2.1. Open **php.ini** located under C:\PHP

2.2. Press **ctrl+f** and type **include_path** in the *Find what box* and click **Find Next**. Because we're installing PEAR on Windows, we are going to change the path under the Windows section which should be: **include_path=".;C:\PHP\PEAR"**.

```
;;;;;;;;;;;;;;;;;;;;;;;;;;;;
;  Paths and Directories  ;
;;;;;;;;;;;;;;;;;;;;;;;;;;;;

;  UNIX:  "/path1:/path2"
;include_path = ".:/php/includes"
;
;  Windows: "\path1;\path2"
include_path = ".;c:\php\pear"
```

Figure 5-12

2.3. Save the file, close it and restart your pc.

The include path created here will be used by PHP as implicit include path which means PHP will already know where to look for the path. So when you use *include* or *require_once* in a PHP page, you don't need to specify the path again.

Step # 3 Update PEAR Installation

3.1. Open your browser and type **http://pear.php.net/go-pear.phar** in the address bar. A small dialog box will appear. Select the **Save File** option and click **OK**. After downloading, locate the file go-pear.phar in your download location (usually in the Download folder under My Documents). Copy this file to C:\PHP folder.

3.2. Open a command prompt (**Start** | **Run** | type **cmd** and press Enter). Type **cd c:\php** and press enter to switch to the PHP folder where we copied go-pear.phar file.

3.3. On C:\PHP> prompt type **php go-pear.phar** to launch the file.

3.4. Press Enter to accept the default system value.

3.5. Press Enter to continue. After completion, you will see the message: *The 'pear' command is now at your service at c:\php\pear.bat.*

3.6. In Windows, go to C:\PHP and double-click **PEAR_ENV.reg** file to create environment variables for the current user.

3.7. On the command prompt, type **pear list** to see a list of installed packages.

3.8. Again on the command prompt, type **pear upgrade**. This will upgrade one or more PEAR packages. When upgrading, your package will be updated if the provided new package has a higher version number. For example, in my scenario the package Console_Getopt was installed with the version 1.3.0. After the upgrade, it was switched to 1.3.1.

Step # 4 The PEAR Mail Package

In the next section, you will send mail from a PHP script. For this purpose, you need PEAR Mail package. Let's see how to download and install this package.

4.1. On C:\PHP> prompt type **pear install -a mail** and hit Enter. The -a option installs all required and optional dependencies. It takes some time to download and install the package in the background so wait for a while till you see the final message: *install ok: channel://par.php.net/Mail-1.2.0* which indicates that the Mail package has been installed along with dependencies.

4.2. Type **pear list** on the command prompt to verify installation. The list now has the Mail package which you will be using in the next section to send an email through a PHP script.

4.3. Close the command prompt.

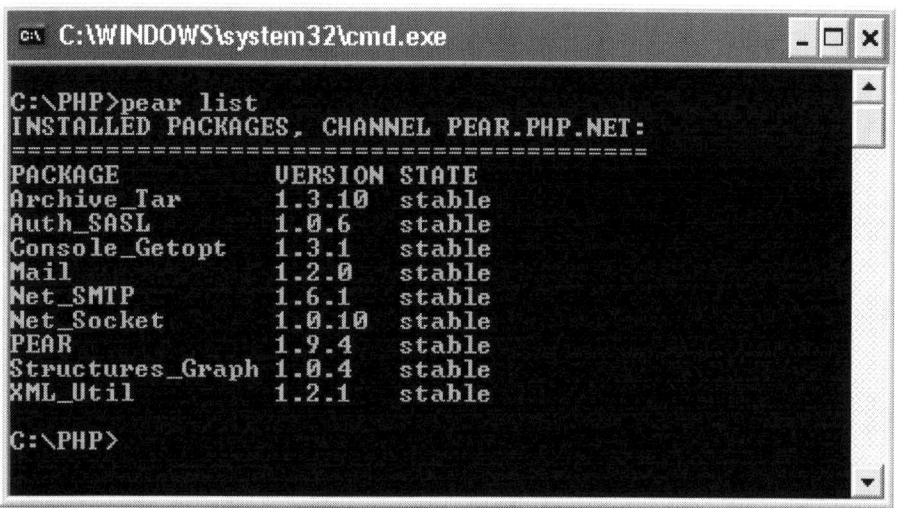

Figure 5-13

Create PHP Script to Send Mail

5.1. Create a PHP script (I named it PearMail.php) using the code below and save it in:
   C:\Inetpub\wwwroot folder.

PHP Code (PearMail.php)

```php
<?php
require_once "Mail.php";
$from = "Riaz Ahmed <realech@cyber.net.pk>";
$to = "Riaz Ahmed <oratech69@gmail.com>";
$subject = "Test message from RT Account";
$body = "Hi Riaz,\n\nHow are you?";
$host = "Your SMTP Server address";
// $username = "";
// $password = "";
$headers = array ('From' => $from, 'To' => $to, 'Subject' => $subject);
$smtp = Mail::factory('smtp', array ('host' => $host, 'port' => 25));
//    'auth' => true,
//    'username' => $username,
//    'password' => $password));
$mail = $smtp->send($to, $headers, $body);
 if (PEAR::isError($mail))
 {
  echo("<p>" . $mail->getMessage() . "</p>");
 }
  else
 {
  echo("<p>Message successfully sent!</p>");
 }
?>
```

Example Explained:

In the example above, you included the PEAR Mail package (Mail.php), so your script can use it. It has to be done only once, therefore you used require_once (require_once is same as require, but the former one makes sure that the file is included only once). Then you assigned data (from, to, subject, body, and host) to appropriate variables. You are required to assign your SMTP server to the $host variable. This is the same value you usually specify in your Outlook client Outgoing mail (SMTP) setting on the Servers tab during account creation. I commented out the variables ($username and $password) because my SMTP server doesn't need this information. You must provide these values if your server need them. Mail::factory() creates a new instance of a specific Mail-Backend with the factory() method. Its syntax is:

   factory (string $backend , array $params = array())

The string $backend parameter can have mail, smtp, or sendmail as the name of the backend while the array $params holds an array of backend specific parameters. Since we used 'smtp' as a mail backend type to send a mail directly connecting to an smtp server, the specific parameters would be:

- $params["host"] - The server to connect. Default is localhost.
- $params["port"] - The port to connect. Default is 25.
- $params["auth"] - Whether or not to use SMTP authentication. Default is FALSE.
- $params["username"] - The username to use for SMTP authentication.
- $params["password"] - The password to use for SMTP authentication.

Again, I ignored auth, username, and password parameters as they were not required by my server. If your sever need authentication then you should write the code as mentioned below. Do not forget to assign username and password to the variables under $host above in the code.

$smtp = Mail::factory('smtp', array ('host' => $host, 'port' => 25, 'auth' => true, 'username' => $username, 'password' => $password));

The value returned by the code above would be a specific Mail instance on success or a PEAR_Error object on failure.

The mail is sent using the send() method. The send() method is provided by the object ($smtp) returned from factory(). Its syntax is:

send (mixed $recipients , array $headers , string $body)

Where mixed $recipients is an array or a string with comma separated recipients. Associative array of headers are contained in array $headers while string $body holds the body of the email. This method returns a Boolean value (true or false) that we stored in the variable $mail and checked in the final IF statement. isError() examines whether a variable is a PEAR_Error object and contains a specific error message or code. getMessage() returns the error message coming with the error object. For example, if you set the value of $host to "localhost2", you will get an error: *Failed to connect to localhost2:25 [SMTP: Failed to connect socket: php_network_getaddresses: getaddrinfo failed: No such host is known. (code: -1, response:)].*

5.2. Open a browser session and type **http://localhost/pearmail.php**. If followed all the steps in order, you'll see *Message successfully sent!* You can check the "to" email account which should receive a message as shown in the following illustration.

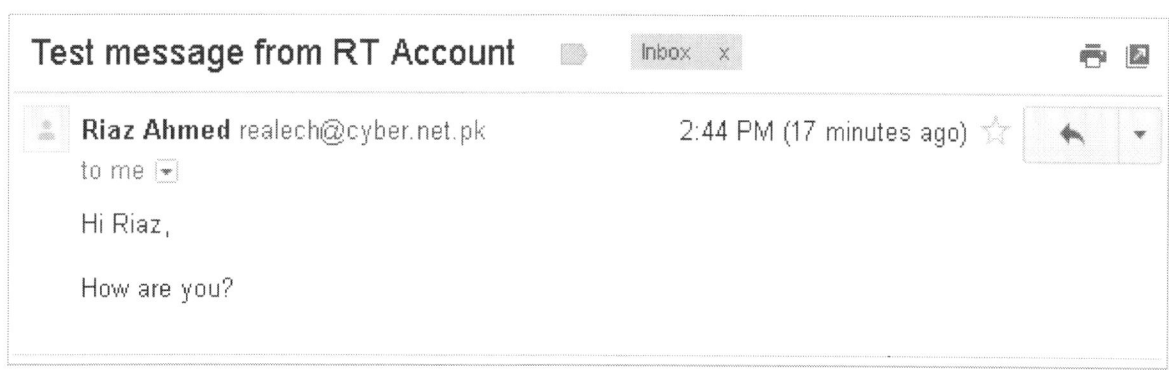

Figure 5-14

193

The PHP code used in the above listing was intended to test Pear mail package on your local machine. However, the real world deployment requires some additional information as defined in the following code:

```
PHP Code in a Host Environment
1    $to = $_POST['subemail'];
2    $headers['To'] = $to;
3    $headers['From'] = '"ABCGLOBAL Consulting" <info@abcglobal.com>';
4    $headers['Reply-To'] = 'info@abcglobal.com';
5    $headers['Subject'] = 'Newsletter Subscription Confirmation';
6    $body = "Hi,\n\nThis message is sent to you from ABC Global Consulting as a confirmation to your
     newsletter subscription request.";
7    $host = "mail.abcglobal.com";
8    $user = "info@abcglobal.com";
9    $pw = "gemini";
10   $auth = array('host' => $host, 'auth' => true, 'username' => $user, 'password' => $pw);
11   $smtp = Mail::factory('smtp', $auth);
12   $mail = $smtp->send($to, $headers, $body);
```

Code Explained:

This code assumes that you've hosted your website on abcglobal.com domain. Line # 3 uses info e-mail account to inform where the mail came from. This code displays the text ABCGLOBAL Consulting in the 'From' column. Line # 4 uses the same e-mail account when the user clicks the Reply button on his e-mail client. The $host variable on line # 7 uses the mail server of the hosting company to process e-mails. The hosting server requires authentication, so, on line # 8 and 9 we supplied user name and password respectively. This information is then used for authentication on line # 10. Note that user names and passwords are defined when you create e-mail accounts through control panel provided by your hosting company.

All the examples till now warmed you up for the next and final part of the book where you will undergo a web site project for ABC Global Consulting Company and will apply most of the techniques you learned throughout this book. In that project you will create a Contact Form, a Newsletter subscription module and an E-Commerce module.

YOU WILL LEARN

- Build a website comprising static & dynamic pages

- Difference between static & dynamic web pages

- How to create web Contact Form

- Newsletter Subscription Module

- E-Commerce Module comprising various Admin & Member modules

- Manage dynamic content through the Admin modules

- Place Online Orders through the Member modules

- Website Deployment on hosting server

CHAPTER 6

WEBSITE PROJECT

YOU must be the CHANGE that you wish to see in the world.

6.1   Project's Introduction

You've landed to the most interesting part of this book. Here, you'll create a professional website for ABC Global Consulting and will apply the techniques you've learned so far. The project is divided into two categories:

Dynamic

Dynamic web pages are generated at the time of access by a user or change as a result of interaction with the user. These pages can give the website owner the ability to simply update and add new content to the site. For example, news and events could be posted to the site through a simple browser interface. Dynamic features of a site are only limited by imagination. Some examples of dynamic website features could be: content management system, e-commerce system, bulletin / discussion boards, intranet or extranet facilities, ability for clients or users to upload documents, ability for administrators or users to create content or add information to a site. In this part of the book, you'll create an e-commerce system and couple of more interfaces with the help of PHP and MySQL database:

- **Contact Form** - This html page is meant to interact with the site visitors. A form will be provided to the visitors of the website to add their comments and feedback. This form will use PHP and MySQL to store the comments in a database table. Besides, it will receive contact details such as e-mail address and other relevant information.

- **Newsletter Subscription** - Using a form site visitors would enter their e-mail address to subscribe to company's newsletters. This form will be added to the home page (index.html). A process will be created with the help of PHP and MySQL to interact with site visitors.

- **Admin Interface** - In the dynamic part, you'll create an e-commerce prototype application that will comprise admin and members sections. The admin section will be accessible only to the site administrators who will use this interface to manage tasks such as products and orders management. See section 6.7 - *Make the Website Dynamic* later in this part for complete details.

- **Members Interface** - This will allow end users to become site members and will allow them to view and purchase products from the website. For further details, see section 6.7 - *Make the Website Dynamic*.

STATIC VS DYNAMIC

When you create a normal web page with HTML and CSS, all the content is fixed by the webmaster. Everyone who visits the page sees the same content—it's static.

By contrast, the content of a dynamic web page frequently changes. For example, the Products page in our project would displays three most recent products (marked as featured products) from the database. When a new item is added to the database, the PHP code in the page automatically displays it. Whenever this page is called, the content changes to display a list of newly added featured products. The code in the page controls the content depending on the request it receives from the browser.

Static

A static web page is a page that is delivered to the user exactly as stored. An obvious example of a static page is an old style HTML document which can only be changed by uploading a new or updated version. Every time a static file is downloaded, the file contents that are sent to the browser are the same for everyone who access that file. In this project you'll be taught to create the following static pages:

- **Index.html** - This is the Home page of our website. Everyone who visits the website will be greeted by this page.
- **Company.html** - This page will contain information about the company i.e. ABC Global Consulting.
- **Services.html** - Services provided by the company will be displayed through this page.
- **Success.html** - This page is related to contact form (dynamic category) and informs users of successful submission of their comments.

6.2 Website Security

A Web site designed, built, and deployed with security as a prime feature is more robust than one deployed with security features added as an afterthought. However, as Web sites become more complex, it also becomes more difficult to make them secure. Security cannot be achieved by setting a few particular properties, or using a specific tool; instead you must take a holistic approach and address security in all stages of site planning, development, and deployment. People just consider the job is done once the website is up. It definitely is not. There are no point and click software available to secure a website. Protecting a website or web server is possible only by continued efforts. Unlike a poorly protected desktop in your place of business, a hacked website will reflect poorly on you, your business or brand. There may not be *fit it and forget* solutions for protecting a website in a world where threats emit constantly. But there are always some time tested fundamental ground work that should be done to get the first line of defense up while figuring out a detailed security plan. This section is aimed at detailing some basic proactive security considerations that can help you lay the foundation for your site security.

6.2.1 Use a Secure Connection

If you web application receives sensitive data such as credit card number or passwords from visitors, you must use a secure connection to transmit data. Failing to do so may allow hackers or other malicious minds to intercept and view this data. Regular HTTP connections send data in plain text and are not suitable for sites like online stores or e-commerce websites. For such sites, you should consider HTTPS (HyperText Transfer Protocol with Secure Sockets Layer). HTTPS is a protocol to transfer encrypted data over the Web. Although hackers can still intercept this data, they cannot read it unless they break the encryption code. Most Web customers know that they should look for the https in the URL and the lock icon in their browser when they are making a transaction. So if your storefront is not using HTTPS, you will lose customers.

> **NOTE**
>
> *It is possible to run your entire Web site on https, but it slows down the connection. You should only secure those pages that request and collect data.*

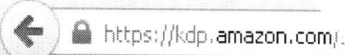

6.2.2 What is SSL Certificate?

An SSL Certificate (Secure Sockets Layer), also called a Digital Certificate, creates a secure link between a website and a visitor's browser. With SSL, the browser encrypts all data that's sent to the server and decrypts all data that's received from the server. Similarly, the server encrypts all data that's sent to the browser and decrypts all data that's received from the browser. By ensuring that all data passed between the two remains private and secure, SSL encryption prevents hackers from stealing private information. SSL can also determine if data has been tampered with during transit and can also verify both client and server. Another new protocol that is used by the Internet for secured connection is Transport Layer Security (TLS). A successor to SSL, TLS is supported only by latest browsers.

Before establishing a secure connection, the server uses SSL server authentication to authenticate itself by providing a digital secure certificate to the browser. The browser accepts the certificate and a secure connection is established.

A digital secure certificate can be purchased from certification authorities (CA) like VeriSign, Thawte, Instantssl, Entrust etc. These authorities verify with a registration authority the validity of the company or person requesting the certificate. To obtain the certificate, you provide the name of a registration authority (RA) with your company information. After approval from RA, the CA issues a certificate. Once you get the certificate, provide it to your hosting provider who will set up the certificate in your Web server so that every time a page is accessed via the https protocol, it hits the secure server. Once that is set up, you can start building your Web pages that need to be secure.

6.2.3 Use Authentication

Authentication is the process of identifying an individual, usually based on a user id and password. In a web application, you can implement authentication to some or all of the web pages to allow access only to authorized users. Form-based authentication in the most common type of authentication where a web form is presented to the user to get his/her id and password. To prevent hackers from intercepting this sensitive information, a secure connection is used along with an encryption algorithm to send the information to the server. You'll follow this approach in the final website project.

6.2.4 Encrypting Password

In this project you'll store userid and password in a database table. Following the best practice method, you'll encrypt the data before storing it in the database. That way, if a hacker gains access to the database, he will not be able to easily read the password. See List X for further details.

THE BOTTOM LINE TO SECURE YOUR WEBSITE

You should consider the following points in order to host your website in a secured environment:

- *A Web server such as Apache with mod_ssl that supports SSL encryption*
- *A Unique IP address - this is what the certificate providers use to validate the secure certificate*
- *An SSL Certificate from an SSL certificate provider*

6.3 Build Website's Static Pages

Taking the simple route first, you'll build the static pages of your project in this section. While creating these web pages, you'll apply the skills learned in earlier parts of this book with the addition of some more useful stuff.

General Steps:

1. If not yet done, download the book's code from:
   http://www.creating-website.com/TheWebBookCode.rar

2. Extract this file in a folder (I extracted it in c:\bookcode and will refer to this folder as 'source' in subsequent sections).

3. Create a folder named ABCGLOBAL under c:\Inetpub\wwwroot. This folder will be referred to as 'site folder'.

4. Copy Images folder from c:\bookcode\project to c:\Inetpub\wwwroot\abcglobal

6.4   The Home Page

Usually a site is visited by typing its URL without specifying a file name like: *www.abcglobal.com*. Every web server needs a file in order to serve a website. This file is called the default file that you set in chapter 5 - section 5.2.2. On most Web servers, this default file is named "index.html". What this means is that when you go to a URL without a file named at the end, the server looks for a default file and displays that automatically. Just as if you had typed in that file name in the URL:

http://www.abcglobal.com/index.html.

When you start building your website, you should create your main page and name it index.html. That way, when people come to your website, they automatically get your main page. All other pages will have names like "company.html" or "contact.html", but your home page file should be named "index.html".

In this project our home page (shown in the figure below) is named index.html. This will be the initial page that will come up after a user enters website's url (www.abcglobal.com) in a browser. Let's begin the project by creating the home page of the website.

Figure 6-1 - The Home Page

Since you are building and testing this website on your own PC, you'll type *http://localhost/abcglobal/index.html* in your preferred browser. Please note that I used Firefox while creating exercises for this book and created some specific -moz- rules in style.css.

1. From bookcode\project folder, copy index.html to the site folder. Make sure the site folder contains the images sub-directory that we copied in the previous section.
2. Open Firefox and type *http://localhost/abcglobal/index.html* in the address bar and hit Enter. You'll see an un-organized website whose content will be scattered from top to bottom. Why is it so? It's just because we didn't specify any style to this page and that's what we're going to do next.
3. Copy style.css from bookcode\project to the site folder and run index.html again. Now you'll see the page similar to figure 6-1.

Let's dig deeper and see how this page was built and how did the CSS file give it a professional look. To understand the whole process, first you'll see HTML code from index.html file and then we'll move on to style.css to check how the rules specified in this file work. You can open both these files by right-clicking on them and selecting *Open With | Notepad* from the context menu.

Line #	Code	Index.html	Table 6-1
1	`<!DOCTYPE html>`		

Each web page begins with a DOCTYPE declaration which informs the browser about the HTML version the page is using. See Section 2.1 *About Markup Languages* for further explanation. This line defines the document type and is a declaration for the latest HTML5 generation.

2	`<html>`

The starting html tag. See section 2.3 *Elements in HTML* for further details.

3	`<head>`

The starting head tag.

4	`<title>ABC Global Consulting</title>`

Title tag displays page title in the browser.

5	`<link rel="stylesheet" type="text/css" href="style.css" />`

Referencing the external style sheet file (style.css) used for this page. All the rules specified in Style.css file will be explained individually during the development process of each web page.

```
6    <!--[if lt IE 9]>
       <script src="http://html5shiv.googlecode.com/svn/trunk/html5.js"></script>
     <![endif]-->
```

Older browsers that do not know the new HTML5 elements will automatically treat them as inline elements. Therefore, to help older browsers, you should include these lines of CSS which states which new elements should be rendered as block-level elements. In order to style these elements using earlier versions of Internet Explorer (IE), you need to use a simple JavaScript known as the HTML5 shiv or HTML5 shim. This code just links to a copy that Google hosts on its servers. It should be placed inside a conditional comment which checks if the browser version is less than (hence the lt) IE9.

Conditional comments - <!--[if IE 9]><![endif]--> - only work in IE, and are thus excellently suited to give special instructions meant only for IE. They are supported from IE 5 onwards. Their basic structure is the same as an HTML comment (<!-- -->). Therefore all other browsers will see them as normal comments and will ignore them entirely. IE, though, has been programmed to recognize the special <!--[if IE]> syntax, resolves the IF and parses the content of the conditional comment as if it were normal page content. Since conditional comments use the HTML comment structure, they can only be included in HTML files, and not in CSS files.

```
7    </head>
```
The ending head tag.

```
8    <body>
```
The starting body tag.

```
9    <div class="wrapper">
```
The content of the page is put inside a <div> element whose class is wrapper. The <div> element is used as a wrapper for the entire page. It holds all other elements (header, article, aside, footer etc).

```
10   <header>
```
The <header> element contains site name, company logo, head links, main navigation bar, and a search box.

```
11   <h1>ABC Global Consulting</h1>
```
The site name.

```
12-a   <div id="headlinks">
  b      <p><a href="member/index.php">Login/Register</a> | <a href="">Sitemap</a></p>
  c    </div>
```
Two links (Login/Register and Sitemap) are created inside a paragraph held in a <div> element having id headlinks. The first link (Login/Register) calls a file index.php located in the member folder to present login interface to the user. This module is described in section 6.17 - Task 8.

```
13-a    <nav>
   b      <ul>
   c        <li><a href="" class="current">Home</a></li>
   d        <li><a href="company.html">Company</a></li>
   e        <li><a href="services.html">Services</a></li>
   f        <li><a href="products.php">Products</a></li>
   g        <li><a href="contact.html">Contact</a></li>
   h      </ul>
   I      <script type="text/javascript">
   j        //Enter domain of site to search.
   k         var domainroot="www.maqcon.com"
   l         function Gsitesearch(curobj){
   m          curobj.q.value="site:"+domainroot+" "+curobj.qfront.value
   n         }
   o      </script>
   p      <form id="search" action="http://www.google.com/search" method="get"
                                          onSubmit="Gsitesearch(this)">
   q        <input name="q" type="hidden" />
   r        <input name="qfront" type="search" value="search..."/><input type="submit" value="Go!"/>
   s      </form>
   t    </nav>
```

The <nav> element is used to contain the major navigational blocks on the site such as the primary site navigation. Navigational items are shown using unordered list <ul> and are linked to appropriate pages through anchor tags <a>. It also contains a form that displays a search box (p-s). The search box uses Google Internal Site Search script (i-o) that uses Google to enable comprehensive search on your site. Since this site in not live yet, we used www.maqcon.com for testing purpose. Type **import** in the search box and hit the Go button. You'll see the search result from this site through Google.

```
14     </header>
```

The ending header tag.

```
15-a    <section class="content">
  b       <article>
  c         <figure class="slide">
  d           <img src="images/slide6.png" alt="slide1"/>
  e           <img src="images/slide5.png" alt="slide2"/>
  f           <img src="images/slide4.png" alt="slide3"/>
  g           <img src="images/slide3.png" alt="slide4"/>
  h           <img src="images/slide2.png" alt="slide5"/>
  i           <img src="images/slide1.png" alt="slide6"/>
  j         </figure>
  k         <hgroup>
  l           <h2>What We Do</h2>
  m         </hgroup>
  n         <p>ABC Global Consulting help organizations achieve their goals by... </p>
            <p>We provide better decision making tools to business owners and...</p><br>
  o       </article>
  p     </section>
```

The <section> element groups related content together, and typically each section would have its own heading. Because the <section> element groups related items together, it may contain several distinct <article> elements that have a common theme or purpose. In our home page, we created a single section having a class named content (15-a). This section holds an <article> element (15-b) that contains <figure> (15-c), <hgroup> (15-k), and <p> (15-n) elements. The <img> elements (d-i) under the <figure> class *slide* are the six png files located under the images folder that are rotated in sequence to create a slide show using @-moz-keyframes myAnimation rule in the css file (we'll talk about this rule shortly). The <figure> element can be used to contain any content that is referenced from the main flow of an article (not just images). You can include: Images, Videos, Graphs, Diagrams, Code samples, Text that supports the main body of an article. The <figure> element can also have a <figcaption> element which provides a text description for the content of the <figure> element. The purpose of the <hgroup> element is to group together a set of one or more <h1> through <h6> elements so that they are treated as one single heading. For example, the <hgroup> element could be used to contain both a title inside an <h2> element and a subtitle within an <h3> element. We'll use h2 and h3 <hgroup> headings in servcies.html page. The two <p> elements are used to show some stuff about the company in two separate paragraphs.

```
16-a    <aside>
    b       <section class="services">
    c         <h2>Our Services</h2>
    d         <a href="services.html">Accounting & Taxation</a>
    e         <a href=" services.html ">Audit & Assurance</a>
    f         <a href=" services.html ">Recruitment Consultancy</a>
    g         <a href=" services.html ">Software Designing</a>
    h       </section>
    I       <section class="newsletter">
    J         <form id="letter" action="subscribe.php" method="post">
    K           <label><b>Subscribe to our newsletter</b></label><br>
    l           <label>E-mail Address:<br>
    m           <input type="email" name="subemail" maxlength="35" size="35" required="vital"
                                                placeholder="me@example.com"/></label><br>
    n           <p><input type="image" alt="Subscribe" class="button"
                                                src="images/subscribe.png"></p>
    o         </form>
    p       </section>
    q    </aside>
```

The <aside> element will be used throughout this project to act as a container for content that is related to the entire page. It can be used to contain links to other sections of the site, a list of recent posts, a search box, or recent tweets by the author. We created two sections (services and newsletter) under the aside tag. The services section (b-h) displays a heading "Our Services" on top of it and shows four linked services the company deals in. Clicking each link would call services.html (which is not yet created) to provide additional details. The newsletter section (i-p) allows site visitors to subscribe to company's newsletter. This section contains a form (j) that calls a PHP script (subscribe.php) to process subscription. The complete subscription procedure is detailed in section 6.9 Newsletter Subscription Module. Also see section 2.31.2 Form Validation for *required* and *placeholder* attributes (m).

```
17-a    <footer>
    b       <p id="copyright">&copy; 2013 ABC Global Consulting</p>
    c       <p id="footlinks"><a href="">Legal Information</a> | <a href="">Privacy Policy</a> |
                                                <a href="">Subscribe </a></p>
    d    </footer>
```

The <footer> element contains copyright information, along with links to the legal information, privacy policy and newsletter subscription. Besides main header and footer that appears at the top and bottom of every page, the <header> and <footer> elements can be used for an individual <article> or <section> within the page. For example, on a page with several blog posts, each individual post can be thought of as a separate section. The <header> element can therefore be used to contain the title and date of each individual post, and the <footer> might contain links to share the article on social networking sites.

```
18   </div><!-- .wrapper -->
```
Closed the <div> element named wrapper. <!-- .wrapper --> is a comment. This type of comment is used by developers for better code understanding.

```
19   </body>
```
Body tag closed.

```
20   </html>
```
End of html document.

This section merely introduced you to the main page of our site and briefed some common elements that you'll see on all pages. From the next section, you'll be provided step by step guidance to create these pages individually.

Do It Yourself

The real essence to learn something is to do some practical work on it. After reading the previous section, you might have some questions on your mind, especially about styling and proper placement of elements on a web page. The rest of this book will answer all these questions and will explain each and every aspect of a web page. The up-coming sections will walk you through to create all the pages on your own. You'll be completing all these exercises in sequential steps where each step comprises HTML, CSS and PHP code along with resulting output and necessary explanations to help you assess how a website is built.

Step-1   Create a Blank HTML Page

1. In the site folder, change the name of style.css to All_Rules.css. This file holds all the css rules for the website and you'll fetch them according to the instructions mentioned in each exercise.
2. Delete index.html from the site folder because you're going to create this file yourself.
3. Open Notepad and enter the html code listed below. You can paste this code from index.html located in bookcode\project folder.
4. Save this new file as index.html in the site folder.
5. Open another session of Notepad and copy Rule-1 from All_Rules.css file. Save the new file as style.css in the site folder.
6. Open your browser and type http://localhost/abcglobal/index.html in the address bar and hit Enter.
7. A blank page with a light orange background will appear.

Below is the code from the two files along with explanation.

Line #	HTML Code
1	`<!DOCTYPE html>`
2	`<html>`
3	`<head>`
4	`<title>ABC Global Consulting</title>`
5	`<link rel="stylesheet" type="text/css" href="style.css" />`
6	`<!--[if lt IE 9]>`
7	`<script src="http://html5shiv.googlecode.com/svn/trunk/html5.js"></script>`
8	`<![endif]-->`
9	`</head>`
10	`<body>`
11	`</body>`
12	`</html>`

> **NOTE**
>
> *The markers (1,2,3... and A, B, C...) in front of html and css codes are used for explanation and should not be included in actual files.*
>
> *To avoid repetition, we ignored meta elements here. These elements provide metadata about the HTML document and must be added to every web page. For further details see chapter 2 section 2.2 - Your First HTML Page.*

CSS Code

Rule-1	**body** {
A	color: #666666;
B	**background-color: #fbf6e2;**
C	font-family: Verdana, Geneva, sans-serif;
D	font-size: 11px;
E	line-height: 20px;
F	margin: 0px;}

> **NOTE**
>
> *The file Style.css contains many rules properly marked with numbers. Most of these rules apply generally to all page elements such as the body rule defined here applies to all pages within the site.*

Explanation

In this step, you created a blank html page without any stuff and associated a css rule to the body section of the html file. Since we do not have any other element in the html file, the only property that was applied here was the background-color that changed the page color from default white to light orange. You are free to test these properties by changing their values in style.css to see different effects. Right now, you can only change the background color because there are no other elements on the page yet.

Rule 1	Created for the <body> element.
A	Set the font color to grey. This color will be applied to every element contained within the <body> element such as paragraphs, links and some sub-headings.
B	Set a light orange color for the page.
C	Set Verdana as the main font for the page along with alternatives.
D	Set font size to 11px.
E	Set line height between two elements.
F	No surrounding margin for any element.

Step-2 Create Main Wrapper and <header> Elements

Add the following code (marked in bold) to both html and css files. The html code should go inside the <body> tag. You can copy the css code from All_Rules.css to the end of style.css file.

Line #	HTML Code
1	<body>
2	<div class="wrapper">
3	<header>
4	<h1>ABC Global Consulting</h1>
5	<div id="headlinks">
6	<p><a href="member/index.php">Login/Register</a> | <a href="">Sitemap</a></p>
7	</div>
8	</header>
9	</div><!-- .wrapper -->
10	</body>

CSS Code

```
Rule-2    .wrapper {
A           width: 950px;
B           margin: 20px auto 20px auto;
C           background-color: #ffffff;
D           -moz-box-shadow: 0 0 10px #111111;
E           position: relative;}
```

```
Rule-3    header {
A           height: 100px;
B           background-image: url(images/logo.png);
C           background-repeat:no-repeat;
D           background-position:left center; }
```

```
Rule-4    #headlinks {
A           float: right;
B           position:absolute;
C           top: 30px;
D           right: 30px;}
```

```
Rule-5    h1 {
A           text-indent: -9999px;
B           width: 950px;
C           height: 100px;
D           margin: 0px;}
```

```
Rule-23   a {
            color: #666666;
            text-decoration: none;}
```

```
Rule-24   a:hover {
            color: #FF9900;}
```

Output & Explanation

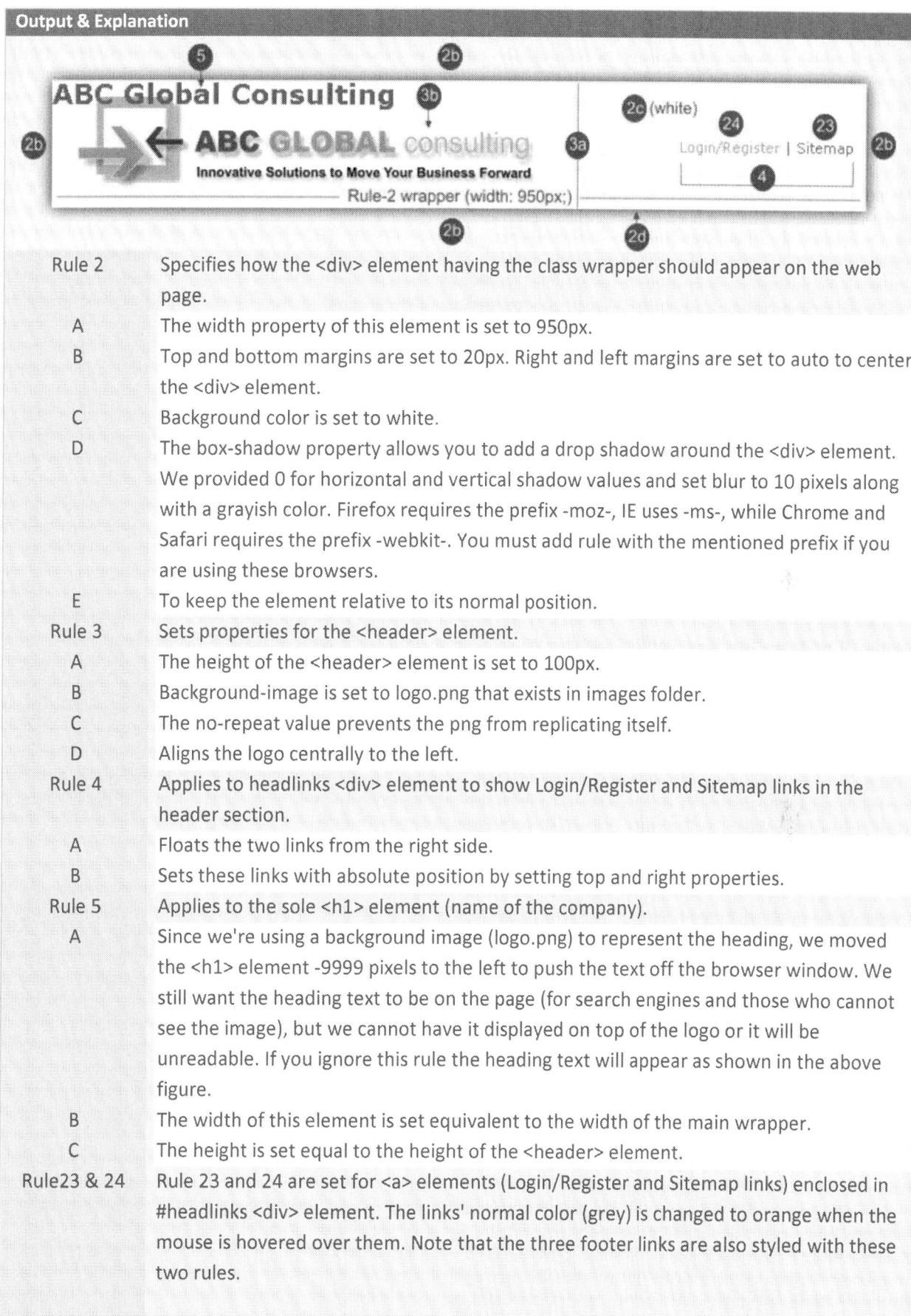

ABC Global Consulting

ABC GLOBAL consulting
Innovative Solutions to Move Your Business Forward
Rule-2 wrapper (width: 950px;)

(white)
Login/Register | Sitemap

Rule 2	Specifies how the <div> element having the class wrapper should appear on the web page.
A	The width property of this element is set to 950px.
B	Top and bottom margins are set to 20px. Right and left margins are set to auto to center the <div> element.
C	Background color is set to white.
D	The box-shadow property allows you to add a drop shadow around the <div> element. We provided 0 for horizontal and vertical shadow values and set blur to 10 pixels along with a grayish color. Firefox requires the prefix -moz-, IE uses -ms-, while Chrome and Safari requires the prefix -webkit-. You must add rule with the mentioned prefix if you are using these browsers.
E	To keep the element relative to its normal position.
Rule 3	Sets properties for the <header> element.
A	The height of the <header> element is set to 100px.
B	Background-image is set to logo.png that exists in images folder.
C	The no-repeat value prevents the png from replicating itself.
D	Aligns the logo centrally to the left.
Rule 4	Applies to headlinks <div> element to show Login/Register and Sitemap links in the header section.
A	Floats the two links from the right side.
B	Sets these links with absolute position by setting top and right properties.
Rule 5	Applies to the sole <h1> element (name of the company).
A	Since we're using a background image (logo.png) to represent the heading, we moved the <h1> element -9999 pixels to the left to push the text off the browser window. We still want the heading text to be on the page (for search engines and those who cannot see the image), but we cannot have it displayed on top of the logo or it will be unreadable. If you ignore this rule the heading text will appear as shown in the above figure.
B	The width of this element is set equivalent to the width of the main wrapper.
C	The height is set equal to the height of the <header> element.
Rule23 & 24	Rule 23 and 24 are set for <a> elements (Login/Register and Sitemap links) enclosed in #headlinks <div> element. The links' normal color (grey) is changed to orange when the mouse is hovered over them. Note that the three footer links are also styled with these two rules.

Step-3 Create Main Navigation Bar

Add the following html code after 12-c (Table 6-1). You can also refer index.html in the source folder for proper positioning of this code. The code creates main navigation bar to link to other pages of the website and adds a search box.

Line	HTML Code
1	`<nav>`
2	`<ul>`
3	`<li><a href="" class="current">Home</a></li>`
4	`<li><a href="company.html">Company</a></li>`
5	`<li><a href="services.html">Services</a></li>`
6	`<li><a href="products.php">Products</a></li>`
7	`<li><a href="contact.html">Contact</a></li>`
8	`</ul>`
9	`<script type="text/javascript">`
10	`//Enter domain of site to search`
11	`var domainroot="www.maqcon.com"`
12	`function Gsitesearch(curobj){`
13	`curobj.q.value="site:"+domainroot+" "+curobj.qfront.value`
14	`}`
15	`</script>`
16	`<form id="search" action="http://www.google.com/search" method="get" onSubmit="Gsitesearch(this)">`
17	`<input name="q" type="hidden" />`
18	`<input name="qfront" type="search" value="search..."/> <input type="submit" value="Go!" />`
19	`</form>`
20	`</nav>`

Output

CSS Code & Explanation

Rule-6	nav {
A	clear: both;
B	background-image: url(images/menu-bg.gif);
C	background-repeat:repeat-x;
D	background-color: orange;
E	height: 30px;}

Rule 6 is defined for the <nav> element that holds the main navigational bar. The <nav> element contains an unordered list <ul> that carries five list items each pointing to a web page.

A	No floating elements are allowed on both sides. For details see section 3.17 - Floating Elements.
B	Background image is set to menu-bg.gif located in the images folder.
C	Menu-bg.gif is a slim image that is repeated horizontally to form a background bar.
D	Added this rule to show the navigational bar in orange color if menu-bg.gif fails to load. Comment out this rule and refresh your browser to see the effect.
E	Sets the height of the navigational bar.

Rule-7	nav ul {
A	margin: 0px;
B	padding: 5px 0px 5px 30px;}

Rule 7 defines properties for the <nav> <ul> element.

A	The margin is set to 0px to keep the bar close to the company logo. If you set some margin, for example 10px, the navigation bar would drop down to create some space from the logo.
B	Padding is added to each <ul> element by setting values 5, 0, 5, and 30 pixels (top, right, bottom, and left respectively). Changing the left padding value from 30 to 0px would drag the menu bar to the left edge. A single value (as done with margin), would apply to all four sides.

Rule-8	nav li {
A	float:left;
B	width:80px;
C	height:20px;
D	display: inline;
E	margin-right: 20px;
F	background: url(images/menu-divider.gif) right top no-repeat;}

Rule 8 sets properties for each <li> element in the <nav> element.

A	Floats each <li> element from the left side. The first element Home is floated first. Then the Company is seated inline next to it and so on.
B	Each element will have a width of 80 pixels.
C	Height of each element is 20 pixels.
D	Displays all <li> elements inline.
E	Sets right margin to 20 pixels for each element.
F	Sets a divider between two <li> elements using menu-divider.gif. This is a shorthand property. CSS shorthand style properties allow you to write some CSS properties in a more compact form, saving space, download time, and development time. The shorthand property for background is simply "background". The position of the image is specified by the background-position property i.e. right top. No-repeat prevents the gif from replication.

CSS Code & Explanation

Rule-9
```
nav li a {
  color: #ffffff;
  font-weight:bold;}
```
Rule 9 renders each navigation item bold faced and in white.

Rule-10
```
nav li a:hover, nav li a.current {
  color: #000000;}
```
Rule 10 displays each navigation item in black color when the mouse is hovered over the item. The second part of this rule applies to the current page to display corresponding label in black in the navigation bar. In html, the <a> element in the first <li> element for the Home page is associated with a class named "current". The second part of this rule is specified for such elements to show the label of the current page in black.

Rule-11
```
#search {
  position:absolute;
  top:103px;
  right:30px;}
```
Rule 11 applies to the form having the id "search" that shows a search box (html code line # 16). We applied absolute positioning by setting top and right properties to display it in the navigation bar. See section 3.16 for further details on absolute positioning.

Step-4 Create Content Section

Add the following html code after line number 14 </header> (Table 6-1). The code creates a section named content to display image slides and couple of paragraphs about the company.

Line #	HTML Code
1	`<section class="content">`
2	`  <article>`
3	`    <figure class="slide">`
4	`      <img src="images/slide6.png" alt="slide1"/>`
5	`      <img src="images/slide5.png" alt="slide2"/>`
6	`      <img src="images/slide4.png" alt="slide3"/>`
7	`      <img src="images/slide3.png" alt="slide4"/>`
8	`      <img src="images/slide2.png" alt="slide5"/>`
9	`      <img src="images/slide1.png" alt="slide6"/>`
10	`    </figure>`
11	`    <hgroup>`
12	`      <h2>What We Do</h2>`
13	`    </hgroup>`
14	`    <p>ABC Global Consulting help organizations achieve their goals by providing scalable...</p>`
15	`    <p>We provide better decision making tools to business owners and specialize in...</p> `
16	`  </article>`
17	`</section>`

Output

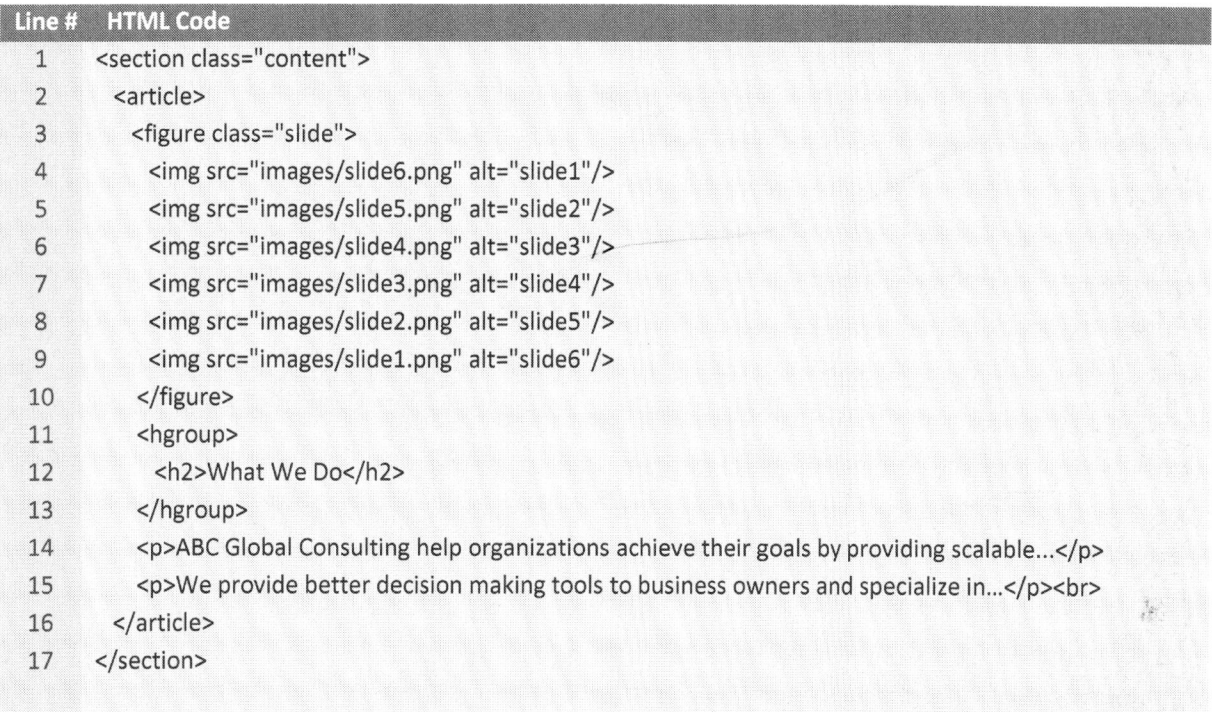
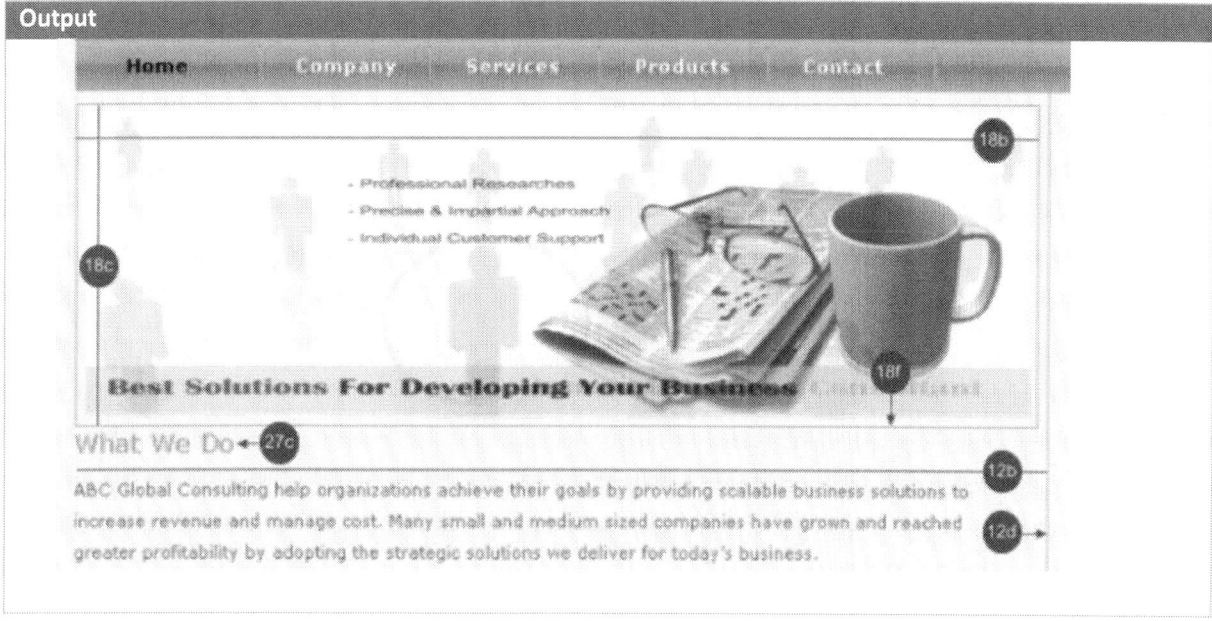

CSS Code & Explanation

Rule-12	section.content {
A	float: left;
B	width: 670px;
C	margin-top: 5px;
D	border-right: 1px solid #eeeeee;}

Rule 12 sets style for the <section> element named "content".

A	The element floats from the left side.
B	The width of this element is set to 670 pixels.
C	Creates a 5 pixels top margin to create some space between this element and the navigational bar.
D	This one creates a border to the right of this element to act as a separator between <section> and <aside> elements.

Rule-13	section.content p{
	margin: 10px 20px 10px 20px;}

Rule 13 styles paragraph <p> elements defined under the content section by specifying top, right, bottom, and left margins.

Rule-16	article {
A	clear: both;
B	overflow: auto;
C	width: 100%;}

Rule 16 applies to the <article> element.

B	This property adds a scroll bar when needed to see the rest of the content.
C	Utilizes 100% width i.e. 670 pixels of the <section> element it resides in.

Rule-18	figure {
A	float: left;
B	width: 632px;
C	height: 328px;
D	padding: 5px;
E	margin: 20px;
F	border: 1px solid #eeeeee;}

Rule 18 formats the <figure> element. This rule works in conjunction with rules 37, 38, 39, and 40 to create a slide animation. If these four rules are ignored, only one static image will be displayed. You will use a static image in the next page (company.html).

A	Floats images from the left side.
B	Sets a width of 632 pixels to contain the image. Each image used in this slide animation is approximately 632 x 328 pixels.
C	Sets the height to fit the image in.
D	Sets 5 pixels padding on all sides.
E	Sets 20 pixels margins on all sides.
F	Draws a border around the image.

CSS Code & Explanation

Rule-37
```
@-moz-keyframes myAnimation {
    0% {opacity:1;}
    17% {opacity:0;}
    34% {opacity:0;}
    51% {opacity:0;}
    68% {opacity:0;}
    85% {opacity:0;}
    100% {opacity:1;}
}
```

Rule-38
```
figure.slide img {position:absolute;}
```

Rule-39
```
figure.slide img{
    -moz-animation-name: myAnimation;
    -moz-animation-timing-function: ease-in-out;
    -moz-animation-iteration-count: infinite;
    -moz-animation-duration: 30s;}
```

Rule-40
```
figure.slide img:nth-of-type(1) {-moz-animation-delay: 25s;}
figure.slide img:nth-of-type(2) {-moz-animation-delay: 20s;}
figure.slide img:nth-of-type(3) {-moz-animation-delay: 15s;}
figure.slide img:nth-of-type(4) {-moz-animation-delay: 10s;}
figure.slide img:nth-of-type(5) {-moz-animation-delay: 5s;}
figure.slide img:nth-of-type(6) {-moz-animation-delay: 0s;}
```

Rules 37-40 are established to create a slide animation using six different images. To distinguish the slide animation from a static figure, we provided it a unique class named "slide" (HTML code 15-c Table 6-1). See section 3.22 - CSS3 Animation for further details.

Rule-17
```
hgroup {
    margin-top: 15px;}
```

Rule 17 is set for <hgroup> element and defines a top margin of 15 pixels for it. This page contains a single <h2> element - What We Do. By adding a suffix, -top, we used an alternate method to set the top margin. You can use right, bottom, and left to specify the margin for individual sides.

Rule-26
```
h1, h2, h3 {
    font-weight: normal;}
```

Rule 26 is created for <h1>, <h2>, and <h3> elements used throughout the web site. We used <h2> element in this page.

Rule-27
```
h2 {
    margin: 0px 0px 5px 20px;
    padding: 0px;
    color: #FF9900;}
```

Rule 27 is specific for <h2> and presents it in orange color.

Step-5	Create Aside Area

The <aside> element is added to every page of the website to create an area that holds additional information related to the page. The home page displays Services and Newsletter sections. The services section carries links which take user to services.html page to provide further details about the services provided by the company. The newsletter section holds a subscription form (line # 10-15) to allow site visitors to subscribe to company's newsletters to get updates for new products, services and other information. The visitor provides his/her e-mail address and submits the form by clicking the subscribe button. Upon submission, line # 10 calls a php file (subscribe.php) and passes the e-mail address to it using the post method. This file is listed and briefed in section 6.8 - Task 2 Newsletter Subscription module.

Add the following html code after line number 15-p </section> (Table 6-1).

Line	HTML Code
1	<aside>
2	<section class="services">
3	<h2>Our Services</h2>
4	<a href="services.html">Accounting & Taxation</a>
5	<a href="services.html">Audit & Assurance</a>
6	<a href="services.html">Recruitment Consultancy</a>
7	<a href="services.html">Software Designing</a>
8	</section>
9	<section class="newsletter">
10	<form id="letter" action="subscribe.php" method="post">
11	<label><b>Subscribe to our newsletter</b></label>
12	<label>E-mail Address:
13	<input type="email" name="subemail" maxlength="35" size="35" required="vital" placeholder="me@example.com"/></label>
14	<p><input type="image" alt="Subscribe" class="button src="images/subscribe.png"></p>
15	</form>
16	</section>
17	</aside>

Output, CSS Code & Explanation

Rule 19
```
aside {
    width: 250px;
    float: left;
    margin: 5px;
    padding: 20px 0px 0px 0px;}
```

Rule 19 is a general rule and applies to the <aside> element in all website pages. The width of the <aside> area is set to 250 pixels. Note that we assigned a width of 670 pixels to the <section> element in Rule 12. Also note that the overall area for the page content was set to 950 pixels in Rule 2. These numbers were set to keep content within the maximum limit.

Rule 20
```
aside h2 {
    margin-left: 0px;
    padding: 10px 0px 5px 5px;
    color: #FF9900;}
```
Rule 20 is specifically defined for <h2> element in the aside area by setting margin, padding, and color properties.

Rule 41
```
aside section.services a {
A       display: block;
        padding: 10px;
B       border-bottom: 1px solid #eeeeee;}
```
Rule 41 sets properties for <a> elements in section's Services class. This section holds links that show services provided by the company.

A   Display links in block form. The element is displayed as a block-level element (like paragraphs and headers).

B   Adds a bottom border to each link that acts as a separator.

Rule 42
```
aside section.services a:hover {
A       color: #ffffff;
B       background-color: #FF9900;}
```
Rule 42 is related to Rule 41 and assigns properties when mouse moves over the links.

A   Sets font color to white.

B   Sets background color to orange.

Output, CSS Code & Explanation

Rule 43	aside section.newsletter {
A	border: 1px solid #f2e19f;
B	margin-top: 9px;
C	padding: 5px 0px 5px 0px;
D	background-color: #fbf6e2;
E	-moz-box-shadow: inset 0 0 10px #f2e19f;
F	-moz-border-radius: 10px;}

NOTE

In this static page you're creating Newsletter Subscription interface. The complete module is discussed later in section 6.9.

Rule 43 styles Newsletter section.

A	Creates a border around the element.
B	Specifies space between Services and Newsletter sections.
C	Creates top and bottom space of 5 pixels between the border and form elements.
D	Sets background color.
E	The box-shadow property puts a drop shadow around the Newsletter section. We set 0 for horizontal and vertical shadow values and set blur to 10 pixels with a light orange color. The inner shadow is created using the inset keyword specified before these values.
F	The border-radius property makes the border rounded around the Newsletter section. See section 3.20 CSS3 Borders for further explanation.

Rule 44	aside section.newsletter form{
	width: 200px;
	padding: 0px 5px 0px 5px;}

Rule 44 sets Newsletter subscription form's width and padding. The right and left padding values assigns space of 5 pixels between the border edges and form elements.

Step-6 Create Page Footer

The page footer is a general area that will appear on every page of the website. The left side will have a copyright message while the right side will display three links: Legal Information, Privacy Policy, and Subscribe.

Line #	HTML Code
1	`<footer>`
2	`<p id="copyright">&copy; 2013 ABC Global Consulting</p>`
3	`<p id="footlinks"><a href="">Legal Information</a>	<a href="">Privacy Policy</a> |`
	`<a href="">Subscribe</a>`
4	`</p>`
5	`</footer>`

Output

© 2013 ABC Global Consulting   Legal Information | Privacy Policy | Subscribe

CSS Code and Explanation

Rule 29	`footer {`
	`clear: both;`
B	`color: #ffffff;`
C	`font-size: 80%;`
	`background-color: orange;`
	`height: 40px;}`

Rule 29 assigns properties to style the `<footer>` element.

B   Sets font color to white. This applies to the copyright message.

C   Marginally reduces the font from the normal font size. 100% is the normal font size.

Rule 30	`footer a{`
	`color: #ffffff;}`
Rule 31	`footer a:hover{`
	`color: #666666;}`

Rule 30 and 31 are used to set normal and hover colors for the `<a>` element.

Rule 32	`footer #copyright{`
	`float: left;`
	`padding: 0px 0px 0px 20px;}`

Rule 32 sets properties for the copyright paragraph. The copyright text is floated from the left side with a left padding of 20 pixels.

Rule 33	`footer #footlinks{`
	`float: right;`
	`padding: 0px 20px 0px 0px;}`

Rule 33 assigns values to style the "footlinks" paragraph. The three footer links are floated from the right with a value of 20 pixels for the right padding.

6.5   The Company Page

This page will be shown when the Company link is clicked on the main navigation bar from any page on the website. Just like index.html page, this page too will be created in a sequence of steps.

Figure 6-2 - The Company Page

The page has some similar and distinct areas (outlined below) as compared to the home page.

- The active page link (Company) in the main navigation bar is shown in black.
- This page shows a static image replacing the slide show displayed on the home page.
- An <h3> heading element (Business Solution Provider) is used in the <hgroup> element.
- Created links in the main content area and presented them with a customized image instead of bullet markers.
- The aside area demonstrates how to add multiple sections to it. The first section exhibits how to use different background images for a link.
- The Events section displays scrolling text using <marquee> element.
- The Latest News section also consists of links with a customized image.

Step-1 Create Header, Navigation Bar, and Footer

1. Open Notepad and enter the html code mentioned in the table below. You can paste this code from company.html located in the source folder.
2. Save this new file as company.html in the site folder.
3. Open your browser and type http://localhost/abcglobal/company.html in the address bar and hit Enter. You'll see the page as shown in Figure 6-2.

Following is the code for the html file. At this stage, the page will utilize all the style rules we defined for the home page.

Line	HTML Code
1	`<!DOCTYPE html>`
2	`<html>`
3	`<head>`
4	`<title>ABC Global Consulting</title>`
5	`<link rel="stylesheet" type="text/css" href="style.css" />`
6	`<!--[if lt IE 9]>`
7	`<script src="http://html5shiv.googlecode.com/svn/trunk/html5.js"></script>`
8	`<![endif]-->`
9	`</head>`
10	`<body>`
11	`<div class="wrapper">`
12	`<header>`
13	`<h1>ABC Global Consulting</h1>`
14	`<div id="headlinks">`
15	`<p><a href="member/index.php">Login/Register</a>	<a href="">Sitemap</a></p>`
16	`</div>`
17	`<nav>`
18	`<ul>`
19	`<li><a href="index.html">Home</a></li>`
20	`<li><a href="" class="current">Company</a></li>`
21	`<li><a href="services.html">Services</a></li>`
22	`<li><a href="products.php">Products</a></li>`
23	`<li><a href="contact.html">Contact</a></li>`
24	`</ul>`
25	`<script type="text/javascript">`
26	`//Enter domain of site to search.`
27	`var domainroot="www.maqcon.com"`
28	`function Gsitesearch(curobj){`
29	`curobj.q.value="site:"+domainroot+" "+curobj.qfront.value`
30	`}`
31	`</script>`
32	`<form id="search" action="http://www.google.com/search" method="get" onSubmit="Gsitesearch(this)">`
33	`<input name="q" type="hidden" />`
34	`<input name="qfront" type="search" value="search..."/> <input type="submit" value="Go!" />`

Line	HTML Code (Continued)
35	`</form>`
36	`</nav>`
37	`</header>`
38	`<footer>`
39	`<p id="copyright">&copy; 2013 ABC Global Consulting</p>`
40	`<p id="footlinks"><a href="">Legal Information</a> | <a href="">Privacy Policy</a> |` `<a href="index.html">Subscribe </a></p>`
41	`</footer>`
42	`</div><!-- .wrapper -->`
43	`</body>`
44	`</html>`

Explanation

The above code is the same as used in index.html page except the one presented in bold which indicates the current page and shows the Company label in black in the main navigation bar. This code will display only header, navigation bar, and the page footer.

Step-2   Create and Style Main Content

Add the following code to both html and css files. The html code should go after the </header> tag (line # 37).

Line	HTML Code
1	`<section class="content">`
2	`<article>`
3	`<figure>`
4	`<img src="images/slide2.png" alt="slide2"/>`
5	`</figure>`
6	`<hgroup>`
7	`<h2>ABC Global Consulting</h2>`
8	`<h3>Business Solution Provider</h3>`
9	`</hgroup>`
10	`<p>ABC Global Consulting was established in October 2008 to ... </p>`
11	`<p>The Spheres of our services are broadly categorized as follows:</p>`
12	`<ul>`
13	`<li><a href="">Accountancy Consultancy</a></li>`
14	`<li><a href="">Taxation Services</a></li>`
15	`<li><a href="">Audit & Assurance</a></li>`
16	`<li><a href="">Software Designing & Implementation</a></li>`
17	`<li><a href="">Human Resource Consultancy</a></li>`
18	`</ul> `
19	`</article>`
20	`</section>`

CSS Code	

Rule 14	`section.content li{`
	`background:url(images/arrow1.png) 0px 6px no-repeat;`
	`padding: 0 0 0 20px;}`

Rule 15	`section.content li a{` `text-decoration:underline;}`
Rule 25	`ul {list-style-type: none;}`

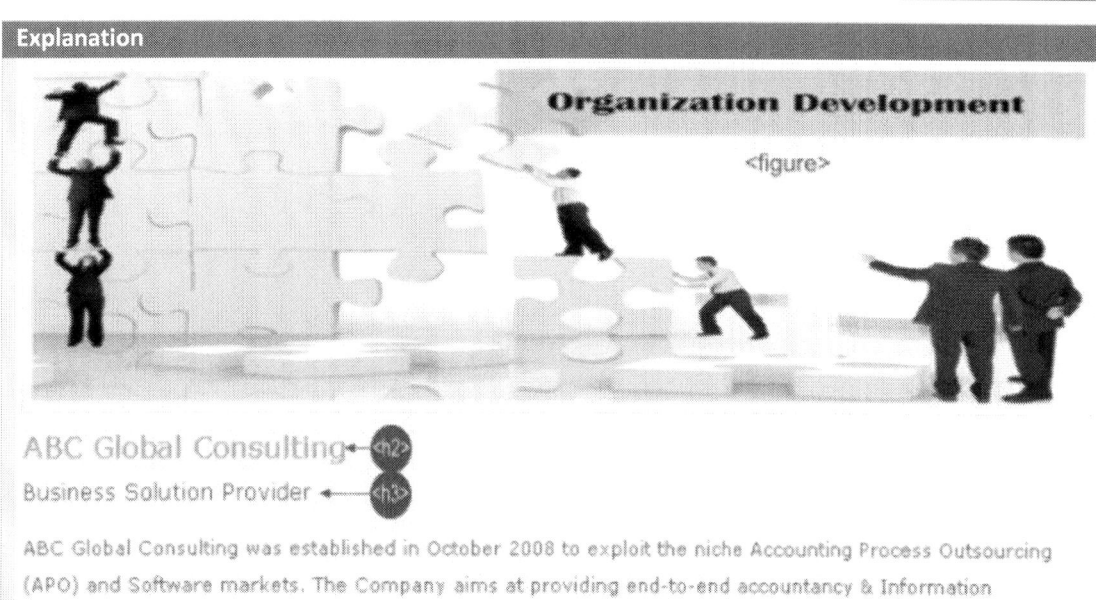

The content section shows a static relevant image instead of the slide show. It uses an image from the slide show and utilizes same dimensions. The <hgroup> element now has an additional heading element <h3> to demonstrate use of multiple headings in the element. The unordered list is added to the content area to show how links are created in this section using a custom image instead of default markers.

Rule 14 styles each list item with a custom image (arrow1.png).

Rule 15 underlines each link.

Rule 25 sets list style type to none which removes default bullet markers from the list.

Step-3 Create List of Services

Add the following html code after the </section> tag (line # 20).

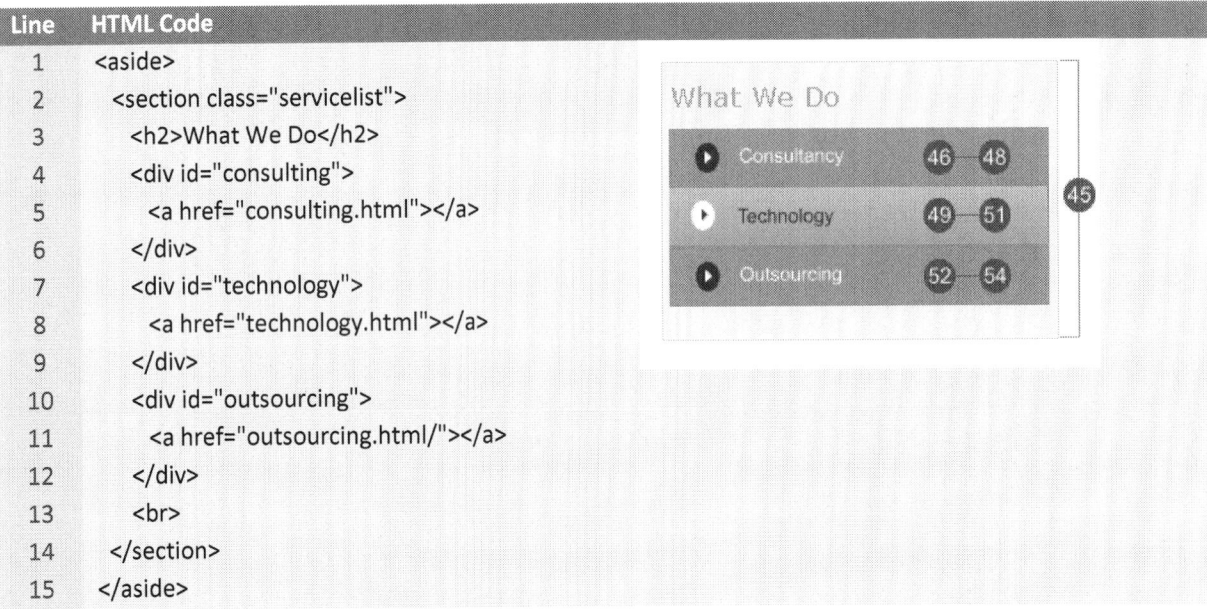

Line	HTML Code
1	<aside>
2	<section class="servicelist">
3	<h2>What We Do</h2>
4	<div id="consulting">
5	<a href="consulting.html"></a>
6	</div>
7	<div id="technology">
8	<a href="technology.html"></a>
9	</div>
10	<div id="outsourcing">
11	<a href="outsourcing.html/"></a>
12	</div>
13	
14	</section>
15	</aside>

The <aside> element contains three sections to display different information. The first section, servicelist, is created to provide links to the services provided by the company. These links are different from the previous links in the way that they use two background images for each link; one for normal display and the other one when the mouse hovers over the link.

CSS Code

Rule 45
```
aside section.servicelist {
    border: 1px solid #f2e19f;
    padding: 0px;
    background-color: #fbf6e2;}
```
Rule 45 draws a container to hold three <div> elements. Each one has an <a> element. This rule puts a border of 1 pixel having f2e19f color and gives this container fbf6e2 background color.

Rule 46
```
aside section.servicelist #consulting {
A    width:239px;
B    height:36px;
C    background:url(images/consulting.gif) 0 0 no-repeat;
D    margin: 0 auto;}
```
Rule 46 applies to the first <div> element named consulting.

A The width is set to 239 pixels. Note that the total width of the aside area is 250 pixels (Rule 19), leaving some space on both sides of the <div> element.

C An image, consulting.gif, is used in the background. This image is shown when the mouse pointer is away from or leaves the <div> element.

D The <div> element is centered in the container.

Rule 47
```
aside section.servicelist #consulting a{
    width:239px;
    height:36px;
    text-decoration:none;
    display: block;}
```
Rule 47 sets style for <a> element under the Consulting <div> element. The "none" value of text-decoration property removes underline from the links.

Rule 48
```
aside section.servicelist #consulting a:hover{
    background:url(images/consulting2.gif) 0 0 no-repeat;}
```
Rule 48 changes the background image to consulting2.gif when mouse moves over the <div> element.

CSS Code

Rule 49
```
aside section.servicelist #technology {
    width:239px;
    height:36px;
    background:url(images/technology.gif) 0 0 no-repeat;
    margin: 0 auto;}
```

Rule 50
```
aside section.servicelist #technology a{
    width:239px;
    height:36px;
    text-decoration:none;
    display: block;}
```

Rule 51
```
aside section.servicelist #technology a:hover{
    background:url(images/technology2.gif) 0 0 no-repeat;}
```
Rule 49 to 51 apply to the technology <div> element and are similar to Rule 46, 47, and 48 with the exception of background image.

Rule 52
```
aside section.servicelist #outsourcing {
    width:239px;
    height:36px;
    background:url(images/outsourcing.gif) 0 0 no-repeat;
    margin: 0 auto;}
```

Rule 53
```
aside section.servicelist #outsourcing a{
    width:239px;
    height:36px;
    text-decoration:none;
    display: block;}
```

Rule 54
```
aside section.servicelist #outsourcing a:hover{
    background:url(images/outsourcing2.gif) 0 0 no-repeat;}
```
Rule 52 to 54 are created for the <div> element outsourcing and are similar to Rule 46, 47, and 48 except for the background image.

Step-4 Create Events List Using Marquee

Add the following html code before the closing </aside> tag. This code generates a scrolling list using marquee element. The direction is set to "up" while the value of the scrollamount property is set to 1 which indicates the scrolling speed.

Line	HTML Code
1	`<section class="events">`
2	`  <h2>Events</h2>`
3	`  <marquee  class="`**`scrollevents`**`" behavior="scroll" direction="up" scrollamount="1">`
4	`    <a href="">Finance Conference</a> `
5	`    <a href="">Best Practices Day</a> `
6	`    <a href="">Compensation Survey</a> `
7	`    <a href="">Identifying Training Needs</a> `
8	`    <a href="">HR Audit Workshop</a>`
9	`  </marquee>`
10	`</section>`

CSS Code

Rule 55
```
aside section.events {
    margin-top: 5px;
    border: 1px solid #f2e19f;
    padding: 5px;
    background-color: #fbf6e2;
    height:150px;}
```

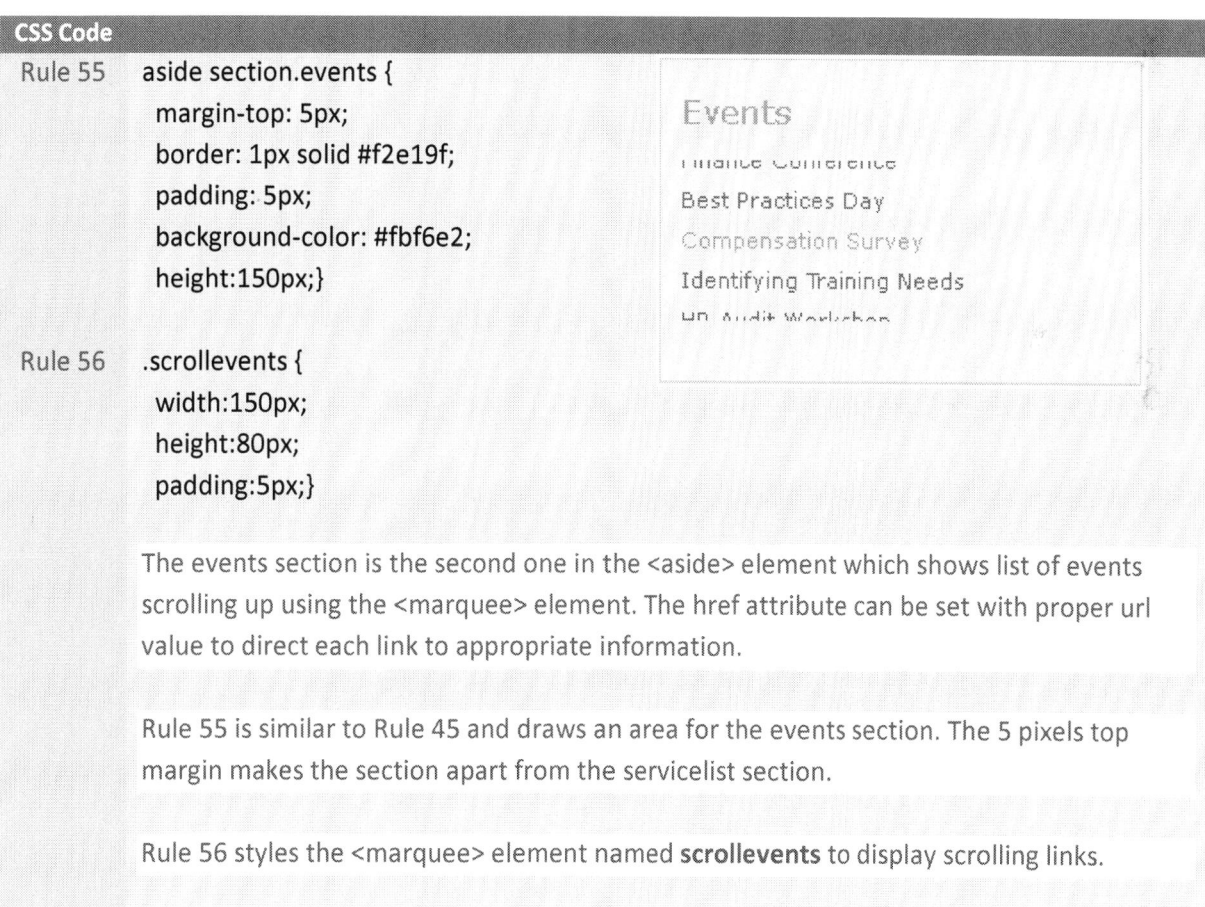

Rule 56
```
.scrollevents {
    width:150px;
    height:80px;
    padding:5px;}
```

The events section is the second one in the <aside> element which shows list of events scrolling up using the <marquee> element. The href attribute can be set with proper url value to direct each link to appropriate information.

Rule 55 is similar to Rule 45 and draws an area for the events section. The 5 pixels top margin makes the section apart from the servicelist section.

Rule 56 styles the <marquee> element named **scrollevents** to display scrolling links.

Step-5   Create Latest News Section

Add the following html code again before the closing </aside> tag.

Line #	HTML Code
1	<section class="news">
2	<h2>Latest News</h2>
3	<ul>
4	<li><a href="#">Budget Commentary</a></li>
5	<li><a href="#">Corporate Updates</a> </li>
6	<li><a href="#">Easy Exit Scheme</a></li>
7	<li><a href="#">Taxation Updates</a></li>
8	<li><a href="#">Financial Reporting</a></li>
9	<li><a href="#">Business planning</a> </li>
10	<li><a href="#">Objectives planning</a></li>
11	<li><a href="#">Corporate culture issues</a> </li>
12	<li><a href="#">Management training programs</a></li>
13	<li><a href="#">Succession planning</a> </li>
14	</ul>
15	</section>

CSS Code

Rule 57	aside section.news { 　border: 1px solid #f2e19f; 　padding: 0px; 　background-color: #fbf6e2; 　margin-top: 5px;}
Rule 58	aside section.news a { 　display: block; 　padding: 2px; 　border-bottom: 1px solid #eeeeee;}
Rule 59	aside section.news ul { 　padding: 0 0 0 15px;}
Rule 60	aside section.news ul li { background:url(images/arrow2.pn g) 5px 10px no-repeat; 　padding: 0 0 0 20px;}

Latest News

» Budget Commentary

» Corporate Updates

» Easy Exit Scheme

» Taxation Updates

» Financial Reporting

» Business planning

» Objectives planning

» Corporate culture issues

» Management training programs

» Succession planning

The News section is the last one in the <aside> element. You can create sections like these in your pages to show list of recent blog posts or links to the latest tweets.

Rules 57-60 are used to style the third section that is News. Almost all properties are similar to the previous two sections with some minor changes. Due to these differences, we created separate rules for each section. We could have created a single rule for all (such as Rule 26) if there were no differences. Also note that we didn't specifically set normal and hover color effects for <a> element under the Events and News sections. These effects were taken from the general rules 23 and 24.

6.6 The Services Page

This page demonstrates the use of multiple <article> elements in the main content area. There are two distinct articles with separate pictures, headings, and text content. Using this technique you can add as many articles as you want. The new stuff will be appended below in the same format. Like distinct headings, you can also add separate <footer> to each article where you can put stuff like social media or additional information links.

Figure 6-3 - The Services Page

Do It Yourself

Follow the steps mentioned below to create this page.

1. Open Notepad and enter the html code from the following table. You can paste this code from services.html in the source folder.
2. Save this new file as services.html in the site folder.

Line	HTML Code
1	<!DOCTYPE html>
2	<html>
	...
3	<nav>
4	<ul>
5	<li><a href="index.html">Home</a></li>
6	<li><a href="company.html">Company</a></li>
7	**<li><a href="" class="current">Services</a></li>**
8	<li><a href="products.php">Products</a></li>
9	<li><a href="contact.html">Contact</a></li>
10	</ul>
	...
11	<section class="content">
12	<article> ← Article # 1
13	<figure class="small">
14	<img src="images/accounting.jpg" alt="Accounting Services"/>
15	</figure>
16	<hgroup>
17	<h2>Accountancy</h2>
18	**<h3>We provide Accountancy & Book Keeping Services</h3>**
19	</hgroup>
20	<p>Reporting complete and accurate financial data is of paramount importance...</p>
21	<p>The Key areas of accountancy are:</p>
22	<ul>
23	<li>Proper Maintaining of all Books of Accounts such as Cash & Bank Book, General Ledgers.</li>
24	<li>Preparation of Periodic Financial Reporting</li>
25	<li>Cash, Bank, Debtors, Creditors & Stock Monthly Reconciliation Statements</li>
26	<li>Any other Reports as per the requirement of the client</li>
27	<li>Analytical Review on Financial Statements</li>
28	<li>Payroll Accounting & Records maintenance</li>
29	<li>Proper maintaining of Stock Ledger</li>
30	<li>Provident Funds & Gratuity Funds Accounts</li>
31	</ul>
32	</article>

Line	HTML Code (Continued)
33	`<article>` ← Article # 2
34	`<figure class="small">`
35	`<img src="images/software.jpg" alt="Software Development"/>`
36	`</figure>`
37	`<hgroup>`
38	`<h2>Software Development</h2>`
39	`<h3>We design tailor cut software to meet your business needs</h3>`
40	`</hgroup>`
41	`<p>Organizations opting for implementing contemporary technology solutions...</p>`
42	`<p>The phenomenal growth of information technology is changing the business ...</p>`
43	`<p>We provide solutions for Business Systems ...</p>`
44	`<p>We manage these engagements with project teams including...</p> `
45	`</article>`
46	`</section>`
47	`<aside>`
48	`<section class="servicelist">`
49	`<h2>Consulting</h2>`
50	`<ul>`
51	`<li>Strategy</li>`
52	`<li>Finance</li>`
53	`<li>Technology</li>`
54	`<li>Governance, risk and compliance</li>`
55	`<li>Operations</li>`
56	`<li>People & change</li>`
57	`<li>Revenue growth</li>`
58	`<li>Shared services and outsourcing</li>`
59	`<li>Sustainability</li>`
60	`<li>Delivering deal value</li>`
61	`<li>Investigations</li>`
62	`</ul>`
63	`<h2>Audit & Assurance</h2>`
64	`<ul>`
65	`<li>Financial statement audit</li>`
66	`<li>Corporate reporting</li>`
67	`<li>Regulatory compliance</li>`
68	`<li>Internal Audit</li>`
69	`</ul>`
70	`<h2>Human Resource</h2>`
71	`<ul>`
72	`<li>HR Management</li>`
73	`<li>Recruitment</li>`
74	`</ul>`

Line	HTML Code (Continued)
75	`<h2>Legal</h2>`
76	`<ul>`
77	`<li>Asset Management</li>`
78	`<li>Corporate and commercial</li>`
79	`<li>Corporate secretarial</li>`
80	`<li>Dispute resolution</li>`
81	`<li>Employment</li>`
82	`<li>Financial Services</li>`
83	`<li>Public law</li>`
84	`<li>...</li>`
85	`</ul>`
86	`</section>`
87	`</aside>`
88	`<footer>`
89	`<p id="copyright">&copy; 2013 ABC Global Consulting</p>`
90	`<p id="footlinks"><a href="">Legal Information</a> | <a href="">Privacy Policy</a> | <a href="index.html">Subscribe </a></p>`
91	`</footer>`
92	`</div><!-- .wrapper -->`
93	`</body>`
94	`</html>`

CSS Code			

Rule 61	`figure.small {`
	`  float: left;`
	`  width: 200px;`
	`  height: 200px;`
	`  padding: 5px;`
	`  margin: 20px;`
	`  border: 1px solid #eeeeee;}`
		Rule 28	`h3 {`
			`  margin: 0px 0px 5px 20px;`
			`  color: #666666;}`

This page uses the same servicelist rule (Rule 45) that we discussed while creating the Company page to create a bordered section in the aside area. All general rules (.wrapper, nav, header etc.) apply to this page as well. The only specific one for this page is Rule 61, which styles the small images used here by setting a square area of 200 pixels. Rule 28 is a general rule that applied to <h3> elements on all pages.

In Company.html, you used a large static picture. Here, you utilized small images of 200x200 pixels. Also note how the text content enclosed in the <p> element flows automatically next to these images. We left out some redundant html code in the above table that we've already discussed in previous sections.

This concludes the part of static web page creation. These exercises were destined to consolidate the crumbs you went through in HTML and CSS parts earlier in this book. The foundation has been laid. If you firmly grasp these techniques, you'll be able to design almost any website. Things are not finished yet, let's move on to buff up our skills even more and learn how to put life into a website.

6.7 Make the Website Dynamic

In previous sections you completed the static parts of the website. Now it's time to create the dynamic segments using PHP and MySQL. In this part you will enable your website to interact with its visitors by adding the following modules.

Contact Form

All modern websites provide some means of communication with their visitors; a contact form is one of them. You'll be guided to add a contact form to the website so that visitors could input their comments. This data will then be stored in a table named Contact in the MySQL database. The form will be created in section 6.8 - Task 1.

Newsletter Subscription

E-mail newsletters are a very popular way to open a channel of communication with your site visitors. Newsletters provide great benefit of keeping a site's user base up-to-date on the latest news and offerings from an organization. Moreover, they have the potential for turning site visitors into customers. For newsletters to be successful, they have to be easy to subscribe to and—just as importantly—unsubscribe from. Recall that while creating the Home page we added the interface of this module. That will be put to work in section 6.9 - Task 2.

E-Commerce Module

Besides consulting services, ABC Global Consulting also deals in IT related products and intends to sell them through their website. To achieve this task you have to add interactive functionalities to the website. You have to build a products page that will show relevant information (image, description, price etc.) from a database and will allow users to buy those products. But before that, you have to create few modules that will manage administrative tasks such as uploading categories and products information. These modules will be accessible only to the site administrators.

6.7.1 Tasks List

The following table lists the tasks you will be performing in this chapter:

Task	Module	Description
General Tasks		
Task 1	Contact Form	Add contact form to receive visitor's comments and store them in the database.
Task 2	Newsletter Subscription	Allow visitors to subscribe to company's newsletter.
Admin Interface Tasks		
Task 3	Admin Login Module	Create login interface for site administrators
Task 4	Manage Categories	View, add, update and delete product categories
Task 5	Manage Products	View, add, update and delete individual products
Task 6	Manage Orders	View, ship, and delete orders placed by customers
Task 7	Manage Accounts	Add, update, and delete admin users
Member Interface Tasks		
Task 8	Member Login Module	Interface for site members
Task 9	Register New Member	Allow new users to become members
Task 10	Reset Password	Provides new passwords to site members.
Task 11	My Account	This page lets users edit their information and review their orders.
Task 12	Featured Products Catalog	This page will be added to the website and will be accessible to all through the *Products* main navigation link. This page will show featured products along with images, short description, and prices.
Task 13	Product Details	This page will provide complete details about a particular product and will have an Add to Cart button.
Task 14	Shopping Cart	Once the member clicks the Add to Cart button, he will be brought to this page to check his cart.
Task 15	Checkout (Confirm Order)	The cart page will contain a checkout link. The module will ask the member to login before placing an order. Once logged in successfully, he or she will proceed to the payment page which will accept credit card information from the member.
Task 16	Website Deployment	After completion, the website will be deployed on a host server so that the world could access it.

6.7.2 Directory Structure

The table on the next page presents the directory structure for the tasks mentioned above. Each module is stored in a separate directory. For example, Checkout module files are stored in the checkout directory. Member, Catalog, Cart, and Checkout directories hold files for the end users of the web site.

In contrast, administrative modules are stored under the Admin directory. This directory has four sub-directories (Users, Category, Product, and Orders) to manage admin users, categories, products, and orders placed by customers respectively.

Each directory contains a controller file (index.php) which is the default file that runs for each directory. This file in turn calls relevant functions and view files stored in respective directories. The web site's root directory has a product.php file that is executed when the user clicks the Products link on the main navigation bar. This file calls show_product.php file to display featured products from the database.

The errors directory contains PHP scripts for displaying application errors, the images directory holds all the image files used in the web site. Files in the model directory provide database functions whereas the utility directory carries files that provide parsing, global and session functions. The view directory contains files (header, footer, sidebar etc.) that are used by all modules to provide a consistent look.

This directory structure is ideal to maintain and enhance a web site. For instance, if you decide to use two different headers, one for the end user and one for the administrators, you just add a new header file to the view directory and modify the files that use it. You will create separate headers for admin and end users to display separate navigation bar. Similarly, if you wish to change something in the cart module, you can go to the cart directory that contains all relevant files to this module. The following illustration presents a general PHP process pattern called MVC (Model, View, and Controller).

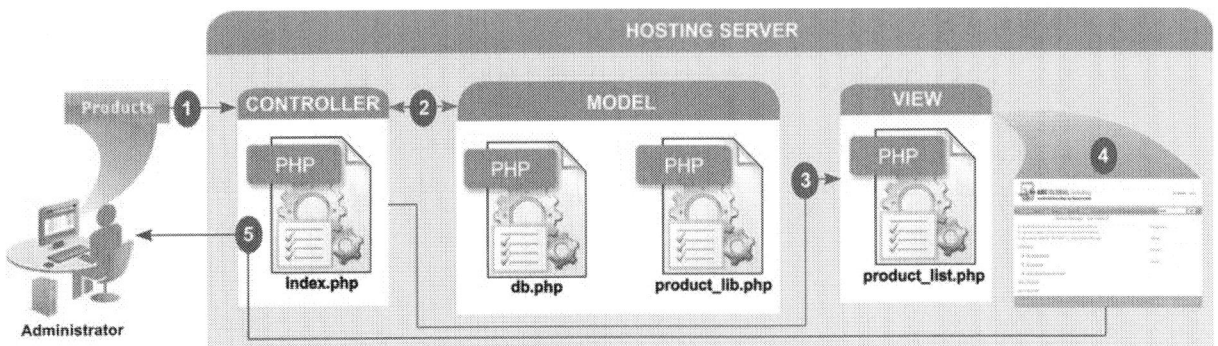

Figure 6-4

In this example, the process initiates when an administrator clicks the Products link on the main navigation bar. The flow is received by the controller: index.php file (Point 1). Then, the controller gets appropriate data from the model (Point 2). The model connects to the database and fetches data through various functions. For instance, here the administrator requested for products data. So, a file product_lib.php is called to fetch the information. After receiving the information, the controller calls a file (product_list.php) from the view layer (Point 3). This file consists of HTML and PHP code to render the list of products (Point 4). The products list is then presented to the administrator through the controller (Point 5).

Directory	Sub-Directory	PHP Files
ABCGLOBAL (root)	-	contact.html, success.html, contact.php, subscribe.php, confirm_subscribe.php, products.php, show_product.php,
Admin		index.php
	Category	index.php, category_list.php
	Orders	index.php, order.php, order_delete.php, order_status.php
	Product	index.php, product_add_edit.php, product_list.php, product_view.php
	Users	index.php, admin_delete.php, admin_edit.php, admin_login.php, admin_view.php
Cart	-	index.php, cart_view.php
Catalog	-	index.php, category_view.php, product_view.php
Checkout	-	index.php, checkout_confirm.php, checkout_payment.php
Errors	-	db_error_connect.php, error.php, member_db_connect_error.php, member_error.php
Images	-	All images used in the website
Member	-	index.php, member_address.php, member_edit.php, member_login.php, member_orders.php, member_password.php, member_pw_sent.php, member_register.php, member_view.php
Model	-	address_db.php, admin_lib.php, cart.php, category_lib.php, db.php, member_lib.php, order_lib.php, product_lib.php
Utility	-	check_admin.php, images.php, main.php, secure.php, tags.php, validation.php
View	-	footer.php, header_admin.php, header_member.php, product.php, sidebar_admin.php, sidebar_member.php

6.7.3 Anatomy of Controller File (Index.php)

Before commencing the project, it is important to get some know how about the structure of controller files. As pointed out in the previous section, index.php exist under all module directories. The main purpose of this file is to control the process of a module it represents. The directory structure you saw in the previous section contains several directories that basically fall under the following two categories:

Main Module Folders

These are the directories that hold php files to process a specific segment of the project. For example, the Cart directory carries couple of files to control the process of shopping cart module. Other main folders in this category are: Admin, Member, Catalog, and Checkout. The Admin folder has four child folders and each one of them takes care of individual admin task.

Subordinate Folders

This category has Errors, Images, Model, Utility, and View directories. All these five directories assist the files in the main directories, mentioned above, in several different ways. For instance, files in the Errors directory handle errors and display appropriate message whenever an error is encountered while executing a task through the main module.

Each main module folder has a controller file that calls files listed under the subordinate folders to achieve some task and all the controller files have more or less the same structure as illustrated in the figure presented on the next page.

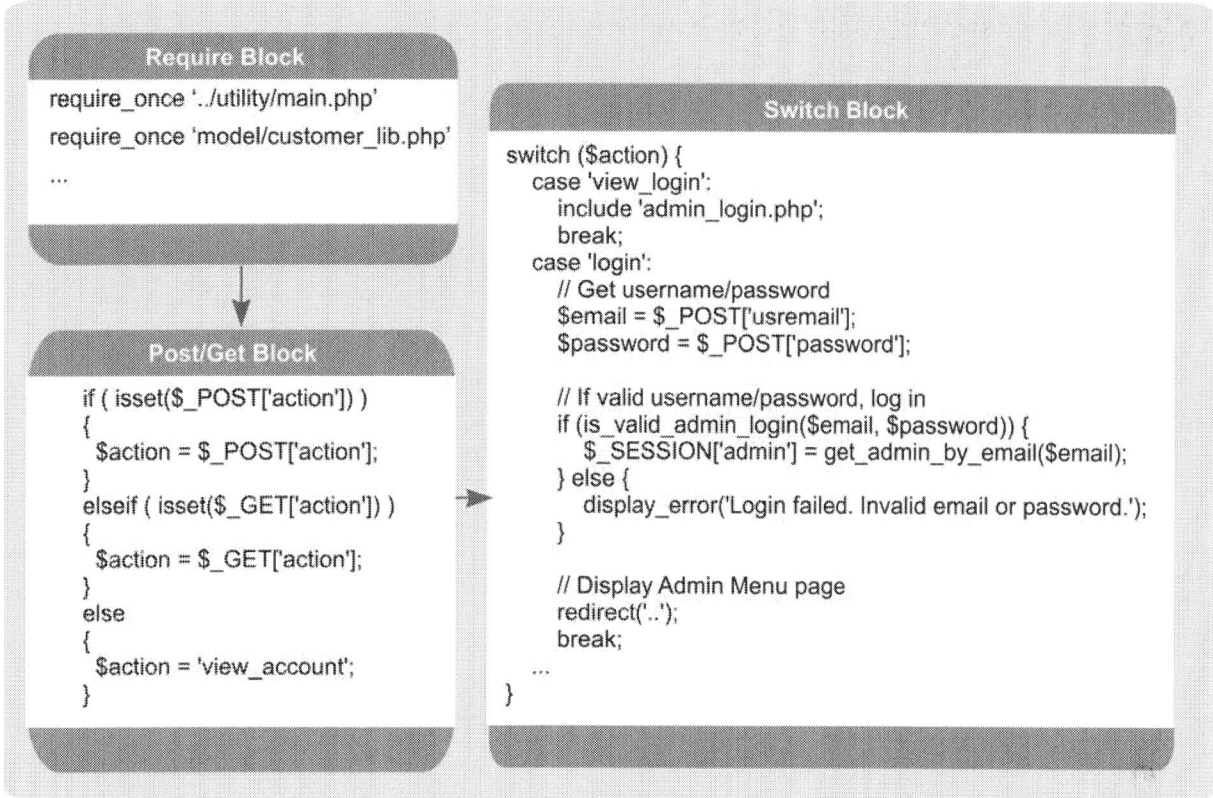

Figure 6-5

As the illustration depicts, every controller file has three blocks: Require, Post/Get, and Switch.

The Require block includes several files from the subordinate directories to perform a job. For example, every controller file includes Main.php file. This file is responsible to prepare the environment by setting some global variables and database connection.

The second block is a conditional block which evaluates whether the received request is either POST or GET. A request is sent to the controller through a parameter defined as 'action' and holds a value which indicates which action to perform. The block also has a default ELSE statement which executes if the request is neither POST nor GET.

The final block evaluates the received request using several Case statements sorted under the main Switch statement. Each case is assessed based on the received request stored in a variable $action. The Switch statement in php is similar to the one you saw in Javascript section 4.12. When a case match is found, statements under that case are executed. Just like the second block, this one also has a default case that executes when no case is satisfied. You'll go through almost all the controller files in this project individually while performing a particular task in subsequent sections.

6.7.4 Database Structure

To accomplish the above tasks, you need to define the following tables in the MySQL database to store information. You'll be guided on how to create these tables in the TESTDB database that you created in Handling Databases (section 5.4).

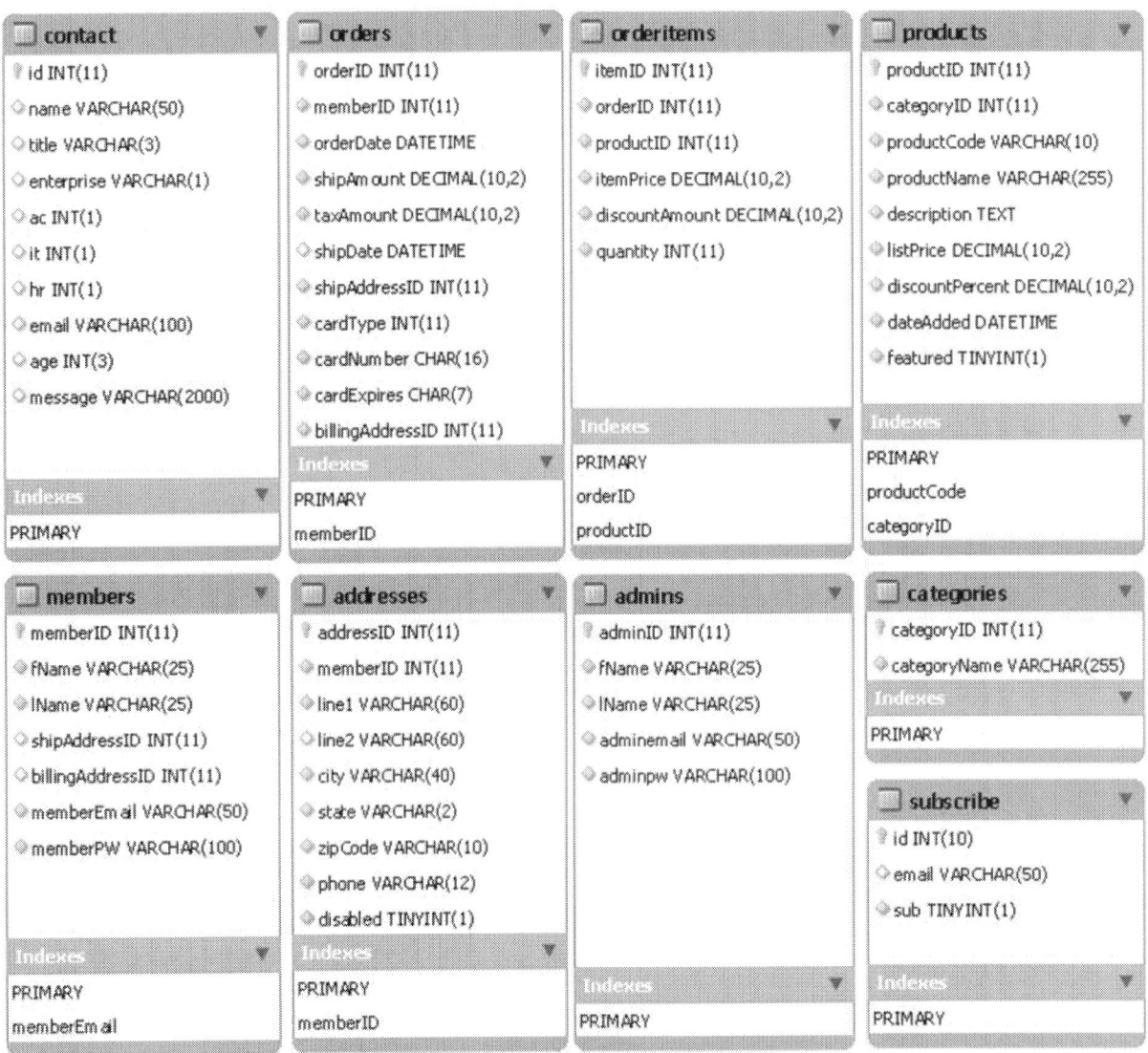

Figure 6-6

6.8 Task 1 - Contact Form

You did some work in the contact page (section 5.12 - Dealing with Forms) where you took users' comments and stored them in the MySQL database through a PHP script. Let's take a step forward and enhance that form by adding some more input elements (radio, checkbox etc.) and incorporate website theme to give it a consistent look as shown below.

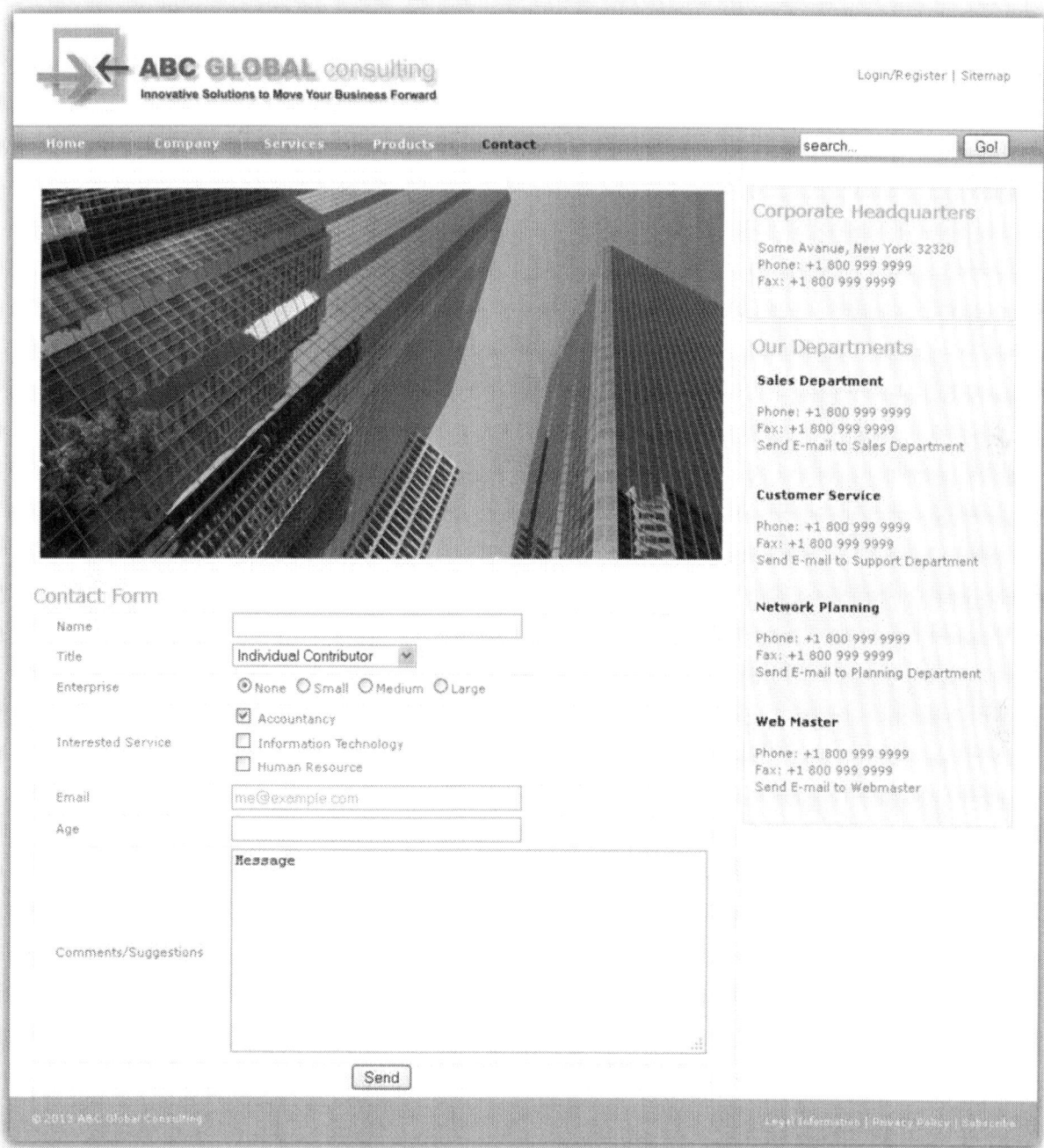

Figure 6-7

Do It Yourself

Perform the following steps to create this page.

Step-1 Create Database Table

Since we're adding new input elements to get more information from the visitor, we need to drop and re-create the Contact table in the TESTDB database. Note that we created this table earlier in section 5.6 for initial testing.

1. Click **Start | All Programs | MySQL | MySQL Server 5.5** and select **MySQL 5.5 Command Line Client**.
2. Enter **gemini** in the password. Enter your own password if you set a different one.
3. On mysql prompt, type **use testdb** and hit Enter.
4. Type **source c:\bookcode\project\contact.sql** and hit Enter. The script, contact.sql, removes and re-creates the Contact table. (For Task3 you'll type *source c:\bookcode\project\db.txt* to create all tables).
5. Type **desc contact** and hit Enter to see structure of the new table. You can see that the first column, ID, is set as the primary key and given the attribute of auto increment. With this attribute set, you do not need to provide a value for this column while saving a record, as you did in the form example earlier. We also added some more columns (title, enterprise, ac, it, and hr) to store additional information. (For Task3 type **show tables** to see all the tables created through db.txt file).

Step-2 Create Header, Navigation, Contact Form & Footer

1. Open Notepad and enter the html code mentioned in table 9.9 below. You can paste this code from contact.html located in the source folder.
2. Save this new file as **contact.html** in the site folder.
3. Open style.css file and copy rules from All_styles.css mentioned in the CSS Code section below.
4. Open your browser and type **http://localhost/abcglobal/contact.html** in the address bar and hit Enter. You'll see the complete web page illustrated in the above figure without the aside section that you'll create next.
5. From the source folder copy and paste **contact.php** and **success.html** files in the site folder.

Following is the code from the two files along with explanation.

Line	HTML Code - Contact Form
1	`<!DOCTYPE html>`
2	`<html>`
3	...
4	`<nav>`
5	`<ul>`
6	...
7	`<li><a href="" class="current">Contact</a></li>`
8	`</ul>`
9	...

Line	HTML Code - Contact Form (Continued)
10	`<section class="content">`
11	`<article>`
12	`<figure class="static">`
13	`<img src="images/office.jpg" alt="office"/>`
14	`</figure>`
15	`<hgroup>`
16	`<h2>Contact Form</h2>`
17	`</hgroup>`
18	`<form action="contact.php" method="POST" id="insert">`
19	`<table id="contact">`
20	`<tr>`
21	`<td>Name</td>`
22	`<td><input type="text" size=40 name="s_Name" required="vital"></td>`
23	`</tr>`
24	`<tr>`
25	`<td>Title</td>`
26	`<td>`
27	`<select name="s_Title">`
28	`<option selected="selected" value="ind">Individual Contributor</option>`
29	`<option value="ceo">CEO/Managing Director</option>`
30	`<option value="cfo">CFO/Finance Director</option>`
31	`<option value="cio">IT Director</option>`
32	`<option value="vp">Vice President</option>`
33	`<option value="dir">Director</option>`
34	`<option value="mgr">Manager</option>`
35	`</select>`
36	`</td>`
37	`</tr>`
38	`<tr>`
39	`<td>Enterprise</td>`
40	`<td>`
41	`<input type="radio" name="s_Enterprise" value="N" checked="checked"/>None`
42	`<input type="radio" name="s_Enterprise" value="S"/>Small`
43	`<input type="radio" name="s_Enterprise" value="M"/>Medium`
44	`<input type="radio" name="s_Enterprise" value="L"/>Large`
45	`</td>`
46	`</tr>`
47	`<tr>`
48	`<td>Interested Service</td>`
49	`<td>`
50	`<input type="checkbox" name="ac" checked="checked" /> Accountancy`
51	` `
52	`<input type="checkbox" name="it" /> Information Technology`
53	` `
54	`<input type="checkbox" name="hr" /> Human Resource`
55	`</td>`
56	`</tr>`

Line	HTML Code - Contact Form (Continued)

```
57          <tr>
58           <td>Email</td>
59           <td><input type="email" size=40 name="s_Email" required="vital"
60                   placeholder="me@example.com"/></td>
61          </tr>
62          <tr>
63           <td>Age</td>
64           <td><input type="text" size=40 name="n_Age"></td>
65          </tr>
66          <tr>
67           <td>Comments/Suggestions</td>
68           <td><textarea  name="s_Message" cols=52 rows=10>Message</textarea></td>
69          </tr>
70          <tr>
71           <td colspan=2 id="sub"><input type="submit" name="submit" value="Send" ></td>
72          </tr>
73          </table>
74        </form>
75      </article>
76     </section>
77     <footer>
        ...
78     </footer>
79     </div><!-- .wrapper -->
80    </body>
81   </html>
```

CSS Code - Contact Form	

```
Rule 62     #contact{
            border:1px solid #eeeeee;
            border-collapse:collapse;
            margin: 0 auto;}


Rule 63     #contact td{
            border-bottom: 1px solid #eeeeee;
            padding: 0 5px 5px 20px;}


Rule 36     #sub{ text-align:center;}
```

Explanation

The html code generates the contact form while the css code styles it in a desired format. We added an image office.jpg in the <figure> section (line 13) and provided an appropriate heading on top of the form (line 16). Next we created a form with the POST method (line 18-74). The form, when submitted, calls contact.php to store information in the Contact database table. The form incorporates new fields from the contact table. These fields - Title, Enterprise, and Interested Service - are sorted in an html <table> element bearing id "contact" (line 19-73). This id is referenced in Rule 62 and 63 to style the <table> and its child <td> elements. The <table> element has 8 rows and 2 columns.

The first new field "Title" is a drop-down list named "s_Title" with some pre-defined values (line 24-37). It is defined using the <select> html element and holds six designations. A visitor can optionally select one of these values to represent him/her.

The second new field is labeled "Enterprise" (line 38-46). It is named "s_Enterprise" and demonstrates how a radio input element could be used to receive a single value in a web page. It presents four options (None, Small, Medium, and Large) to the visitor to select a single value from.

The final new field "Interested Service" (line 47-56) allows visitor to select one or more options from the provided values. We used three checkbox input elements with different names. Each checkbox corresponds to a column in the Contact database table. The checked attribute of the first checkbox is turned on and that's why it contains a small checked icon when the page is run.

The last row of the form (line 70-72) carries a button labeled "send". When clicked, this button calls contact.php file (listed below) to process the form. The last <td> element, identified by the id "sub" (line 71), contains an attribute called colspan. The colspan attribute defines the number of columns a cell should span. The value of this attribute is set to 2 because we have two columns in the <table> element. This attribute is set to display the submit button in the center of the table and which is done through Rule-36. For further details see section 5.12 - Dealing with Forms.

Line	PHP Code (Contact.php)
1	`<?php`
2	`$con = mysql_connect("localhost","root","gemini");`
3	`if (!$con)`
4	`{`
5	`die('Could not connect: ' . mysql_error($con));`
6	`}`
7	`mysql_select_db("testdb", $con);`
8	`$s_Name = $_POST['s_Name'];`
9	`$s_Title = $_POST['s_Title'];`
10	`$s_Enterprise = $_POST['s_Enterprise'];`
11	`if (isset($_POST['ac'])) {`
12	`$n_Ac = 1;`
13	`}`
14	`else {`
15	`$n_Ac = 0;`
16	`}`
17	`if (isset($_POST['it'])) {`
18	`$n_It = 1;`
19	`}`
20	`else {`
21	`$n_It = 0;`
22	`}`
23	`if (isset($_POST['hr'])) {`
24	`$n_Hr = 1;`
25	`}`
26	`else {`
27	`$n_Hr = 0;`
28	`}`
29	`$s_Email = $_POST['s_Email'];`
30	`$n_Age = (is_numeric($_POST['n_Age']) ? (int)$_POST['n_Age'] : 0);`
31	`$s_Message = $_POST['s_Message'];`
32	`$sql="INSERT INTO Contact (name,title,enterprise,ac,it,hr,email,age,message) VALUES`
33	`('$s_Name','$s_Title','$s_Enterprise','$n_Ac','$n_It','$n_Hr','$s_Email',$n_Age,'$s_Message')";`
34	`if (!mysql_query($sql,$con))`
35	`{`
36	`die('Error: ' . mysql_error($con));`
37	`}`
38	`header('Location: ' . 'success.html');`
39	`mysql_close($con);`
40	`?>`

Explanation

When you press the *send* button, information entered in the form elements is passed to "contact.php" file (html line 18). This file initiates connection with the database, inserts data in the contact table and displays a message through success.html page.

You already went through most of this stuff in section 5.12 - Dealing with Forms. Here, we will discuss the untouched areas.

We used checkbox input element to present multiple options to the visitor. Now it's up to the visitor to select any number of options from none to all or a mix of them. To evaluate the selections, we used isset() function. The isset() PHP function determines whether a certain variable has already been declared. It returns a Boolean value true if the variable has already been set, or false otherwise. In the first IF condition (line 11) we checked whether the built-in $_POST array carries the value 'ac' (this value is passed to this script by the html form when the send button is pressed). If so, the variable $n_Ac is assigned the value 1 indicating the visitor has selected the Accountancy option. If the 'ac' value is not set in $_POST, a value of 0 is moved to the $n_Ac variable. The same process is repeated for the other two options with different variables.

Note that this time the INSERT SQL statement doesn't have the ID column because we set this column's attribute to generate automatically while creating the table.

Finally, a message is displayed through the header() PHP function by calling success.html page (line 38). Success.html is a simple html page that displays a successful submission message of form and doesn't contain any technical stuff to discuss.

Step-3 Create Aside Sections

The aside section in the Contact page shows company address, phone numbers, e-mail addresses and departmental contact details. Add the following code to relevant files. The html code should sit after the </section> tag.

Line	HTML Code
1	`<aside>`
2	`<section class="contact">`
3	`<h2>Corporate Headquarters</h2>`
4	`<p>Some Avanue, New York 32320 `
5	`Phone: +1 800 999 9999 `
6	`Fax:  +1 800 999 9999 `
7	` `
8	`</p>`
9	`</section>`
10	`<section class="contact">`
11	`<h2>Our Departments</h2>`
12	`<h4>Sales Department</h4>`
13	`<p>Phone: +1 800 999 9999 `
14	`Fax:  +1 800 999 9999 `
15	`<a href="mailto:sales@abcglobal.com?Subject=Inquiry%20Ticket">Send E-mail to Sales Department</a>  `
16	`</p>`
17	`<h4>Customer Service</h4>`
18	`<p>Phone: +1 800 999 9999 `
19	`Fax:  +1 800 999 9999 `
20	`<a href="mailto:customer@abcglobal.com?Subject=Support%20Ticket">Send E-mail to Support Department</a>  `
21	`</p>`
22	`<h4>Network Planning</h4>`
23	`<p>Phone: +1 800 999 9999 `
24	`Fax:  +1 800 999 9999 `
25	`<a href="mailto:planning@abcglobal.com?Subject=Inquiry%20Ticket">Send E-mail to Planning Department</a>  `
26	`</p>`
27	`<h4>Web Master</h4>`
28	`<p>Phone: +1 800 999 9999 `
29	`Fax:  +1 800 999 9999 `
30	`<a href="mailto:webmaster@abcglobal.com?Subject=Website Inquiry%20Ticket">Send E-mail to Webmaster</a>  `
31	`</p>`
32	`</section>`
33	`</aside>`

CSS Code

Rule 64	`aside section.contact {`	Rule 65	`aside section.contact p {`
	`margin-top: 2px;`		`padding: 0 0 0 10px;`
	`border: 1px solid #f2e19f;`		`background-color: #fbf6e2;`
	`padding: 0;`		`line-height: 15px;}`
	`background-color: #fbf6e2;}`		

```
Rule 66    h4 {
           margin: 0px 0px 5px 10px;
           color: #000000;}
```

Output & Explanation

Corporate Headquarters

Some Avanue, New York 32320
Phone: +1 800 999 9999
Fax: +1 800 999 9999

Our Departments

Sales Department

Phone: +1 800 999 9999
Fax: +1 800 999 9999
Send E-mail to Sales Department

Customer Service

Phone: +1 800 999 9999
Fax: +1 800 999 9999
Send E-mail to Support Department

Network Planning

Phone: +1 800 999 9999
Fax: +1 800 999 9999
Send E-mail to Planning Department

Web Master

Phone: +1 800 999 9999
Fax: +1 800 999 9999
Send E-mail to Webmaster

The aside area has two sections. Both these sections use the same "contact" class referenced in Rule 64 and 65. The first section displays contact details for the company's headquarters whereas the second section lists contact information about different departments in the company.

We also added e-mail links that, when clicked, invoke email client such as Microsoft Outlook with a new message window and a default subject line. See section 2.14 - Email Links in HTML for further reading.

CSS rules 64 and 65 are not different from those we have already seen in the previous exercises. Rule 66 applies to <h4> elements that we used in the html code to display department names (Sales, Customer Service etc.).

The page is ready to launch.

1. Type **http://localhost/abcglobal/contact.html** in the browser and hit Enter. The page illustrated in Figure 6-7 should appear.

2. Enter and select values from the provided options and click the **Send** button. If everything went well, you'll see success.html page with the message "**Thank you for contacting us - We have received your message**".

3. Use the statement **select * from contact** to check this record on MySQL command line.

6.9 Task 2 - Newsletter Subscription

In this section, you'll learn how subscription application works in a website. Here, a visitor will sign up for a subscription on the site - to receive newsletters from the company - and will receive a confirmation e-mail.

Step-1 Create Table in MySQL Database

In this part you'll use MySQL Workbench to create a new table named *Subscribe* to hold data of users who request subscription. The Subscribe table has three data columns: ID, Email, and Sub (see the following figure). The ID column is the primary key and uses an integer format that is automatically incremented. The Email column has a text format and is intended to hold the subscribers e-mail addresses. The final column, Sub, is a Boolean field, intended to note whether a user is currently subscribed or not: 1 indicates subscribed, 0 for unsubscribed. Unsubscribed records are usually deleted but you may keep users' e-mail addresses on file this way in case your site offers other e-mail opportunities other than just the newsletter.

1. Click **Start | Program Group | MySQL | MySQL Workbench**
2. On the main menu, select **Database** and then **Query Database**
3. In *Connect to Database* dialog, select **Local instance MySQL55** from the *Stored Connection* and click **OK**. If asked, enter *gemini* in the password box.
4. To your left, right click **TESTDB** under schemas pane and select **Set as Default Schema**.
5. On the toolbar, click the icon **Create a new table**.
6. In *Table Name* type **Subscribe**.
7. Double click the first row under the Column Name section and type **id**. Set Datatype to **INT(10)**, put checks in PK (primary key), NN (not null), and AI (auto-increment)
8. Double click subsequent blank rows to add other columns as shown in the figure below.
9. After completion, click the **Apply** button to create the table.
10. Click **Apply** in the review dialog box. A message *SQL script was successfully applied to the database* should appear. Click **Finish** to dismiss this window.

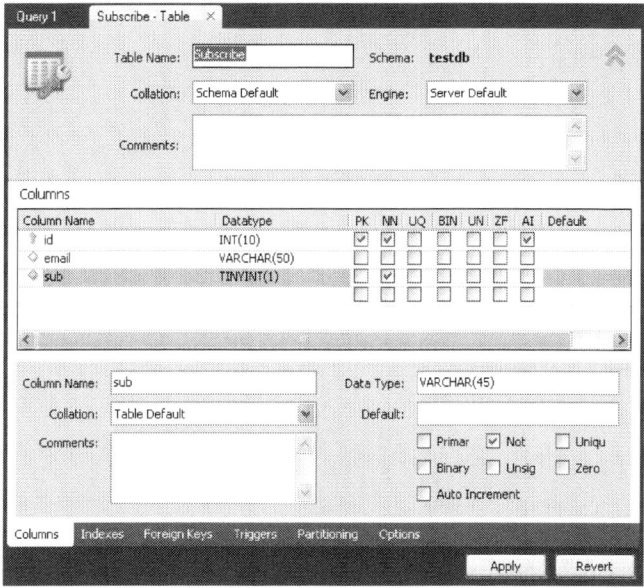

Figure 6-8

Step-2 Copy PHP Files

1. From project source folder copy *subscribe.php* and *confirm_subscribe.php* and paste them into the site folder.

2. From project source copy the *view* folder under the site folder (abcglobal\view).

The code presented below already exist in relevant files, therefore nothing is to be done on your part. The html code exists in index.html page and corresponding rules (43 and 44) have already been incorporated in styles.css and discussed while creating the Home page.

Line	HTML Code
1	`<section class="newsletter">`
2	`<form id="letter" action="`**`subscribe.php`**`" method="post">`
3	`<label><b>Subscribe to our newsletter</b></label> `
4	`<label>E-mail Address: `
5	`<input type="email" name="subemail" maxlength="35" size="35" required="vital"` `placeholder="me@example.com"/></label> `
6	`<p><input type="image" alt="Subscribe" class="button" src="images/subscribe.png"></p>`
7	`</form>`
8	`</section>`

Line	PHP Code - Subscribe.php
1	`<?php`
2	`$con = mysql_connect("localhost","root","gemini");`
3	`if (!$con)`
4	`{`
5	`  die('Could not connect: ' . mysql_error($con));`
6	`}`
7	`mysql_select_db("testdb", $con);`
8	`$s_Email = $_POST['subemail'];`
9	`$sql="INSERT INTO Subscribe (email,sub) VALUES ('$s_Email', 1)";`
10	`if (!mysql_query($sql,$con))`
11	`{`
12	`  die('Error: ' . mysql_error($con));`
13	`}`
14	`mysql_close($con);`
	`// Send a confirmation e-mail`
15	`require_once "Mail.php";`
16	`$from = "Administrator <admin@abc.com>";`
17	`$to = $_POST['subemail'];`
18	`$subject = "Newsletter Subscription Confirmation";`
19	`$body = "Hi,\n\nThis message is sent to you from ABC Global Consulting as a confirmation to your newsletter subscription request.";`
20	`$host = "localhost";  // Enter SMTP provided by your ISP like $host = "smtp.xyz.net";`
21	`$headers = array ('From' => $from, 'To' => $to, 'Subject' => $subject);`
22	`$smtp = Mail::factory('smtp', array ('host' => $host, 'port' => 25));`
23	`$mail = $smtp->send($to, $headers, $body);`
24	`if (PEAR::isError($mail))`
25	`{`
26	`  echo("<p>" . $mail->getMessage() . "</p>");`

Line	PHP Code - Subscribe.php
27	}
28	else
29	{
30	include 'confirm_subscribe.php';
31	}
32	?>

PHP Code Explanation

Code 1-14 establishes connection with the TESTDB database and inserts email address of the subscriber along with a constant value of 1 (which stands for subscribe) in the Subscribe table.

Code 15-31 sends a confirmation e-mail to the subscriber. This process was described in section 5.16 Step # 5 - Create PHP Script to Send Mail.

Code 30 calls another PHP file named confirm_subscribe (listed below) if the e-mail is sent successfully. See section 5.15 *Include and Require Statements* for details.

Line	PHP Code - Confirm_Subscribe.php
1	<?php include **'view/header_member.php'**; ?>
2	<section class="content">
3	<article>
4	<hgroup>
5	<h2>Thank you for subscribing to our newsletter</h2>
6	</hgroup>
7	<p>A confirmation of your subscription has been sent to your email address **<?php echo $to ; ?>**, with instructions for unsubscribing.</p>
8	</article>
9	</section>
10	<?php include **'view/footer.php'**; ?>

Explanation

This script is called when the previous script Subscribe.php executes successfully.

Line number 1 passes control to header_member.php file (listed below) in the View folder to display page headers. Note that this line is terminated with '?>' indicating that the PHP code ends here.

Code 2-9 comprises html elements that you've been working with in the static part of this project. These elements carry successful subscription message. A PHP code is embedded in line 7 that concatenates e-mail of the subscriber, stored in the variable $to, with the message.

Code 10 calls footer.php (listed below) in the View folder to add page footer.

Line	PHP Code - Header_Member.php
1	`<!DOCTYPE html>`
2	`<html>`
	`<!-- the head section -->`
3	`<head>`
4	`<title>ABC Global Consulting</title>`
5	`<link rel="stylesheet" type="text/css" href="`**`<?php echo $app_path ?>`**`style.css" />`
6	`<!--[if lt IE 9]>`
7	`<script src="http://html5shiv.googlecode.com/svn/trunk/html5.js"></script>`
8	`<![endif]-->`
9	`</head>`
	`<!-- the body section -->`
10	`<body>`
11	`<div class="wrapper">`
12	`<header>`
13	`<h1>ABC Global Consulting</h1>`
14	`<?php`
	`// Check if member is logged in and display login status`
15	`$account_url = $app_path . 'member';  // /abcglobal/member`
16	`$logout_url = $account_url . '?action=logout'; // /abcglobal/member?action=logout`
17	`if (`**`isset($_SESSION['user'])`**`) :`
18	`?>`
19	`<div id="headlinks">`
20	`<p>`
21	`<b><?php echo 'Hi, ' .` **`$_SESSION['user'][3]`** `. ' ' .` **`$_SESSION['user'][4]`** `.'!'; ?></b>`
	`  <a href="`**`<?php echo $logout_url; ?>`**`">Logout</a>	<a href="">Sitemap</a>`
22	`</p>`
23	`</div>`
24	`<?php else: ?>`
25	`<div id="headlinks">`
26	`<p><a href="`**`<?php echo $account_url; ?>`**`">Login/Register</a>	<a href="">Sitemap</a></p>`
27	`</div>`
28	`<?php endif; ?>`
29	`<nav>`
30	`<ul>`
31	`<li><a href="<?php echo $app_path ?>index.html">Home</a></li>`
32	`<li><a href="<?php echo $app_path ?>company.html">Company</a></li>`
33	`<li><a href="<?php echo $app_path ?>services.html">Services</a></li>`
34	`<li><a href="<?php echo $app_path ?>products.php">Products</a></li>`
35	`<li><a href="<?php echo $app_path ?>contact.html">Contact</a></li>`
36	`</ul>`
37	`<script type="text/javascript">`
	`//Enter domain of site to search.`
38	`var domainroot="www.maqcon.com"`
39	`function Gsitesearch(curobj){`
40	`curobj.q.value="site:"+domainroot+" "+curobj.qfront.value`
41	`}`
42	`</script>`
43	`<form id="search" action="http://www.google.com/search" method="get"`
	`onSubmit="Gsitesearch(this)">`
44	`<input name="q" type="hidden" />`
45	`<input name="qfront" type="search" value="search..."/> <input type="submit" value="Go!" />`
46	`</form>`
47	`</nav>`
48	`</header>`

Explanation

This file is basically connected to E-commerce module. But due to PHP inclusion, we are going to discuss it here. Note that we have two different PHP header files in the View folder one each for members and administrators.

Line 5 has a PHP code that echoes a variable $app_path. This variable is basically assigned in Main.php file in the Utility folder and holds the path that tells PHP where to look for the specified files. Initially, it holds the application root path - in our case it is /abcglobal/. Since this variable is not defined in this module, a notice entry "*Undefined variable: app_path*" will be logged in PHP log file. Because the file style.css is lying in the root folder, it will be executed to style the web page. You'll learn about this variable in a subsequent section where we'll discuss Main.php file - List II.

Code 12-24 checks if a member is logged in and displays the login status.

Line 15 assigns /abcglobal/member to a variable $account_url. This value is used in a link on line 26 behind the label "Login/Register" and calls index.php in the member folder to present the login form to the user. The variable $app_path is initialized in Main.php.

Line 16 appends a parameter "action" with a value "logout" to the application path before assigning it to the variable $logout_url. This variable is used on line 21.

Line 17 checks whether a user session exist. If true, line 19-23 are executed to display a greeting text with the name of the logged in user using values in the session variable. It also creates a link using the $logout_url variable value that holds the path /abcglobal/member?action=logout. The url link is echoed using the link name Logout. If you hover over this link, it will display the value http://localhost/abcglobal/member?action=logout in the status bar. Clicking this link calls index.php file in the member folder where user session is unset.

Code 31-35 creates main navigation links using the application path variable. Rest of the code till the </header> tag has already been discussed (see Table 6-1).

Don't worry if you couldn't understand the code here; just move on. Once you read files like Index.php and Main.php, you'll start getting the concept more easily. For the time being, just remember that these php files create header, footer, and sidebar in dynamic web pages in our project.

Line	PHP Code - Footer.php
1	`<footer>`
2	`<p id="copyright">&copy; <?php echo date("Y"); ?> ABC Global Consulting</p>`
3	`<p id="footlinks"><a href="">Legal Information</a>	<a href="">Privacy Policy</a> |` `<a href="index.html">Subscribe </a></p>`
4	`</footer>`
5	`</div><!-- .wrapper -->`
6	`</body>`
7	`</html>`

Explanation

This file displays the page footer. In static web pages we used a static value to show year in the copyright message. Here, we tried to show current date from the system. On line 2 we used PHP date() function which returns a string formatted as a date. By default, this function works with the current date and time. The capital 'Y' represents four digits year i.e. 2013 that we intend to display here.

Try this module:

1. Type **http://localhost/abcglobal/index.html** in the browser and hit Enter.
2. In the newsletter subscription box enter your e-mail address and click the **Subscribe** button.
3. The next page will acknowledge your subscription with the text "*Thank you for subscribing to our newsletter*". Check your e-mail account for a message similar to the one shown below.

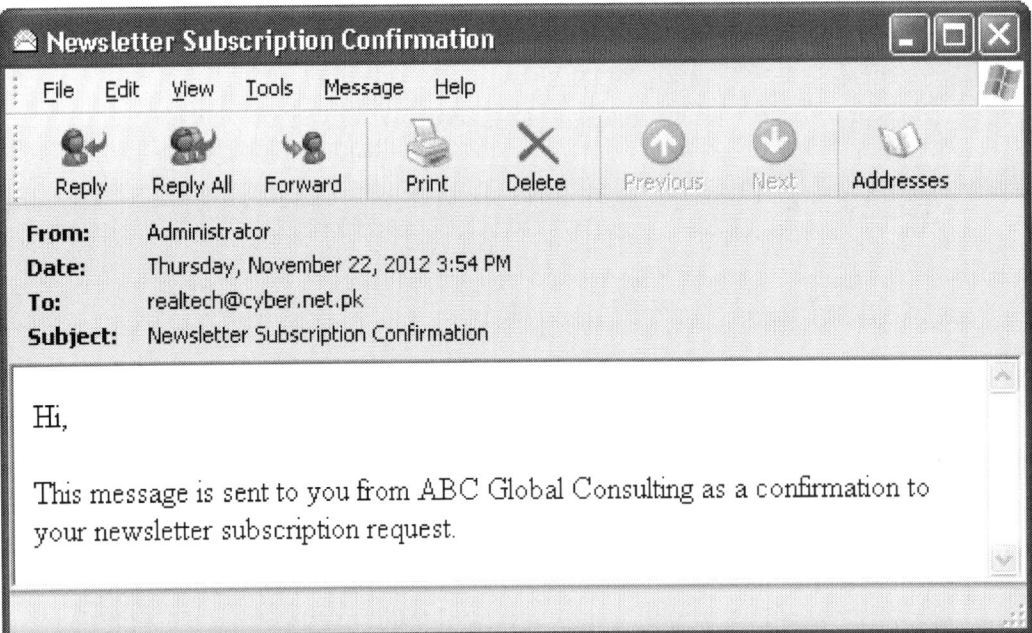

Figure 6-9

6.10 Manage Website Dynamically - Admin Modules

In this part, you'll create different modules to help administrators manage the site. Starting with the login module, you will create pages that will allow site admins to manage categories, products, orders, and their own accounts. Now that you've become familiar with the page creation procedure; from here onward, I'm going to explain code from relevant files with the process flow of individual module.

6.11 Task 3 - Admin Login Module

1. Copy all files and folders from the source project directory to the site folder (abcglobal) - overwriting all existing files and folders in the site directory.
2. Using the steps defined in Task1 (Step 1 - Create Database Table), run db.txt script.
3. Type **http://localhost/abcglobal/admin**. The admin login page, as shown in Figure 6-10, should come up.
4. Enter **admin@abc.com** in the E-mail Address box and **gemini** for the Password and click the **Login** button. This account was created through db.txt script. However, if there are no accounts in the Admins table, the application will present a form to create the initial admin account. The next page will show Admin menu with four links. Each link is a separate task that you'll evaluate in this part of the book. Also note that the main navigation bar is replaced by these admin task links and the Login link is changed to Logout with a welcome text displaying the name of the logged in admin user.
5. Click the Logout link. This is the whole process that will be explained in the next few page. Let's first take a look at how the admin login process flows.

Figure 6-10

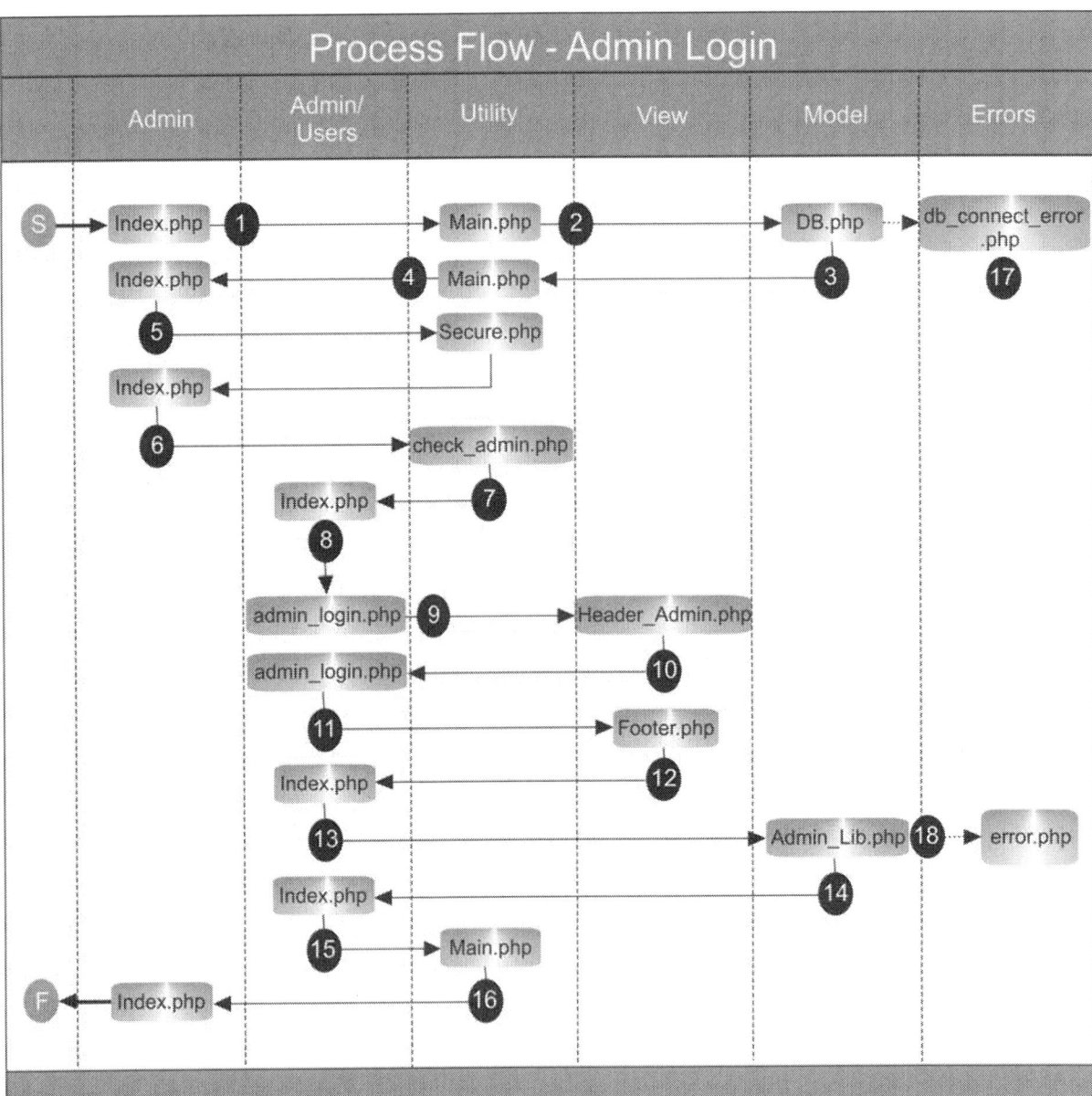

Diagram 1 - Admin Login Process

Diagram Explained

S. The process starts when you enter http://localhost/abcglobal/admin in the browser. This url calls index.php file under the Admin directory. Every folder in this PHP project has its own default index.php file that controls subsequent related processes.

1. The first line of index.php file (List-I next page) calls Main.php (List-II) in the Utility folder. This file sets some global variables, global functions, and calls the start_session function to start a session. It is included at the start of all index.php files.

2. Another file DB.php (List-III) is called from Main.php to initiate database connection. If the database is down or is inaccessible due to any reason, the file DB_Connect_Error.php (point 17 List-IV) is called which is located in the Errors folder to handle the situation.

3. If there are no database errors and the connection is established successfully, process flow returns to Main.php - the calling script.

4. Main.php returns the flow back to index.php (admin directory).

5. Index.php calls Secure.php (List-V) that makes a secure connection (https) and returns to Index.php.

6. Check_Admin.php (List-VI) is called to verify whether the administrator is logged in.

7. Since the administrator is not logged in, the flow transfers to the Users directory - a child directory under Admin. The default Index.php file (List-VII) in this directory is executed.

8. Admin_Login.php file (List-VIII) is invoked from the above Index.php file. This is the file that actually holds the login form for administrators.

9. Header_Admin.php file is called to display page headers.

10. Login form is displayed.

11. Page footer is displayed through Footer.php file.

12. Flow returns to Index.php file to continue the process.

13. User enters admin credentials in the login form and presses the login button. The file Admin_Lib.php (List-X) is called which contains various functions. Here, it is called to verify the provided credentials through a function called "is_valid_admin_login". If either the e-mail address or the password is incorrect, a message is displayed to the user through Error.php file (List-XI).

14. Control is returned to Index.php file.

15. At the end of the evaluated case statement (case 'login' - List IX) in Index.php file, a function named redirect() in Main.php file is called passing a parameter ('..').

16. The redirect function moves the flow back to the root Index.php file which in turn displays the Admin menu.

F. The process finishes here.

This is the simplest explanation of the admin login process. However, there is some iteration that takes place during the execution. Whenever the controller file (Index.php) is called it executes from the start and calls the required files again. For example, secure.php is displayed only once in the above diagram, however, it is called more than once to check the secured connection. Once a secured connection is established, the code within the file is bypassed. All the files mentioned in the above process are listed and explained ahead to make things more clear.

List I - Index.php - Admin

```php
1    <?php
2      require_once('../utility/main.php');          List II→
3      require_once('utility/secure.php');           List V→
4      require_once('utility/check_admin.php');      List VI→
5    ?>
6    <?php include 'view/header_admin.php'; ?>
7    <section class="content">
8     <article>
9      <h2>Admin Menu</h1>
10     <ul>
11      <p><li><a href="category">Category Manager</a></li></p>
12      <p><li><a href="product">Product Manager</a></li></p>
13      <p><li><a href="orders">Order Manager</a></li></p>
14      <p><li><a href="users">Account Manager</a></li></p>
15     </ul>
16    </article>
17   </section>
18   <?php   include 'view/footer.php'; ?>
```

Explanation

The Index.php file is also called the controller file because it controls the execution of a particular process. It comprises both PHP and HTML code to process and display web pages. Under the Admin directory, this file initiates the admin login process by calling some files from the Utility directory (line # 2, 3, and 4). The Utility directory lies under the root (ABCGLOBAL). The files under this directory perform some basic functions and are discussed in subsequent sections after this. The require_once function is used to forward request to relevant files. The double dot (..) prefix is pointing to the parent directory i.e. the application root directory (ABCGLOBAL in the current scenario, because the Utility is a child directory to ABCGLOBAL). A single dot represents current directory.

Line # 6 uses header_admin.php in the View directory to set page headings. This file is similar to header_member.php - that we discussed earlier in the Newsletter Subscription module - with some minor changes to display appropriate navigation bar to site administrators.

Line 7-17 lists the same stuff you're already acquainted with. These lines display the Admin Menu in the main content section using an unordered list of links. These options help administrator manage different segments of the website. For example, the Category Manager option lets him/her add, modify, or remove product categories. You will read about all these options later on.

Finally, on line # 18 the file Footer.php (also under the View directory) is called to show page footer. This one too was discussed in the Newsletter module.

Note that line 6 through 18 are executed only when the user is authenticated as an administrator. This stage is indicated in point 16 in the process flow diagram. If at any stage the authentication process fails, the procedure is repeated automatically unless the user provides valid credentials. Once the user successfully logs into the admin interface, he is provided with the above four options to perform administrative tasks.

List II - Main.php - Utility

```php
1   <?php
2   // Get the document root
3   $doc_root = $_SERVER['DOCUMENT_ROOT'];
4   // Get the application path
5   $uri = $_SERVER['REQUEST_URI'];
6   $dirs = explode('/', $uri);
7   $app_path = '/' . $dirs[1] . '/'; //Only ABCGLOBAL directory
8   // Set the include path
9   set_include_path($doc_root . $app_path .PATH_SEPARATOR. 'c:\php\pear');
10  // Get common code
11  require_once('utility/tags.php');
12  require_once('model/db.php');    List III →
13  // Function to handle database errors
14  function display_db_error($error_message) {
15    global $app_path;
16    include 'errors/db_connect_error.php';   List IV →
17    exit;
18  }
19  // Function to handle general errors (With Admin headers)
20  function display_error($error_message) {
21    global $app_path;
22    include 'errors/error.php';    List XI →
23    exit;
24  }
25  // Function to handle general errors (With Members headers)
26  function member_error($error_message) {
27    global $app_path;
28    include 'errors/member_error.php';
29    exit;
30  }
31  // Redirect Function
32  function redirect($url) {
33    session_write_close();
34    header("Location: " . $url);
35    exit;
36  }
37  // Start session to store user and cart data
38  session_start();
39  ?>
```

Forward vs Redirect

*In PHP, you call one file from another either through **include** or **require** functions; as done in List I. This is called request forwarding. In this case, all processing takes place on the server and there is only one round trip to the server. In PHP, another term **redirect** exist which is used instead of forwarding a request. A redirect should be used if you need to transfer control to a different domain or to achieve separation of tasks. For example, database update and data display can be separated by redirect. Do the PaymentProcess and then redirect to displayPaymentInfo. If the client refreshes the browser only the displayPaymentInfo will be done again and PaymenProcess will not be repeated. But if you use forward in this scenario, both PaymentProcess and displayPaymentInfo will be re-executed sequentially, which may result in incosistent data. For other than the above two scenarios, forwarding is efficient to use since it is faster than redirect. To redirect a request, you use the header() function as done in line 34. This function returns an HTTP response to the browser that contains a Location header. The header causes the browser to request the specified URL resulting in a second round trip to the server.*

Explanation

The purpose of this file is to set the include path, some global variables, global functions, and to start or resume a user session using the session_start() function. This file is included at the beginning of all the controller files (index.php).

Line # 3 stores the document root in a variable. $_SERVER is a super global array in PHP containing information such as headers, paths, and script locations. DOCUMENT_ROOT is a variable which points to the directory under which the current script is executing. For our project, the value "c:\inetpub\wwwroot" will be stored in the variable $doc_root because we are running our website under IIS. For Apache it would be "\htdocs".

Line # 5, 6, and 7 gets the name of the root directory in the application path. The variable $uri holds a value from REQUEST_URI. This is the value that usually appears in browser's address bar. For example, when you call the admin login form, the value of $uri would be "/ABCGLOBAL/admin/users/". The explode() function breaks a string into an array. On line # 6 the value of variable $uri is broken at the symbol "/". This creates an array that is stored in the variable $dirs like this:

> $dirs[1] = "ABCGLOBAL"
> $dirs[2] ="admin"
> $dirs[3]="users"

On line # 7, we stored the value of the first element i.e. ABCGLOBAL (after concatenating it with a preceding and following directory separating symbol "/") in a variable $app_path. The value of $app_path becomes "/ABCGLOBAL/" and is appended to $doc_root on line 9.

Line # 9 sets the include path. This path tells PHP where to look for the files specified in "include" and "require" functions. The resulting concatenated value is c:\inetpub\wwwroot/abcglobal/. We also added another path - 'c:\php\pear' - to include PEAR Mail.php package. Using this package automated emails carrying new passwords will be sent to members of the website (see Task 10). The *PATH_SEPARATOR* is used to separate the two paths. On deployment server, the second path would be added something like this:

> *set_include_path($doc_root . $app_path .PATH_SEPARATOR.* **'/home/abcglobal/php');**

If you receive a warning along with a fatal error mentioning that the process failed to open Mail.php file, indicates that either the Mail or the PEAR package or both of them are not installed on your hosted server. See section 6.25 - Website Deployment to learn how these packages are installed on host servers.

Tags.php on line # 11 is not applicable to this module. The file (discussed later) contains couple of functions to format text and to add HTML tags.

Line # 12 shifts control to DB.php in the Model directory to establish connection with the database. This file is also explained later.

Explanation (continued)

From line # 14-18 a function named display_db_error is defined to handle database errors. Whenever a database error occurs, this function is called by passing a message ($error_message) to it. This function makes the variable $app_path global so that it is accessible to other files. Then the function calls db_connect_error.php file under the Errors directory to post the message. Exit is used to terminate the current script.

The function display_errors (line # 20-24) is called to handle general errors. For example, when invalid login credentials are entered, this function calls error.php file to display appropriate message to the user. Note that this function is called from a file Error.php in the Errors directory and is specific to the Admin modules. For Member modules, another file Member_Error.php is created to display corresponding page headings while displaying error messages.

The last function, redirect() (line # 32-36), ends the current session and stores session data through session_write_close() built-in function and redirects the user to another location passed to it using the variable $url. For example, it is called by List IX - Line # 15 to invoke Admin/Index.php file to show the Admin menu after a successful login attempt.

The session_start() function creates a session or resumes the current one based on a session identifier passed via a GET or POST request, or passed via a cookie. The session_start() function prompts PHP to check for a session ID in the request and to create a new session ID and session cookie if one doesn't exit. See section 5.10 for details on PHP Sessions.

List III - DB.php - Model

```php
1    <?php
2    // Connect to the TESTDB database
3    $dsn = 'mysql:host=localhost;dbname=testdb';
4    $username = 'root';
5    $password = 'gemini';
6    $options = array(PDO::ATTR_ERRMODE => PDO::ERRMODE_EXCEPTION);
7    try
8    {
9      $db = new PDO($dsn, $username, $password, $options);
10   }
11   catch (PDOException $e)
12   {
13     $error_message = $e->getMessage();
14     include('errors/db_connect_error.php');
15     exit();
16   }
17   ?>
```

List IV - DB_Connect_Error.php - Errors

```php
<?php include 'view/header_admin.php'; ?>
<section class="content">
 <article>
   <h2>Database Error</h2>
   <p>The following error encountered while connecting to the database.</p>
   <p>Error message: <?php echo $error_message; ?></p>
 </article>
</section>
<?php include 'view/footer.php'; ?>
```

Explanation

The file DB.php is called to establish a connection with the TESTDB database. As we have already discussed most of the stuff presented in this file earlier, we will only look at the un-touched areas here.

On line # 6, we set error handling options for the PDO connection using the fourth argument ($options) to the PDO constructor. By default, PDO sets an error message that can be retrieved through PDO::errorInfo() and an SQLCODE that can be retrieved through PDO::errorCode() when any error occurs; to request this mode explicitly, we set PDO::ATTR_ERRMODE => PDO::ERRMODE_EXCEPTION to throw a PHP exception to handle the error that we did in the catch block (line 11-16).

PDO gives you the option of handling errors as warnings, errors, or exceptions. However, when you create a new PDO connection object, PDO always throws a PDOException object if an error occurs. If you do not catch the exception, PHP prints a backtrace of the error information which might expose your database connection credentials, including your id and password.

To catch a PDOException object and handle the associated error gracefully, we:
- Wrapped the call to the PDO constructor in a try block (line 7-10).
- Included a catch block that catches the PDOException object (line 11-16).
- Retrieved the error message associated with the error by invoking the Exception::getMessage() method on the PDOException object (line 13).
- Finally, called the .php file to display the error.

When any database error is encountered, the catch block activates and calls db_connect_error.php file (List IV) in the Errors directory to display the exact error message in a new page.

List V - Secure.php - Utility

```php
1    <?php
2        // Add https prefix for secure connection
3        if (!isset($_SERVER['HTTPS'])) {
4            $url = 'https://' . $_SERVER['HTTP_HOST'] . $_SERVER['REQUEST_URI'];
5            header("Location: " . $url);
6            exit();
7        }
8    ?>
```

Explanation

This file is called to add https prefix to urls to make connections secured.

Line # 3 checks if the sever is not already using a secured connection. If so, a variable ($url) is created to hold the address with the https prefix concatenated to it. In our scenario, the HTTP_HOST element holds the value "localhost" whereas REQUEST_URI carries the remaining requesting address such as "abcglobal/admin/index.php". After concatenation, the url becomes "localhost/abcglobal/admin/index.php". This url is then passed to the header() function. The header() function sends a raw HTTP header to a client. The values within the parenthesis specify the header string to send. This whole action calls Index.php again using a secured connection.

For further details, see section 6.2 - *Website Security*. Moreover, read the following articles to make a secured connection in IIS.

How To Set Up an HTTPS Service in IIS - http://support.microsoft.com/?id=324069
How to enable SSL in IIS - http://support.microsoft.com/?id=298805

List VI - Check_Admin.php - Utility

```php
1    <?php
2        // If administrator is not logged in, call index.php to show login form
3        if (!isset($_SESSION['admin'])) {
4            header('Location: ' . $app_path . 'admin/users/' );
5        }
6    ?>
```

Explanation

This file is called from the root Index.php file to check whether the array "admin" exist under the superglobal $_SESSION variable. This array is created in Index.php (List IX) under the Admin/Users folder. Initially, the admin session is not set so the code on line # 4 is executed and invokes Index.php file under Admin/Users directory to create one.

List VII - Index.php - Admin/Users

```php
1    <?php
2    require_once('../../utility/main.php');
3    require_once('utility/secure.php');
4    require_once('model/admin_lib.php');
     ...
5    else
6    {
7      $action = 'view_login';
8    }
9    switch ($action) {
10     case 'view_login':
11       include 'admin_login.php';
12       break;
     ...
13   ?>
```

Explanation

In this listing only the relevant code is shown to understand the current process flow. The remaining code will be discussed as and when needed. This controller file exists in the Users child directory under Admin and evaluates which interface is to be provided based on various conditions sorted under the Switch statement. For example, in the current scenario a user is trying to login to the administrative interface so the first case in the Switch statement 'view_login' is evaluated and processed.

Line # 4 calls admin_lib.php file under the Model directory. This file contains some functions to validate administrative credentials and is described in detail in a subsequent listings.

The code in the else block (line 5-8) is executed first to present the login form using admin_login.php file located in the same Users directory. The break statement is used to terminate further processing of the script.

List VIII - Admin_Login.php - Admin/Users

```
1     <?php include 'view/header_admin.php'; ?>
2      <section class="content">
3       <section class="signin">
4         <h2>Admin Login</h2>
5         <form action="index.php" method="post" id="login_form">
6          <input type="hidden" name="action" value="login" />
7          <label>E-mail Address:<br>
8          <input type="email" name="usremail" maxlength="35" size="35" required="vital" autofocus
                                      placeholder="me@example.com"/></label><br>
9          <label>Password:<br>
10         <input type="password" name="password" required="vital"/></label>
11         <p><input type="image" alt="Login" src="<?php echo $app_path;?>images/login.png"></p>
12        </form>
13       </section>
14      </section>
15    <?php include 'view/footer.php'; ?>
```

Explanation

This is the file that actually presents the login form. Once again, we used PHP and HTML code combination to create the admin login page. It creates the web page by first including the header_admin.php file (line # 1). Next, it defines the login form in the content section (lines 5-12) using four HTML input elements - hidden, email, password, and image - in the signin class section. The form is named "login_form" and calls Index.php file in the same Users directory using the post method.

On line # 6 a hidden input element is used. Hidden fields are text fields that are not displayed on the web page. This type of field allows you to add hard-coded values to a form. In addition, programmers often use hidden fields to pass data from one web page to another as is done here. When the form is posted (either by pressing the Enter key or by pressing the provided Login button), the value of this element (login) is passed to the called Index.php file.

The page footer is displayed using the code on line # 15. Footer.php is same for both admin and member interfaces. See Newsletter Subscription module for its code and explanation.

The login form is styled using rule # 67, 68, 69, and 70 duly numbered in style.css file.

List IX - Index.php - Admin/Users	Explanation

1 ...
 2 elseif (isset($_POST['action']) == 'login')
 3 {
 4    $action = 'login';
 5 }
  ...
 6 switch ($action) {
  ...
 7   case 'login':
     // Get username & password
 8     $email = $_POST['usremail'];
 9     $password = $_POST['password'];
     // If valid username/password, log in
 10   if (is_valid_admin_login($email, $password)) {
 11      $_SESSION['admin'] = get_admin_by_email($email);
 12   } else {
 13   display_error('Login failed. Invalid email or password.');
 14   }
     // Display Admin Menu page
 15   redirect('..');
 16   break;
	When the control is received again by Index.php file from the previous section, the elseif condition (line # 2) is evaluated and processed because the value of 'action' is 'login' passed on by the hidden element in the previous listing. This value is moved to the variable $action (line # 4) and is evaluated in the Switch statement (line # 7). E-mail and password of the administrator are retrieved from the calling script (Admin_Login.php) and stored in corresponding variables (line # 8 and 9). On line # 10 a function named is_valid_admin_login is called passing the two variables to validate the provided information. This function exists in admin_lib.php file which was included in the process on line 4 - List VII.

If the provided credentials are correct, another function named get_admin_by_email (line # 11) from the same file is called using the email id supplied by the administrator. This function fetches the complete record of the user. The record is then stored in an array named admin that is created under the $_SESSION global variable. The following behind the scene illustration presents this array and the corresponding values that it holds:

If the login information provided by the user is incorrect, line # 13 calls display_error function (List II - Line 20) passing the message *Login failed. Invalid email or password*. The function displays the message in a new page and terminates the script.

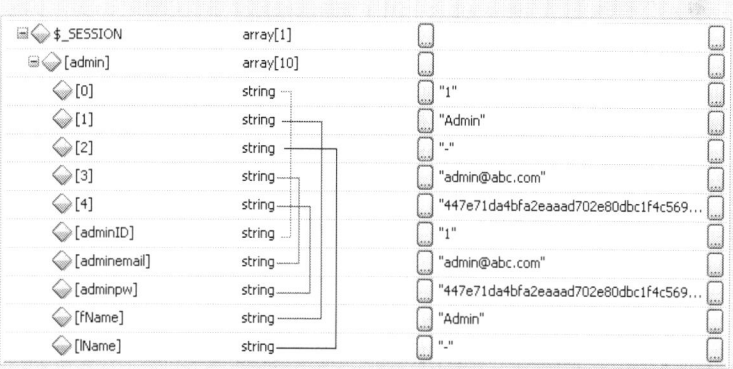

If the provided information is correct, line # 15 calls the redirect() function (List II - Line 32) and passes parent directory argument (i.e. Admin - Note that the current process is executing in the Users child directory which is under the parent Admin directory). This action invokes Admin/index.php file and displays the Admin menu.

List X - Admin_Lib.php - Model

```php
1    <?php
2    function is_valid_admin_login($email, $password) {
3      global $db;
4      $password = sha1($email . $password);
5      $query = 'SELECT * FROM admins WHERE adminemail = :email AND adminpw = :password';
6      $statement = $db->prepare($query);
7      $statement->bindValue(':email', $email);
8      $statement->bindValue(':password', $password);
9      $statement->execute();
10     $valid = ($statement->rowCount() == 1);
11     $statement->closeCursor();
12     return $valid;
13   }
14   function get_admin_by_email($email) {
15     global $db;
16     $query = 'SELECT * FROM admins WHERE adminemail = :email';
17     $statement = $db->prepare($query);
18     $statement->bindValue(':email', $email);
19     $statement->execute();
20     $admin = $statement->fetch();
21     $statement->closeCursor();
22     return $admin;
23   }
24   ?>
```

Explanation

The file Admin_Lib.php is a library of admin related functions. Right now you'll be looking at the two functions used in the current task.

The is_valid_admin_login function validates an administrator by receiving his/her email id and password. The most common type of authentication is to store the encrypted user email address and password in a database.

On line # 2, it uses the $db variable by making it global. Note that this variable was created in List III (line 9) and carries a PDO object to connect to the database.

Line # 4 concatenates the email address with the password and uses the sha1 function to encrypt this data. Here, the email address has been included to make the password longer and more complex which makes it more difficult to crack. The sha1 function, which uses the Secure Hash Alogrithm 1, converts the password to a 40-character hexadecimal string. This function is a hash function that accepts a variable-size string and returns a fixed-size string known as the hash value. The four types of SHA are: SHA-0, SHA-1, SHA-2, and SHA-3. Of these, SHA-1 is the most widely used.

Line # 5 stores a SELECT statement in the variable $query. This statement retrieves complete record of the administrator - trying to login - from the Admins table. The WHERE clause compares the email and password stored in the database with those provided by the user. Here, *adminemail* is a column in the Admins table, whereas, *:email* is a bind variable that holds the supplied email address.

Explanation (continued)

Line # 6 prepares the SQL statement by binding the variable value ($email and $password) to the place holder parameter (:email and :password).

Line # 7 binds $email to :email and line # 8 binds $password to :password.

Line # 9 executes the prepared SQL statement and sends the query to the database.

On line # 10, we used the rowCount() function that returns the number of rows affected by the last SQL statement. If the record is found in the database i.e. rowCount() == 1; a value TRUE or 1 is stored in the variable $valid to indicate that the provided credentials are valid. If no record is found i.e. rowCount() == 0; a value FALSE or 0 is stored in the $valid variable.

Line # 11 uses closeCursor() that frees up the connection to the server so that other SQL statements may be issued.

Line # 12 returns either TRUE or FALSE to the calling script for further processing.

The second function get_admin_by_email receives $email parameter. This function is called to fetch complete record of the logged in administrator by using the email address. Note that this function is executed only when the previous one validates the administrator and returns TRUE in $valid variable. The process is same as mentioned before. The only difference is line # 20 where the fetch() statement gets a row from a result set associated with a PDOStatement object. This statement fetches the complete record in an array ($admin). The array is then returned to the calling script (List IX Line # 11) that creates an admin session and displays the Admin Menu to manage categories, products, orders, and admin accounts.

List XI - Error.php - Errors

```
1    <?php include 'view/header_admin.php'; ?>
2    <section class="content">
3      <article>
4        <h2>Error</h2>
5        <p><?php echo $error_message; ?></p>
6      </article>
7    </section>
8    <?php include 'view/footer.php'; ?>
```

Explanation

This script is called to display generic errors in a new web page. For example, it is called from Main.php to display a message to the user if the supplied login information doesn't match with those in the database.

6.12 Task 4 - Manage Categories

After successfully logging in to the website, the following page is displayed to perform administrative tasks. The welcome text displays the first name of the logged in administrator along with the Logout link.

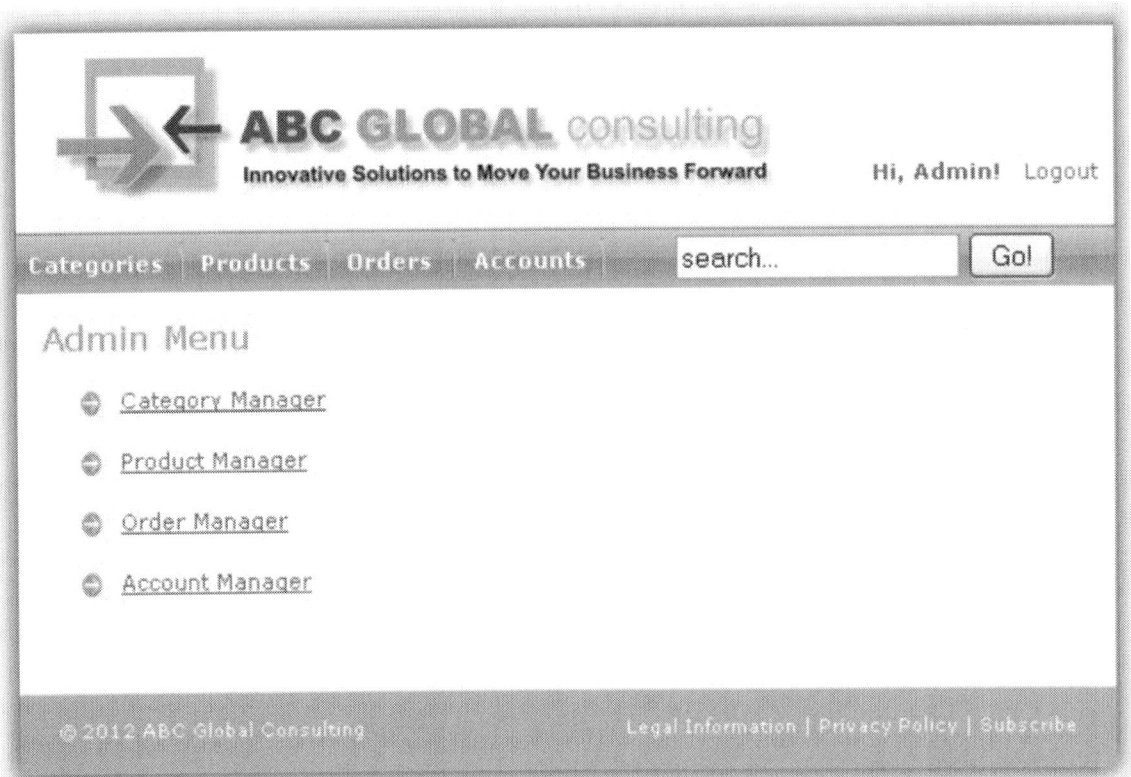

Figure 6-11

The Admin Menu

As you can see, the Admin Menu has four options:

Category Manager - Task 4: This option lets administrators add, modify, or delete a product category. In this section you'll be looking at how to perform these tasks.

Product Manager - Task 5: This module will allow administrators to add, modify, or delete an individual product.

Order Manager - Task 6: With the help of this module, an administrator can view, process, or delete an order.

Account Manager - Task7: You can add more administrators and modify or delete existing admin accounts.

When you click the Category Manager link in the Admin Menu, the following page appears. The Category Manager section lets you update or delete an existing category. The *Add Category* section has a text box where you can input a new category. When you press the *Add* button next to the text box, the category is added to the above list as well as to the aside *Categories* section to the right.

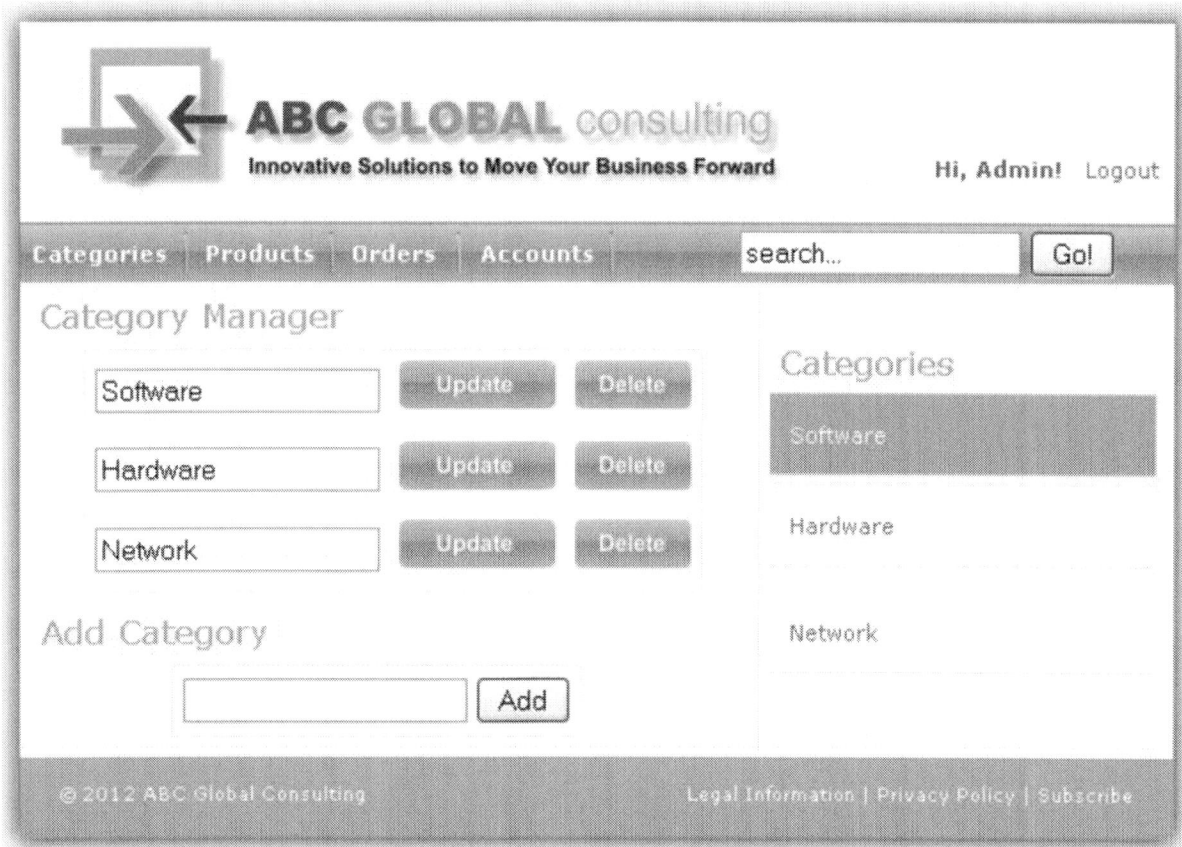

Figure 6-12

This page has four main processes:

1. View categories
2. Update category
3. Delete category
4. Add a new category

To better understand, you'll see all these processes individually. Let's begin with the first one: View categories.

Process Flow - Manage Categories

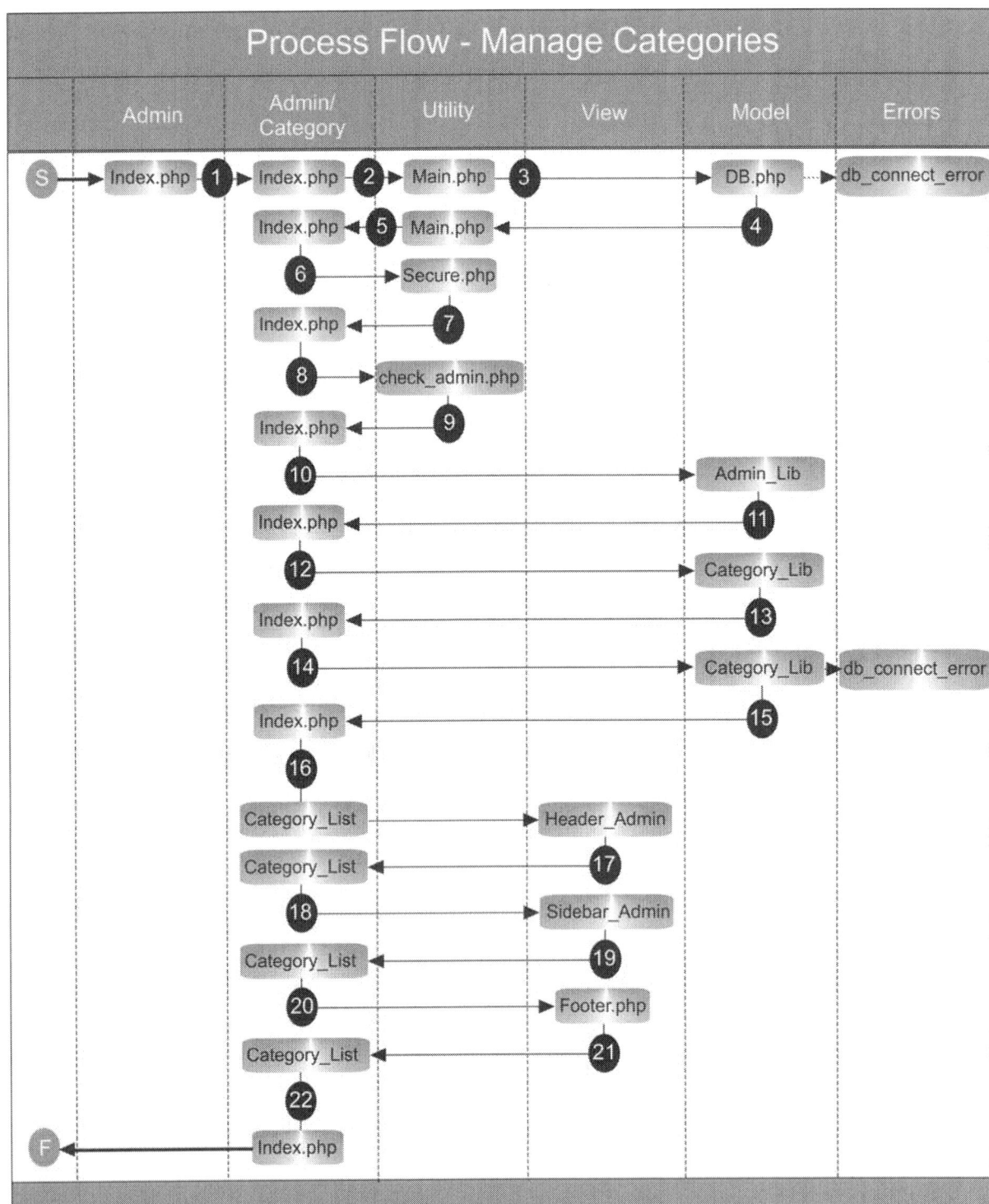

Diagram 2 - Categories Management Process

Diagram Explained

Point S. The process initiates when you click the Category Manager link under the Admin Menu. This invokes the underlying script in Admin/Index.php file - *<a href="category">Category Manager</a>* (List I Line 11).

1. The href attribute above is referencing "category" folder under the Admin directory. Note that whenever you create a link like this, the default Index.php file under that particular folder executes.

See details of point 3-11 in the Admin Login section. Code in Secure and Check_Admin files is ignored by PHP because you're already using the secured connection and are logged in as administrator.

12. Category_Lib is also a library of functions related to categories. Here, this file is included in the process and the functions it contains are utilized subsequently.

14. When the option Category Manager is initially clicked in the Admin menu, the case condition 'list_categories' under the Switch statement is executed. The code under this case calls a function named get_categories() from the Category_Lib file to fetch all categories from the relevant table.

16. The file Category_List displays all categories as shown above in Figure 6-12.

18. The Sidebar_Admin file shows all saved categories from the database in the aside section. Whenever you create a new category or update an existing one, this area reflects the changes immediately.

List XII - Index.php - Admin/Category

```php
1    <?php
2    ...
3    require_once('model/category_lib.php');
4    ...
5    else {
6      $action = 'list_categories';
7    }
8    $action = strtolower($action);
9    switch ($action) {
10     case 'list_categories':
11       $categories = get_categories();
12       include('category_list.php');
13       break;
14   }
15   ?>
```

Explanation

This controller file is located under Admin/Category directory to control category management process. The initial function of this file is to display a list of categories. On the same page, administrators have the option to add, modify, and remove categories from the database. The file category_lib.php specified on line # 3 is exclusive to this module. It's a library file that contains various functions related to category management. All other files such as Main.php, Secure.php etc. have already been discussed.

Initially, the code specified in the else block (line # 5-7) is executed which assigns a string value 'list_categories' to a variable named $action.

Line # 8 contains the strtolower() function which converts a string to lowercase to match it with the static lower case values defined in the Swith statement.

The first case condition 'list_categories' is processed and executed. On line # 11, a function get_categories() (List XIII) from the category_lib.php file is called to fetch all records from the categories table. The result is stored in an array named $categories.

Line # 12 calls category_list.php to display the fetched records.

The break statement on line # 13 terminates the script and no other case statement is evaluated at this stage.

List XIII - Category_Lib.php - Model

```php
1    <?php
2    function get_categories() {
3      global $db;
4      $query = 'SELECT *,
5            (SELECT COUNT(*)
6             FROM products
7             WHERE products.categoryID = categories.categoryID)
8             AS productCount
9          FROM categories
10         ORDER BY categoryID';
11     try {
12       $statement = $db->prepare($query);
13       $statement->execute();
14       $result = $statement->fetchAll();
15       $statement->closeCursor();
16       return $result;
17     }
18     catch (PDOException $e) {
19       $error_message = $e->getMessage();
20       display_db_error($error_message);
21     }
...  }
       ...
```

Explanation

As mentioned before, this file carries five functions to handle this module. The one listed above get_categories() is the first among them. The SELECT statement (line # 4-10) retrieves all records from the categories table. There is a sub-query defined within the main SELECT statement (line # 5-7) to evaluate how many products exist under a specific category. The result of this sub-query is stored in a column named productCount. This evaluation is done to eliminate deletion of those categories that have associated products. If the productCount column holds a value greater than zero, the Delete button hides on the web page.

Line # 12 prepares the query which is executed on line # 13. The fetchAll() statement on line # 14 returns an array containing all of the result set rows that are stored subsequently in the variable $result. This result is returned to the calling script on line # 16.

See List III DB.php for details on the catch block. Line # 20 of this block calls a function display_db_error with the argument $error_message. This function exists in Main.php, which calls db_connect_error.php in the Errors directory to display the error message. The catch block usually throws an error message if any database table used in the SELECT statement is missing. Also note that the catch block used in List III (DB.php) only handles connectivity exceptions. After connecting to the database, the block defined here handles further exceptions such as a missing table.

After executing the function the flow returns to List XII - Line # 12 where the file category_list.php is called.

List XIV - Category_List.php - Admin/Category

```php
1    <?php include 'view/header_admin.php'; ?>
2    <section class="content">
3     <article>
4      <h2>Category Manager</h2>
5      <table>
6       <?php foreach ($categories as $category) : ?>
7       <tr>
8         <form action="index.php" method="post" >
9         <td>
10          <input type="text" name="name" value="<?php echo $category['categoryName']; ?>"/>
11         </td>
12         <td>
13          <input type="hidden" name="action" value="update_category" />
14          <input type="hidden" name="category_id" value="<?php echo $category['categoryID']; ?>"/>
15          <input type="image" alt="Update" src="<?php echo $app_path; ?>images/update.png">
16         </td>
17         </form>
18         <td>
19          <?php if ($category['productCount'] == 0) : ?>
20          <form action="index.php" method="post" >
21           <input type="hidden" name="action" value="delete_category" />
22           <input type="hidden" name="category_id" value="<?php echo $category['categoryID']; ?>"/>
23           <input type="image" alt="Delete" src="<?php echo $app_path; ?>images/delete.png">
24          </form>
25          <?php endif; ?>
26         </td>
27       </tr>
28       <?php endforeach; ?>
29      </table>
30      <h2>Add Category</h2>
31      <table>
32       <tr>
33        <td>
34        <form action="index.php" method="post">
35         <input type="hidden" name="action" value="add_category" />
36         <input type="input" name="name" />
37         <input type="submit" value="Add"/>
38        </form>
39        </td>
40       </tr>
41      </table>
42     </article>
43    </section>
44    <?php include 'view/sidebar_admin.php'; ?>
45    <?php include 'view/footer.php'; ?>
```

Explanation

This script creates a page, as illustrated in Figure 6-12, to manage categories. The page displays a list of categories in a table (Line # 5-29) fetched through the get_categories() function. This file is a good example to understand how to embed PHP code in HTML.

Line # 6-28 uses a foreach loop to iterate through all the rows of the result set, one row at a time. The array $categories stores the PDOStatement object for a multi-row result set which was:
   a. Retrieved from List XIII,
   b. Returned to List XII line 11 and
   c. Forwarded to this list by List XII line 12

Line # 8 defines a form and calls index.php file under Admin/Category when the form is posted.

Line # 10 created a text input element to hold the category name.

Line # 13 creates a hidden element having a value 'update_category'. This element is created to tell the controller that an update operation is performed. Line # 14 creates another hidden element and holds value from the column categoryID. Line # 15 puts an image (update.png) to act as a button. This image, when clicked, carries value of the selected categoryID from the array $category to index.php along with the action value 'update_category'. After receiving these values, the index.php file executes the code under the update_category case.

Code on line # 19-25 is evaluating whether the productCount column is equal to zero. This column was created in the previous script to show number of products under each category. If the condition is true and there are not products under the current category, a delete button is placed to allow the administrator to remove the category from the database. Note that this evaluation is done for each category record because we're in the foreach loop. If the productCount has a value greater than zero for any category, the delete button will not be displayed in front of that category. Here again, we used some hidden elements to delete the exact record.

Line # 30-41 forms a sub-section to add a new category. When the administrator enters a new category and presses the Add button, the form is posted to index.php file along with a hidden element value 'add_category'. In the next listing we're going to see how these hidden values are handled by index.php file.

On line # 44 we included sidebar_admin.php file (List XXI) to show a list of stored categories from the database in the side bar.

List XV - Index.php - Admin/Category

```
      ...
1     if (isset($_POST['action'])) {
2        $action = $_POST['action'];
3     } else if (isset($_GET['action'])) {
4        $action = $_GET['action'];
5     } else {
6        $action = 'list_categories';
7     }
      ...
8        case 'delete_category':
9          $category_id = $_POST['category_id'];
10         delete_category($category_id);
11         header("Location: .");
12         break;
      ...
```

List XVI - Category_Lib.php - Model

```
1     function delete_category($category_id) {
2        global $db;
3        $query = 'DELETE FROM categories WHERE categoryID = :category_id';
4        try {
5          $statement = $db->prepare($query);
6          $statement->bindValue(':category_id', $category_id);
7          $statement->execute();
8          $statement->closeCursor();
9        } catch (PDOException $e) {
10         $error_message = $e->getMessage();
11         display_db_error($error_message);
12       }
13    }
```

Explanation

When the administrator clicks the delete button corresponding to a category, the process flows back to Index.php file as shown in List XV. This time, the first if statement (presented in bold) is executed since the delete process uses the post method. The case 'delete_category' which was forwarded through a hidden form element (list XIV - Line 21) is assessed and executed.

Line # 9 stores the received category id in a variable. This variable is passed as an argument to the function delete_category(). After removing the record from the database, the page is refreshed through line # 11 which again runs the controller to display a fresh list.

The delete_category function in Category_Lib.php file (List XVI) receives the category id and stores a DELETE SQL statement on line # 3. This statement is executed on line # 7 in the try block and thus the category record is deleted from the database.

List XVII - Index.php - Admin/Category

```
      ...
1     if (isset($_POST['action'])) {
2       $action = $_POST['action'];
      ...
3       case 'add_category':
4         $name = $_POST['name'];
5         // Validate input
6         if (empty($name)) {
7           display_error('You must include a name for the category. Please try again.');
8         }
9         else {
10          $category_id = add_category($name);
11        }
12        header("Location: .");
13        break;
      ...
```

List XVIII - Category_Lib.php - Model

```
1     function add_category($name) {
2       global $db;
3       $query = 'INSERT INTO categories
4             (categoryName)
5           VALUES
6             (:name)';
7       try {
8         $statement = $db->prepare($query);
9         $statement->bindValue(':name', $name);
10        $statement->execute();
11        $statement->closeCursor();
12        // Get the last category ID
13        $category_id = $db->lastInsertId();
14        return $category_id;
15      } catch (PDOException $e) {
16        $error_message = $e->getMessage();
17        display_db_error($error_message);
18      }
19    }
```

> The add_category function receives the category name and uses the INSERT SQL statement to add the new category to the database. On line 13, a built-in function, lastInsertID(), is called to store id of the last category in a variable.

Explanation

The value 'add_category' of the hidden input element is passed to Index.php when the Add button is clicked. Another information that this files receives through the post method is the 'name' of the category. The categories table has two columns: categoryID and categoryName. The property of the id column is set to increment automatically, therefore, we do not need to consider a new value for it. On line # 6 we put a condition to check whether the received name value is empty. If so, the function display_error is invoked in Main.php file to display the associated message. The else block calls add_category function from the category library. After insertion, the header() function on line # 12 calls Index.php that repeats the process to display the newly added category both in the main content section and in the aside area.

List XIX - Index.php - Admin/Category

```
    ...
1   if (isset($_POST['action'])) {
2     $action = $_POST['action'];
    ...
3     case 'update_category':
4       $category_id = $_POST['category_id'];
5       $name = $_POST['name'];
6       // Validate input
7       if (empty($name)) {
8         display_error('You must include a name for the category. Please try again.');
9       }
10      else {
11        update_category($category_id, $name);
12      }
13      header("Location: .");
14      break;
    ...
```

List XX - Category_Lib.php - Model

```
1    function update_category($category_id, $name) {
2      global $db;
3      $query = '
4        UPDATE categories
5        SET categoryName = :name
6        WHERE categoryID = :category_id';
7      try {
8        $statement = $db->prepare($query);
9        $statement->bindValue(':name', $name);
10       $statement->bindValue(':category_id', $category_id);
11       $statement->execute();
12       $statement->closeCursor();
13     }
14     catch (PDOException $e) {
15       $error_message = $e->getMessage();
16       display_db_error($error_message);
17     }
18   }
```

Explanation

This process helps administrators update the only data i.e. name in the categories table. The web page displaying the categories list carries an update button next to each category. The administrator just modifies the category name and presses this button. The process is executed using the UPDATE SQL statement and the new name is reflected in both sections of the page.

List XXI - Sidebar_Admin.php - View

```
1    <aside>
2      <section class="services">
       <!-- display links for all categories -->
3        <?php if (isset($categories)) : ?>
4          <h2>Categories</h2>
5          <?php foreach ($categories as $category) : ?>
6            <a href="<?php echo $app_path .
               'admin/product?action=list_products' .
               '&amp;category_id=' . $category['categoryID']; ?>">
               <?php echo $category['categoryName']; ?>
             </a>
7          <?php endforeach; ?>
8        <?php endif; ?>
9      </section>
10   </aside>
```

Explanation

The logged in administrator could see a list of categories from the database in the aside section to the right of the web page. Clicking a link brings up a page with all the products under that particular category. The product management module is not yet designed, therefore, you'll get an Object Not Found message if you try to click any link in this section. But let's go through the code.

The list is displayed only when the array $categories exist (line # 3). All categories are displayed using the foreach loop. Line # 6 creates a link for each category. For example, if the Software category is clicked, the following url is formed:

https://localhost/abcglobal/admin/product/?action=list_products&category_id=1

Here the id of the software category is 1. The Admin/Product clause invokes Index.php file in the Product directory and passes a parameter "action" with a value "list_products". The Index.php file has a case statement with the name *list_products* which gets all products for the selected category from the database and calls Product_List.php file to show a list of those products. The final clause &category_id=1 is also a parameter that is also passed to Index.php file and is evaluated in the same case statement to fetch related products for the provided category id.

6.13 Task 5 - Manage Products

This module will allow administrators to manage individual product information. It is similar in functionality to the categories management section. Here, you'll learn some more techniques such as how to handle product images on a dynamic website. Another area that will be addressed in this module is how to process HTML tags at run time.

This module has the following processes to help administrators view, modify, delete, and add products:

1. **List Products:** When the administrator selects the Product Manager link in the Admin Menu or clicks the Products link in the main navigation bar, a page appears that lists all the products under a specified category.
2. **View Product:** This page presents details of a selected product such as its image, price, description and more.
3. **Delete Product:** A Delete button will be provided on the View Product page to remove the selected product from the database.
4. **Edit Product:** This process allows administrators modify products' information. For example, the administrator can change a product's category from one to another, put a new price, add more features in the description section etc.
5. **Image Manager:** On product detail page, a sub-section will be provided to upload product images. These images will be displayed along with other details.
6. **Add Product:** As the name implies, this process allows administrators to add new products to the database through this interface.

After looking at the main processes, let's go through all of them individually.

6.13.1 Listing Products on a Web Page from the Database

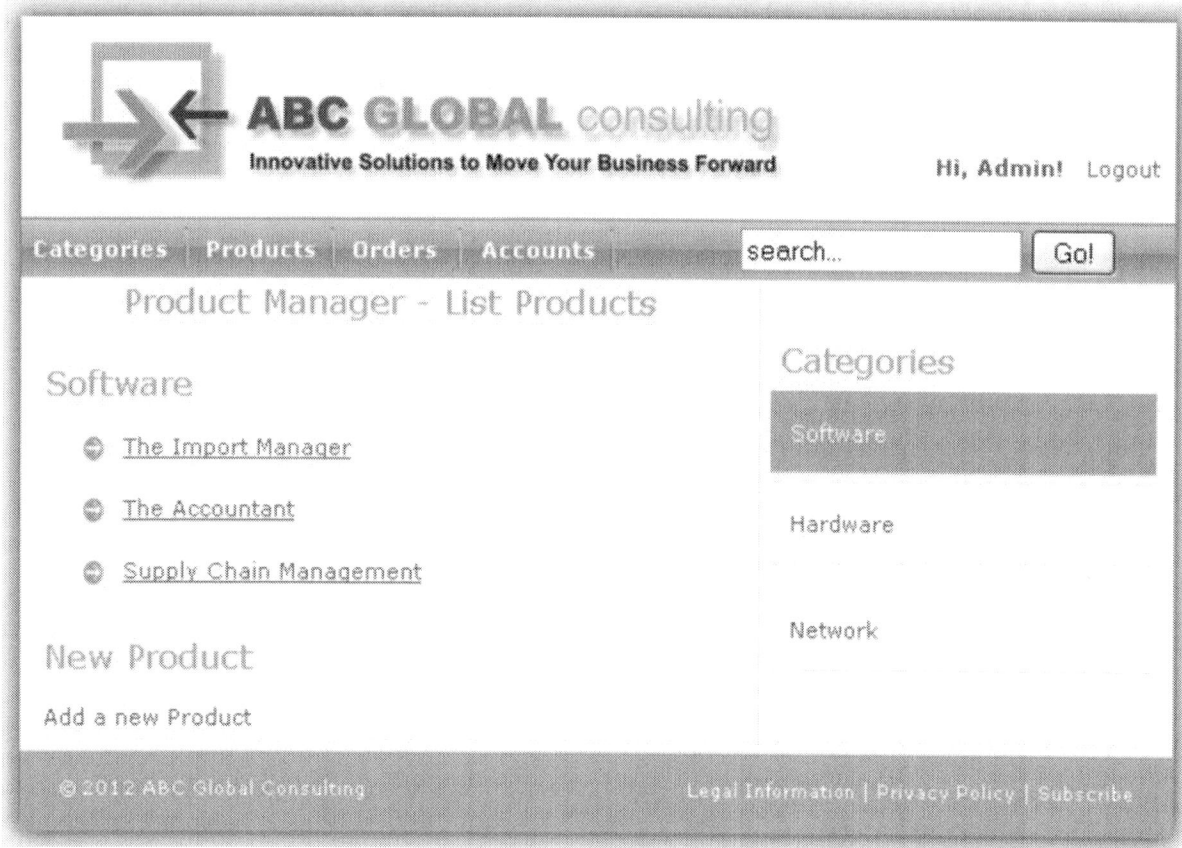

Figure 6-13

As mentioned, the page illustrated above lists all products from a selected category. This page is divided into three sections.

1. The Category section (left) displays the category name and a list of associated products. For instance, the above figure displays the Software category and a list of all software products. Clicking a product link calls a page that holds all the details about that product. The administrator can modify product's content, upload image, and can also delete it from the database on the details page.

2. The "Add a new Product" link under the New Product section calls another page to add a new product to the database.

3. Selecting a category in the Categories section (right) refreshes this page and products related to the selected category are displayed on the left side along with the category name.

Process Flow - List Products

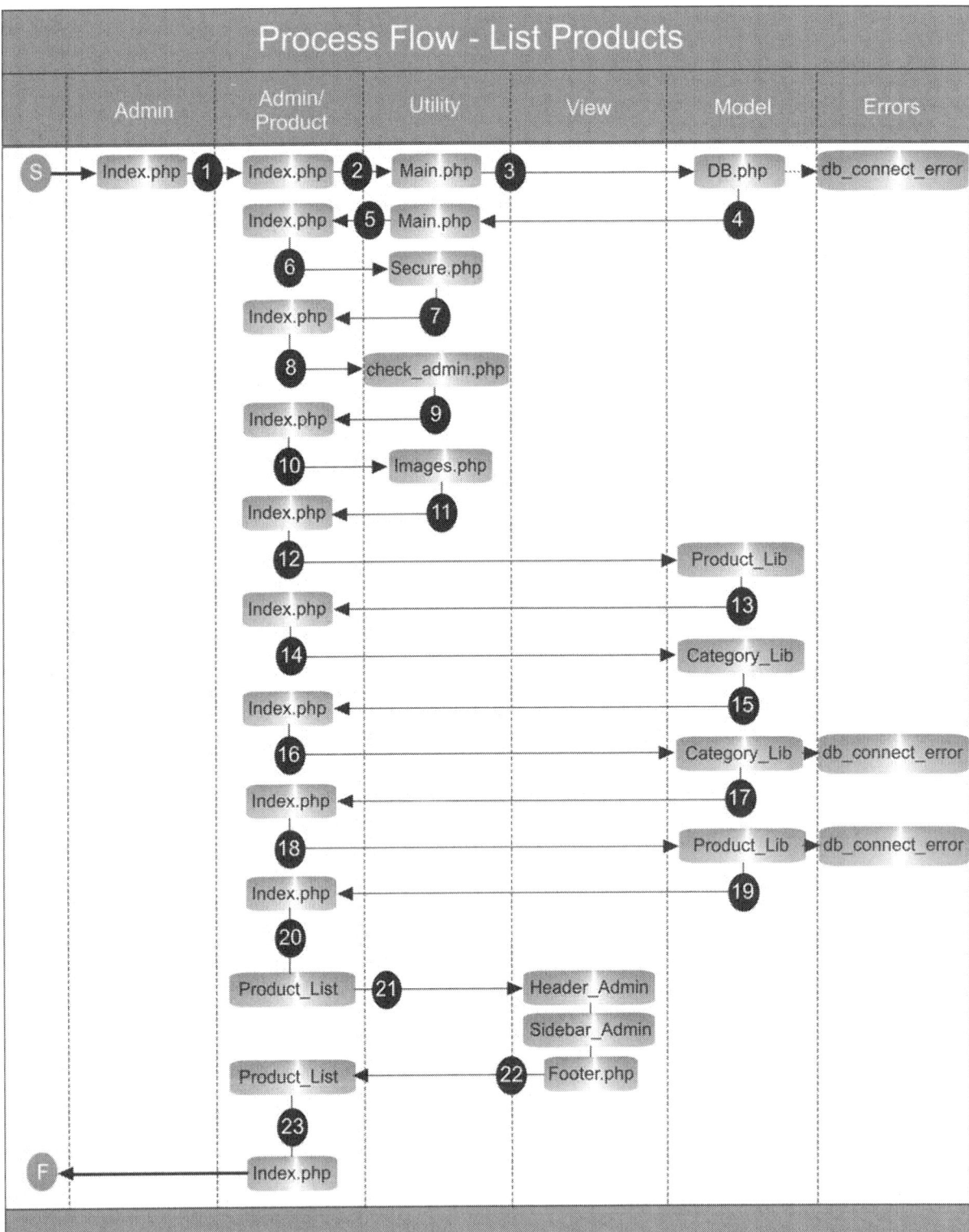

Diagram 3 - List Products Process

Diagram Explained

Point S. The process kicks off when the administrator clicks the link Product Manager in the Admin Menu. The underlying script in Admin/Index.php file *<a href="product">Product Manager</a>* (List I Line 12) is executed.

Index.php file under Admin/Product directory comes into play in point 1.

Points 3-9 are similar to the previous processes and have been briefed.

Point 10 includes Images.php file from the Utility directory. You'll shortly see in detail what this file does.

The Product_Lib.php file called in point 12 contains a library of functions to process the product module.

Category_Lib.php file that you've already seen is also included in point 14.

In point 16, a function named getCategories() is called from the Index.php file. This function exists in Category_Lib.php file. If any database error occurs, the file db_connect_error.php is executed.

Point 18 calls a function get_products_by_category from the product functions library (Product_Lib.php).

Point 21 displays the Product List page shown in Figure 6-13.

List XXII - Index.php - Admin/Product

```
1    <?php
     ...
2    require_once('utility/images.php');          List XXXVII, List XXXVII-A, List XXXVII-B➜
3    require_once('model/product_lib.php');        List XXIII➜
     ...
4    else {
5      $action = 'list_products';
6    }
7    $action = strtolower($action);
8    switch ($action) {
9      case 'list_products':
         // get categories and products
10       if (isset($_GET['category_id'])) {
11         $category_id = $_GET['category_id'];
12       }
13       else {
14         $category_id = 1;
15       }
16       $current_category = get_category($category_id);       List XIII➜
17       $categories = get_categories();
18       $products = get_products_by_category($category_id);   List XXIII➜
         // display product list
19       include('product_list.php');    List XXIV➜
20       break;
21   ?>
```

Explanation

As usual, this file includes six other files from different folders required to smoothly execute the process. Since no Post or Get actions are set so far, the else block runs and assigns the value 'list_products' to the variable $action. This variable is then assessed in the first case statement (line # 9).

The IF/ELSE block (line 10-15) checks whether the value category_id is set. If so, this value is moved to a variable $category_id (line # 11) to fetch products pertaining to this category. Usually, the IF block is not executed the first time you call this page. Instead, the ELSE block triggers and a default value of 1 is moved into the variable to get all products for the first category.

Line # 16 calls a function get_category() from the file Category_Lib by passing the value $category_id as a parameter. The function returns id and name of the specified category which is then stored in $current_category array.

Line # 17 stores the returning result from the get_categories() function in an array $categories. You went through this function in List-XIII.

Line # 18 also calls a function get_products_by_category. It passes the argument $category_id and fetches all products for the specified category in the array $products.

List XXIII - Product_Lib.php - Model

```
1    function get_products_by_category($category_id) {
2      global $db;
3      $query = '
4        SELECT *
5        FROM products p
6          INNER JOIN categories c
7          ON p.categoryID = c.categoryID
8          WHERE p.categoryID = :category_id';
9      try {
10         $statement = $db->prepare($query);
11         $statement->bindValue(':category_id', $category_id);
12         $statement->execute();
13         $result = $statement->fetchAll();
14         $statement->closeCursor();
15         return $result;
16     } catch (PDOException $e) {
17         $error_message = $e->getMessage();
18         display_db_error($error_message);
19     }
20   }
```

Explanation

This function returns all products for a given category. The SELECT statement uses an inner join on the categoryID column from both products and categories tables. If you use the above SELECT statement in MySQL Workbench, the output would be something like this:

productID	categoryID	productCode	productName	categoryID	categoryName
1	1	TIM	The Import Manager	1	Software
6	1	TMA	The Accountant	1	Software
7	1	SCM	Supply Chain Management	1	Software

SQL joins are used to query data from two or more tables, based on a relationship between certain columns in these tables using the JOIN keyword. The INNER JOIN keyword returns rows when there is at least one match in both tables. If there are rows in "Categories" that do not have matches in "Products", those rows will NOT be listed.

Note that the provided script (DB.TXT) has only one product for each category. I added two software products, product # 6 and 7, through the Add Product interface. The first four columns (productID, categoryID, productCode, and productName) in the above figure arrived from the table Products, while the last two (categoryID and categoryName) came from the Categories table.

List XXIV - Product_List.php - Admin/Product

```php
1    <?php include '../../view/header_admin.php'; ?>
2    <section class="content">
3     <article>
4      <h2 class="center">Product Manager - List Products</h2>
5      <p>To see a list of products, select the desired category from the left side.<br>
6          To view, edit, or delete a product, select the product from the list below.<br>
7          To add a product, select the "Add Product" link at the bottom of this page.</p>
8      <?php if (count($products) == 0) : ?>
9        <p>There are no products for this category.</p>
10     <?php else : ?>
11       <h2><?php echo $current_category['categoryName']; ?></h2>
12        <?php foreach ($products as $product) : ?>
13        <p>
14          <ul>
15           <li><a href="?action=view_product&amp;product_id=
                 <?php echo $product['productID']; ?>">
                 <?php echo $product['productName']; ?></a>
16           </li>
19          </ul>
20        </p>
21        <?php endforeach; ?>
22     <?php endif; ?>
       ...
```

Explanation

This PHP file creates the web page and displays the category title and a list of associated products in the main content section.

Line # 8 uses the count() function to check whether the $products array carries any record. If not, the message defined on line # 9 is displayed.

Line # 10 forms the ELSE block. The category name is displayed through line # 11. Line # 12 creates a foreach loop to fetch products from the $products array.

Line # 15 displays the name of each product as a link which, when clicked, passes a parameter named action with a value (view_product) and the productID to the controller (Index.php). The value, view_product, is assessed in a Case statement and another file (product_view.php - coming up next) is called to display details of the selected product. The code echo $product['productID'] is enclosed in the opening <a> tag and is associated with the = operator. If you click the first product, the complete expression would appear in the browser like this:

http://localhost/abcglobal/admin/product/?action=view_product&product_id=1

To further check, hover your mouse over each link in the list and see the complete expression in the status bar. The code echo $product['productName'] is used to displays product name as a link text.

6.13.2 View Product Details

Figure 6-14

After clicking a link in the Product List page, you'll see this one. The main Content section displays details of the selected product. It has an Add to Cart button that is provided for placing order and will be discussed in the members module. The Delete button removes the product from the database. Note that this button appears only if no orders are placed against a product. We will discuss it shortly. Using the Edit button administrators can modify the product's content.

The page also contains the Image Manager sub-section which is used to upload images of products. Using the Browse button you can locate the image. After selecting the image, clicking the Upload Image button moves the selected image to the Images folder in the site directory. This process creates three versions of an image: actual, medium, and small. The one you see on this page is the actual one. You can see other versions using the links provided under the Upload Image button.

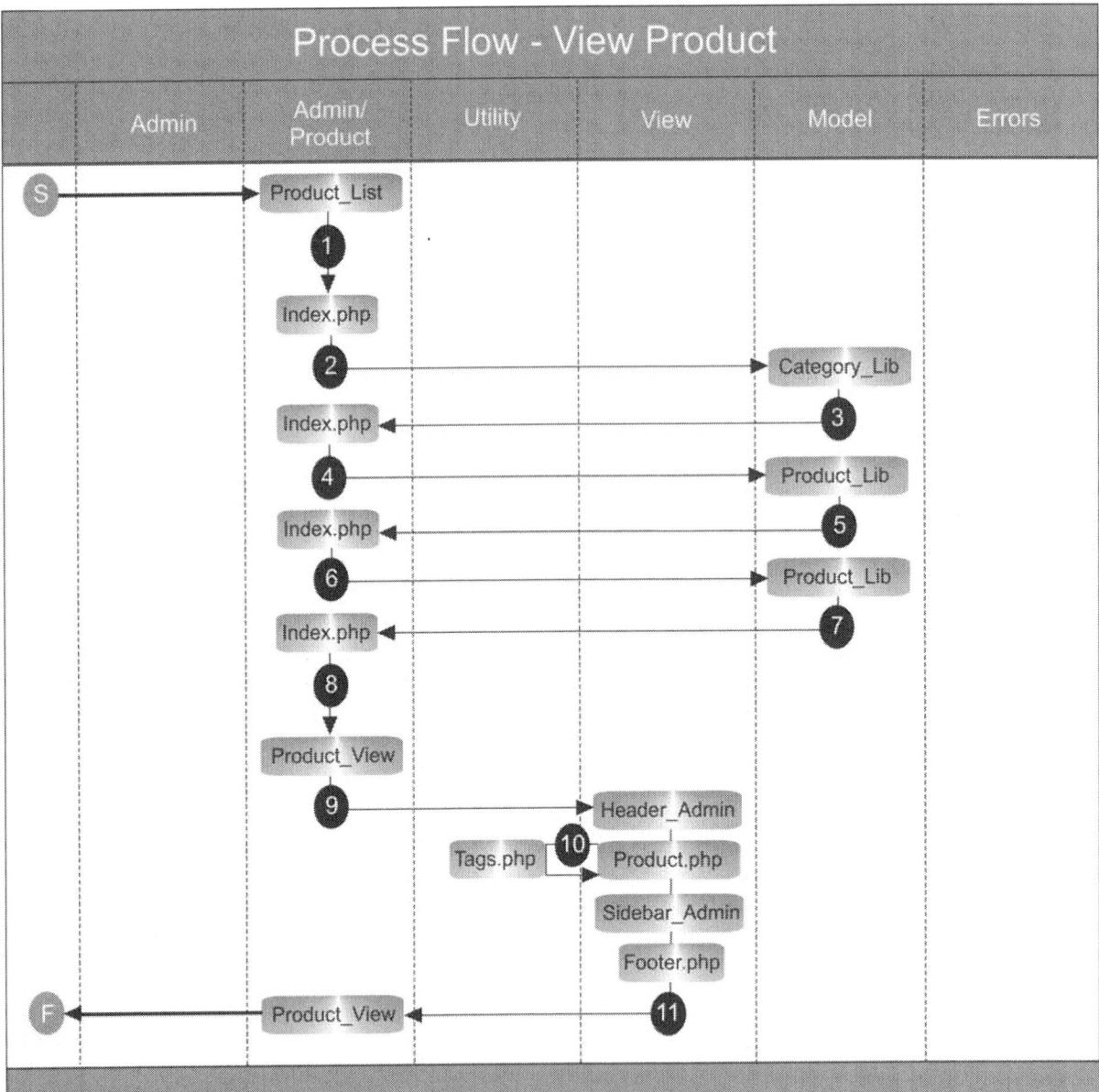

Diagram 4 - View Product Process

Diagram Explained

The process of displaying details begins when an administrator clicks the link defined in List XXIV - Line # 15. The href attribute of the <a> tag passes the value 'view_product' with the productID to Index.php file.

Point 1 - This time, the ELSE IF condition is processed because the request is received appended to the URL which corresponds to the GET method. In the current scenario, the $_GET array (as shown in the figure below) is defined and has two elements. The first element [action] has a value 'view_product' while the second one is [product_id] with a value of 1. The variable $action is assigned the value 'view_product' and is processed in the Case statement. See List XXV below.

$_GET	array[2]	
[action]	string	"view_product"
[product_id]	string	"1"

Figure 6-15 - $_GET Array Structure

Point 2-7 - The code in the Case block fetches required data through function calls.

Point 8 - The Product_View.php file generates the targeted page to display product details. This file also calls Product.php from the View directory that actually fetches database values from the array into respective variables and performs calculations.

Point 10 - Product.php makes a call to Tags.php to handle HTML tags in the Description column.

List XXV - Index.php - Admin/Product

```
1    <?php
     ...
2    else if (isset($_GET['action'])) {
3        $action = $_GET['action'];
4    }
     ...
5        case 'view_product':
6            $categories = get_categories();
7            $product_id = $_GET['product_id'];
8            $product = get_product($product_id);
9            $product_order_count = get_product_order_count($product_id);
10           include('product_view.php');      List XXVI→
11           break;
     ...
```

Explanation

The link defined in List XXIV - Line # 15 passes two parameters (appended to the url) to Index.php file using the GET method. Since the GET method is defined, the ELSE IF block is executed (line # 2-4).

The Case presented on line # 5 is found true and processed.

All categories are fetched through the get_categories() function on line # 6.

Line # 7 assigns product_id from the $_GET array to $product_id variable.

Line # 8 calls get_product function from the product function library. This function retrieves complete record of the selected product into an array $product.

Line # 9 calls a function get_product_order_count from the product function library to check whether there are any orders already placed for the selected product. This check is performed on the Orderitems table. Since there are no orders, a zero value will be stored in the corresponding variable to the left. This check is performed to evaluate either to show the Delete button or not. If the value indicates zero, the Delete button will appear on the web page and the administrator will be able to remove the product. If in case a single order is placed for it, the product could not be deleted and the Delete button will not appear on the page.

Line # 10 calls Product_View.php file (next) to display complete details of the selected product.

List XXVI - Product_View.php - Admin/Product

```php
1    <?php include '../../view/header_admin.php'; ?>
2    <section class="content">
3     <article>
4      <h2 class="center">Product Manager - View Product</h2>
5      <!-- display product -->
6      <?php include '../../view/product.php'; ?>
7      <!-- display Delete and Edit buttons -->
       ...
8      <h2>Image Manager</h2>
       ...
9     </article>
10   </section>
11   <?php include '../../view/sidebar_admin.php'; ?>
12   <?php include '../../view/footer.php'; ?>
```

Explanation

This file generates the product detail page. Besides usual header, sidebar, and footer calls, it has three parts marked in bold in the above script. The display product part (line # 6) calls Product.php in the View directory. This file moves information received from the database into appropriate variables and performs some calculations as well. After performing the process the values from the variables are displayed on the page.

When the flow transfers back to this file, couple of form elements are created to display Delete and Edit button (line # 7). This code is omitted here intentionally because these two processes need individual attention and are discussed later.

Similar to buttons, the Image Manager part is also discussed later on to show how to upload a product image.

List XXVII A - Product.php - View

```php
1   <?php
      // Parse data
2     $category_id = $product['categoryID'];
3     $product_code = $product['productCode'];
4     $product_name = $product['productName'];
5     $description = $product['description'];
6     $list_price = $product['listPrice'];
7     $discount_percent = $product['discountPercent'];
      // Add HMTL tags to the description
8     $description = add_tags($description);    List XXVIII➔
      // Calculate discounts
9     $discount_amount = round($list_price * ($discount_percent / 100), 2);
10    $unit_price = $list_price - $discount_amount;
      // Format discounts
11    $discount_percent = number_format($discount_percent, 0); // 10
12    $discount_amount = number_format($discount_amount, 2); // 10.00
13    $unit_price = number_format($unit_price, 2);
      // Get image URL and alternate text
14    $image_filename = $product_code . '_m.png';
15    $image_path = $app_path . 'images/' . $image_filename;
16    $image_alt = 'Image filename: ' . $image_filename;
17  ?>
```

Explanation

This file is listed in two parts: A & B. This part (part A) discusses data handling process.

It fetches values from the $product array and stores them in relevant variables (line # 2-7). For example, the database value productCode (line 3) is retrieved from the array element $product['productCode'] and is stored in the variable $product_code.

Line # 8 calls a function add_tags placed in Tags.php file under the Utility directory. This function will be discussed soon.

Line # 9 calculates the discount value. It initially divides the value of $discount_percent by 100, then multiplies it with $list_price and rounds the resulting value up to 2 decimal places. Suppose the values of $discount_percent and $list_price are 10 and 100 respectively. The value received after the initial division would be 0.1. Multiplied with 100 would yield 10 which is the discount value.

Line # 10 subtracts discount value from the list price to give actual unit price.

The number_format() function on line # 11, 12 and 13 formats a number with grouped thousands. The first one formats value in the $discount_percent variable with zero, while in the remaining variables two digits are added.

Line # 14 concatenates the product code with a string '_m.png'. Here the letter m represents medium sized image file. After joining, the value is stored in a variable $image_filename. For example, the product code retrieved from the database is TIM. After concatenation, the value 'TIM_m.png' will be stored in the designated variable.

The value of $image_path variable on line # 15 would be formed as /abcglobal/images/TIM_m.png.

Line # 16 creates an alternate text for the image. This text is displayed when the browser fails to show the image on a web page.

List XXVII B - Product.php - View

```
1    <h2><?php echo $product_name; ?></h2>
2    <figure class="small">
3      <p><img src="<?php echo $image_path; ?>" alt="<?php echo $image_alt; ?>" /></p>
4    </figure>
5    <p><b>List Price:</b>
6      <?php echo '$' . $list_price; ?>
7    </p>
8    <p><b>Discount:</b>
9      <?php echo $discount_percent . '%'; ?>
10   </p>
11   <p><b>Your Price:</b>
12     <?php echo '$' . $unit_price; ?>
13     (You save <?php echo '$' . $discount_amount; ?>)
14   </p>
15   <form action="<?php echo $app_path . 'cart' ?>" method="get" id="add_to_cart_form">
16     <input type="hidden" name="action" value="add" />
17     <input type="hidden" name="product_id" value="<?php echo $product_id; ?>" />
18     <b>Quantity:</b> 
19     <input type="text" name="quantity" value="1" size="2" />
20     <input type="submit" value="Add to Cart" />
21   </form>
22   <br>
23   <h2>Description</h2>
24   <?php echo $description; ?>
```

Explanation

This part of the Product.php file carries HTML elements with embedded PHP code to display product details.

Line # 1 show product's name in <h2> element.

Lines 2-4 forms a <figure> block to show a medium size picture of the product using rule # 61 in the style sheet. This rule was used earlier while creating the Services pages. The $image_path variable holds the full path to the image including the Images directory and the image file name (see line # 15 in the previous listing).

Lines 5-7 create a paragraph element to display List Price. Similarly, lines 8-10 and 11-14 also contain paragraphs to display Discount value and discounted price.

Lines 15-21 create a form to display the quantity a member wishes to place in the cart. Note that this form uses the GET method and passes a value 'add' in a hidden element named 'action' to the controller in the Cart directory. The controller evaluates the value in a Case statement for further processing and which is described in detail in the Cart module (Task 14). Line # 19 shows a text input element to receive the desired quantity from a member. This element receives a maximum value of 99 (size="2") and has a default value of 1.

Lines 23 and 24 display formatted description of the product. The next listing describes how to format content of the description column.

List XXVIII - Tags.php - Utility

```php
1    function add_tags($text) {
        // Convert return characters to the Windows new lines
2        $text = str_replace("\r\n", "\n", $text);  // For Windows
3        $text = str_replace("\r", "\n", $text);     // For Mac
         // Get an array of paragraphs
4        $paragraphs = explode("\n\n", $text);
         // Add tags to each paragraph
5        $text = '';
6        foreach($paragraphs as $p) {
7            $p = ltrim($p);
8            $first_char = substr($p, 0, 1);
9            if ($first_char == '*') {
                 // Add <ul> and <li> tags
10               $p = '<ul>' . $p . '</li></ul>';
11               $p = str_replace("*", '<li>', $p);
12               $p = str_replace("\n", '</li>', $p);
13           } else {
                 // Add <p> tags
14               $p = '<p>' . $p . '</p>';
15           }
16           $text .= $p;
17       }
18       return $text;
19   }
```

Explanation

In listing XXVII-A line # 8 we called this function to add HTML tags to the Description column before displaying it on the product's details page. If you had a chance to look at the INSERT statement that added three products in db.txt file, you might have noticed some special tags such as \r, \n and * used in the content for the Description column. This technique is called escape sequences to include special characters in strings. The \r is used for carriage return while \n adds a new line. The last one '*' is used to represent <li> tags. You can see the effect of these special characters by browsing the description column using either MySQL Workbench or the command line utility.

The function begins by receiving raw description in a variable $text. The next two lines (2 & 3) use a built-in function str_replace which replaces all occurrences of the search string with the replacement string. On line # 2, the string "\r\n" is searched in the variable $text and is replaced with "\n".

"The Import Manager is a unique imports information and management software ....
.... in any part of the world.

Features:

* Streamlines your import processes
......
......
* Enables intelligent sourcing decisions by calculating accurate landed costs"

Explanation

Line # 4 breaks (explodes) content in the $text variable and stores the result in an array $paragraphs. The string "\n\n" specifies where to break the string. The following picture depicts the values held in the $paragraphs array. The first element [0] stores the main description from *"The Import Manager"* to *"any part of the world"*. The second element [1] stores the sub-heading *"Features:"* and the third element [2] stores the eight features, each preceded by the symbol '*'.

Line # 5 empties the $text string to create fresh content with HTML tags (on line # 16).

Line # 6 begins a foreach loop. In this loop all special characters are replaced with relevant HTML tags.

Line # 7 uses ltrim() function to remove whitespaces or other predefined character from the left side of the string $p.

Line # 8 uses the substr() function to return a part of the string $p. It fetches one character (1) from the first position (0 is the starting point) in the string $p.

Line # 9 checks whether the first character is '*'. If so, lines 10-12 add <ul> and <li> tags to the string $p.

```
"<ul><li> Streamlines your import processes</li><li> Maintains database of your
imports</li><li> Instantly provides current & historical data of imports</li><li> Gives you greater
control over the import flow</li><li> Manages custom duty and government levies</li><li>
Increases management information</li><li> Provides significant financial benefits & work
efficiency to importers</li><li> Enables intelligent sourcing decisions by calculating accurate
landed costs</li></ul>"
```

The ELSE block (line 13-15) adds the <p> tag to the rest of the paragraphs.

```
"<p>The Import Manager is a unique imports information and management software for importers
......
......
operating in any part of the world. </p><p>Features: </p>"
```

Line # 16 re-creates the $text variable content by adding text from the variable $p and returns this content (containing HTML tags) to Product.php.

6.13.3 Delete Product

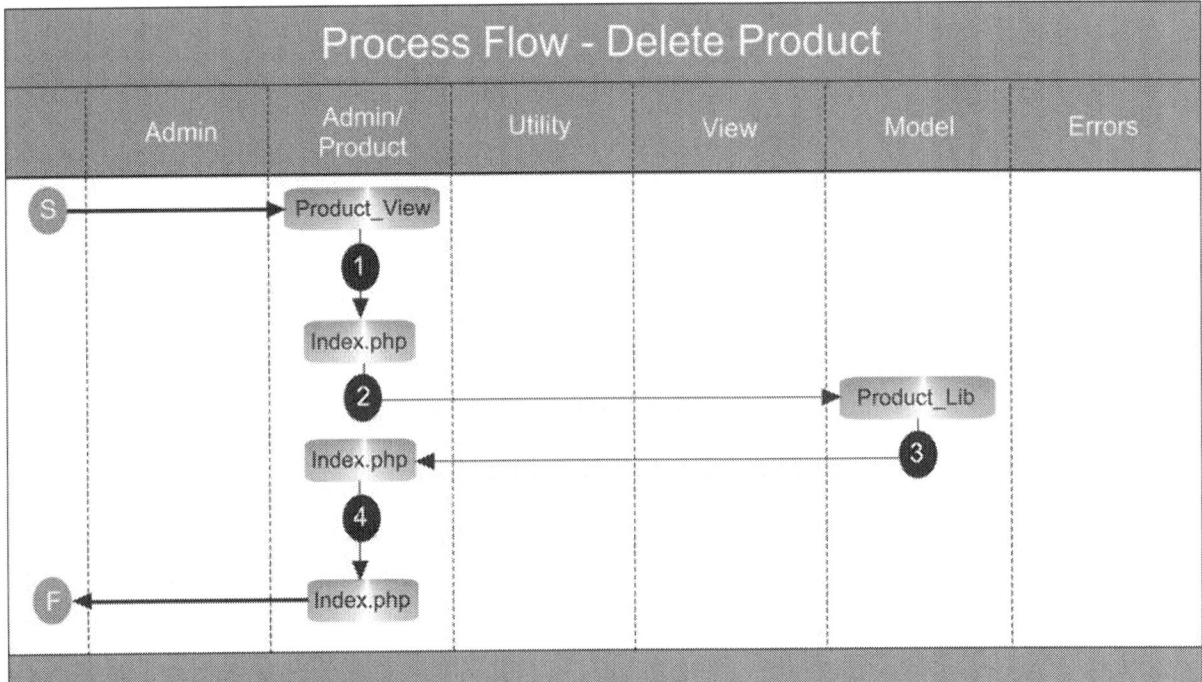

Diagram 5 - Product Deletion Process

Diagram Explained

The purpose of this process is to remove only those product records from the database which are not used in any order.

Point S - The process begins when the administrator clicks the Delete button on the product details page. This action takes a hidden element value 'delete_product ' to the controller.

Point 1 - The controller assesses the value 'delete_product'.

Point 2 - Based on its assessment, the controller calls a function delete_product in the functions library file. The function removes the specified product record from the database.

Point 3 - After deletion, the process is switched back to the controller.

Point 4 - Using the Header() function, controller calls itself to refresh the products page.

List XXIX - Product_View.php - Admin/Product

```
    ...
1       <?php if ($product_order_count == 0) : ?>
2       <form action="index.php" method="post" id="delete_button_form" >
3         <input type="hidden" name="action" value="delete_product"/>
4         <input type="hidden" name="product_id" value="<?php echo $product['productID']; ?>" />
5         <input type="hidden" name="category_id" value="<?php echo $product['categoryID']; ?>" />
6         <input type="image" alt="Delete Product" id="right_button" src="<?php echo $app_path;?>
                                                          images/delete.png">
7       </form>
8       <?php endif; ?>
    ...
```

Explanation

This is a partial code taken from the file Product_View.php. We saw some part of it in the List XXVI earlier. This is the point where the administrator initiates the product deletion process.

Line # 1 ensures whether to show the Delete button on the web page. It does so by testing the value of $product_order_count, a variable declared in listing XXV that holds number of orders the product is used in. If the variable has a value of zero (as mentioned in the IF condition), a form is created.

Lines 2-7 create a form with the post method to hold the Delete button and relevant hidden elements to complete the process.

The first hidden element on line # 3 possesses the value "delete_product". When the button is clicked, this value is passed to the controller for further processing.

Hidden elements on line 4 and 5 are created to hold product and category id and are forwarded to the controller through the post method.

Line # 6 creates an image button from the Images directory. This button is positioned using rule 72A. The src attribute has two sections. The first one is a php code that renders the variable $app_path holding the value /ABCGLOBAL/. The second section defines the remaining path to the image. Combined together, the src attribute becomes /abcglobal/images/delete.png. When this button is clicked, the control transfers to index.php - listed next - in the current directory.

List XXX - Index.php - Admin/Product

```
     ...
1    if (isset($_POST['action'])) {
2      $action = $_POST['action'];
3    }

     ...
4      case 'delete_product':
5        $category_id = $_POST['category_id'];
6        $product_id = $_POST['product_id'];
7        delete_product($product_id);
         // Display the Product List page for the current category
8        header("Location: .?category_id=$category_id");
9        break;
```

Explanation

The controller evaluates and processes the POST condition (line 1) and moves the value *delete_product* into the variable *$action* (line 2). The controller also receives product and category ids from the previous list through the POST method (line 4 & 5) and calls the delete_product() function (line 7) in the library file. After deletion, the flow return to line # 8 where the controller calls itself through the header() function to refresh the products list page.

List XXXI - Index.php - Admin/Product

```
1    function delete_product($product_id) {
2      global $db;
3      $query = 'DELETE FROM products WHERE productID = :product_id';
4      try {
5        $statement = $db->prepare($query);
6        $statement->bindValue(':product_id', $product_id);
7        $statement->execute();
8        $statement->closeCursor();
9      }
10     catch (PDOException $e) {
11       $error_message = $e->getMessage();
12       display_db_error($error_message);
13     }
14   }
```

Explanation

The function receives product id on line # 1 from the previous list and uses the DELETE SQL statement for record removal using the forwarded parameter.

6.13.4 Update Product

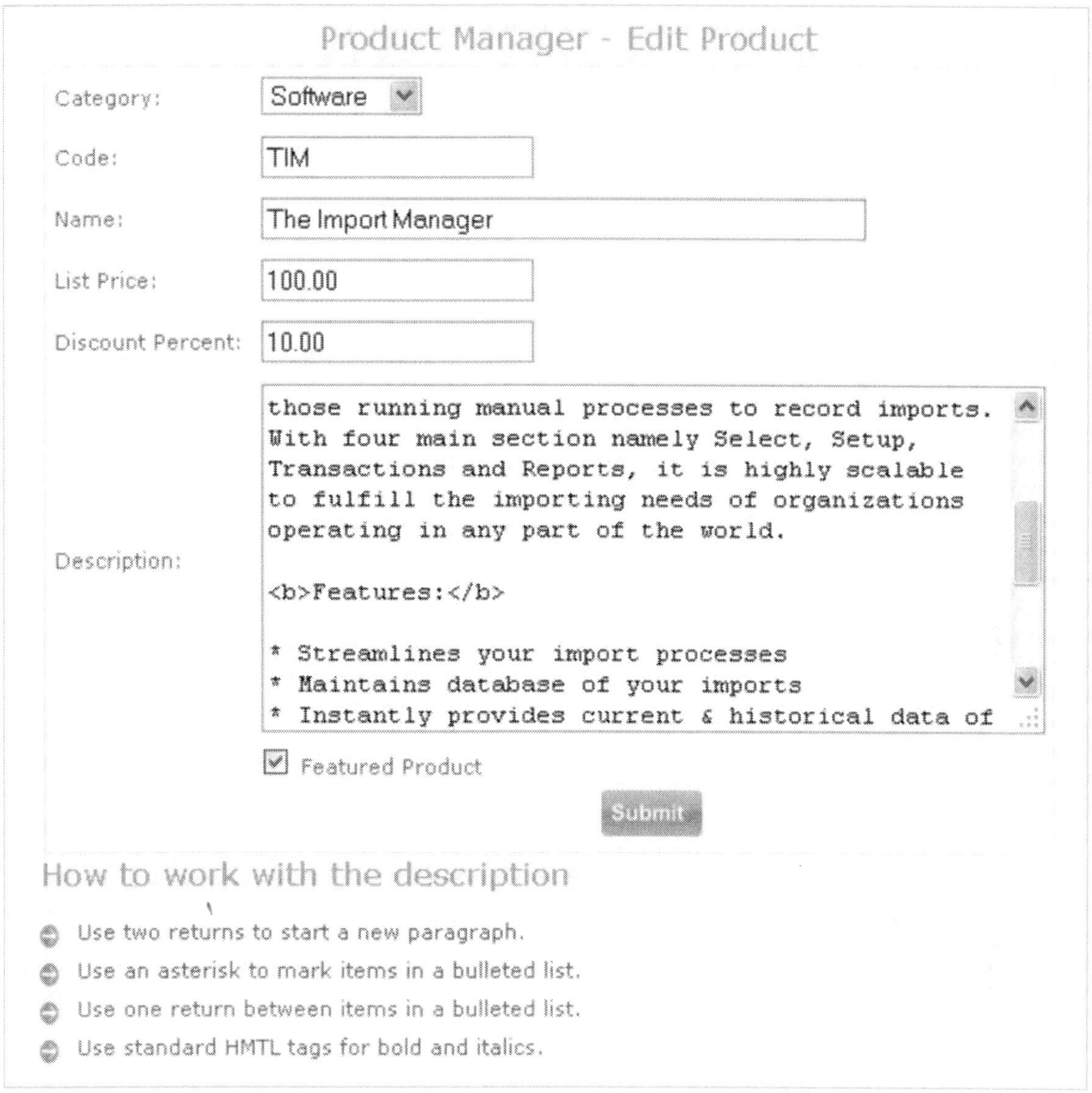

Product Manager - Edit Product

Category: Software

Code: TIM

Name: The Import Manager

List Price: 100.00

Discount Percent: 10.00

Description:

```
those running manual processes to record imports.
With four main section namely Select, Setup,
Transactions and Reports, it is highly scalable
to fulfill the importing needs of organizations
operating in any part of the world.

<b>Features:</b>

* Streamlines  your  import  processes
* Maintains database of your imports
* Instantly provides current & historical data of
```

☑ Featured Product

Submit

How to work with the description

- Use two returns to start a new paragraph.
- Use an asterisk to mark items in a bulleted list.
- Use one return between items in a bulleted list.
- Use standard HMTL tags for bold and italics.

Figure 6-16

After adding a product, an administrator can always modify its content through the interface illustrated above. In this section you'll learn how this process works. The Add Product process is described in section 6.13.6. Note that both these processes are very similar and use same set of php files either to update or to add a product.

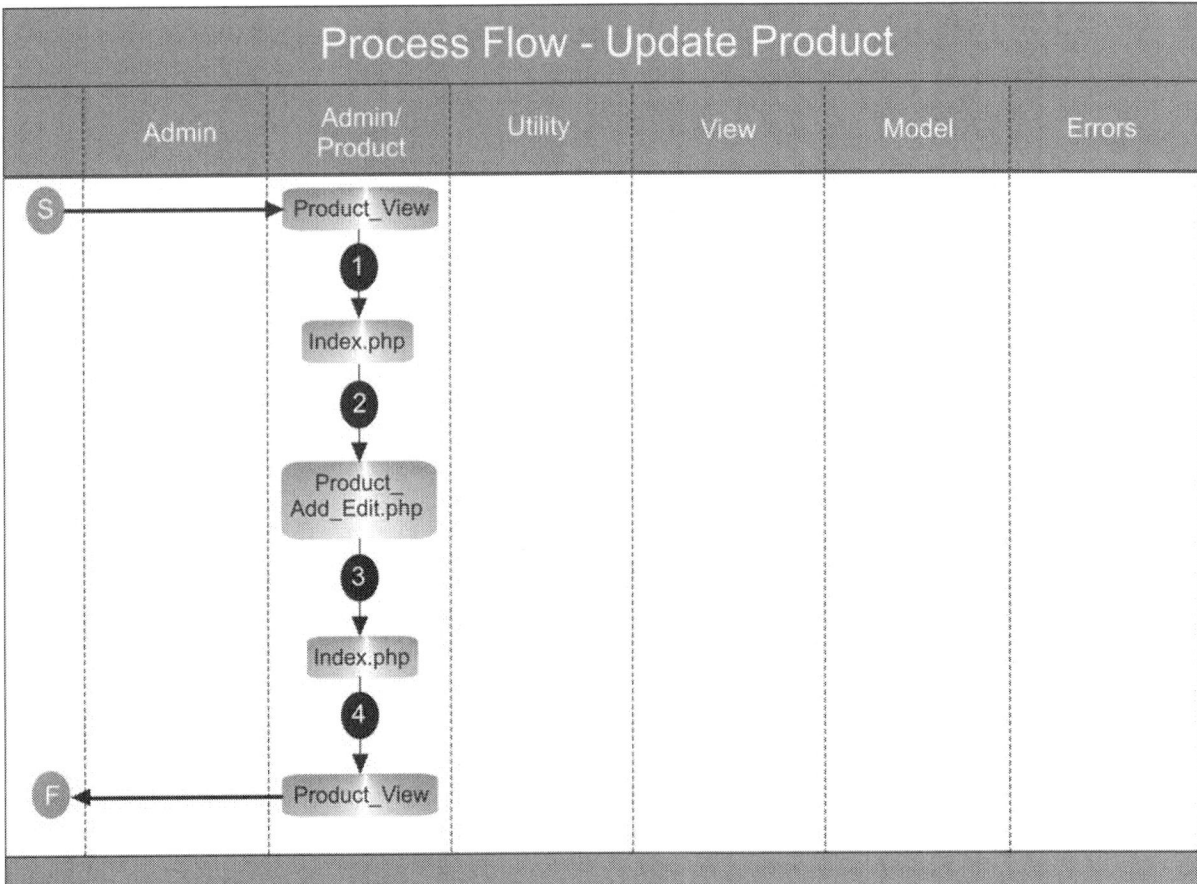

Diagram 6 - Product Update Process

Diagram Explained

Point S - The process starts when the administrator clicks the Edit button on the product details page.

Point 1 - A hidden element having value 'show_add_edit_form' is passed to the controller.

Point 2 - The controller calls product_add_edit.php file based on the above parameter.

Point 3 - The file product_add_edit.php contains a form comprising text elements to allow modification - see Figure 6-16 above. After amendment, the form is submitted back to the controller through a hidden element's parameter value 'update_product'.

Point 4 - After receiving the parameter, the controller evaluates it through the Case statement and calls Product_View.php file. At this point, the update process terminates and the called file Product_view.php displays the product with updated content. Note that the display process has already been discussed in:
- Diagram 4 - points 9, 10, and 11
- List XXVI - XXVIII

List XXXII - Product_View.php - Admin/Product

```
1    <form action="index.php" method="post" id="edit_button_form" >
2      <input type="hidden" name="action" value="show_add_edit_form"/>
3      <input type="hidden" name="product_id" value="<?php echo $product['productID']; ?>" />
4      <input type="hidden" name="category_id" value="<?php echo $product['categoryID']; ?>" />
5      <input type="image" alt="Edit Product" id="right_button" src="<?php echo $app_path;
                                                            ?>images/edit.png">
6    </form>
```

Explanation

This code is similar to the delete process listed under XXIX. The only exception is the value parameter which passes a string "show_add_edit_form" to the controller. We also used an image button named edit.png that processes the code upon click.

List XXXIII - Index.php - Admin/Product

```
1     case 'show_add_edit_form':
2       if (isset($_GET['product_id'])) {
3         $product_id = $_GET['product_id'];
4       } else {
5         $product_id = $_POST['product_id'];
6       }
7       $product = get_product($product_id);
8       $categories = get_categories();
9       include('product_add_edit.php');
10      break;
```

Explanation

After receiving the control, the Index.php file processes the ELSE condition mentioning $_POST (line 5), executes couple of functions, and calls Product_Add_Edit.php file located in the same directory. Note that this case (show_add_edit_form) is executed for both add and edit operations. When a new product is added through the link <a href="index.php?action=show_add_edit_form">Add a new Product</a> listed in Product_List.php file under Admin\Product directory, this case is evaluated again and the IF condition assessing $_GET (line 2) is executed because the parameter (action) and the corresponding value (show_add_edit_form) are forwarded to the controller in the url. Whenever this type of call is made, php creates a $_GET array which is accordingly evaluated in the IF condition.

List XXXIV A - Product_Add_Edit.php - Admin/Product

```php
1    <?php include '../../view/header_admin.php'; ?>
2    <section class="content">
3     <article>
4      <?php
5       if (isset($product_id)) {
6         $heading_text = 'Edit Product';
7       }
8       else {
9         $heading_text = 'Add Product';
10      }
11     ?>
12     <h2 class="center">Product Manager - <?php echo $heading_text; ?></h2>
13     <form action="index.php" method="post" id="add_product_form">
14      <table>
15       <?php if (isset($product_id)) : ?>
16         <input type="hidden" name="action" value="update_product" />
17         <input type="hidden" name="product_id" value="<?php echo $product_id; ?>" />
18       <?php else: ?>
19         <input type="hidden" name="action" value="add_product" />
20       <?php endif; ?>
21       <input type="hidden" name="category_id" value="<?php echo $product['categoryID']; ?>" />
     ...
```

Explanation

As the name indicates, this file generates a page that is used both for editing and adding a product. Note that the code of this file is divided into three listings including this one.

The first IF/ELSE condition (line 5-10) determines an appropriate page heading according to the selected process. Existence of the variable $product_id is an indication that a product is being edited; else, the file is called to add a new product.

Line # 12 puts the evaluated heading in an <h2> element along with a fixed text - Product Manager. The heading takes effect from Rule # 71, shown below, to place the heading in the center of the web page.

.center{ text-align:center;}

Line # 13 places a form on the page to display product's content for amendment or for addition. The form contains a table that holds individual input elements.

Lines 15-20 again establish a condition based on the variable $_product_id. If it exists, two hidden elements are created to inform the controller that an 'update_product' process is being executed for a product whose identity is held in $product_id. The code under ELSE block is executed when a new product is added. It passes a value 'add_product'. Note that here we used an alternate IF/ELSE block which uses the colon symbol instead of curly braces as used in the block just above (line 5-10).

Line # 21 creates another hidden element to hold category id.

List XXXIV B - Product_Add_Edit.php - Admin/Product

```
...
22        <tr>
23         <td><label>Category:</label></td>
24         <td><select name="category_id">
25           <?php foreach ($categories as $category) :
26             if ($category['categoryID'] == $product['categoryID']) {
27                $selected = 'selected';
28             }
29             else {
30                $selected = '';
31             }
32           ?>
33           <option value="<?php echo $category['categoryID']; ?>"<?php echo $selected ?>>
34              <?php echo $category['categoryName']; ?>
35           </option>
36         <?php endforeach; ?>
37         </select></td>
38        </tr>
39        <tr>
40         <td><label>Code:</label></td>
41         <td><input type="input" name="code" value="<?php echo $product['productCode']; ?>" /></td>
42        </tr>
43        <tr>
44         <td><label>Name:</label></td>
45         <td><input type="input" name="name" value="<?php echo $product['productName']; ?>
                                                        "size="50" /></td>
46        </tr>
47        <tr>
48         <td><label>List Price:</label></td>
49         <td><input type="input" name="price" value="<?php echo $product['listPrice']; ?>" /></td>
50        </tr>
51        <tr>
52         <td><label>Discount Percent:</label></td>
53         <td><input type="input" name="discount_percent" value="<?php echo
                                   $product['discountPercent']; ?>" /></td>
54        </tr>
55        <tr>
56         <td><label>Description:</label></td>
57         <td><textarea name="description" rows="10" cols="50"><?php echo $product['description'];
                                                        ?></textarea></td>
58        </tr>
59        <tr>
60         <td><label> </label></td>
61         <td><input type="checkbox" name="featured"
               <?php if ($product['featured']) : ?> checked="checked"
               <?php endif; ?>
               size="30" /> Featured Product
```

```
62        </td>
          </tr>
63        <tr>
64          <td><label> </label></td>
65          <td colspan=2 id="sub"><input type="image" alt="submit" src="<?php echo $app_path;
                                              ?>images/submit.png"></td>
66        </tr>
67      </table>
68    </form>
      ...
```

Explanation

Lines 24-37 display categories in a drop-down list and which is done using the <select> and <option> elements. Line 25 starts a FOREACH loop to populate the list with all categories. The IF condition on line 26 matches the value of categoryID in both $category and $product arrays. If the match is found, the category is marked as *selected* on line # 27. This marking indicates that the category was initially selected by the administrator while creating this product record. Conversely, if no match is found, a null value is moved into the variable $selected (line 30) which generally means that a new product is being added and no value is selected yet. In case of editing, line # 33 will echo 'selected' and will display the selected category (saved previously in the database) in the drop-down list. On the other hand, a null string will be put to mark no selection in case of a new product and the drop-down list will be filled with all categories with first category on top.

This small piece of code is a good example of how to display values in a drop-down list from a database column and to restore the previous selection in the list when a record is called for editing.

The code from line # 39-58 simply generates input and textarea elements to display product information. The elements are presented as blank text boxes when the process is called to enter a new product.

The row created from line 59-62 puts a check box labeled *Featured Products*. Products marked as featured products are displayed on the main Product page of the website. If the administrator checks this box while adding or updating a product, a value of 1 is inserted in the Featured column of the Products table. The administrator can always remove a product from the featured product list by un-checking this box which moves a value of zero into the specified column.

Line # 65 places an image button which, when clicked, passes control to Index.php file defined in the form's action attribute on line # 13 in the previous listing.

List XXXIV C - Product_Add_Edit.php - Admin/Product

```
...
        <!--Inline style applied because this section is unique and appeared only once-->
69      <h2 style="margin-left:60px">How to work with the description</h2>
70      <ul style="margin-left:20px">
71        <li>Use two returns to start a new paragraph.</li>
72        <li>Use an asterisk to mark items in a bulleted list.</li>
73        <li>Use one return between items in a bulleted list.</li>
74        <li>Use standard HMTL tags for bold and italics.</li>
75      </ul>
76      </article>
77    </section>
78    <?php include '../../view/sidebar_admin.php'; ?>
79    <?php include '../../view/footer.php'; ?>
```

Explanation

The rest of the code in this file provides help to administrators on how to enter data in the Description column. Note that we applied inline styles to <h2> and <ul> elements to align them with other page content. The last point of this guidance (line # 74) suggests using standard HTML tags to make text bold and italicized. Let's see how it's done. Follow the steps to make the "Features:" subtitle bold:

1. Login to the admin interface by typing **localhost/abcglobal/admin** in your browser.
2. Enter **admin@abc.com** in the E-mail address box and **gemini** in the password. Click the Login button.
3. Click the **Product Manager** link in the Admin Menu.
4. Under Software, click **The Import Manager**.
5. Click the **Edit** button.
6. Scroll down in the Description area and add tags to the Features subtitle like this: **Features:**
7. Click the **Submit** button and note the sub-heading that will be shown bold-faced.

6.13.5 Image Manager

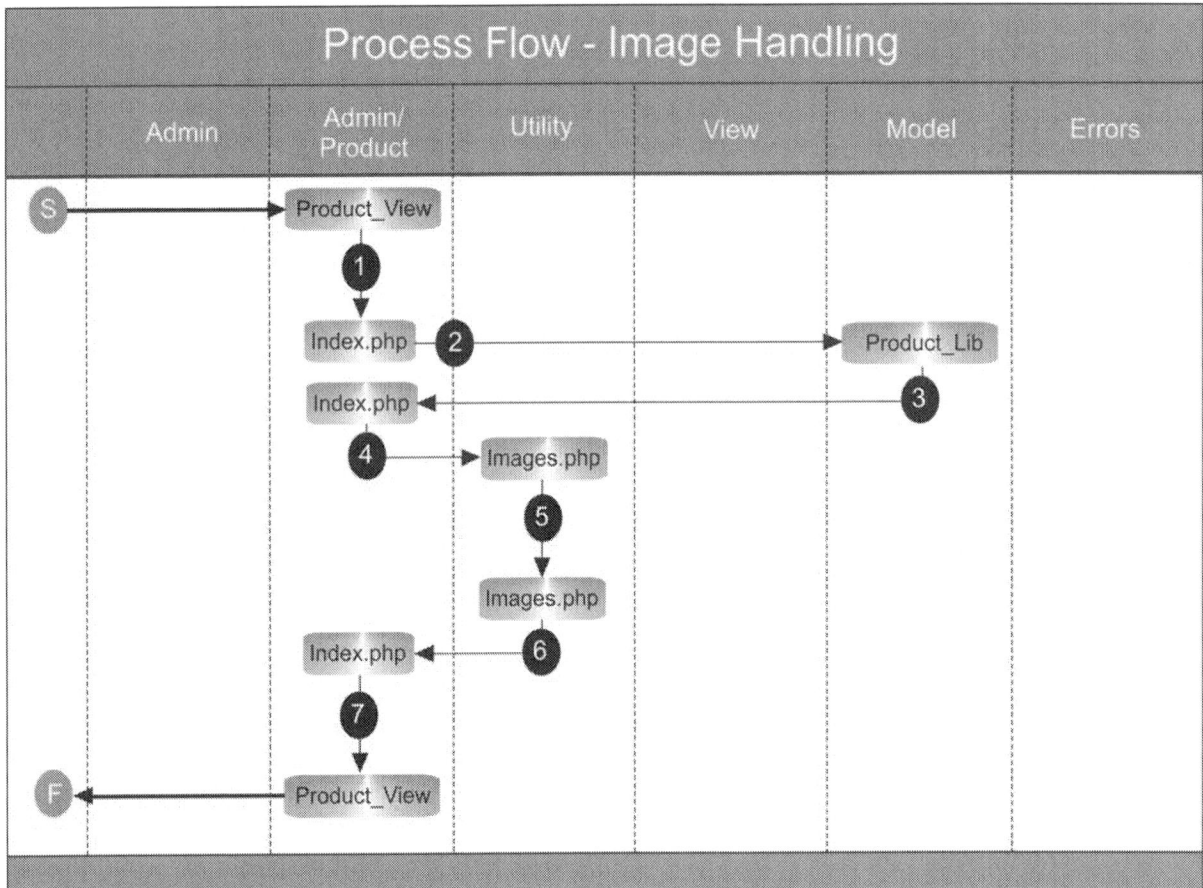

Diagram 7 - Image Handling Process

Diagram Explained

The image upload process is handled through the GD library. It is an image processing library that lets you to work with most image types including GIF, JPEG, and PNG. We enabled this library for our website project in section 5.2.3 7(k) - Download and Configure PHP.

Point S - The process initiates when the administrator selects an image and clicks the upload image button.

Point 1 - The controller is called to handle the process.

Point 2 - The controller calls the get_product() function from the Product_Lib.php file

Point 3 - The function returns complete record of the selected product.

Point 4 - The controller calls Images.php in the Utility directory to process the uploaded image.

Point 5 - The function resize_image() in the Images.php file is called twice to create medium and small versions of the uploaded image.

Point 6 - After adding three image versions (Large - which is the actual uploaded image, Medium, and Small), the flow returns to the controller.

Point 7 - The controller calls Product_View.php file to display the new image.

```
1    <h2>Image Manager</h2>
2    <form action="index.php" method="post" enctype="multipart/form-data" id="upload_image_form">
3      <input type="hidden" name="action" value="upload_image"/>
     <!--Inline style applied to this unique section because it appeared only once-->
4      <input type="file" name="file1" style="margin-left:20px"/><br>
5      <input type="hidden" name="product_id" value="<?php echo $product['productID']; ?>"/>
6      <input type="image" alt="Upload Image" src="<?php echo $app_path; ?>images/upload.png"
                                                        style="margin-left:20px">
7    </form>
8    <p><a href="../../images/<?php echo $product['productCode']; ?>.png">View large image</a></p>
9    <p><a href="../../images/<?php echo $product['productCode']; ?>_s.png">View small image</a></p>
```

Explanation

The second line creates a form to hold image handling elements. Note that we added a new attribute enctype to the form which sends form-data encoded as "multipart/form-data". The enctype attribute specifies how the form-data should be encoded when submitting it to the server. This value is required when you are using forms that have a file upload control - *input type="file"* line # 4. It can be used only if method="post". When you make a POST request, you have to encode the data that forms the body of the request in some way. HTML forms provide three methods of encoding. In the default *application/x-www-form-urlencoded* all characters are encoded before sent (spaces are converted to "+" symbols, and special characters are converted to ASCII HEX values). The one we used here, *multipart/form-data*, is a more complicated encoding. In this method, no characters are encoded but it allows entire files to be included in the data. In the third method, *text/plain*, spaces are converted to "+" symbols, but no special characters are encoded.

Line # 3 sets a value in a hidden element for controller.

On line # 4 we used the required file input type - see section 2.28 File Input Control. This control permits administrators to upload a product image to the web server. We used an inline style to properly place this unique control.

Line # 5 passes the product's id through a hidden control.

Line # 6 places an image button captioned 'Upload Image'. When clicked, this button passes the values mentioned above to the controller in Admin/Product directory.

One line # 8 and 9 two links are created to display large and small images of the product being viewed. When a product image is uploaded, the Image Manager process creates three versions of the image: large, medium, and small. The actual uploaded file is considered as a large image. The remaining two versions are created by the process that we'll see shortly. The medium size image is saved in the Images directory with a '_m' suffix. Similarly, '_s' is added to the small thumbnail version. For example, the code of the first software product provided in the dummy data (db.txt) is TIM. The three versions of this image file would be: TIM.png, TIM_m.png, and TIM_s.png. Note that the image files are moved to the Images folder under the site directory. The above code forms links by providing complete path (../../images/) and file name ($product['productCode'] _s.png).

List XXXVI - Index.php - Admin/Product

```
1      case 'upload_image':
2          $product_id = $_POST['product_id'];
3          $product = get_product($product_id);
4          $product_code = $product['productCode'];
5          $image_filename = $product_code . '.png';
6          $image_dir = $doc_root . $app_path . 'images/';
7          if (isset($_FILES['file1'])) {
8              $source = $_FILES['file1']['tmp_name'];
9              $target = $image_dir . DIRECTORY_SEPARATOR . $image_filename;
               // save uploaded file with correct filename
10             move_uploaded_file($source, $target);
               // add code that creates the medium and small versions of the image
11             process_image($image_dir, $image_filename);
               // display product with new image
12             include('product_view.php');
13         }
14         break;
```

Explanation

The controller receives the process flow from Product_View.php file and executes code under the 'upload_image' Case statement. Assume that you're uploading file for the first software product - The Import Manager -; the following values will be stored in the variables defined above.

Line # 2: $product_id = 1

Line # 3: The $product array stores complete record of product # 1 fetched through the function get_product.

Line # 4: $product_code = TIM

Line # 5: $image_filename = TIM.png

Line # 6: $image_dir = c:\inetpub\wwwroot/abcglobal/images/

Line # 7: The array $_FILES has the following values:

$_FILES	array[1]	
[file1]	array[5]	
[name]	string	"TIM.PNG"
[type]	string	"image/png"
[tmp_name]	string	"C:\WINDOWS\Temp\php5D.tmp"
[error]	integer	0
[size]	integer	21581

> **NOTE**
> By using the global PHP $_FILES array you can upload files from a client computer to the remote server.

Line # 8: $source = C:\WINDOWS\Temp\php5D.tmp

Line # 9: $target = c:\inetpub\wwwroot/abcglobal/images/\TIM.png

Line # 10: The PHP built-in *move_uploaded_file()* function moves an uploaded file to a new location. It returns TRUE on success, or FALSE on failure. The syntax of this function is:

move_uploaded_file(file,newloc) where the file parameter specifies the file to be moved and the newloc parameter tells the new location for the file.

Line # 11 calls a function process_image() from Images.php file positioned under the Utility directory.

Line # 12 displays the product's page with the uploaded image.

List XXXVII - Images.php - Utility

```
1    function process_image($dir, $filename) {
         // Set up the variables
2        $i = strrpos($filename, '.');
3        $image_name = substr($filename, 0, $i);
4        $ext = substr($filename, $i);
         // Set up the read path
5        $image_path = $dir . $filename;
         // Set up the write paths
6        $image_path_m = $dir . $image_name . '_m' . $ext;
7        $image_path_s = $dir . $image_name . '_s' . $ext;
         // Create an image that's a maximum of 200x200 pixels
8        resize_image($image_path, $image_path_m, 200, 200);
         // Create a thumbnail image that's a maximum of 100x100 pixels
9        resize_image($image_path, $image_path_s, 100, 100);
10   }
```

Explanation

This function is called by Index.php (line # 11) to process product's images. The two parameters $dir and $filename receive values *c:\inetpub\wwwroot/abcglobal/images* and *TIM.png* respectively from the controller file. Values held in other variables are:

Line # 2: $i = 3 - The strrpos() function finds the position of the last occurrence of a string (.) inside another string ($filename). This function returns 3 as the position of the sought period character starting with 0 as the first position.

Line # 3: $image_name = TIM - The substr() function returns a part of a string. Here, the function fetches 3 characters ($i) from the string ($filename) and from the starting position (0).

Line # 4: $ext = .png - Stores the extension part of the file name along with period by taking all onward characters from the third position. Remember that zero posses the first place in the string.

Line # 5: $image_path = c:\inetpub\wwwroot/abcglobal/images/TIM.png

Line # 6: $image_path_m = c:\inetpub\wwwroot/abcglobal/images/TIM_m.png

Line # 7: $image_path_s = c:\inetpub\wwwroot/abcglobal/images/TIM_s.png

Line # 8 calls a function resize_image() residing in the same Images.php file to create a medium sized version of the provided product image.

Line # 9 calls the function again to create a thumbnail version of the image. The resize_image function is called twice to create the two smaller versions of the image 200x200 and 100x100 pixels. Since the image we are using is smaller than the first measure, only the second image will be created in the called function.

List XXXVIII A - Images.php - Utility

```php
1    function resize_image($old_image_path, $new_image_path, $max_width, $max_height) {
         // Get image type
2        $image_info = getimagesize($old_image_path);
3        $image_type = $image_info[2];
         // Set up the function names
4        switch($image_type) {
5          case IMAGETYPE_JPEG:
6            $image_from_file = 'imagecreatefromjpeg';
7            $image_to_file = 'imagejpeg';
8            break;
9          case IMAGETYPE_GIF:
10           $image_from_file = 'imagecreatefromgif';
11           $image_to_file = 'imagegif';
12           break;
13         case IMAGETYPE_PNG:
14           $image_from_file = 'imagecreatefrompng';
15           $image_to_file = 'imagepng';
16           break;
17         default:
18           echo 'File must be a JPEG, GIF, or PNG image.';
19           exit;
20       }
         ...
```

This function exhibits how to resize an image and is described in two parts. As mentioned earlier, the uploaded image file has three versions: Large (the original one), medium, and small. This function creates the last two after receiving all the required parameters from the previous one.

Line # 2: The getimagesize() function determines the size of any given image file and returns the dimensions along with the file type and a height/width text string. The following figure presents values from the $image_info array for TIM.png got through the function getimagesize().

$image_info	array[6]	
[0]	integer	163
[1]	integer	178
[2]	integer	3
[3]	string	"width="163" height="178""
[bits]	integer	8
[mime]	string	"image/png"

Line # 3-20: The value of $image_type is 3 which is obtained from index [2]. Index 2 returns a constant that identifies the type of the image. Here, the image is a PNG, so index 2 returns the IMAGETYPE_PNG constant. If the image were a JPEG or GIF, this index would return the IMAGETYPE_JPEG and IMAGETYPE_GIF constants respectively. This constant is evaluated in the Switch statement to set up an appropriate function name to read and write the image to and from a file. For example, in the current scenario, the third Case statement (line # 13), for PNG image type, will be executed because we are using a .png file. PHP provides three functions: imagecreatefromjpeg, imagecreatefromgif, and imagecreatefrompng to create an image from a file. After assessing the image type, the code creates the new image using the function name stored as a string in the $image_from_file variable. The code uses the imagecreatefrompng function because we're using a PNG type image. However, if the image were of the JPEG or GIF type, this code would use the other functions mentioned in other Case statements. If the image isn't among the listed types, the message on line # 18 will be displayed. Sometimes this message is displayed even if you're uploading the correct image type. In such situation, check the PHP log file (php-error.log). See point 7(b) under section 5.2.3 Download and Configure PHP for the log file location. If you see a message like "unlink: Permission denied" in the log file, grant full control to Internet Guest User (IUSR) on the Images directory. After granting permission, the file will be uploaded to the Images folder on your PC. Once this code processes the image, it uses the function that's stored in the $image_to_file variable to write the image to the second file path. Again, since this example uses a PNG image, this code uses the appropriate function for writing a PNG image: the imagepng function on line 15.

List XXXVIII B - Images.php - Utility

```
    ...
    // Get the old image and its height and width
21  $old_image = $image_from_file($old_image_path);
22  $old_width = imagesx($old_image);
23  $old_height = imagesy($old_image);
    // Calculate height and width ratios
24  $width_ratio = $old_width / $max_width;
25  $height_ratio = $old_height / $max_height;
    // If image is larger than specified ratio, create the new image
26  if ($width_ratio > 1 || $height_ratio > 1) {
      // Calculate height and width for the new image
27    $ratio = max($width_ratio, $height_ratio);
28    $new_width = round($old_width / $ratio);
29    $new_height = round($old_height / $ratio);
      // Create the new image
30    $new_image = imagecreatetruecolor($new_width, $new_height);
      // Set transparency according to image type
31    if ($image_type == IMAGETYPE_GIF) {
32      $alpha = imagecolorallocatealpha($new_image, 0, 0, 0, 127);
33      imagecolortransparent($new_image, $alpha);
34    }
35    if ($image_type == IMAGETYPE_PNG || $image_type == IMAGETYPE_GIF) {
36      imagealphablending($new_image, false);
37      imagesavealpha($new_image, true);
38    }
      // Copy old image to new image - this resizes the image
39    $new_x = 0;
40    $new_y = 0;
41    $old_x = 0;
42    $old_y = 0;
43    imagecopyresampled($new_image, $old_image,
                $new_x, $new_y, $old_x, $old_y,
                $new_width, $new_height, $old_width, $old_height);
      // Write the new image to a new file
44    $image_to_file($new_image, $new_image_path);
      // Free any memory associated with the new image
45    imagedestroy($new_image);
46  } else {
      // Write the old image to a new file
47    $image_to_file($old_image, $new_image_path);
48  }
    // Free any memory associated with the old image
49  imagedestroy($old_image);
50 }
```

Explanation

Line # 21: This code reads the image from the specified file. To do so, it uses the function *imagecreatefrompng* that's stored as a string in the $image_from_file variable (line # 14), and passes the argument $old_image_path. This path is also received as an argument from the function process_image() (line # 8-9 List XXXVII and Line # 1 List XXXVIII A).

Line # 22: This code gets the width of the old image through the function imagesx(). Since the width of the image TIM.PNG is 163, the value is stored in the variable $old_width.

Line # 23: Just like the previous code, this one uses imagesy() function to get the height of the uploaded image. The height, 178 is stored in the variable $old_height.

Line # 24: Calculates the width ratio. The result stored in the variable $width_ratio will be 1.63 (163/100).

Line # 25: Calculates the height ratio. The current height ratio is 1.78 (178/100). These ratios are calculated to keep the image within the specified limit.

Line # 26: The IF condition checks that either the height ratio or the width ratio is greater than 1; the old image is larger than maximum height or width.

Line # 27: This code uses the max() function to get the larger of the two ratios. The values stored in the variable $ratio will be the $height_ratio (1.78) because it is the maximum between the two.

Line # 28: Calculates the new image width. The value, after rounding, will be 92 (163/1.78).

Line # 29: Determines the new height. This value will be 100 (178/1.78).

Line # 30: This line uses the function *imagecreatetruecolor* to create a new truecolor image of 92 x 100 pixels.

Line # 31-38: In this block of code transparency for GIF and PNG is handled. Note that JPEG doesn't allow parts of an image to be transparent. Lines 31-34 perform some processing that needs to be done only for GIF images. The first statement (line # 32) calls the *imagecolorallocatealpha* function that allocate black color (RGB value 0, 0, 0) as alpha color and an alpha value of 127 to indicate that the alpha color should be completely transparent. The next statement uses the *imagecolortransparent* function to set the alpha color as the transparent color in the image. The IF statement from line 35-38 checks whether the image is a GIF image or a PNG image. The first statement (line # 36) turns off alpha blending which is necessary to save complete alpha channel information that is done using code on line # 37.

Line # 39-43: This block of code creates the new image and copies the old image to the new image. To do that, this code uses a value of 0 for the x and y values of the old and new images to indicate that both images should start at the upper left corner. In addition, it specifies the correct values for the height and width of the old and new images. The function *imagecopyresampled* copies a rectangular portion of the source image (old) to the destination image (new) resizing the image if necessary.

Line # 44: This code writes the new image to the specified file path.

Line # 45: This line uses the imagedestroy() function to free any memory used by the new image.

Line # 46-48: The ELSE block is executed when the old image is smaller than the maximum width and height limits. In such situation, the image is not resized and a copy of the old image is written to the new path (line # 47).

Line # 49: Frees any memory used by the old image.

6.13.6 Add Product

The Add Product process is similar to the update process and uses the same PHP files that we used while editing a product.

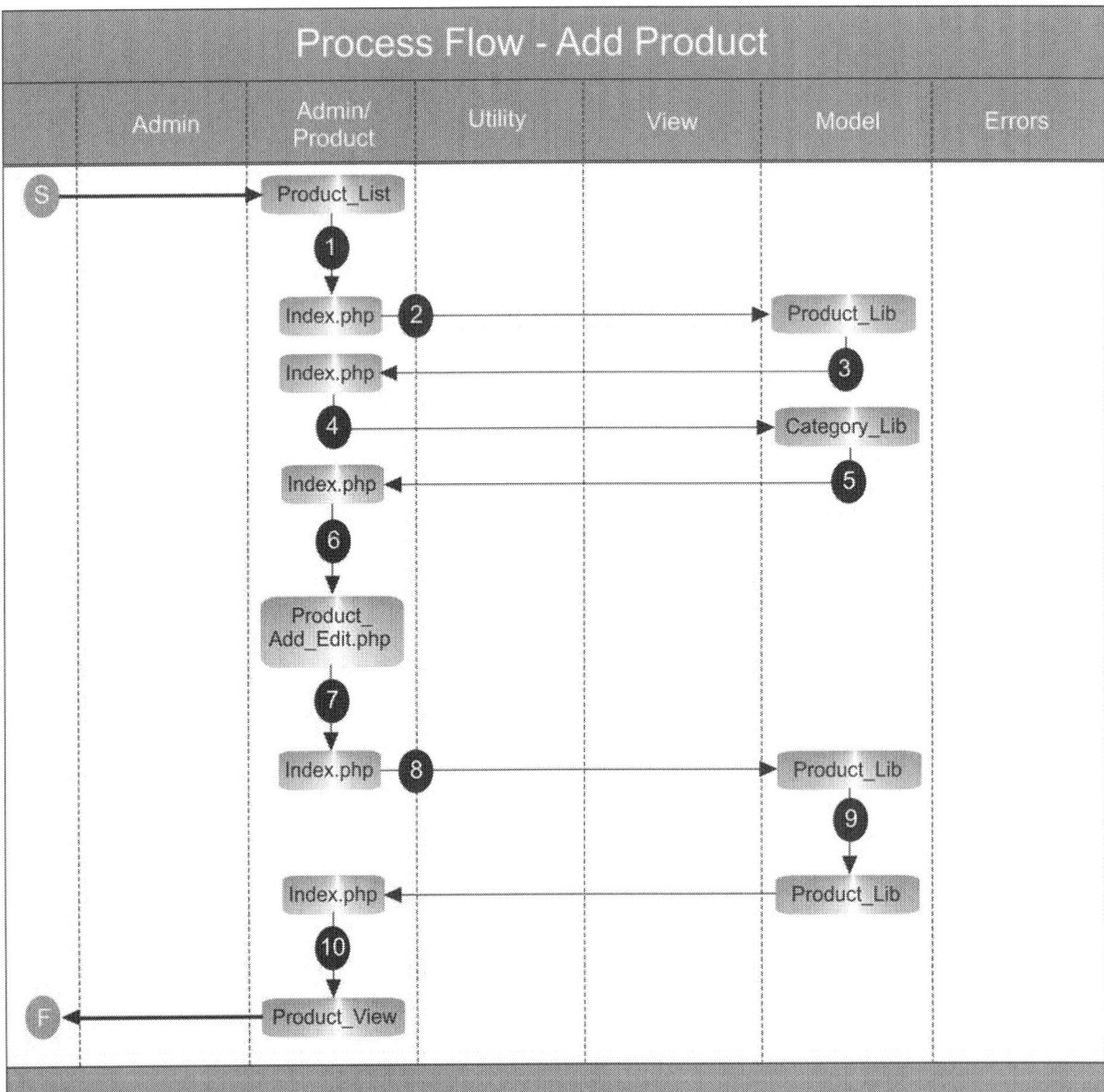

Diagram 8 - Product Addition Process

Diagram Explained

Point S - The process starts when the administrator clicks the 'Add a New Product' link under the list of products.

Point 1 - The controller executes the code under the case 'show_add_edit_form'. This parameter is passed to it through the GET method when the above link is clicked.

Point 2 - The function get_product() is called from Product_Lib.php file.

Point 4 - get_categories() function is called from Category_Lib.php file.

Point 6 - This file presents the form to input content for the new product. It was discussed in listing XXXIV.

Point 8 and 9 - The new product is added to the database through the add_product() function in the library file. The get_product() function is executed again to get details of the newly added product.

Point 10 - Displays the new product.

As most of the code in this process has already been discussed, we'll move on to the next task - Manage Orders.

6.14 Task 6 - Manage Orders

The administrators can view, process and delete orders placed by members of the website with the help of this module which has the following three pages:

1. **Orders List:** After clicking the initial Order Manager link in the Admin Menu, the administrator is presented with a list of Outstanding and Shipped orders.

2. **Order Information:** Both these sections (Outstanding and Shipped Orders) carry links to corresponding orders which, when clicked, display details of individual orders on Order Information page. The page has two buttons - Delete and Ship Order. An administrator can either process the order through the Ship Order button or cancel the order by using the Delete button. Note that these buttons are displayed only when an order is outstanding.

3. **Delete Order:** If an order is not shipped, the administrator can delete it. The Delete Order page confirms the process before removing the order from the database.

Let's see how this process works beginning with the first one: Orders List.

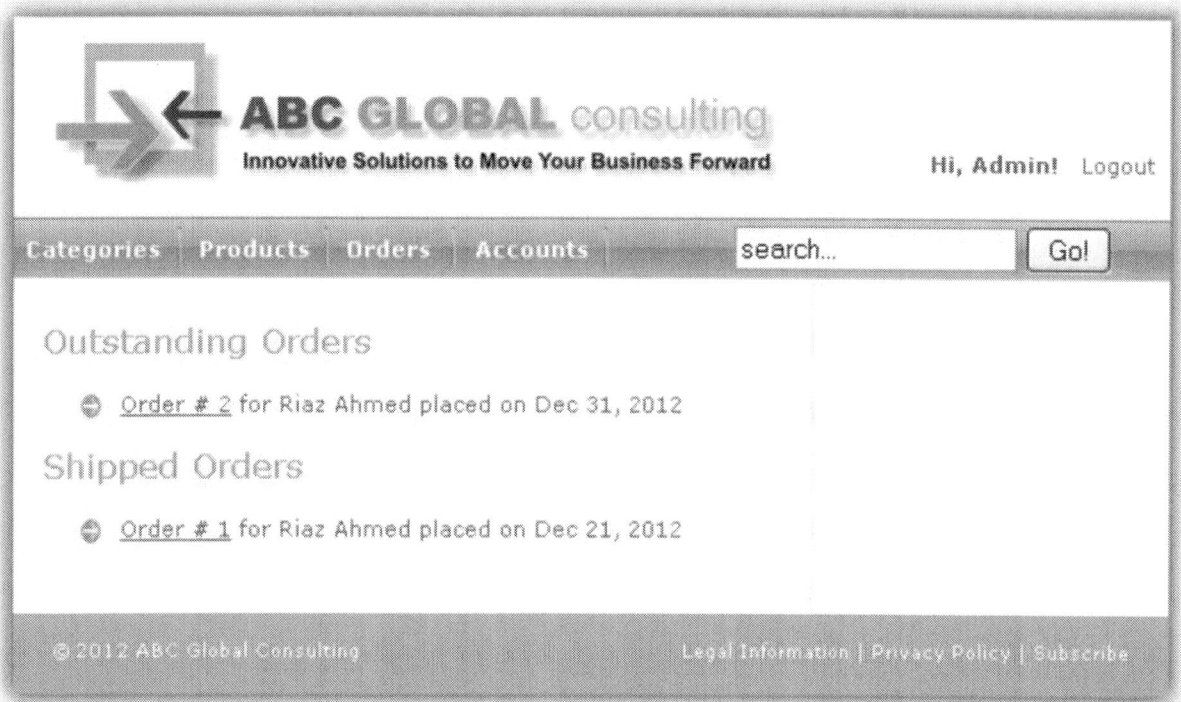

Figure 6-17

The page illustrated above lists all orders, either shipped or yet to be shipped, under two sections. Each section has links to individual orders. These links call another page to display details of the order. Orders under the Shipped section can only be viewed, while those under the outstanding category can either by shipped or deleted through the order details page.

6.14.1 Orders List

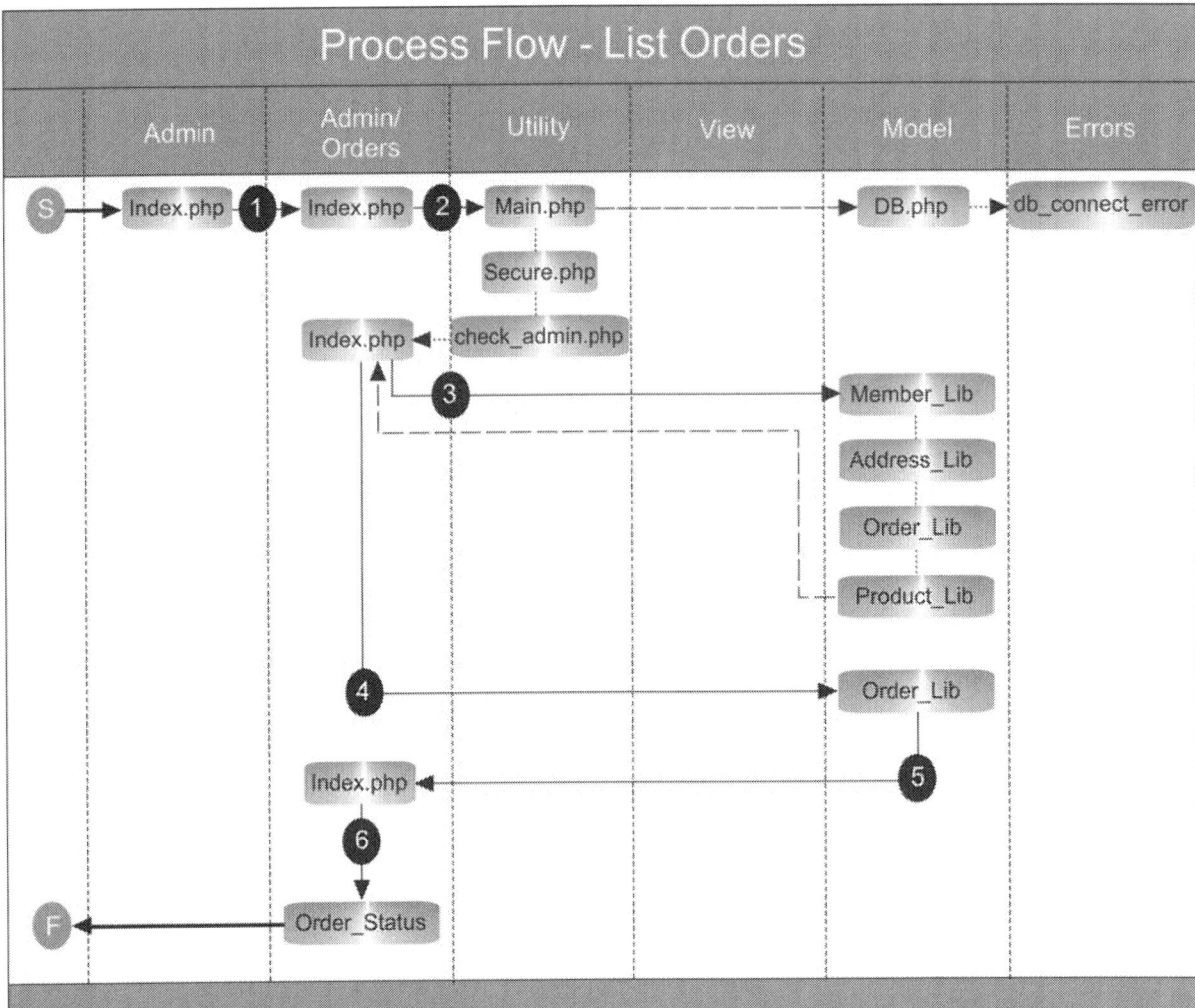

Diagram 9 - List Orders

Diagram Explained

Point S - The process starts when the link Order Manager link is clicked in the Admin Menu.

Point 1 - The control is transferred to Index.php in the Orders directory.

Point 2 - It's a usual process that calls some utility files to check connectivity.

Point 3 - Here, some new files are included in the process. These files are Member_Lib, Address_Lib, and Order_Lib. All these library files contain several functions to interact with the database.

Point 4 - Two functions, Outstanding_Orders and Shipped_Orders, are called from the library file Order_Lib.php. These functions return matching orders for display.

Point 6 - The controller calls Order_Status.php file which displays the result returned in Point 5.

List XXXIX - Index.php - Admin/Orders & Order_Lib.php - Model

Index.php

```
1    case 'list_orders':
2      $new_orders = outstanding_orders();
3      $old_orders = shipped_orders();
4      include 'order_status.php';
5      break;
```

Order_Lib.php

```
6    function outstanding_orders() {
7      global $db;
8      $query =
          'SELECT * FROM orders
          INNER JOIN members
          ON members.memberID = orders.memberID
          WHERE shipDate IS NULL ORDER BY orderDate';
       ...
     }
9    function shipped_orders() {
10     global $db;
11     $query =
          'SELECT * FROM orders
          INNER JOIN members
          ON members.memberID = orders.memberID
          WHERE shipDate IS NOT NULL ORDER BY orderDate';
       ...
     }
```

Explanation

At this stage you must be comfortable with the process flow and can also understand what's happening. In the above listing we've merged related code from two different files. The code from Index.php file is executed when the orders' list page is initially called.

Line # 2 and 3 receive results from the two functions in the defined variables: $new_orders and $old_orders.

Line # 4 calls Order_Status.php from Admin/Orders directory to display the result.

The two functions outstanding_orders() and shipped_orders() use the SELECT SQL statement to collect order data. The first query filters data on IS NULL basis while the second one uses the reverse IS NOT NULL criterion.

The output of the two queries is show below:

Outstanding Orders Query		Shipped Orders Query	
orderID	2	orderID	1
memberID	1	memberID	1
orderDate	2012-12-31 10:35:15	orderDate	2012-12-31 10:35:15
shipAmount	200.00	shipAmount	200.00
taxAmount	64.64	taxAmount	64.64
shipDate	NULL	shipDate	2013-01-01 09:43:13
shipAddressID	1	shipAddressID	1
cardType	2	cardType	2
cardNumber	1111111111111111	cardNumber	1111111111111111
cardExpires	04/2015	cardExpires	04/2015
billingAddressID	2	billingAddressID	2
memberID	1	memberID	1
fName	Riaz	fName	Riaz
lName	Ahmed	lName	Ahmed
shipAddressID	1	shipAddressID	1
billingAddressID	2	billingAddressID	2
memberEmail	realtech@cyber.net.pk	memberEmail	realtech@cyber.net.pk
memberPW	4ee29c1079121336a....	memberPW	4ee29c1079121336a....

List XXXX - Order_Status.php - Admin/Orders

```
...
1    <h2>Outstanding Orders</h2>
2    <?php if (count($new_orders) > 0 ) : ?>
3      <ul>
4        <?php foreach($new_orders as $order) :
5          $order_id = $order['orderID'];
6          $order_date = strtotime($order['orderDate']);
7          $order_date = date('M j, Y', $order_date);
8          $url = $app_path . 'admin/orders' . '?action=view_order&order_id=' . $order_id;
9        ?>
10         <li>
11           <a href="<?php echo $url; ?>">Order #
12           <?php echo $order_id; ?></a> for
13           <?php echo $order['fName'] . ' ' . $order['lName']; ?> placed on <?php echo $order_date; ?>
14         </li>
15       <?php endforeach; ?>
16      </ul>
17   <?php else: ?>
18     <p>There are no outstanding orders.</p>
19   <?php endif; ?>
20   <h2>Shipped Orders</h2>
21   <?php if (count($old_orders) > 0 ) : ?>
22      <ul>
23        <?php foreach($old_orders as $order) :
24          $order_id = $order['orderID'];
25          $order_date = strtotime($order['orderDate']);
26          $order_date = date('M j, Y', $order_date);
27          $url = $app_path . 'admin/orders' . '?action=view_order&order_id=' . $order_id;
28        ?>
29         <li>
30           <a href="<?php echo $url; ?>">Order #
31           <?php echo $order_id; ?></a> for
32           <?php echo $order['fName'] . ' ' . $order['lName']; ?> placed on <?php echo $order_date; ?>
33         </li>
34       <?php endforeach; ?>
35      </ul>
36   <?php else: ?>
37     <p>There are no shipped orders.</p>
38   <?php endif; ?>
...
```

Explanation

Line 1-19 form a section to display outstanding orders. These orders are judged through the count of $new_orders. If the value of this variable is greater than zero, a list of outstanding orders is generated from line 3-16. If the value is zero, line # 18 is executed to display the message.

The strtotime() function on line # 6 parses an English textual date or time. It parses the time string parameter - $order['orderDate'].

The code on line # 7 uses the date() function to present value in the $order_date variable in Mon dd, YYYY format. Here, the three letters represent:

> M: For three letters month (Jan-Dec)
>
> j: For day of month (1-31)
>
> Y: For four digits year (2012)

When the administrator clicks an order link, line # 8 calls Index.php (Admin/Orders). It passes two values view_order and $order_id to the controller. The former one is evaluated in a Case statement and the later one is used to fetch details of the specified order.

```
elseif ( isset($_GET['action']) ) {
    $action = $_GET['action'];
}
```

```
case 'view_order':
    $order_id = $_GET['order_id'];
    // Get order data
    $order = get_order($order_id);
    $order_date = date('M j, Y', strtotime($order['orderDate']));
    $order_items = get_order_items($order_id);
    ...
```

Lines 10-14 display order links specified on line # 8 and concatenate other values such as member name and order date to it. The code produces a text like: *Order # 2 for Riaz Ahmed placed on Dec 31, 2012*. The text, *Order # 2*, is a link that calls details of the specified order when clicked.

Code from line # 20-38 generates list of shipped orders. It is similar to the previous code with one distinction and that is: the $old_orders variable which is used to check number of shipped orders to display.

6.14.2 Order Information, Confirmation and Deletion

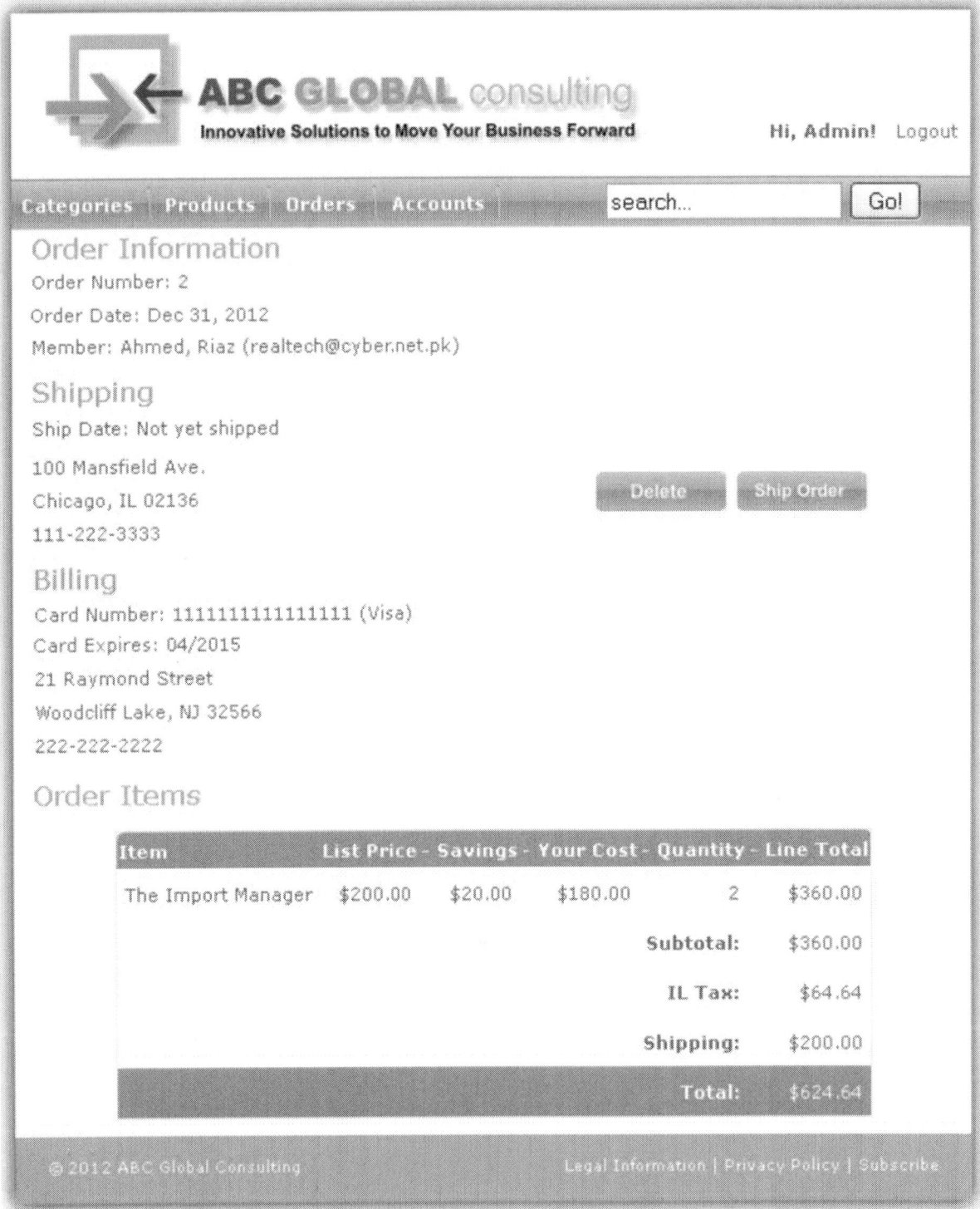

Figure 6-18

In the illustrated web page, details of a selected order are presented. The existence of two buttons (Delete and Ship Order) is an indication that the order is yet to be shipped. An administrator can either delete or process it using these two buttons.

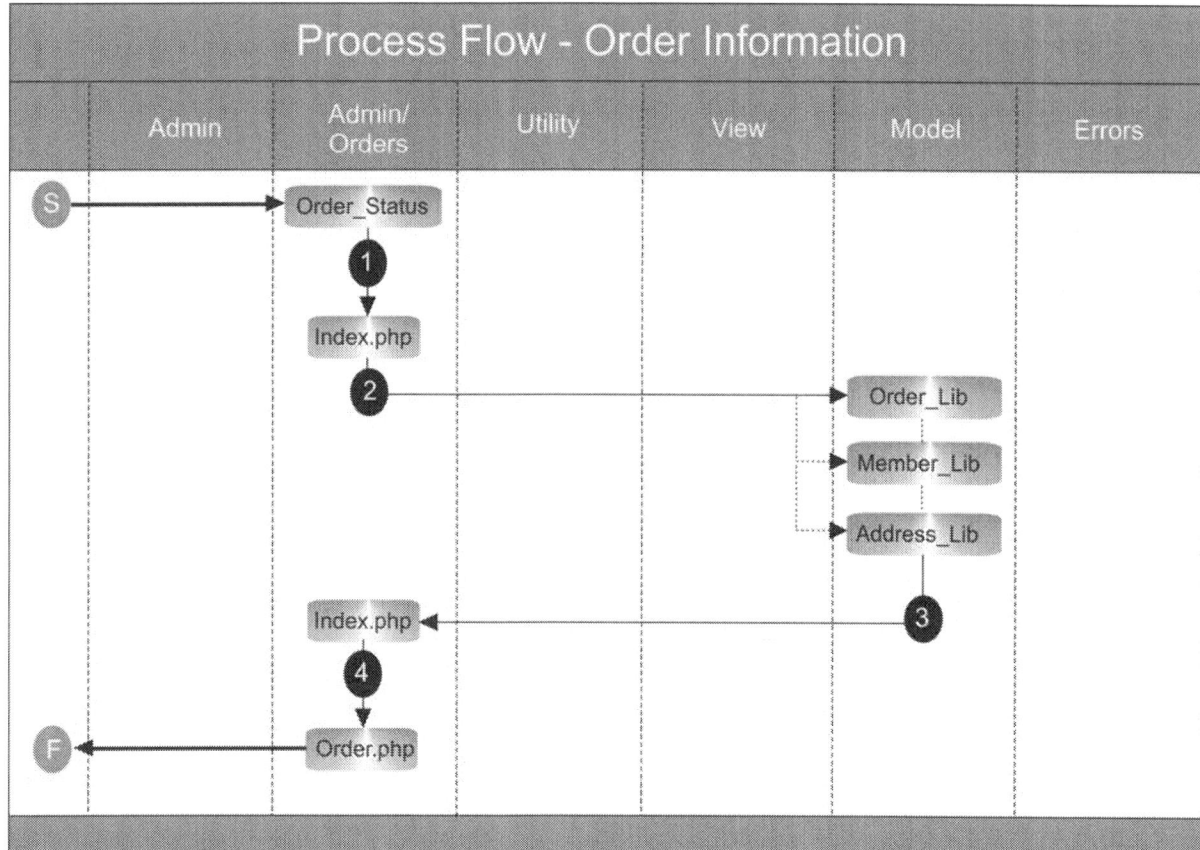

Diagram 10 - Order Information

Diagram Explained

Point S - This process starts when an order link is clicked in either the outstanding or the shipped orders list.

Point 1 - Two parameters, view_order and $order_id, are passed to the controller which executes the code associated with the case view_order.

Point 2 - The three library files are called from the Model directory to fetch relevant records. The first one is called to execute get_order() and get_order_items() functions, the second one is accessed to run get_member() function, while the last one fetches shipping and billing addresses through get_address() function.

Point 4 - After receiving the required data (point 3), the controller calls Order.php file which displays order details as illustrated in figure 6-18.

List XXXXI - Index.php - Admin/Orders

```
    ...
1   elseif ( isset($_GET['action']) ) {
2       $action = $_GET['action'];
3   }

    ...
4     case 'view_order':
5         $order_id = $_GET['order_id'];
          // Get order data
6         $order = get_order($order_id);
7         $order_date = date('M j, Y', strtotime($order['orderDate']));
8         $order_items = get_order_items($order_id);
          // Get member data
9         $member = get_member($order['memberID']);
10        $name = $member['lName'] . ', ' . $member['fName'];
11        $email = $member['memberEmail'];
12        $card_number = $order['cardNumber'];
13        $card_expires = $order['cardExpires'];
14        $card_name = card_name($order['cardType']);
          //Get Shipping Address
15        $shipping_address = get_address($order['shipAddressID']);
16        $ship_line1 = $shipping_address['line1'];
17        $ship_line2 = $shipping_address['line2'];
18        $ship_city = $shipping_address['city'];
19        $ship_state = $shipping_address['state'];
20        $ship_zip = $shipping_address['zipCode'];
21        $ship_phone = $shipping_address['phone'];
          //Get Billing Address
22        $billing_address = get_address($order['billingAddressID']);
23        $bill_line1 = $billing_address['line1'];
24        $bill_line2 = $billing_address['line2'];
25        $bill_city = $billing_address['city'];
26        $bill_state = $billing_address['state'];
27        $bill_zip = $billing_address['zipCode'];
28        $bill_phone = $billing_address['phone'];
29        include 'order.php';
30        break;
    ...
```

Explanation

The controller makes all the files available to this process using the initial require_once statements. Then, it executes the ELSEIF code (line 1) which provides couple of arguments to it. One of these arguments is view_order which, in this case, is evaluated and found true. Note that the two arguments that this code received came from List XXXX line 8 & 27.

Line # 5 stores the parameter value order_id into $order_id. This primary key is required to tell subsequent processes about which order details to fetch.

Line # 6 retrieves data from the master table i.e. *Orders* through a call to the function get_order() in Order_Lib.php file.

Line # 7 formats order date in the specified format. See previous listing for details.

Line # 8 gets all rows from the detail table i.e. *OrderItems* for the selected order.

Line # 9 fetches complete record of the member who placed that order. After retrieving the row, information contained within columns is stored in corresponding variables (line 10-14).

Lines 15-28 store shipping and billing address data in appropriate variables after fetching them from the database through the get_address() function. Note that this function is called twice but with different parameters to fetch the two addresses - *$order['shipAddressID']* & *$order['billingAddressID']*.

One line # 29, the controller calls order.php file to display the gathered information on the Order Information page.

List XXXXII - Order.php - Admin/Orders

...

```
1    <h2>Order Information</h2>
2    <p>Order Number: <?php echo $order_id; ?></p>
3    <p>Order Date: <?php echo $order_date; ?></p>
4    <p>Member: <?php echo $name . ' (' . $email . ')'; ?></p>
5    <h2>Shipping</h2>
6    <?php if ($order['shipDate'] === NULL) : ?>
7      <p>Ship Date: Not yet shipped</p>
8      <p>
9        <form action="index.php" method="post" >
10         <input type="hidden" name="action" value="set_ship_date" />
11         <input type="hidden" name="order_id" value="<?php echo $order_id; ?>" />
12         <input type="image" id="right_button" src="<?php echo $app_path;?>images/shiporder.png">
13       </form>
14       <form action="index.php" method="post" >
15         <input type="hidden" name="action" value="confirm_delete" />
16         <input type="hidden" name="order_id" value="<?php echo $order_id; ?>" />
17         <input type="image" id="right_button" src="<?php echo $app_path;?>images/delete.png">
18       </form>
19     </p>
20   <?php else:
21     $ship_date = date('M j, Y', strtotime($order['shipDate']));   ?>
22     <p>Ship Date: <?php echo $ship_date; ?></p>
23   <?php endif; ?>
24   <p><?php echo $ship_line1; ?><br>
25     <?php if ( strlen($ship_line2) > 0 ) : ?>
26       <?php echo $ship_line2; ?><br>
27     <?php endif; ?>
28     <?php echo $ship_city; ?>, <?php echo $ship_state; ?>
29     <?php echo $ship_zip; ?><br>
30     <?php echo $ship_phone; ?>
31   </p>
```

...

Explanation

This file is used to display both outstanding and shipped orders. Using the shipDate column value (line # 6), it distinguishes the two. If the value of shipDate is NULL (as mentioned on line 6), code from line 7-19 is executed. The identical operator (===) checks that the two values are true and have the same type. This block of code displays the two buttons we've been talking about to either delete or ship the selected order. After clicking any one of these buttons, the process takes hidden values (set_ship_date or confirm_delete) to Index.php file. Based on these values the controller proceeds. The value set_ship_date indicates that the administrator has requested to ship the order. On the other hand, the value confirm_delete sends a request to delete the selected order. In the former case, the controller calls a function set_ship_date() from the order library file (order_lib.php) which uses the UPDATE SQL statement to put current system date in the shipdate column. A date value in this column signifies that the order has been shipped. NULL stands for outstanding orders. Once the administrator processes an order, it is listed in the shipped category and the two buttons are removed as well.

Clicking the Delete button executes the confirm_delete case in the controller file. The code under this block fetches some basic information such as order date and member details. Next, it calls order_delete.php file. This file displays a confirmation page with two buttons and the above basic information. If the administrator clicks the Cancel button, nothing happens; but, if he/she clicks the Delete button, the process flows back to Index.php file with a hidden value 'delete'. The 'delete' case in the controller file calls delete_order() function which removes the selected order from two database tables (orders and orderitems).

Both these case statements use a built-in intval() function which gets the integer value of a variable. In our case, it returns the integer value of the variable order_id on success, or 0 on failure.

A table is also created to display records from the detail table (orderitems) in the database. This table is styled using rule # 73-78. For further information, see section 3.14 - Styling Tables. Open style.css file to see the six rules. All these rules use similar properties and attributes that you saw earlier while creating the static pages for this project.

6.15 Task 7 - Manage Admin Accounts

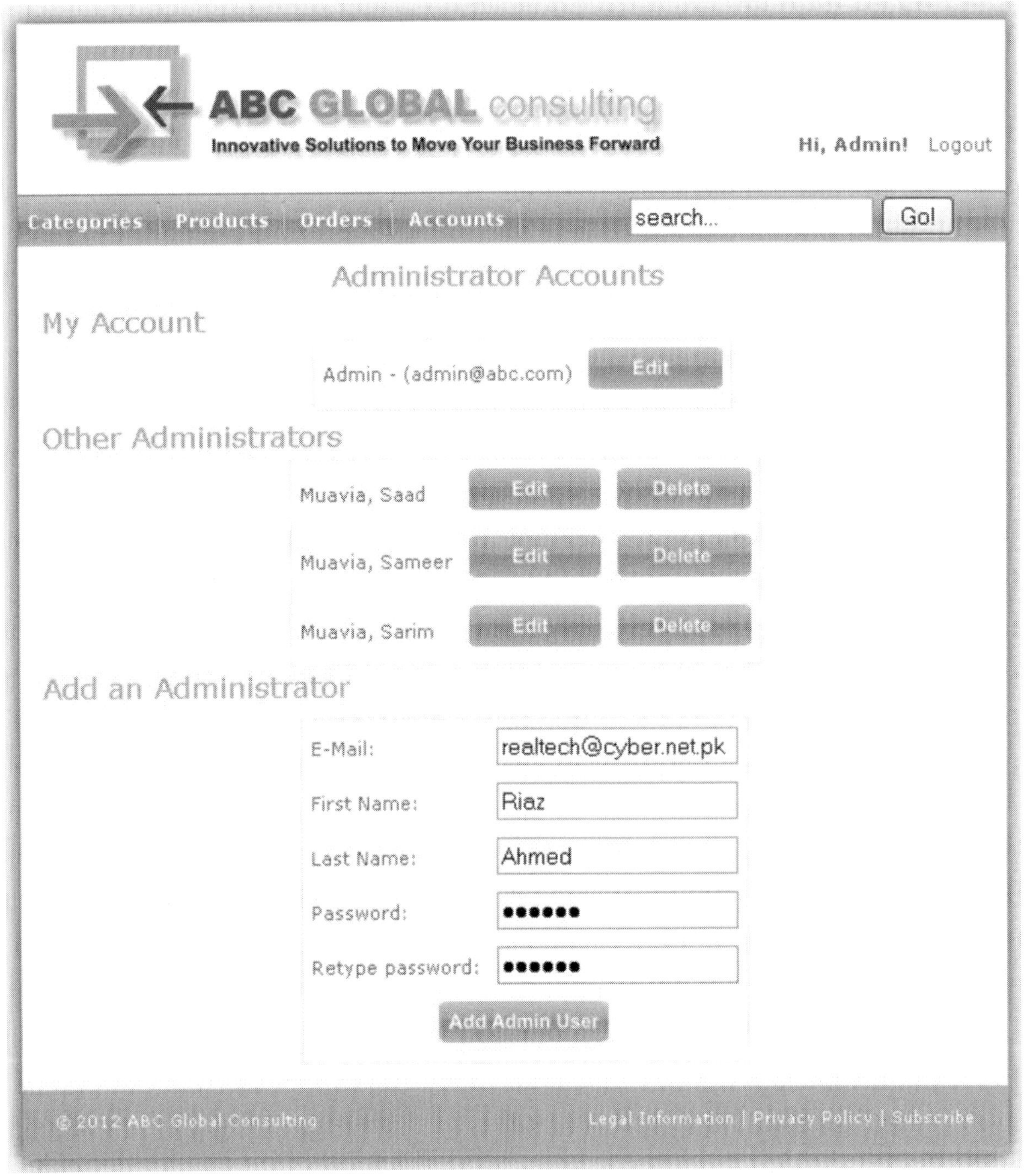

Figure 6-19

Using this module, an administrator can view, add, modify, or delete admin accounts, as illustrated in figure 6-19. The first section, My Account, allows the logged in administrator to modify his credentials. The second one, Other Administrators, lets him modify or delete other admin accounts. The last one, Add an Administrator, is used to add new site administrators. Let's see how this Administrator Accounts page is generated.

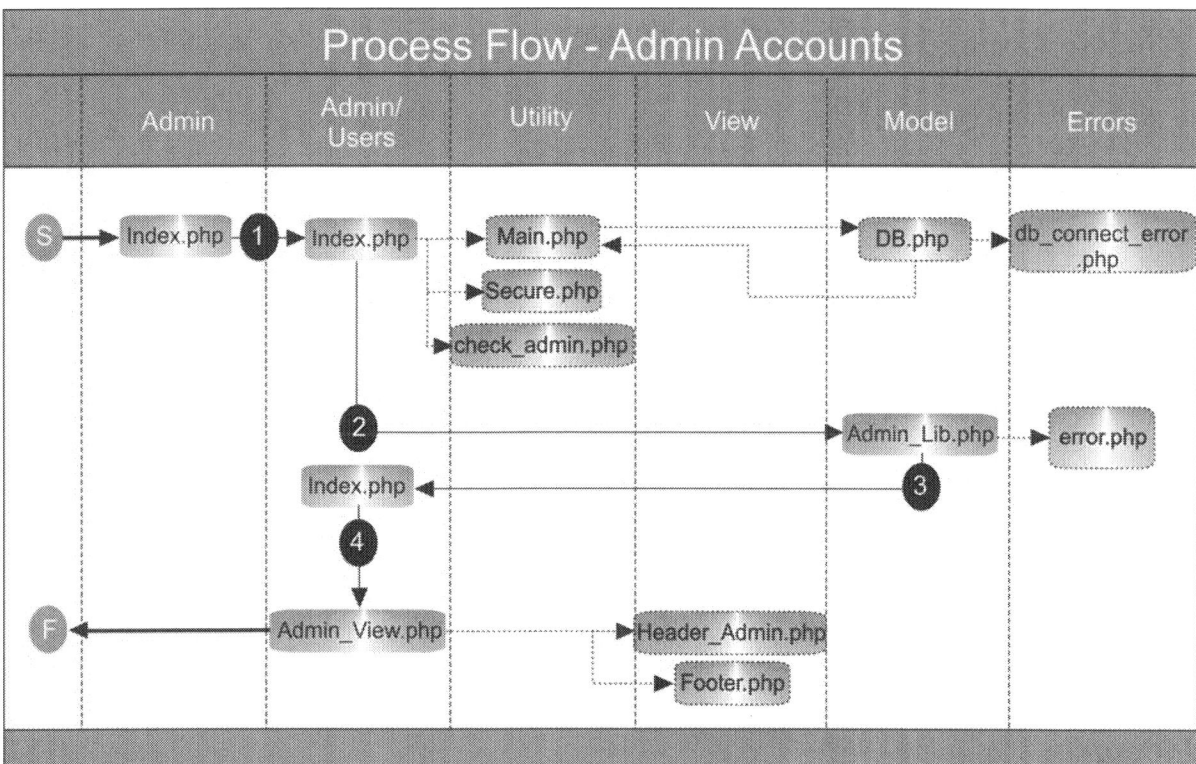

Diagram 11 - Admin Accounts

Diagram Explained

Point S - The process starts when the link Account Manager is clicked in the Admin Menu.

Point 1 - As usual, the main controller passes flow to the respective controller in the Admin/Users directory which initially calls subordinate routine files under the Utility and View directories.

Point 2 - Index.php calls Admin_Lib.php library file to collect data from Admins table.

Point 4 - After receiving the data, the controller calls Admin_View file from the same directory to display all admin records.

In the above diagram, regular processes are marked with dotted lines that you're already familiar with.

List XXXXIII - Index.php - Admin/Users

```
      ...
1     if (isset($_SESSION['user'])) {
2       display_error('Already logged in as a member.');
3     }
4     if ( admin_count() == 0 ) {
5       if ( $_POST['action'] == 'create' ) {
6         $action = 'create';
7       }
8       else {
9         $action = 'view_account';
10      }
11    }

      ...
12      case 'view_account':
          // Get admin user data from session
13        $name = $_SESSION['admin']['fName'] . ' ' . $_SESSION['admin']['lName'];
14        $email = $_SESSION['admin']['adminemail'];
15        $admin_id = $_SESSION['admin']['adminID'];
          // Get all accounts from database
16        $admins = get_all_admins();
          // View admin accounts
17        include 'admin_view.php';
18        break;

      ...
```

Explanation

The code on line 1-3 checks if you're already logged in as a member. In a situation like this, you'll have to log off before performing any administrative tasks.

Lines 4-7 are incorporated to present the 'Add Administrator' interface when there are no admin accounts in the database. You can test it by removing the sole admin record from the Admins table. Once the record is removed, type http://localhost/abcglobal/admin in the browser and you'll be asked to create the first admin account. The admin_count() function exists in the Admin_Lib.php file which counts number of admin records in the Admins table. Upon return, code in the ELSE block (line # 9) is executed to store a string 'view_account' in $action variable. Based on this value, code under the Case statement 'view_account' (line # 12) is executed.

Lines 13-15 fetches values from the admin session (credentials of the currently logged in administrator) into appropriate variables for display in the My Account section.

Line # 16 calls get_all_admins() function and stores all records from the Admins table in the array $admins. These records are displayed under the Other Administrators section.

Line # 17 includes Admin_View.php file to display the two sections along with a blank form, to add a new admin account, as shown in the above figure.

Note that if the admin session is empty and the Admins database is also blank, only the 'Add Administrator' section will be displayed. This situation happens when the first admin account is created, as discussed above.

List XXXXIV A - Admin_View.php - Admin/Users

```
...
1      <h2 class="center">Administrator Accounts</h2>
2      <?php if (isset($_SESSION['admin'])) : ?>
3        <h2>My Account</h2>
4        <form action="index.php" method="post">
5          <input type="hidden" name="action" value="view_edit" />
6          <table>
7            <tr>
8              <td><?php echo $name . ' (' . $email . ')'; ?>
9                <input type="hidden" name="admin_id" value="<?php echo $admin_id; ?>" />
10             </td>
11             <td><input type="image" alt="Edit" src="<?php echo $app_path; ?>images/edit.png"></td>
12           </tr>
13         </table>
14       </form>
15     <?php endif; ?>
...
```

Explanation

The code of this file is explained in three parts (A, B, and C). This one elaborates the Administrator Accounts section. As discussed, the Administrator Accounts page holds three sections. The above code structures the first one - My Account.

This section displays information of the currently logged in administrator and allows him/her to modify personal credentials. It uses a table inside a form to put the information on the web page. The information it displays using the variables $name, $email, and $admin_id arrive from lines 13-15 in the previous listing. The admin id is stored in a hidden element for further referencing.

Line # 11 defines an image button (edit.png) that passes the view_edit parameter (line # 5) to the controller which calls another interface (admin_edit.php) where administrators can change their e-mail address, first name, last name and even their passwords.

After modification, a hidden value 'update' is forwarded to the controller which executes instructions under the update case. These instructions are straight forward. First, the admin id value received through $_POST is converted to integer using the intval() function. This conversion is done to match the variable value with the table column value (which is an integer) in the WHERE clause of the UPDATE statement. Next, the update_admin() function is called from the functions library to put new values in the Admin table. Finally, the admin session is re-created to get updated values from the database and the page is refreshed through the redirect() function to reflect updates.

List XXXXIV B - Admin_View.php - Admin/Users

```
...
1   <?php if ( count($admins) > 1 ) : ?>
2     <h2>Other Administrators</h2>
3     <table>
4     <?php foreach($admins as $admin):
5        if ( $admin['adminID'] != $admin_id ) : ?>
6          <tr>
7            <td><?php echo $admin['lName'] . ', ' . $admin['fName']; ?> </td>
8            <td>
9              <form action="index.php" method="post">
10               <input type="hidden" name="action" value="view_edit" />
11               <input type="hidden" name="admin_id" value="<?php echo $admin['adminID']; ?>" />
12               <input type="image" alt="Edit" src="<?php echo $app_path; ?>images/edit.png">
13             </form>
14           </td>
15           <td>
16             <form action="index.php" method="post">
17               <input type="hidden" name="action" value="view_delete_confirm" />
18               <input type="hidden" name="admin_id"  value="<?php echo $admin['adminID']; ?>" />
19               <input type="image" alt="Delete" src="<?php echo $app_path;?>images/delete.png">
20             </form>
21           </td>
22         </tr>
23       <?php endif; ?>
24     <?php endforeach; ?>
25     </table>
26   <?php endif; ?>
...
```

Explanation

Other Administrators is the second section that is listed here. The FOREACH loop on line # 4 loops through all admin records fetched in list XXXXIII line # 16. The IF statement on line # 5 ensures that only other admin records are displayed in this section (because detail of the logged in administrator has already been displayed in the My Account section through the previous listing). You also have two buttons (Edit and Delete) for each admin account. These buttons are defined in separate forms and take hidden values (view_edit and view_delete_confirm respectively) to the controller, when clicked. An administrator can use these buttons to either modify an account or delete it altogether.

List XXXXIV C - Admin_View.php - Admin/Users

```
    ...
1   <h2>Add an Administrator</h2>
2   <form action="index.php" method="post">
3    <input type="hidden" name="action" value="create" />
4    <table>
5     <tr>
6      <td><label for="email">E-Mail:</label></td>
7      <td><input type="text" name="email" value="<?php echo $_SESSION['form_data']['email'];
                                                    ?>"/> </td>
8     </tr>
9     <tr>
10     <td><label for="first_name">First Name:</label></td>
11     <td><input type="text" name="first_name" value="<?php echo
               $_SESSION['form_data']['first_name']; ?>" /></td>
12    </tr>
13    <tr>
14     <td><label for="last_name">Last Name:</label></td>
15     <td><input type="text" name="last_name" value="<?php echo $_SESSION['form_data']['last_name'];
                                                    ?>" /></td>
16    </tr>
17    <tr>
18     <td><label for="password_1">Password:</label></td>
19     <td><input type="password" name="password_1" /></td>
20    </tr>
21    <tr>
22     <td><label for="password_2">Retype password:</label></td>
23     <td><input type="password" name="password_2" /></td>
24    </tr>
25    <tr>
26     <td colspan=2 id="sub"><input type="image" alt="Add Admin User" src="<?php echo $app_path;
                                                    ?>images/adminuser.png"></td>
27    </tr>
28   </table>
29  </form><br>
30  </article>
31  </section>
32  <?php
33  if (isset($_SESSION['form_data'])) {
34     unset($_SESSION['form_data']);
35  }
36  ?>
    ...
```

Explanation

The third and final section, Add an Administrator, of this web page enables an administrator to add more admin accounts.

One line # 3, the hidden element named action takes the value 'create' to the controller when the button 'Add Admin User' (line # 26) is clicked.

Lines 5-27 generate table rows to take input for the new admin account. The <label> tag defines a label for an <input> element. The FOR attribute of the <label> tag should be equal to the id attribute of the related element to bind them together. It specifies which form element a label is bound to. For example, on line 10 we used the FOR attribute of the label First Name to bind it to the input element named first_name on line 11. The $_SESSION['form_data'] is a session variable array declared under the 'create' case in Index.php file (discussed later). It sets new admin user data in session and is used to preserve form values. If not used, the user will have to re-type the data as in the two password elements on line # 19 and 23.

Line # 34 releases memory space by unsetting form_data session.

List XXXXV - Index.php - Admin/Users

```
      ...
1     case 'create':
         // Get admin user data
2        $email = $_POST['email'];
3        $first_name = $_POST['first_name'];
4        $last_name = $_POST['last_name'];
5        $password_1 = $_POST['password_1'];
6        $password_2 = $_POST['password_2'];
         // Set new admin user data in session
7        $_SESSION['form_data'] = array();
8        $_SESSION['form_data']['email'] = $email;
9        $_SESSION['form_data']['first_name'] = $first_name;
10       $_SESSION['form_data']['last_name'] = $last_name;
         // Validate admin user data
11       if (!filter_var($email, FILTER_VALIDATE_EMAIL)) {
12          display_error('The e-mail address ' . $email . ' is not valid.');
13       } elseif (is_valid_admin_email($email)) {
14          display_error('The e-mail address ' . $email . ' is already in use.');
15       }
16       if (empty($first_name)) {
17          display_error('First name is a required field.');
18       }
19       if (empty($last_name)) {
20          display_error('Last name is a required field.');
21       }
22       if (empty($password_1) || empty($password_2)) {
23          display_error('Password is a required field.');
24       } elseif ($password_1 !== $password_2) {
25          display_error('Passwords do not match.');
26       } elseif (strlen($password_1) < 6) {
27          display_error('Password must be at least six characters.');
28       }
         // Add admin user
29       $admin_id = add_admin($email, $first_name, $last_name, $password_1, $password_2);
         // Set up session data
30       unset($_SESSION['form_data']);
31       if (!isset($_SESSION['admin'])) {
32          $_SESSION['admin'] = get_admin($admin_id);
33       }
34       redirect('.');
35       break;
      ...
```

Explanation

This part of the file Index.php is executed when the button 'Add Admin User' is clicked. The code takes in values from the $_POST superglobal variable (lines 2-6).

We saw $_SESSION['form_data'] array in action in the last listing. It is created here to preserve admin user data in a session named form_data (lines 7-10).

On line # 11 we used a built-in function - filter_var(). This function filters a variable with the specified filter. Here, it is filtering the variable $email using the filter FILTER_VALIDATE_EMAIL to validate the value in the variable $email as a valid e-mail address. It returns the filtered data on success or false on failure. For example, if you input *someone@exa mple.com* or *me@example...com*, the invalid e-mail address message defined on line # 12 will be displayed. Line # 13 calls the function is_valid_admin_email() from Admin_Lib.php to check whether the provided e-mail address already exist in the Admins table. If found, the message on line # 14 triggers.

Lines 16-28 are included to check the required fields. Line # 22 checks that both passwords are not empty (the sign || represents the OR operator). Line # 24 ensures that both passwords match. The message is displayed only when they are not equal (!==). Line # 26 uses strlen() function to see whether the minimum length of the provided password is met.

If all the provided information is correct, line # 29 calls add_admin() function by providing it the five parameters. The function executes a routine that inserts the new account in the Admin table.

Line # 30 releases the form_data session array.

Line # 32 sets the admin session if not already exist. Again, this code is executed when the first admin account is created.

Line # 34 runs the file itself to refresh the page with new content.

This concludes the administration part of our website project. Try out different aspects of these modules keeping relevant code in front to observe the process flow. The next section discusses member modules that allow them to register and place orders online.

6.16   Purchase Products Over the Internet - Members Module

This part enables site visitors to become a member and purchase products online. Existing and new member can:

- Login to the website to place orders
- Put desired products into their carts
- Place orders by providing payment information

The following figure illustrates a general process flow for the steps mentioned above.

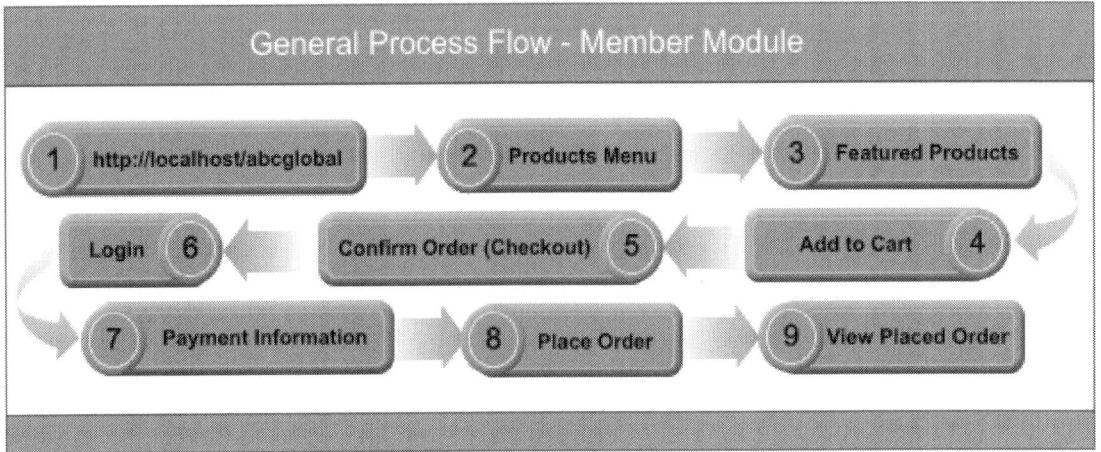

Figure 6-20

1. The process begins when a visitor enters the website by entering the specified url.
2. Clicks Product link on the main navigation bar.
3. Selects a product from the list of featured products.
4. Enters the desired quantity and places the product in his/her cart.
5. Clicks the Checkout link to confirm order.
6. At this stage, the visitor is asked to login. If the visitor doesn't have an account, he/she can register using a link provided on the login form.
7. After successful login/registration, the visitor becomes a member and is presented with a form to enter payment information.
8. On the payment form, the member clicks the Place Order button to complete the process.
9. The final step of this process displays details of the placed order to the member.

Let's continue the project and see in detail how the above mentioned steps work. Realizing that you should now be comfortable with PHP code, we'll be discussing only the unique code in the module files provided for this section.

6.17 Task 8 - Member Login Module

Considering the functionality, this module is similar to the Admin Login Module that we discussed in detail in Task 1. However, there are some additional links provided on the member login page presented in the following figure. For example, the *Register* link allows new visitors to become site members and an existing member can use the *Forgot password* link to receive a new password in his/her e-mail. Similarly the sidebar section, generated through sidebar_member.php file in the View directory, presents some navigation links relevant to site members and visitors. Also note the main navigation bar which is different from the Admin module. This page appears either when the user clicks the Checkout link to confirm order and is not logged in, or, when he/she clicks the Login/Register link provided on top of all static pages. After successful log in attempt, the former case takes users to the payment information page while in the later scenario the members are landed on the My Account page where they can view and change their personal information such as e-mail, passwords and addresses.

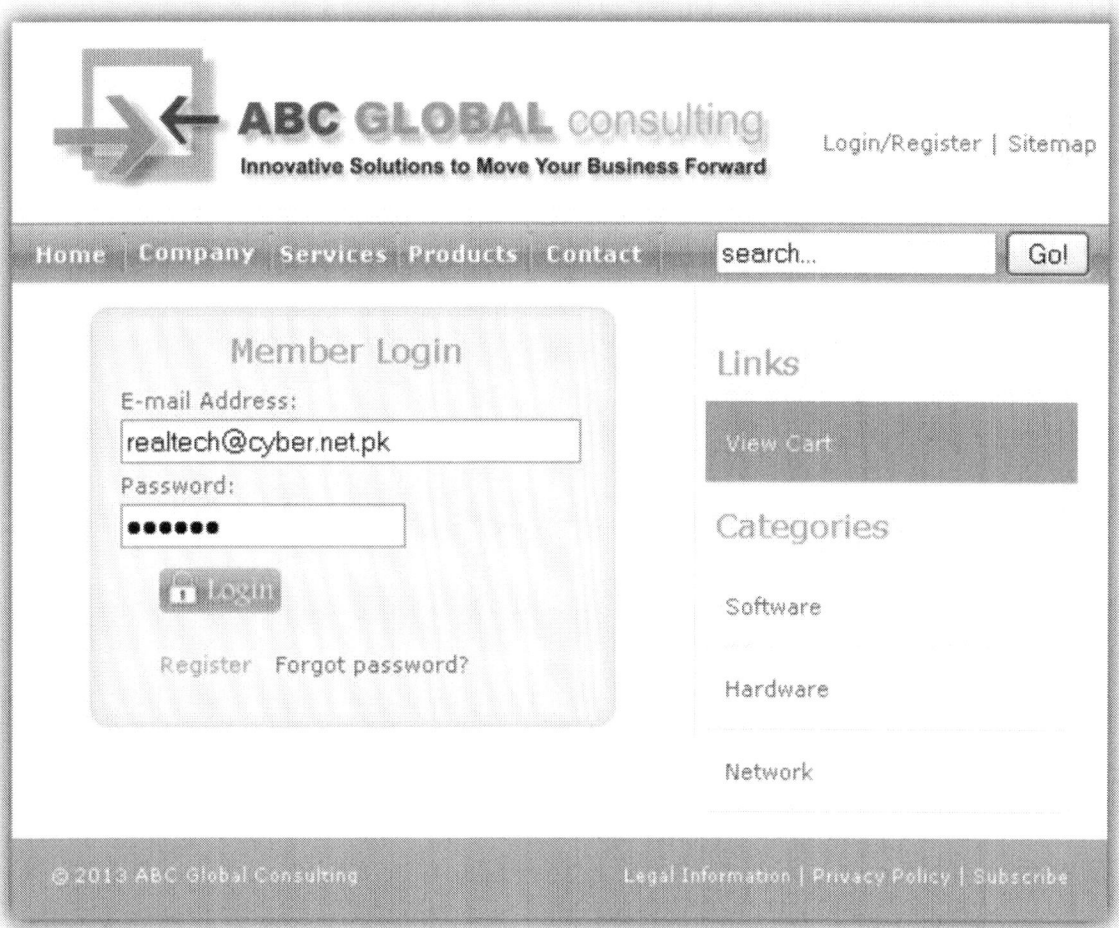

Figure 6-21

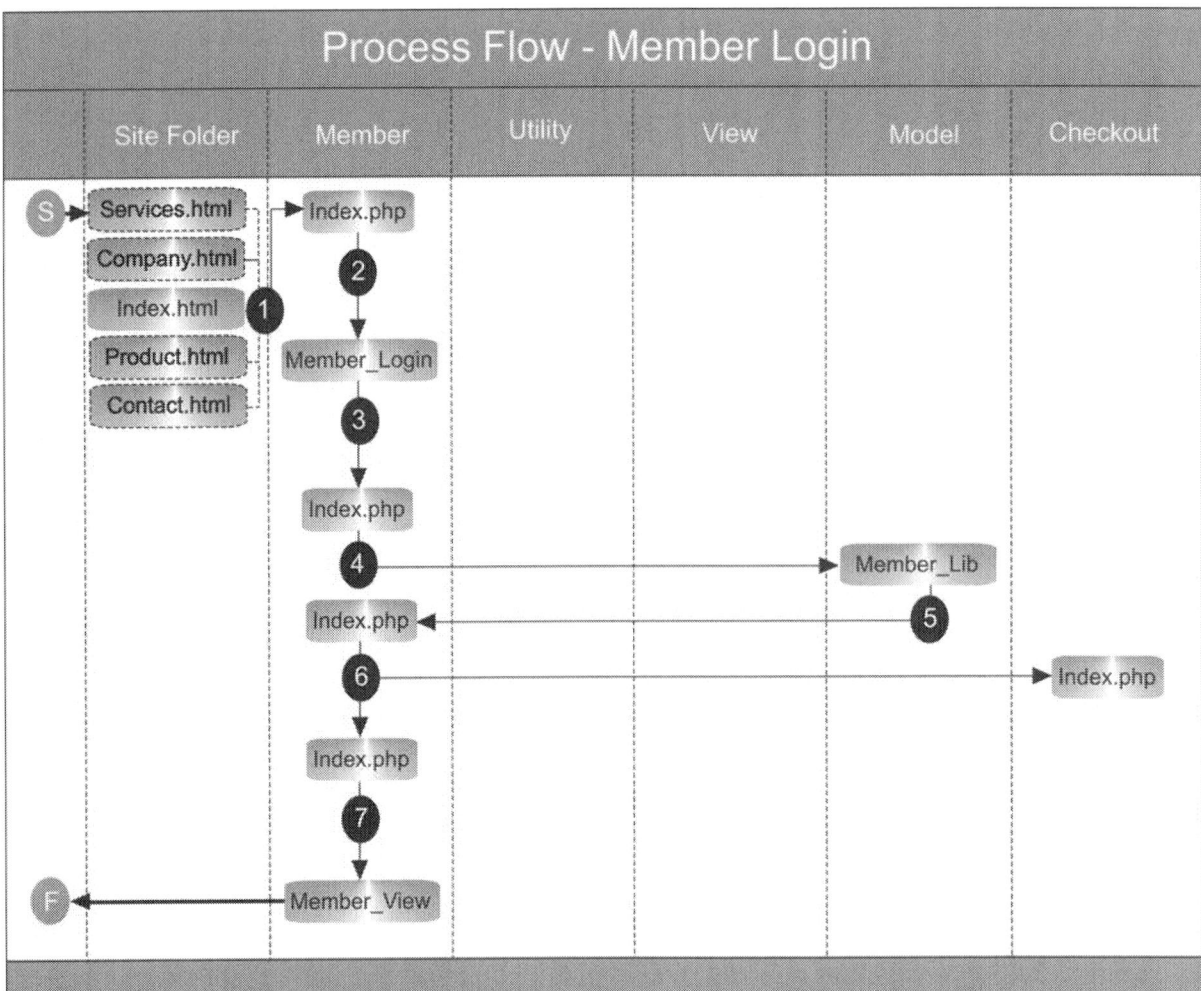

Diagram 12 - Member Login Process

Diagram Explained

Point S - The process initiates when the site visitor clicks the Login/Register link provided on all static (.html) pages as shown in the following code.

List T8-1 [Index.html - The Home Page]

```
      ...
1     <body>
2       <div class="wrapper">
3         <header>
4           <h1>ABC Global Consulting</h1>
5           <div id="headlinks">
6           <p><a href="member/index.php">Login/Register</a> | <a href="">Sitemap</a></p>
7           </div>
      ...
```

Point 1 - After clicking the link, the process passes control to the controller Index.php file under the Member directory.

Point 2 - Index.php executes the initial code under the default *view_login* case and calls Member_Login.php file from the same directory.

List T8-2 [Index.php - Member]

```
      ...
1     else {
2       $action = 'view_login';
3     }

4     switch ($action) {
5       case 'view_login':
6         include 'member_login.php';
7         break;
      ...
```

Point 3 - Member_Login.php file displays the login form. Besides the two e-mail and password boxes, it contains code for the two links: *Register* and *Forgot password*. It calls Member_Register.php when the Register link is clicked to display a form to the visitor to become a member. After taking user's credentials, it passes control back to Index.php file with e-mail address, password and a hidden value: 'login'.

	List T8-3 [Member_Login.php - Member]
1	`<?php include 'view/header_member.php'; ?>`
2	`<section class="content">`
3	`  <section class="signin">`
4	`    <h2>Member Login</h2>`
5	`    <form action="index.php" method="post" id="login_form">`
6	`      <input type="hidden" name="action" value="login" />`
7	`      <label>E-mail Address: `
8	`      <input type="email" name="email" maxlength="35" size="35" required="vital" autofocus` `                        placeholder="me@example.com"/></label> `
9	`      <label>Password: `
10	`      <input type="password" name="password" required="vital"/></label>`
11	`      <p><input type="image" alt="Login" src="<?php echo $app_path; ?>images/login.png"></p>`
12	`      <p>`
13	`        <a href="member_register.php">Register  </a>`
14	`        <a href="member_password.php">Forgot password?</a>`
15	`      </p>`
16	`    </form>`
17	`  </section>`
18	`</section>`
19	`<?php include 'view/sidebar_member.php'; ?>`
20	`<?php include 'view/footer.php'; ?>`

Point 4 - The controller calls couple of functions - *is_valid_member_login()* and *get_member_by_email()* - located in Member_Lib.php file to validate the provided information.

Point 6 - If the provided information is correct, the controller sets a user session. It also checks for the existence of another session named checkout. The existence of checkout session indicates that the user has arrived here from the order confirmation page. So to keep the process in flow, the user is redirected to the checkout process.

List T8-4 [Index.php - Member]

```
1      case 'login':
2        $email = $_POST['email'];
3        $password = $_POST['password'];
5        if (is_valid_member_login($email, $password)) {   // If valid username/password, login
6          $_SESSION['user'] = get_member_by_email($email);
7        } else {
8          member_error('Login failed. Invalid email or password.');
9        }
10       if (isset($_SESSION['checkout'])) {   // If necessary, redirect to the Checkout app
11         unset($_SESSION['checkout']);
12         redirect('../checkout');
13       } else {
14         redirect('.');
15       }
16       break;
       ...
```

List T8-5 [Member_Lib.php - Model]

```
function is_valid_member_login($email, $password) {
  global $db;
  $password = sha1($email . $password);
  $query = '
    SELECT * FROM members
    WHERE memberEmail = :email AND memberPW = :password';
  $statement = $db->prepare($query);
  $statement->bindValue(':email', $email);
  $statement->bindValue(':password', $password);
  $statement->execute();
  $valid = ($statement->rowCount() == 1);
  $statement->closeCursor();
  return $valid;
}
function get_member_by_email($email) {
  global $db;
  $query = 'SELECT * FROM members WHERE memberEmail = :email';
  $statement = $db->prepare($query);
  $statement->bindValue(':email', $email);
  $statement->execute();
  $member = $statement->fetch();
  $statement->closeCursor();
  return $member;
}
```

Point 7 - If the checkout session doesn't exist, the controller runs itself (in point 6) to display the My Account page through Member_View.php file (Task 11). This is a normal flow in which the user tried to login through the provided links on the static pages. For further details on login process, refer to Task1.

6.18 Task 9 - Member Registration Module

It is necessary for the site visitor to become a member before placing orders. The member login form provides a registration link that presents a form, illustrated below, to visitors. The visitor immediately becomes a member after submitting the form.

ABC GLOBAL consulting
Innovative Solutions to Move Your Business Forward

Login/Register | Sitemap

Home | Company | Services | Products | Contact   search...   Go!

Members Registration Form

Member Information

E-Mail:

Password:

Retype Password:

First Name:

Last Name:

Shipping Address

Address:

Line 2:

City:

State:

Zip Code:

Phone:

Billing Address

☐ Use shipping address

Address:

Line 2:

City:

State:

Zip Code:

Phone:

Register

© 2013 ABC Global Consulting   Legal Information | Privacy Policy | Subscribe

Figure 6-22

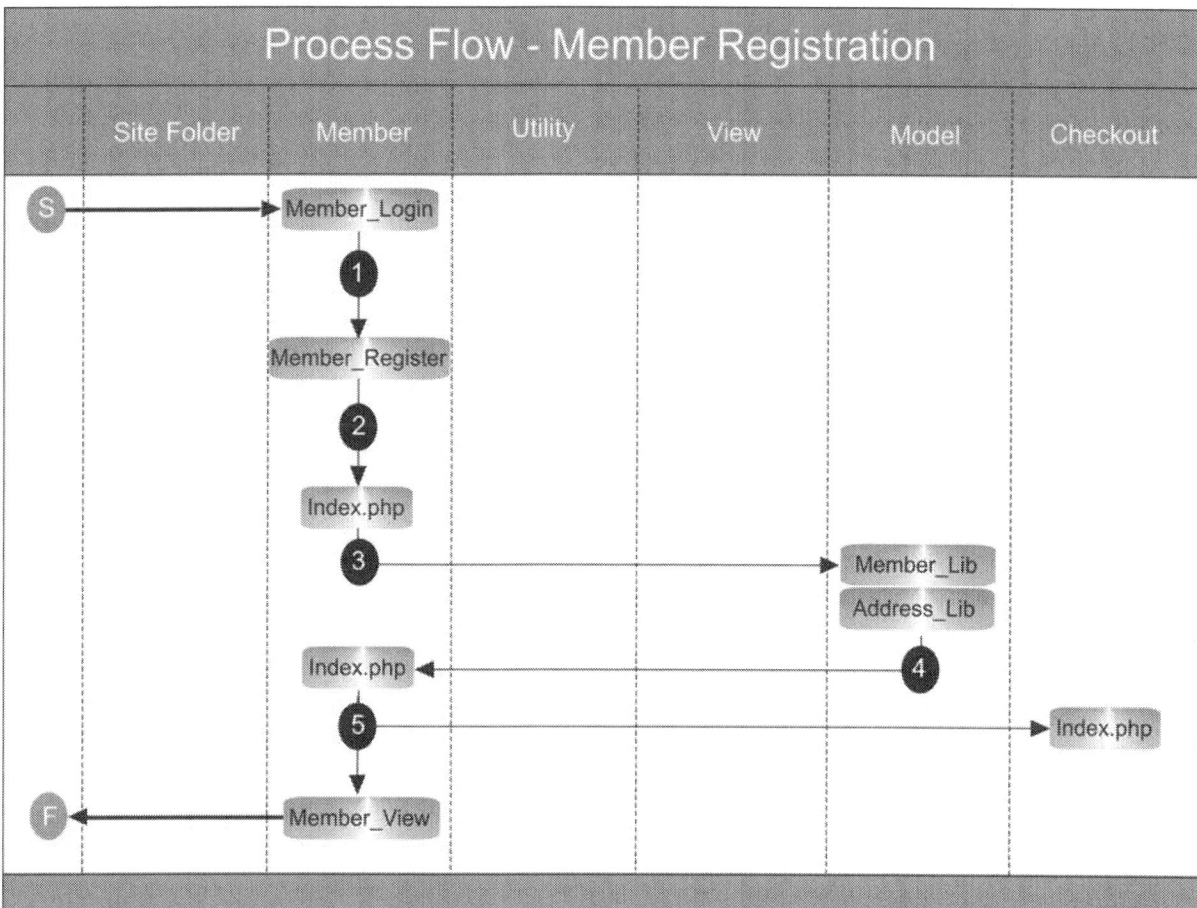

Diagram 13 - Member Registration Process

Diagram Explained

Point S - The member login form has a link named Register which initiates the registration process. See List T8-3 line 13 in Task 8.

Point 1 - The Register link calls Member_Register.php file. This file contains code to display the registration form illustrated in figure 6-22. The code is similar to the one you saw in Add Admin Account - listing XXXXIV C. It also uses the form_data session variable to store all form information except passwords. The form has a checkbox named use_shipping. Its status is also stored in the form_data session variable. A check mark placed in this box indicates that both shipping and billing addresses are same and values entered in the Shipping Address fields are inserted automatically for Billing Address.

```
<input type="checkbox" name="use_shipping"
  <?php if ($_SESSION['form_data']['use_shipping']) : ?> checked="checked" <?php endif; ?>
    size="30" /> Use shipping address
```

List T9-1 [Member_Register.php - Member]

```php
...
<section class="content">
 <article>
  <h2 class='center'>Members Registration Form</h2>
  <table>
  <form action="index.php" method="post" id="register_form">
    <tr>
     <td><h2 class='left'>Member Information</h2></td>
    </tr>
    <input type="hidden" name="action" value="register" />
    <tr>
     <td><label>E-Mail:</label></td>
     <td><input type="text" name="email" value="<?php echo $_SESSION['form_data']['email']; ?>"
         size="30" />
     </td>
    </tr>
    <tr>
     <td><label>Password:</label></td>
     <td><input type="password" name="password_1" size="30" /></td>
     <?php echo $password_message; ?>
    </tr>
    <tr>
     <td><label for="password_2">Retype Password:</label></td>
     <td><input type="password" name="password_2" size="30" /></td>
    </tr>
    <tr>
     <td><label for="first_name">First Name:</label></td>
     <td><input type="text" name="first_name"
         value="<?php echo $_SESSION['form_data']['first_name']; ?>" size="30" /></td>
    </tr>
```

Continued ➜

364

List T9-1 [Member_Register.php - Member] (Continued)

```html
<tr>
  <td><label for="last_name">Last Name:</label></td>
  <td><input type="text" name="last_name"
        value="<?php echo $_SESSION['form_data']['last_name']; ?>" size="30" /></td>
</tr>
<tr>
  <td><h2 class='left'>Shipping Address</h2></td>
</tr>
<tr>
  <td><label for="ship_line1">Address:</label></td>
  <td><input type="text" name="ship_line1"
        value="<?php echo $_SESSION['form_data']['ship_line1']; ?>" size="30" /></td>
</tr>
<tr>
  <td><label for="ship_line2">Line 2:</label></td>
  <td><input type="text" name="ship_line2"
        value="<?php echo $_SESSION['form_data']['ship_line2']; ?>" size="30" /></td>
</tr>
<tr>
  <td><label for="ship_city">City:</label></td>
  <td><input type="text" name="ship_city"
        value="<?php echo $_SESSION['form_data']['ship_city']; ?>" size="30" /></td>
</tr>
<tr>
  <td><label for="ship_state">State:</label></td>
  <td><input type="text" name="ship_state"
        value="<?php echo $_SESSION['form_data']['ship_state']; ?>" size="30" /></td>
</tr>
<tr>
  <td><label for="ship_zip">Zip Code:</label></td>
  <td><input type="text" name="ship_zip"
        value="<?php echo $_SESSION['form_data']['ship_zip']; ?>" size="30" /></td>
</tr>
<tr>
  <td><label for="ship_phone">Phone:</label></td>
  <td><input type="text" name="ship_phone"
        value="<?php echo $_SESSION['form_data']['ship_phone']; ?>" size="30" /></td>
</tr>
<tr>
  <td><h2 class='left'>Billing Address</h2></td>
</tr>
<tr>
  <td><label> </label></td>
  <td><input type="checkbox" name="use_shipping"
      <?php if ($_SESSION['form_data']['use_shipping']) : ?> checked="checked"
      <?php endif; ?>
      size="30" /> Use shipping address
  </td>
</tr>
<tr>
  <td><label for="bill_line1">Address:</label></td>
```

Continued →

```
          <td><input type="text" name="bill_line1"
              value="<?php echo $_SESSION['form_data']['bill_line1']; ?>" size="30" />
          </td>
        </tr>
        <tr>
          <td><label for="bill_line2">Line 2:</label></td>
          <td><input type="text" name="bill_line2"
              value="<?php echo $_SESSION['form_data']['bill_line2']; ?>" size="30" />
          </td>
        </tr>
        <tr>
          <td><label for="bill_city">City:</label></td>
          <td><input type="text" name="bill_city"
              value="<?php echo $_SESSION['form_data']['bill_city']; ?>" size="30" />
          </td>
        </tr>
        <tr>
          <td><label for="bill_state">State:</label></td>
          <td><input type="text" name="bill_state"
              value="<?php echo $_SESSION['form_data']['bill_state']; ?>" size="30" />
          </td>
        </tr>
        <tr>
          <td><label for="bill_zip">Zip Code:</label></td>
          <td><input type="text" name="bill_zip"
              value="<?php echo $_SESSION['form_data']['bill_zip']; ?>" size="30" />
          </td>
        </tr>
        <tr>
          <td><label for="bill_phone">Phone:</label></td>
          <td><input type="text" name="bill_phone"
              value="<?php echo $_SESSION['form_data']['bill_phone']; ?>" size="30" />
          </td>
        </tr>
        <tr>
          <td colspan=2 id='sub'><input type="image" alt='Register' src="<?php echo
                                    $app_path;?>images/register.png">
          </td>
        </tr>
      </form>
      </table>
    </article>
  </section>
<?php
if (isset($_SESSION['form_data'])) {
  unset($_SESSION['form_data']);
}
?>
<?php include '../view/footer.php'; ?>
```

Point 2 - When the visitor clicks the Register button after completing the form, the data is submitted to the controller with a hidden value 'register'.

List T9-2 [Index.php - Member]

```php
case 'register':
  // Store user data in local variables
  $email = $_POST['email'];
  $first_name = $_POST['first_name'];
  $last_name = $_POST['last_name'];
  $ship_line1 = $_POST['ship_line1'];
  $ship_line2 = $_POST['ship_line2'];
  $ship_city = $_POST['ship_city'];
  $ship_state = $_POST['ship_state'];
  $ship_zip = $_POST['ship_zip'];
  $ship_phone = $_POST['ship_phone'];
  $use_shipping = isset($_POST['use_shipping']);
  $bill_line1 = $_POST['bill_line1'];
  $bill_line2 = $_POST['bill_line2'];
  $bill_city = $_POST['bill_city'];
  $bill_state = $_POST['bill_state'];
  $bill_zip = $_POST['bill_zip'];
  $bill_phone = $_POST['bill_phone'];

  // Store data in the session
  $_SESSION['form_data'] = array();
  $_SESSION['form_data']['email'] = $email;
  $_SESSION['form_data']['first_name'] = $first_name;
  $_SESSION['form_data']['last_name'] = $last_name;
  $_SESSION['form_data']['ship_line1'] = $ship_line1;
  $_SESSION['form_data']['ship_line2'] = $ship_line2;
  $_SESSION['form_data']['ship_city'] = $ship_city;
  $_SESSION['form_data']['ship_state'] = $ship_state;
  $_SESSION['form_data']['ship_zip'] = $ship_zip;
  $_SESSION['form_data']['ship_phone'] = $ship_phone;
  $_SESSION['form_data']['use_shipping'] = isset($use_shipping);
  $_SESSION['form_data']['bill_line1'] = $bill_line1;
  $_SESSION['form_data']['bill_line2'] = $bill_line2;
  $_SESSION['form_data']['bill_city'] = $bill_city;
  $_SESSION['form_data']['bill_state'] = $bill_state;
  $_SESSION['form_data']['bill_zip'] = $bill_zip;
  $_SESSION['form_data']['bill_phone'] = $bill_phone;

  $password_1 = $_POST['password_1'];
  $password_2 = $_POST['password_2'];
```

Continued →

```php
// Validate user data
if (!filter_var($email, FILTER_VALIDATE_EMAIL)) {
    member_error('The e-mail address ' . $email . ' is not valid.');
} elseif (is_valid_member_email($email)) {
    member_error('The e-mail address ' . $email . ' is already in use.');
}
if (empty($first_name)) {
    member_error('First name is a required field.');
}
if (empty($last_name)) {
    member_error('Last name is a required field.');
}
if (empty($password_1) || empty($password_2)) {
    member_error('Password is a required field.');
} elseif ($password_1 !== $password_2) {
    member_error('Passwords do not match.');
} elseif (strlen($password_1) < 6) {
    member_error('Password must be at least six characters.');
}


// Validate shipping address
if (empty($ship_line1)) {
    member_error('Shipping address line 1 is required.');
}
if (empty($ship_city)) {
    member_error('Shipping city is required.');
}
if (empty($ship_state)) {
    member_error('Shipping state is required.');
}
if (strlen($ship_state) > 2 ) {
    member_error('Use two-letter code for shipping state.');
}
if (empty($ship_zip)) {
    member_error('Shipping ZIP code is required.');
}
if (empty($ship_phone)) {
    member_error('Shipping phone number is required.');
}



// If necessary, validate billing address
if (!$use_shipping) {
    if (empty($bill_line1)) {
        member_error('Billing address line 1 is required.');
    }
    if (empty($bill_city)) {
        member_error('Billing city is required.');
    }
    if (empty($bill_state)) {
        member_error('Billing state is required.');
    }
```

Continued →

```php
        if (strlen($bill_state) > 2 ) {
            member_error('Use two-letter code for billing state.');
        }
        if (empty($bill_zip)) {
            member_error('Billing ZIP code is required.');
        }
        if (empty($bill_phone)) {
            member_error('Billing phone number is required.');
        }
    }


    // Add the member data to the database
    $member_id = add_member($email, $first_name,
                    $last_name, $password_1, $password_2);


    // Add the shipping address
    $shipping_id = add_address($member_id, $ship_line1, $ship_line2,
                    $ship_city, $ship_state, $ship_zip,
                    $ship_phone);
    member_change_shipping_id($member_id, $shipping_id);


    // Add the billing address
    if ($use_shipping) {
        $billing_id = add_address($member_id, $ship_line1, $ship_line2,
                        $ship_city, $ship_state, $ship_zip,
                        $ship_phone);
    } else {
        $billing_id = add_address($member_id, $bill_line1, $bill_line2,
                        $bill_city, $bill_state, $bill_zip,
                        $bill_phone);
    }
    member_change_billing_id($member_id, $billing_id);


    // Set up session data
    unset($_SESSION['form_data']);
    $_SESSION['user'] = get_member($member_id);


    // Redirect to the Checkout application if necessary
    if (isset($_SESSION['checkout'])) {
        unset($_SESSION['checkout']);
        redirect('../checkout');
    } else {
        redirect('.');
    }
    break;
```

Point 3 - The controller executes code under the Register case. It creates the form_data session array to preserve form values (except the two passwords). Then it validates the e-mail address provided by the visitor through the filter_var function that we've already discussed in the Admin module. If the provided e-mail address is valid, the code checks whether the address already exist in the database using the is_valid_member_email() function. It also validates all the required fields, matches the two passwords and verifies their minimum length. The statement, *if (!$use_shipping)*, evaluates whether the user has put a check mark on the *Use Shipping Address* box. If not, the code under the statement is executed to verify the billing information.

After verification, the controller calls *add_member()* and *add_address()* functions in respective library files to insert the provided information in relevant tables. The add_member() function inserts e-mail address, names, and passwords in the Members table leaving the two address ids. The add_address() function is called twice to insert shipping and billing addresses. Each call returns a value in a variable $address_id which it gets through the built-in lastIndertID() function. The lastInsertID() function returns the ID of the last inserted row. These values are used as arguments in member_change_shipping_id() and member_change_billing_id() functions to replace shipping and billing ids in the Members table that were initially left blank.

Next, the controller sets user's session by calling *get_member()* function. This function retrieves complete record for the member who's just joined.

Point 5 - After successful registration, the member is redirected to the checkout page - *if (isset($_SESSION['checkout'])) ...redirect('../checkout'...* - if he came to the registration page from there, otherwise, the code calls Index.php file - *redirect('.')* - to display My Account page using Member_View.php file (List T8-6).

List T9-3 [Member_Lib.php - Model]

```php
function add_member($email, $first_name, $last_name, $password_1, $password_2) {
  global $db;
  $password = sha1($email . $password_1);
  $query = '
    INSERT INTO members (fName, lName, memberEmail, memberPW)
    VALUES (:first_name, :last_name, :email, :password)';
  $statement = $db->prepare($query);
  $statement->bindValue(':first_name', $first_name);
  $statement->bindValue(':last_name', $last_name);
  $statement->bindValue(':email', $email);
  $statement->bindValue(':password', $password);
  $statement->execute();
  $member_id = $db->lastInsertId();
  $statement->closeCursor();
  return $member_id;
}

function get_member($member_id) {
  global $db;
  $query = 'SELECT * FROM members WHERE memberID = :member_id';
  $statement = $db->prepare($query);
  $statement->bindValue(':member_id', $member_id);
  $statement->execute();
  $member = $statement->fetch();
  $statement->closeCursor();
  return $member;
}
```

List T9-4 [Address_Lib.php - Model]

```php
function add_address($member_id, $line1, $line2, $city, $state, $zip_code, $phone) {
  global $db;
  $query = '
    INSERT INTO addresses (memberID, line1, line2, city, state, zipCode, phone)
    VALUES (:member_id, :line1, :line2, :city, :state, :zip_code, :phone)';
  $statement = $db->prepare($query);
  $statement->bindValue(':member_id', $member_id);
  $statement->bindValue(':line1', $line1);
  $statement->bindValue(':line2', $line2);
  $statement->bindValue(':city', $city);
  $statement->bindValue(':state', $state);
  $statement->bindValue(':zip_code', $zip_code);
  $statement->bindValue(':phone', $phone);
  $statement->execute();
  $address_id = $db->lastInsertId();
  $statement->closeCursor();
  return $address_id;
}
```

6.19 Task 10 - Password Reset Module

This module is included to help website members in recovering their lost passwords. There is a link labeled *Forgot Password* on the member login form. When clicked, this link asks the member to provide his/her e-mail address. After verification, the module creates a new random password, stores it in the database, and sends it to the member's e-mail account. After receiving the e-mail, the member can login with the new password and can change it on My Account page that we'll discuss in the next task.

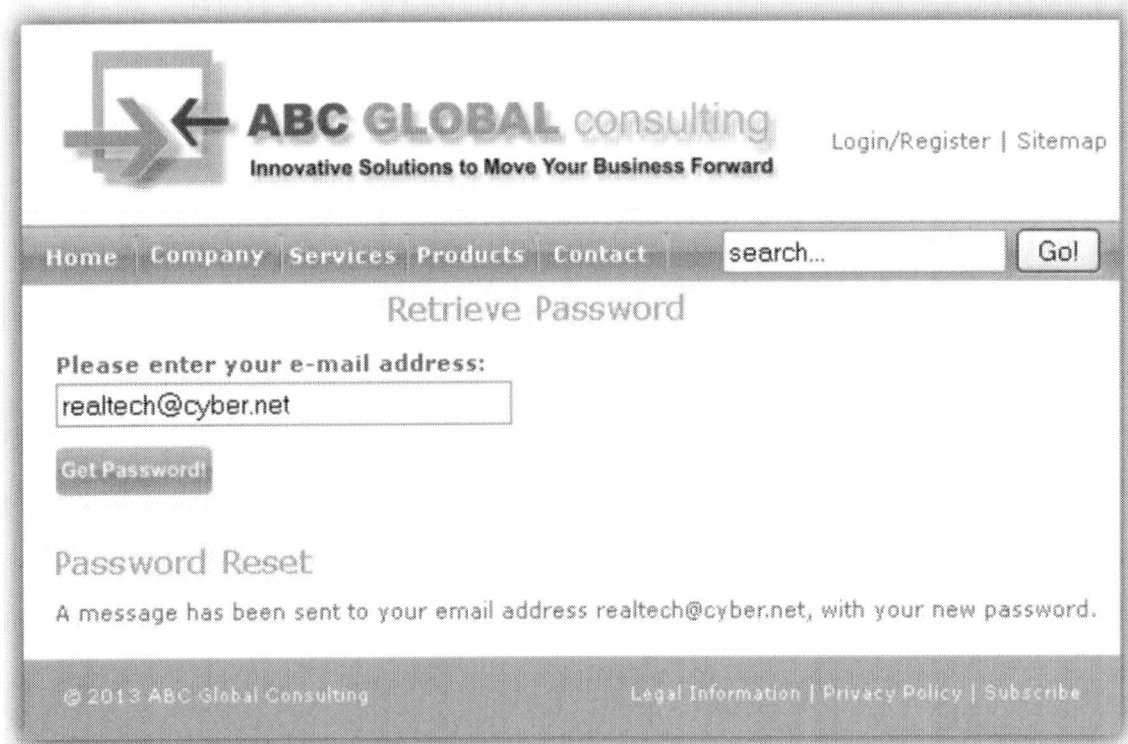

Figure 6-23

Diagram Explained

Point S - The member forgets her password and clicks the *Forgot Password* link on the login form.

Point 1 - The Retrieve Password page, as shown in figure 6-23, comes up and asks the user to provide her e-mail address.

Point 2 - A hidden value *'assign_password'* is forwarded to the controller. Based on this value, the controller runs instructions under the corresponding case.

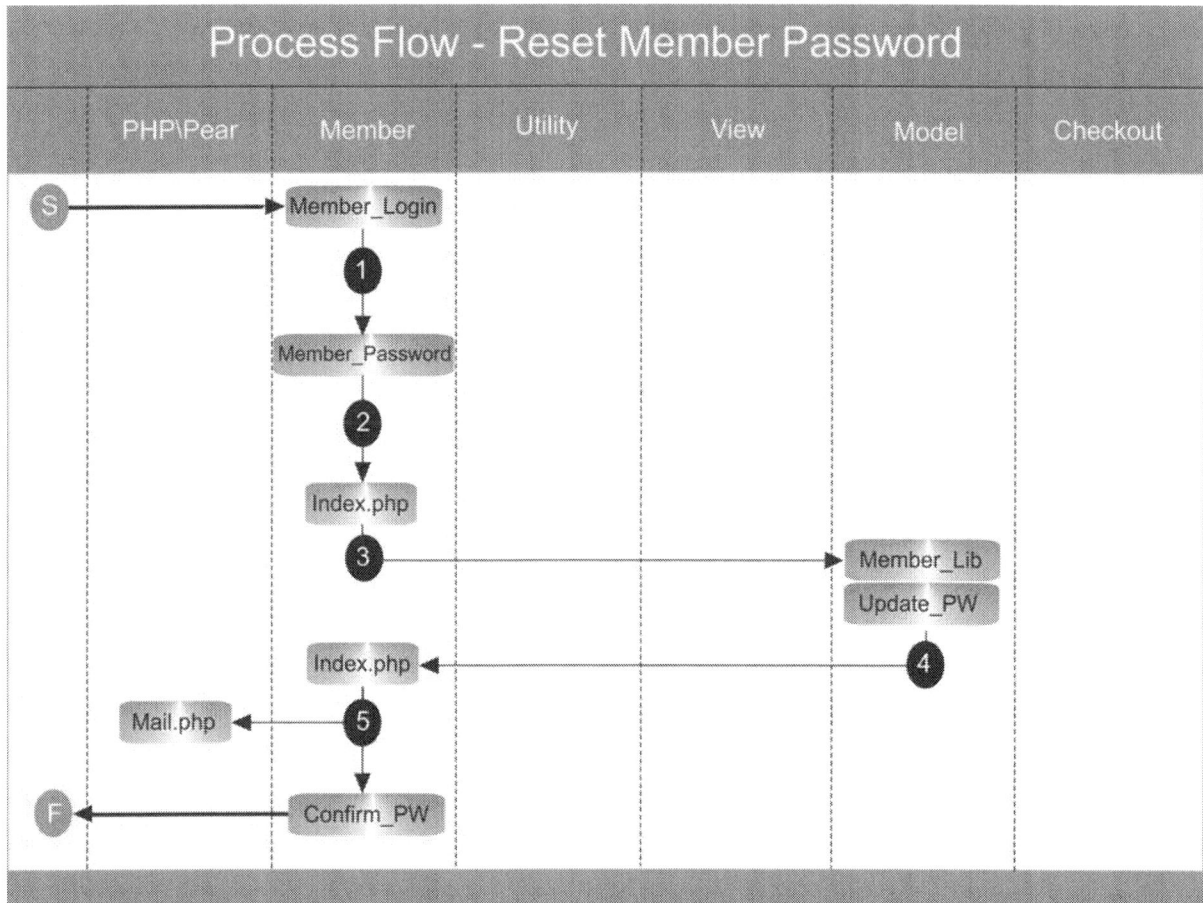

Diagram 14 - Password Reset Process

Point 3 - The controller calls *get_member_by_email()* function in *Member_Lib.php* file and stores the sole returned row in a session named *password*. It takes memberID value from the session variable (password) and stores it in a variable *$member_id*. Next, it evaluates whether the *$member_id* has a value. A value of zero indicates that the database doesn't have any record for the provided e-mail address and thus an appropriate message is displayed to the user. Note that this time we called the *member_error()* function from Main.php file which consequently calls member_error.php in the Errors directory to display the message. To distinguish page headings from the Admin module, we used another file to display appropriate member module headings using header_member.php file. The controller then calls *update_pw()* function by passing two arguments: *$member_id* and *$email*. The returned value (a new random password) is received in *$new_password*. This function is explained ahead in List T10-4. The rest of the code in this case statement is already known to you as it was also used in the Newsletter subscription module. It uses the PHP PEAR Mail package to send the new password to the member through her e-mail address.

Point 4 - After transmitting a successful e-mail, the controller calls *member_pw_sent.php* file. This file informs the member to check her mailbox for the new password.

List T10-1 [Index.php - Member]

```php
1     case 'assign_password':
2       $email = $_POST['email'];
3       $_SESSION['password'] = get_member_by_email($email);
4       $member_id = $_SESSION['password']['memberID'];
5       if ($member_id <= 0) {
6         member_error('E-mail address does not exist in our database.');   List II Line 26 →
7       }
8       $new_password = update_pw($member_id, $email);   List T10-4 →
        // Send new password through e-mail
9       require_once "Mail.php";
10      $from = "Administrator <admin@abc.com>";
11      $to = $email;
12      $subject = "Your New Password";
13      $body = "Hi,\n\nYour new password on ABC Global Consulting domain is: " . $new_password;
14      $host = "localhost"; // Enter SMTP provided by your ISP like $host = "smtp.xyz.net";
15      $headers = array ('From' => $from, 'To' => $to, 'Subject' => $subject);
16      $smtp = Mail::factory('smtp', array ('host' => $host, 'port' => 25));
17      $mail = $smtp->send($to, $headers, $body);
18      //$to = $email;
19      //$headers['To'] = $to;
20      //$headers['From'] = '"Administrator - ABCGLOBAL Consulting" <admin@abc.com>';
21      //$headers['Subject'] = 'Your New Password';
22      //$body = "Hi,\n\nYour new password on ABC Global Consulting domain is: " . $new_password;
23      //$host = "mail.abc.com";
24      //$user = "admin@abc.com";
25      //$pw = "gemini";
26      //$auth = array('host' => $host, 'auth' => true, 'username' => $user, 'password' => $pw);
27      //$smtp = Mail::factory('smtp', $auth);
28      //$mail = $smtp->send($to, $headers, $body);
29      if (PEAR::isError($mail))
30      {
31        member_error("<p>" . $mail->getMessage() . "</p>");
32      }
33      else
34      {
35        include 'member_pw_sent.php';
36      }
37      unset($_SESSION['password']);
38      break;
```

> For explanation, refer to Chapter 5 section 5.14 and Task 2 Newsletter Subscription module.
>
> The code from line 18-28 (for host environment) was also defined in the last paragraph in Chapter 5.

List T10-2 [Member_Error.php - Errors]

```
1    <?php include 'view/header_member.php'; ?>
2    <section class="content">
3     <article>
4      <h2>Error</h2>
5      <p><?php echo $error_message; ?></p>
6     </article>
7    </section>
8    <?php include 'view/footer.php'; ?>
```

List T10-3 [Member_PW_Sent.php - Member]

```
1    <?php include 'view/header_member.php'; ?>
2    <section class="content">
3     <article>
4      <hgroup>
5       <h2>Password Reset</h2>
6      </hgroup>
7      <p>A message has been sent to your email address <?php echo $to ; ?>, with your new password.</p>
8     </article>
9    </section>
10   <?php include 'view/footer.php'; ?>
```

List T10-4 [Member_Lib.php - Model]

```php
1    function update_pw($member_id, $email) {
2      $pw_length= 8;
3      $symbols = '~!@#$%^&*()-_=+[]{};:,.<>?';
4      $symbol_count = strlen($symbols);
5      $index = mt_rand(0, $symbol_count - 1);
6      $password = substr($symbols, $index, 1);
7      $password .= chr(mt_rand(48, 57));
8      $password .= chr(mt_rand(65, 90));
9      while (strlen($password) < $pw_length) {
10       $password .= chr(mt_rand(97, 122));
11     }
12     $new_password = str_shuffle($password);
13     if (!empty($new_password)) {
14       global $db;
15       $password = sha1($email . $new_password);
16       $query = '
17         UPDATE members
18         SET memberPW = :password
19         WHERE memberID = :member_id';
20       $statement = $db->prepare($query);
21       $statement->bindValue(':password', $password);
22       $statement->bindValue(':member_id', $member_id);
23       $statement->execute();
24       $statement->closeCursor();
25     }
26     return $new_password;
27   }
```

Explanation

This function is called from the controller file as mentioned above. It performs two tasks: generate a random password and update member's record with this new password in the database. After updating the new password in the database, it is returned to the controller which sends it through an e-mail to the requesting member.

To start, the first line of this function receives two arguments to identify the member. Line # 2 defines length for the new password. The new password consists of single uppercase letter, number, symbol, and five lowercase letters. Line # 3 defines the list of symbols to be added. Code on line 4-5 selects a random position for the symbol using *strlen()* and *mt_rand()* functions which is then added to the password using the *substr()* function on line # 6. Line # 7 picks a random number while line # 8 gets a random uppercase letter. In the ASCII character set, numbers 0 through 9 have the decimal values 48 to 57 while the uppercase letters fall between 65 and 90. The *while* loop (line 9-11) generates random lowercase letters (using the decimal values 97-122) to fill in the remaining 5 positions. The *str_shuffle()* function used on line # 12 randomly shuffles all the characters in the $password variable and stores it in the variable $new_password which looks something like this: a6zRa_rm.

You can also test this function independently in your browser to see how it returns different values when you refresh the browser. To do so, open a Notepad session and copy code from line 2-12. Add *<?php* to the beginning of this file and *?>* to the end to inform the browser that it's a PHP file. Add *echo $new_password;* on the second last line just above the *?>* symbol. Save this file as pw.php under the wwwroot folder. In your browser type http://localhost/pw.php. You'll see a random password. Press the browser's refresh button and note the symbol position along with the new password.

The IF conditional block from line 13 to 25 updates the memberPW column in the Members database table with this new password using the technique mentioned earlier in List X. This is done to authenticate the member with the new random password created in this function when she attempts to login after receiving the password in her e-mail.

Line # 26 returns the new password to the controller to transmit it to the member. See List T10-1 Line 8 above.

6.20 Task 11 - My Account Module

This module enables site members to:

- Change their e-mail address, names, and passwords
- Change their Shipping and Billing addresses
- View the status of their orders
- View individual order details

Figure 6-24

My Account is the initial page that appears when a member logs into the website and is displayed using Member_View.php file (List T11-1) under the Member directory. It can also be accessed through the MY Account link provided on the sidebar. It passes a value *view_account_edit* to the controller. In reply, the controller calls member_edit.php file to display a page wherein members can modify their accounts. As this module is similar to Task 5 - Manage Admin Accounts, we will not dig deeper.

The first Edit button enables members to modify their personal profile while the next two buttons allow them to edit their shipping and billing addresses. Both shipping and billing addresses use the same Member_Address.php file under the Member directory to change existing data. Based on the member's action, the controller forwards a value either 'Update Shipping Address' or 'Update Billing Address' in a variable named $heading to the Member_Address.php file which uses it to display a suitable heading.

The final section 'Your Orders' will be displayed only when the logged in member has at least one order on record. The Member_View.php file iterates through $orders array using the FOREACH loop to display a list of all orders (either shipped or pending) placed by the current member. Each order is presented as a link which, when clicked, calls the View Order page to display details of an individual order. This page too came under discussion in Order Information section in Task 4 - Manage Orders.

List T11-1 [Member_View.php - Member]

```php
1   <?php include '../view/header_member.php'; ?>
2   <section class="content">
3    <article>
4     <h2 class="center"><b>MY ACCOUNT</b></h2>
5     <p><?php echo $member_name . ' (' . $email . ')'; ?></p>
6     <form action="index.php" method="post">
7      <input type="hidden" name="action" value="view_account_edit" />
8      <input type="image" value="Edit Account" id="left_button" alt="Edit" src="<?php echo $app_path;
                                                   ?>images/edit.png"><br/>
9     </form>
10    <br/>
11    <h2>Shipping Address</h2>
12    <p><?php echo $ship_line1; ?><br />
13     <?php if ( strlen($ship_line2) > 0 ) : ?>
14        <?php echo $ship_line2; ?><br />
15     <?php endif; ?>
16     <?php echo $ship_city; ?>, <?php echo $ship_state; ?>
17     <?php echo $ship_zip; ?><br />
18     <?php echo $ship_phone; ?>
19    </p>
20    <form action="index.php" method="post">   List T11-2 ➔
21     <input type="hidden" name="action" value="view_address_edit" />
22     <input type="hidden" name="address_type" value="shipping" />
23     <input type="image" value="Edit Shipping Address" id="left_button" alt="Edit" src="<?php echo
                                                   $app_path; ?>images/edit.png"><br/>
24    </form>                    Continued ➔
```

List T11-1 [Member_View.php - Member]   (Continued)

```
25  <br/>
26  <h2>Billing Address</h2>
27    <p><?php echo $bill_line1; ?><br />
28      <?php if ( strlen($bill_line2) > 0 ) : ?>
29        <?php echo $bill_line2; ?><br />
30      <?php endif; ?>
31      <?php echo $bill_city; ?>, <?php echo $bill_state; ?>
32      <?php echo $bill_zip; ?><br />
33      <?php echo $bill_phone; ?>
34    </p>
35    <form action="index.php" method="post">   List T11-2
36      <input type="hidden" name="action" value="view_address_edit" />
37      <input type="hidden" name="address_type" value="billing" />
38      <input type="image" value="Edit Billing Address" id="left_button" alt="Edit" src="<?php echo
                                                        $app_path; ?>images/edit.png"><br/>
39    </form>
40    <?php if (count($orders) > 0 ) : ?>
41      <br/>
42      <h2>Your Orders</h2>
43      <ul>
44        <?php foreach($orders as $order) :
45          $order_id = $order['orderID'];
46          $order_date = strtotime($order['orderDate']);
47          $order_date = date('M j, Y', $order_date);
48          if ($order['shipDate'] != NULL){
49            $ship_date = strtotime($order['shipDate']);
50            $ship_date = date('M j, Y', $ship_date);
51          }else{
52            $ship_date='';
53          }
54          $url = $app_path . 'member'.
55              '?action=view_order&order_id=' . $order_id;
56        ?>
57          <li>
58            <a href="<?php echo $url; ?>">Order No.
59            <?php echo $order_id; ?></a> placed on
60            <?php echo $order_date; ?>
61            <?php if ($ship_date != '') {
62            echo ' - Shipped on ' . $ship_date;} else {echo ' - Yet to be shipped';}?>
63          </li>
64        <?php endforeach; ?>
65      </ul>
66    <?php endif; ?><br/>
67    </article>
68  </section>
69  <?php include '../view/sidebar_member.php'; ?>
70  <?php include '../view/footer.php'; ?>
```

List T11-2 [Index.php - Member]

```php
    case 'view_address_edit':          ← List T11-1
      // Set up variables for address type
      $billing = $_POST['address_type'] == 'billing';
      if ($billing) {
        $address_id = $_SESSION['user']['billingAddressID'];
        $heading = 'Update Billing Address';
      } else {
        $address_id = $_SESSION['user']['shipAddressID'];
        $heading = 'Update Shipping Address';
      }
      // Get the data for the address
      $address = get_address($address_id);
      $line1 = $address['line1'];
      $line2 = $address['line2'];
      $city = $address['city'];
      $state = $address['state'];
      $zip = $address['zipCode'];
      $phone = $address['phone'];
      // Display the data on the page
      include 'member_address.php';   List T11-3 →
      break;
```

List T11-3 [Member_Address.php - Member]

```php
<?php include '../view/header_member.php'; ?>   ← List T11-2
<section class="content">
 <article>
  <h2 class='center'><?php echo $heading; ?></h2>
  <table>
  <form action="index.php" method="post" id="edit_address_form">
    <input type="hidden" name="action" value="update_address" />
    <?php if ($billing) : ?>
      <input type="hidden" name="address_type" value="billing" />
    <?php else: ?>
      <input type="hidden" name="address_type" value="shipping" />
    <?php endif; ?>
    <tr>
     <td><label for="line1">Address:</label></td>
     <td><input type="text" name="line1" value="<?php echo $line1; ?>" /></td>
    </tr>
    ...
  </form>
  </table>
 </article>
</section>
<?php include '../view/sidebar_member.php'; ?>
<?php include '../view/footer.php'; ?>
```

6.21 Task 12 - Display Products Catalog

The Products option on the main navigation bar calls a dynamic page. In contrast to other neighboring static pages, this page grabs products from the database marked as featured products through an administrative task performed earlier. The visitor can always see all products, offered by the company, using the sidebar links under the Categories section. Moreover, visitors can click product's title to see further details of that particular product.

Figure 6-25

List T12-1 [Products.php - abcglobal]

```php
<?php
 require_once('utility/main.php');
 require_once('model/product_lib.php');
 $products = get_featured_product();
 // Display products
 include('show_product.php');
?>
```

The page you're looking at in figure 6-25 is generated through Products.php and Show_Product.php files. Both these files are located in the site folder (root directory). The Products.php file is called when the visitor clicks the Products link on the main navigation bar. This file calls a function get_featured_product() from Product_Lib.php file under the Model directory. The function fetches all records from the Products table, marked as featured. After retrieving data, it calls the second file (Show_Product.php) to display featured products.

List T12-2 [Show_Product.php - abcglobal]

```php
<?php include 'view/header_member.php'; ?>
<section class="content">
 <article>
 <br />
 <p>We have a great collection of IT related products including software, hardware, and network that...</p>
 <!-- display products -->
 <h2>Featured products</h2>
 <table>
  <?php foreach ($products as $product) :
    // Get product data
    $list_price = $product['listPrice'];
    $discount_percent = $product['discountPercent'];
    $description = $product['description'];
    // Calculate unit price
    $discount_amount = round($list_price * ($discount_percent / 100.0), 2);
    $unit_price = $list_price - $discount_amount;
    // Get first paragraph of description
    $description = add_tags($description);
    $i = strpos($description, "</p>");
    $description = substr($description, 3, $i);
  ?>
  <tr>
     <td class="right">
       <img src="images/<?php echo $product['productCode']; ?>_s.png"
       alt=" ">
     </td>
     <td>
       <p id="product_title">
         <b><a href="catalog?product_id=<?php echo
         $product['productID']; ?>">
         <?php echo $product['productName']; ?>
         </a></b>
       </p>
       <p>
         <b>Your price:</b>
         $<?php echo number_format($unit_price, 2); ?>
       </p>
       <p>
         <?php echo $description; ?>
       </p>
     </td>
  </tr>
  <?php endforeach; ?>
 </table>
 </article>
</section>
<?php include 'view/sidebar_member.php'; ?>
<?php include 'view/footer.php'; ?>
```

The file Show_Product.php moves product information stored in the $product array to corresponding variables, performs calculation to show discounted price, and displays the information in a table. The function add_tags(), that we saw in List XXVIII, is called to add html tags to product description. Couple of functions - strpos() and substr() - are also applied on the description data to remove features part from being displayed on the current page. If you comment out the following two lines, list of features would also appear on the web page.

```
$i = strpos($description, "</p>");
$description = substr($description, 3, $i);
```

As mentioned, the information is presented in a table comprising two columns. The first column holds product's small image that was generated through an automatic process in the Upload Image module. The second column carries title, price, and description. Each product title is presented as a link which calls its detail page to provide some additional information (product features) and Add to Cart utility.

Besides the featured products, visitors can also see all products under a selected category. For example, if they click the Software link under the Categories section in the sidebar, they'll see a list of all software products available in the database.

List T12-3 [Sidebar_Member.php - View]

```php
1   <aside>
2     <section class="services">
3       <h2>Links</h2>
4       <a href="<?php echo $app_path . 'cart'; ?>">View Cart</a>
5       <?php
        // If user is logged in, display My Account link
6         $account_url = $app_path . 'member';
7         if (isset($_SESSION['user'])) :
8       ?>
9           <a href="<?php echo $account_url; ?>">My Account</a>
10        <?php endif; ?>
11      <h2>Categories</h2>
        <!-- display links for all categories -->
12      <?php
13        require_once('model/db.php');
14        require_once('model/category_lib.php');
15        $categories = get_categories();
16        foreach($categories as $category) :
17          $name = $category['categoryName'];
18          $id = $category['categoryID'];
19          $url = $app_path . 'catalog?category_id=' . $id;
20      ?>
21          <a href="<?php echo $url; ?>">
22            <?php echo $name; ?>
23          </a>
24        <?php endforeach; ?>
25    </section>
26  </aside>
```

Being part of this page, it is feasible to discuss the sidebar that displays some links specific to site members. The bunch of links in the sidebar is generated through Sidebar_Member.php file in the View directory. The first link, View Cart (line 4), calls Index.php from the Cart directory to display member's cart. You'll see member cart in an upcoming task. The second link, My Account (line 9), is displayed only when the user session is set (line 7) i.e. a member is logged in. In such case, the controller from Member directory is called to display profile of the logged in member. Code under the categories section (line 11-24) calls get_categories() function and displays each category as a link using a FOREACH loop. When the member clicks any of these links, a variable $url forwards the selected category id to the controller under the Catalog directory (line 19). The controller executes the Category case, fetches all products for the selected category through get_product_by_category() function, and includes Category_View.php file. The file Category_View.php generates a page that displays title of the selected category followed by a list of associated products as shown in figure 6-26 on the next page.

List T12-4 [Category_View.php - Catalog]

```php
1   <?php include '../view/header_member.php'; ?>
2   <section class="content">
3    <article>
4     <h2><?php echo $category_name; ?></h2>
5     <?php if (count($products) == 0) : ?>
6      <p>There are no products in this category.</p>
7     <?php else: ?>
8      <table>
9      <?php foreach ($products as $product) :
        // Get product data
10       $list_price = $product['listPrice'];
11       $discount_percent = $product['discountPercent'];
12       $description = $product['description'];
        // Calculate unit price
13       $discount_amount = round($list_price * ($discount_percent / 100.0), 2);
14       $unit_price = $list_price - $discount_amount;
        // Get first paragraph of description
15       $description = add_tags($description);
16       $i = strpos($description, "</p>");
17       $description = substr($description, 3, $i);
18     ?>
19      <tr>
20       <td class="right">
21        <img src="../images/<?php echo $product['productCode']; ?>_s.png" alt=" ">
22       </td>
23       <td>
24        <p id="product_title">
25         <b><a href="<?php echo '?product_id=' . $product['productID']; ?>">
26          <?php echo $product['productName']; ?>
27         </a></b>
28        </p>
29        <p>
30         <b>Your price:</b>
31         $<?php echo number_format($unit_price, 2); ?>
32        </p>
33        <p>
34         <?php echo $description; ?>
35        </p>
36       </td>
37      </tr>
38     <?php endforeach; ?>
39     </table>
40    <?php endif; ?>
41   </article>
42  </section>
43  <?php include '../view/sidebar_member.php'; ?>
44  <?php include '../view/footer.php'; ?>
```

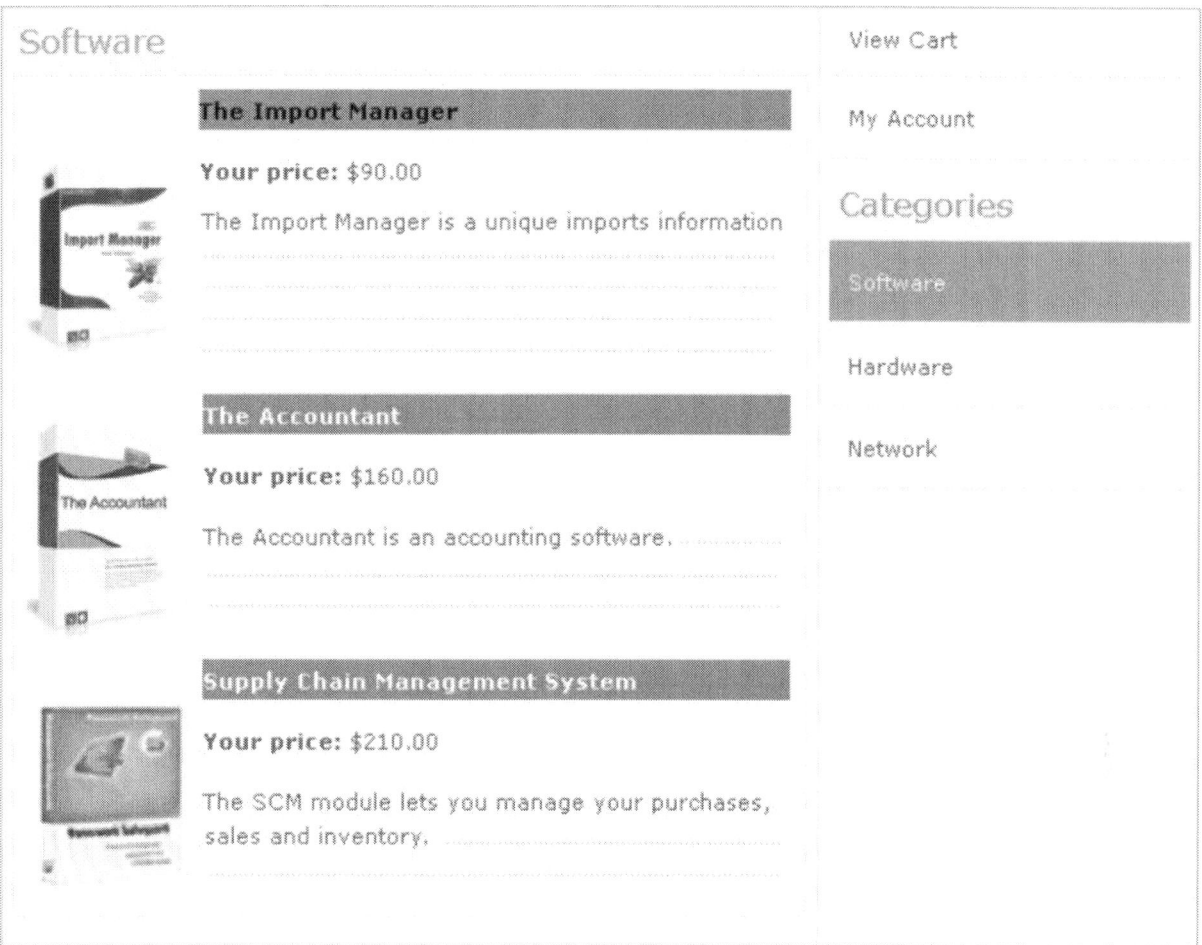

Figure 6-26

List T12-5 [Index.php - Catalog]		List T12-6 [Product_View.php - Catalog]	
	...	1	`<?php include '../view/header_member.php'; ?>`
1	`case 'product':`	2	`<section class="content">`
	`// Get product data`	3	`  <article>`
2	`$product_id = $_GET['product_id'];`		`  <!-- display product -->`
3	`$product = get_product($product_id);`	4	`    <?php include '../view/product.php'; ?>`
	`// Display product`	5	`  </article>`
4	`include('./product_view.php');`	6	`</section>`
5	`break;`	7	`<?php include '../view/sidebar_member.php'; ?>`
	...	8	`<?php include '../view/footer.php'; ?>`

When the member clicks a product's title either from the list presented in the above figure or from the list of featured products, the second case, product, in the controller (Catalog/Index.php) calls Product_View.php file. This file includes Product.php file from the View directory to display details of an individual product. The file, Product.php, was discussed in List XXVII under View Product Details in the Admin section.

6.22 Task 13 - Product Details

Site visitors can see more details such as list of features, list price, and discount offered for a particular product by clicking its title. This action takes them to the details page of the selected product where they can add the product to their cart by entering the desired quantity. If you compare this page with the View Product page in the Admin section (*View Product Details - Section 6.11.2*), you'll observe similarity between the two except Image Manager and the two buttons (Delete and Edit) that were specifically added for administrative purposes. The reason for similarity is that both these module use the same Product.php file under the View directory described in List XXVII-A to display product details. Please refer to *View Product Details* in the Admin section to see how this page is rendered.

6.23 Task 14 - Add Online Shopping Cart

This module shows how to add shopping cart to a website so that visitors could purchase products online. The page illustrated in the following figure comes up when the site visitor clicks Add to Cart button on the product details page. This module has three basic operations: View, Add, and Update cart. The first one, as displayed in the figure hereunder, shows products lying in the cart. The second one, Add, is performed when the visitor moves back using the two 'Return to' links and adds more products. The final Update operation is executed when the visitor increases or decreases values in the quantity box and click the *Update Cart* button. We'll see all these operations individually in this part of the book to understand how online shopping carts work.

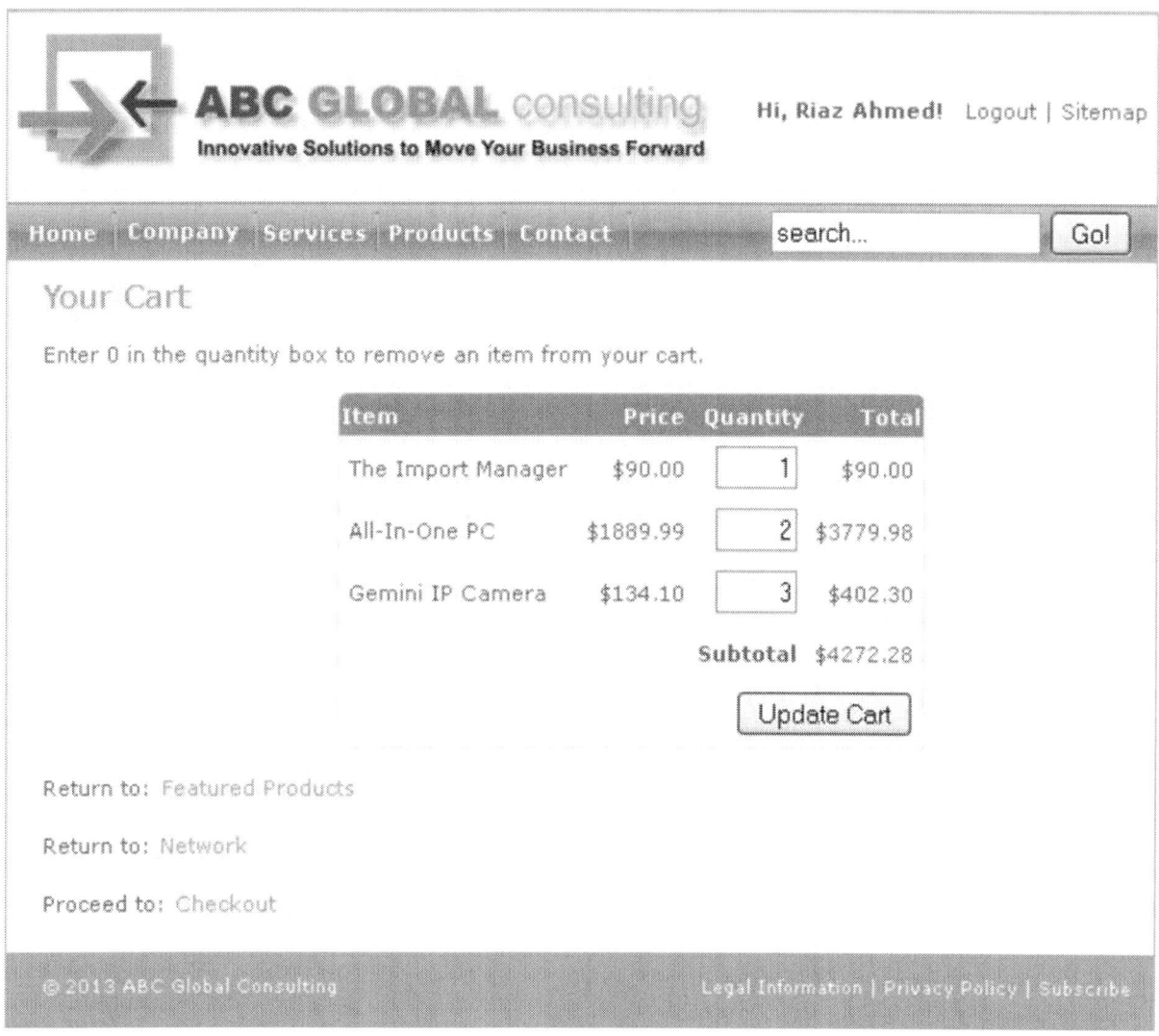

Figure 6-27

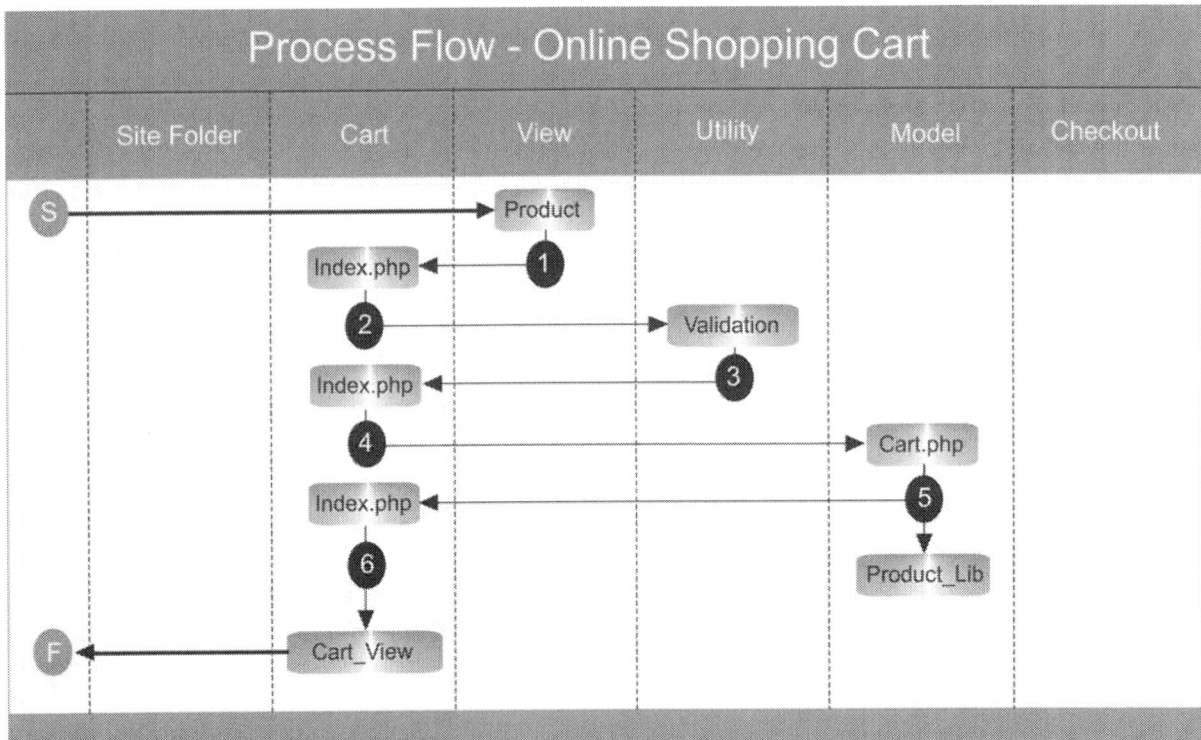

Diagram 15 - Online Shopping Cart Process

Diagram Explained

Point S - As mentioned, this process initiates when the site visitor adds a product to his online shopping cart which is done through Product.php file in the View directory. See List XXVII-B for details.

Point 1 - The file, Product.php, shifts process to the controller under the Cart directory with a hidden value: add. An empty cart - $_SESSION['cart'] - is created through a call to Cart.php using the *require* statement from the controller file.

Point 2 - In the '*add*' case the controller receives product id and quantity from Product.php file. It validates the quantity entry by calling Validation.php file in the Utility directory.

Point 4 - The controller makes some calls to Cart.php file in the Model directory. Depending on user actions, it calls functions defined in the file to perform various operations relevant to the cart module. An internal call from these functions is made to get_product() in the Product_Lib.php file to fetch all details of the added product in $product array. This detail is subsequently used to perform calculations and display other relevant information in the cart.

Point 6 - In this step the controller calls Cart_View.php to display the *Your Cart* page shown in figure 6-27.

6.23.1 Add Products to Shopping Cart

List T14-1A [Index.php - Cart]

```php
1   <?php
2   require_once '../utility/main.php';
3   require_once '../utility/validation.php';
4   require_once '../model/cart.php';
5   require_once '../model/product_lib.php';
    ...
6   elseif (isset($_GET['action'])) {
7     $action = $_GET['action'];
    ...
8   switch ($action) {
    ...
9     case 'add':
10      $product_id = $_GET['product_id'];
11      $quantity = $_GET['quantity'];
        // validate the quantity value
12      if (empty($quantity)) {
13        member_error('You must enter a quantity.');
14      } elseif (!is_valid_number($quantity, 1)) {
15        member_error('Quantity must be 1 or more.');
16      }
17      cart_add_item($product_id, $quantity);
18      $cart = cart_get_items();
19      break;
    ...
20    default:
21      member_error("Unknown cart action: " . $action);
22      break;
23  }
24  include './cart_view.php';
25  ?>
```

Explanation

The controller in the Cart directory requires four files to process this module. Like others, Cart.php file in the Model directory also contains various functions. Besides functions, it has the following code at the beginning of the file:

```
if (!isset($_SESSION['cart']) ) {
    $_SESSION['cart'] = array();
}
```

This code creates an empty cart if one doesn't exist and is executed when the controller makes an initial call to the file it contains in.

The Product.php file passes parameters to the controller through the GET method, so lines 6 and 7 are executed to store the hidden value 'add' in the variable $action which is evaluated and processed from line 9-19.

Code on line 9-19 initially validates the value entered in the quantity box. It does so by calling *is_valid_number()* and *is_present()* functions in Validation.php file.

On line # 17 it calls the function *cart_add_item()*, again from the Model directory, to add product to the cart. The function also sets name and id of the last selected category in two separate sessions which is then displayed to the user in the *'Return to'* section near the bottom of the web page illustrated above. At this point the $_SESSION array will have three arrays: [cart], [last_category_id], and [last_category_name] with the values 1, "1", and "Software" respectively assuming that the user selected the first software product.

Line # 18 calls *cart_get_items()* function which returns an array of items shown in the explanation area on the next page.

Finally, on line # 24 the file Cart_View.php is included to display the cart. Note that this file is included after the SWITCH statement which means that it will be called after executing every case (view, add, and update) defined under the SWITCH statement.

List T14-2 [Cart.php - Model]

```php
1    function cart_get_items() {
2      $items = array();
3      foreach ($_SESSION['cart'] as $product_id => $quantity ) {
        // Get product data from db
4        $product = get_product($product_id);
5        $list_price = $product['listPrice'];
6        $discount_percent = $product['discountPercent'];
7        $quantity = intval($quantity);
        // Calculate discount
8        $discount_amount = round($list_price * ($discount_percent / 100.0), 2);
9        $unit_price = $list_price - $discount_amount;
10       $line_price = round($unit_price * $quantity, 2);
        // Store data in items array
11       $items[$product_id]['name'] = $product['productName'];
12       $items[$product_id]['description'] = $product['description'];
13       $items[$product_id]['list_price'] = $list_price;
14       $items[$product_id]['discount_percent'] = $discount_percent;
15       $items[$product_id]['discount_amount'] = $discount_amount;
16       $items[$product_id]['unit_price'] = $unit_price;
17       $items[$product_id]['quantity'] = $quantity;
18       $items[$product_id]['line_price'] = $line_price;
19     }
20     return $items;
21   }
```

Explanation

The purpose of this function is to get details of the cart products from the database. This information is stored in the array $items initialized on line # 2.

Line # 3 uses the loop to iterate through all cart products. Here, we used the second form (associative array) of the FOREACH loop. For further details, see section 5.14 - Using FOREACH Loop.

Line # 4 calls *get_product()* function from Product_Lib.php using product id as a parameter. Complete record of each product is stored in the array $product.

From line 5-7 individual column values are retrieved from $product array and stored in corresponding variables.

Lines 8-10 perform calculations to set discounts.

All the above variables are then stored in $items array (from line 11-18) and are returned to the calling script (line # 18 - List T14-1A). The calling script stores this result in $cart variable which is then used in Cart_View.php (line # 18 - List T14-3A on the next page). The status of $items is presented in the following figure. The [1] array under $items represents product id and carries sub-arrays comprising product's details.

Name	Type	Value
⊟◇ $items	array[1]	
⊟◇ [1]	array[8]	
◇ [name]	string	"The Import Manager"
◇ [description]	string	"The Import Manager is a unique imports i…
◇ [list_price]	string	"100.00"
◇ [discount_percent]	string	"10.00"
◇ [discount_amount]	float	10
◇ [unit_price]	float	90
◇ [quantity]	integer	1
◇ [line_price]	float	90

List T14-3A [Cart_View.php - Cart]

```php
1    <?php include '../view/header_member.php'; ?>
2    <section class="content">
3     <article>
4      <h2>Your Cart</h2>
5      <?php if (cart_product_count() == 0) : ?>
6        <p>There are no products in your cart.</p>
7      <?php else: ?>
8        <p>Enter 0 in the quantity box to remove an item from your cart.</p>
9        <form action="index.php" method="post">
10          <input type="hidden" name="action" value="update" />
11         <table>
12         <tr class="head">
13           <th class="left">Item</th>
14           <th class="right">Price </th>
15           <th class="right"> Quantity</th>
16           <th class="right">Total</th>
17         </tr>
18         <?php foreach ($cart as $product_id => $item) : ?>
19         <tr>
20           <td><?php echo $item['name']; ?></td>
21           <td class="right">
22             <?php echo sprintf('$%.2f', $item['unit_price']); ?>
23           </td>
24           <td class="right">
25             <input type="text" size="3" class="right"
26                 name="items[<?php echo $product_id; ?>]"
27                 value="<?php echo $item['quantity']; ?>" />
28           </td>
29           <td class="right">
30             <?php echo sprintf('$%.2f', $item['line_price']); ?>
31           </td>
32         </tr>
33         <?php endforeach; ?>
34         <tr>
35           <td colspan="3" class="right" ><b>Subtotal</b></td>
36           <td class="right">
37             <?php echo sprintf('$%.2f', cart_subtotal()); ?>
38           </td>
39         </tr>
40         <tr>
41           <td colspan="4" class="right">
42             <input type="submit" value="Update Cart" />
43           </td>
44         </tr>
45         </table>
46       </form>
47     <?php endif; ?>
         ...
```

Explanation

This file forms the **Your Cart** page and is described in two parts. On line # 5 it checks whether there are any products in the cart through *cart_product_count()* function. If the value is zero, an appropriate message is displayed to the user. A value greater than zero indicates that at least one product exists in the cart, so the else block is executed.

This page allows visitors to update their cart by modifying values in the quantity box. To remove a product, they're required to simply put zero as the quantity. Upon submission, this page is posted with the *update* value.

The cart is displayed in a table and is styled using different classes defined in style.css file. For example, the first row (line 12-17) uses the *'head'* class to style table headings. Similarly, we used 'left' and 'right' classes to align heading labels and product data.

The FOREACH loop uses the associative approach to access each product's data individually from the cart session.

The sprintf() function writes a formatted string. For example, the code *sprintf('$%.2f', $item['unit_price'])* writes unit price preceded with a $ sign and with two decimal places. Line # 37 calls *cart_subtotal()* function from Cart.php file to calculate subtotal value.

List T14-3B [Cart_View.php - Cart]

```
     ...
48      <p>Return to: <a href="../products.php">Featured Products</a></p>
        <!-- display most recent category -->
49      <?php if (isset($_SESSION['last_category_id'])) :
50        $category_url = '../catalog' . '?category_id=' . $_SESSION['last_category_id']; ?>
51        <p>Return to: <a href="<?php echo $category_url; ?>">
            <?php echo $_SESSION['last_category_name']; ?></a></p>
52      <?php endif; ?>
        <!-- if cart has products, display the Checkout link -->
53      <?php if (cart_product_count() > 0) : ?>
54        <p>
55          Proceed to: <a href="../checkout">Checkout</a>
56        </p>
57      <?php endif; ?>
58    </article>
59  </section>
60  <?php include '../view/footer.php'; ?>
```

Explanation

The second part of the Cart_View file provides links such as:

- featured products
- the last category a product was selected from
- Checkout

As the name implies, the Featured Product link (line # 48) returns users to the main products page.

Line # 50 forms a url by taking category id value from the session. It then presents it as a link on line # 51 to return the user to the last selected category.

The final Checkout link (line 55) is displayed only when there is at least one product in the cart. An IF condition is applied from line 53 to 57 to check this status. The link passes the flow to Index.php under the Checkout directory. This process will be discussed in the next task.

6.23.2 Update Product in the Shopping Cart

List T14-1B [Index.php - Cart]

```
    ...
1   if (isset($_POST['action'])) {
2     $action = $_POST['action'];
3   }
    ...
4   switch ($action) {
    ...
5     case 'update':
6       $items = $_POST['items'];
7       foreach ( $items as $product_id => $quantity ) {
8         if ($quantity == 0) {
9           cart_remove_item($product_id);
10        } else {
11          cart_update_item($product_id, $quantity);
12        }
13      }
14      $cart = cart_get_items();
15      break;
    ...
16  include './cart_view.php';
17  ?>
```

Explanation

When the cart is updated, code defined from line 1 to 3 is executed. Since the action is update, the code retrieves the array of added products from the $_POST array on line # 6. The following snapshot illustrates values held under $_POST array. Elements [1], [2], and [3] are product ids with ordered quantity values 10, 20, & 30 respectively.

Name	Type	Value
⊟◇ $_POST	array[2]	
◇ [action]	string	"update"
⊟◇ [items]	array[3]	
◇ [1]	string	"10"
◇ [2]	string	"20"
◇ [3]	string	"30"

The FOREACH loop checks each product's quantity in the $items array. If the quantity is zero, the function *cart_remove_item()* is called to remove the product from the cart using the key: $product_id. The else block calls *cart_update_item()* function to update the quantity for the product. Note that in order to pick existing products we used $items array in this loop. Line 14 calls *cart_get_items()* again to update $cart array.

6.24 Task 15 - Checkout Module

The checkout module asks members to confirm their orders and need their payment information to proceed. It comprises the following two pages:

- **Confirm Order:** The confirm order page (shown below) displays member's cart with tax and shipping charges. At this stage, members have the option to move back and update their carts. The Payment link at the bottom of this page advances them to the next page to complete the process.
- **Payment:** This page accepts payment information to place order and will be discussed shortly.

Figure 6-28

6.24.1 Order Confirmation

List T15-1 [Index.php - Checkout]

```php
1   <?php
2   require_once('../utility/main.php');
3   require_once('../utility/secure.php');
4   require_once('../utility/validation.php');
5   require_once('../model/cart.php');
6   require_once('../model/product_lib.php');
7   require_once('../model/order_lib.php');
8   require_once('../model/member_lib.php');
9   require_once('../model/address_lib.php');
10  if (!isset($_SESSION['user'])) {
11    $_SESSION['checkout'] = true;
12    redirect('../member');
13    exit();
14  }
    ...
15  else {
16    $action = 'confirm';
17  }
18  switch ($action) {
19    case 'confirm':
20      $cart = cart_get_items();
21      if (cart_product_count() == 0) {
22        redirect('../cart');
23      }
24      $subtotal = cart_subtotal();  // Model/Cart
25      $item_count = cart_item_count();  // Model/Cart
26      $shipping_cost = shipping_cost();  // Model/Order_Lib
27      $shipping_address = get_address($_SESSION['user']['shipAddressID']);
28      $state = $shipping_address['state'];
29      $tax = tax_amount($subtotal);  // Model/Order_Lib
30      $total = $subtotal + $tax + $shipping_cost;
31      include 'checkout_confirm.php';
32      break;
33    ...
    }
34  ?>
```

This controller receives focus from the Checkout link on the previous page (Your Cart). To complete the process, it requires various files from Utility and Model directories (line 2-9).

On line # 10 it looks for the user session. The absence of this session means the user is not logged in. In such situation, the visitor is diverted to the Member directory (line # 12) where the respective controller displays the member login form. Line # 11 creates a session named checkout to remember that the user was redirected from the checkout module. For relevant information see Member Registration Module.

The figure presented above fetches information from the confirm case (line 19-32). The code under this case calls cart_get_items() to retrieve complete cart information. If the cart is empty (line 21-23), the flow is redirected to cart/index.php.

From line 24 to 30 four functions (listed next) are called to calculate subtotal, number of items in the cart, shipping cost, and tax value. All these are then presented on the order confirmation page through checkout_confirm.php file (List T15-3).

List T15-2 [Functions]

```php
// Model/Cart.php
function cart_subtotal() {
  $subtotal = 0;
  $cart = cart_get_items();
  foreach ($cart as $item) {
    $subtotal += $item['unit_price'] * $item['quantity'];
  }
  return $subtotal;
}

// Model/Cart.php
function cart_item_count() {
  $count = 0;
  $cart = cart_get_items();
  foreach ($cart as $item) {
    $count += $item['quantity'];
  }
  return $count;
}

// Model/Order_Lib.php
function shipping_cost() {
  $item_count = cart_item_count();
  $item_shipping = 5;  // $5 per item
  if ($item_count > 5) {
    $shipping_cost = $item_shipping * 5;
  } else {
    $shipping_cost = $item_shipping * $item_count;
  }
  return $shipping_cost;
}

// Model/Order_Lib.php
function tax_amount($subtotal) {
  $shipping_address = get_address($_SESSION['user']['shipAddressID']);
  $state = $shipping_address['state'];
  $state = strtoupper($state);
  switch ($state) {
    case 'CA': $tax_rate = 0.09; break;
    default: $tax_rate = 0; break;
  }
  return round($subtotal * $tax_rate, 2);
}
```

Explanation

These are the four functions used in the previous listing.

The cart_subtotal() function calculates and returns cart's subtotal. If fetches complete cart information from current session, uses a loop to multiply unit price with each product's quantity, stores the cumulative result in a variable ($subtotal), and returns it to line # 24 in the previous listing.

The second function, cart_item_count(), adds up values in the quantity field and returns it to $item_count on line # 25 in the previous listing.

The shipping_cost() function calculates a shipping charge of $5 per item for the first five items. The returned value is stored in $shipping_cost variable on line # 26 in the previous listing.

The final tax_amount() function receives $subtotal parameter and calculates sales tax on this value only for orders originating from California (CA) state. This value is returned to line # 29.

List T15-3 [Checkout_Confirm.php - Checkout]

```php
1   <?php include '../view/header_member.php'; ?>
2   <section class="content">
3    <article>
4     <h2>Confirm Order</h2>
5     <table>
6      <tr class="head">
7       <th class="left" >Item</th>
8       <th class="right">Price </th>
9       <th class="right">Quantity </th>
10      <th class="right">Total </th>
11     </tr>
12     <?php foreach ($cart as $product_id => $item) : ?>
13      <tr>
14       <td><?php echo $item['name']; ?></td>
15       <td class="right"> <?php echo sprintf('$%.2f', $item['unit_price']); ?> </td>
16       <td class="right"> <?php echo $item['quantity']; ?> </td>
17       <td class="right"> <?php echo sprintf('$%.2f', $item['line_price']); ?> </td>
18      </tr>
19     <?php endforeach; ?>
20     <tr>
21      <td colspan="3" class="right"><b>Subtotal</b></td>
22      <td class="right"> <?php echo sprintf('$%.2f', $subtotal); ?> </td>
23     </tr>
24     <tr>
25      <td colspan="3" class="right"><?php echo $state; ?> Tax</td>
26      <td class="right"> <?php echo sprintf('$%.2f', $tax); ?> </td>
27     </tr>
28     <tr>
29      <td colspan="3" class="right">Shipping</td>
30      <td class="right"> <?php echo sprintf('$%.2f', $shipping_cost); ?> </td>
31     </tr>
32     <tr id="total">
33      <td colspan="3" class="right"><b>Total</b></td>
34      <td class="right"> <?php echo sprintf('$%.2f', $total); ?> </td>
35     </tr>
36    </table>
37    <p>
38     Proceed to: <a href="<?php echo '?action=payment'; ?>">Payment</a>
39    </p>
40   </article>
41  </section>
42  <?php include '../view/footer.php'; ?>
```

Explanation

The code presented in this listing draws the order confirmation page.

Lines 6-11 form a row to hold table headings using head, right, and left classes from style.css file.

Row created from line 13 to 18 display individual product from the $cart array with price, quantity, and total.

Lines 20-23 display subtotal on a separate row.

The next table row (line 24-27) shows tax figures along with member's state. A tax rate of 0.09 is applied to all orders generating from the California (CA) state.

The second last row (line 28-31) displays shipping cost while the last row (line 32-35) displays grand total for the order.

Line # 38 creates a link named Payment that takes member to the next page where she provides her credit card information.

6.24.2   Payment Information

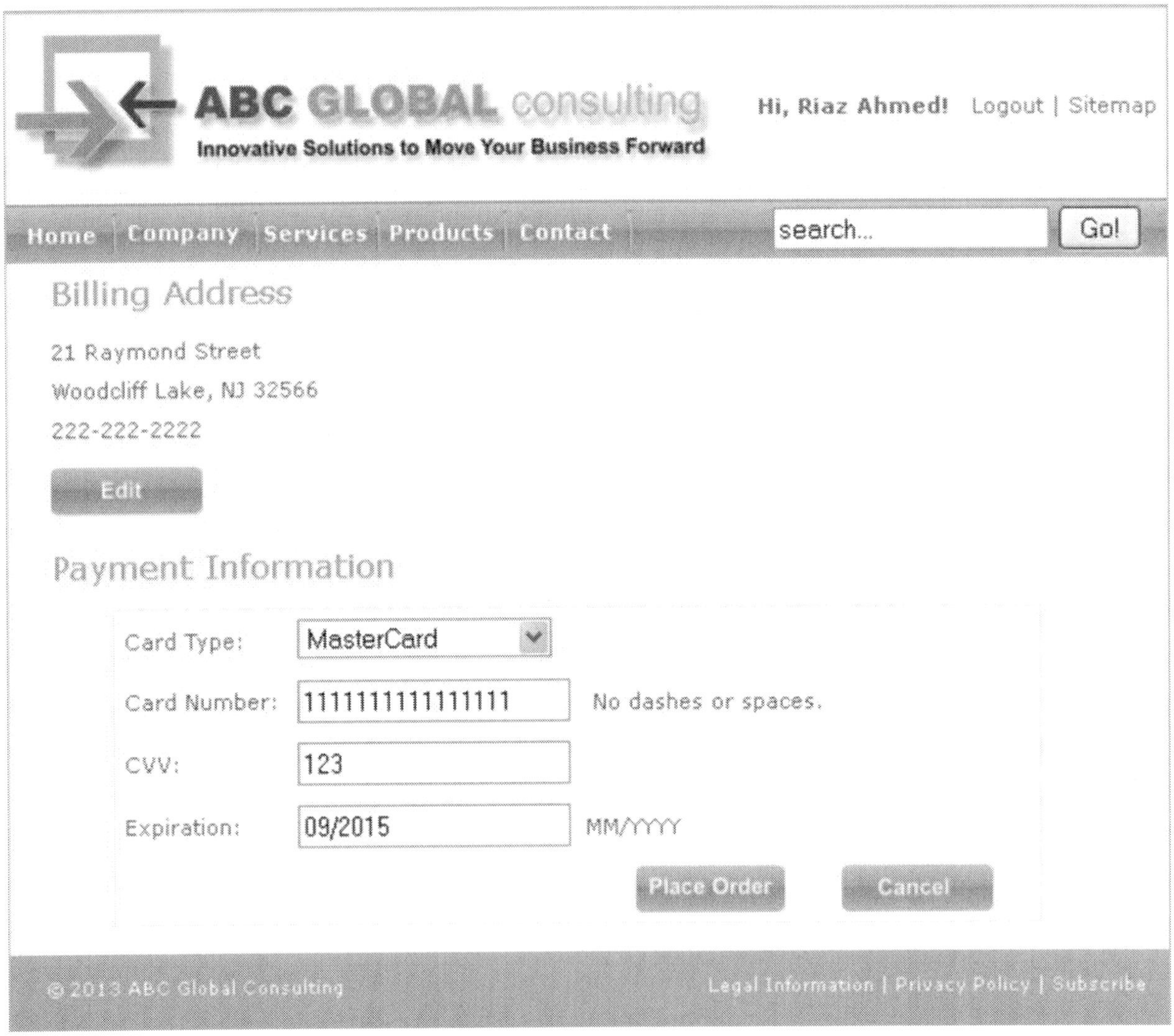

Figure 6-29

This page has two sections: Billing Address and Payment Information. The former one displays member's billing address from the database and presents an Edit button to alter this information. The latter one has a form which takes credit card information from the member. Card Type is a drop down list from which the member can select his card. It carries: Master Card, Visa, Discover, and American Express. The Card Number field accepts 15 digits for American Express and 16 for others. Similarly the CVV box takes 4 digits for American Express and 3 digits for the rest. The card expiration should be entered in MM/YYYY format. For example, 09/2015 represents September, 2015. After filling in this form, the member clicks the Place Order button to confirm his order. The Cancel button takes him back to the cart page.

List T15-4A [Index.php - Checkout]

```
    ...
1   elseif (isset($_GET['action'])) {
2     $action = $_GET['action'];
3   }
4   switch ($action) {
5     case 'payment':
6       if (cart_product_count() == 0) {
7         redirect($app_path . 'cart');
8       }
9       $billing_address = get_address($_SESSION['user']['billingAddressID']);   //Model/Address_Lib.php
10      $bill_line1 = $billing_address['line1'];
11      $bill_line2 = $billing_address['line2'];
12      $bill_city = $billing_address['city'];
13      $bill_state = $billing_address['state'];
14      $bill_zip = $billing_address['zipCode'];
15      $bill_phone = $billing_address['phone'];
16      include 'checkout_payment.php';
17      break;
18    ...
19  }
20  ?>
```

Explanation

The code listed here initiates the payment process. In the previous list, an action named *payment* was forwarded on line # 38. The controller GETS and stores this value in $action (lines 1-3) and executes the 'payment' case (line # 5).

After checking the shopping cart status (lines 6-8), it calls get_address() function by passing billing address id from the user session as a parameter and stores data in individual variables (lines 10-15). This data is displayed on the payment page with an Edit button so that members could change their billing information.

Finally, on line # 16 the file checkout_payment.php is included to display the payment page.

List T15-5 [Checkout_Payment.php - Checkout]

```
...
1     <h2>Billing Address</h2>
2     <p><?php echo $bill_line1; ?><br>
3       <?php if ( strlen($bill_line2) > 0 ) : ?>
4         <?php echo $bill_line2; ?><br>
5       <?php endif; ?>
6       <?php echo $bill_city; ?>, <?php echo $bill_state; ?>
7       <?php echo $bill_zip; ?><br>
8       <?php echo $bill_phone; ?>
9     </p>
10    <form action="../member/index.php" method="post">
11      <input type="hidden" name="action" value="view_address_edit" />
12      <input type="hidden" name="address_type" value="billing" />
13      <input type="image" id="left_button" alt="Edit" src="<?php echo $app_path; ?>images/edit.png">
14    </form>
15    <br><br>
16    <h2>Payment Information</h2>
17    <table>
18    <form action="index.php" method="post" id="payment_form">
19      <input type="hidden" name="action" value="process" />
20      <tr>
21        <td><label for="card_type">Card Type:</label></td>
22        <td><select name="card_type">
23          <option value="1">MasterCard</option>
24          <option value="2">Visa</option>
25          <option value="3">Discover</option>
26          <option value="4">American Express</option>
27        </select></td>
28      </tr>
29      <tr>
30        <td><label for="card_number">Card Number:</label></td>
31        <td><input type="text" name="card_number" />  No dashes or spaces.</td>
32      </tr>
33      <tr>
34        <td><label for="card_cvv">CVV:</label></td>
35        <td><input type="text" name="card_cvv" /></td>
36      </tr>
37      <tr>
38        <td><label for="card_expires">Expiration:</label></td>
39        <td><input type="text" name="card_expires" />  MM/YYYY</td>
40      </tr>
41      <tr>
42        <td colspan=2><input type="image" id="right_button" alt="Place Order"
                      src="<?php echo $app_path; ?>images/order.png"></td>
43    </form>
44      <form action="../cart/index.php" method="post" >
45        <td><input type="image" id="right_button" alt="Cancel"
              src="<?php echo $app_path; ?>images/cancel.png"></td>
46      </form>
47      </tr>
48    </table><br>
...
```

Explanation

This file displays the payment information page. Lines 1-14 generate the first section: Billing Address.

Line # 4 displays second address only when it exist, which is evaluated on line # 3 using strlen() built-in function.

Lines 10-14 create a form with two hidden and one image elements. Upon click, the image (edit.png) POSTS the two hidden values to the controller under the Member directory to present Update Billing Address page.

The second section of this page is created from line # 16 to 48. It has a form having a table and an image button: Place Order. The Place Order button, defined on line # 42, POSTS this form with a hidden value 'process' to the controller. The Cancel button, shown in the above figure, is contained in another form (line # 44-46) and calls the Cart page when clicked.

You can also see the four card types, defined in a <select> element (line 20-28) whereas the other three fields are specified on separate rows supplemented with some help text.

List T15-4B [Index.php - Checkout]

```php
1    if (isset($_POST['action'])) {
2      $action = $_POST['action'];
3    }
     ...
4    switch ($action) {
     ...
5      case 'process':
6        if (cart_product_count() == 0) {
7          redirect('Location: ' . $app_path . 'cart');
8        }
9        $cart = cart_get_items();
10       $card_type = intval($_POST['card_type']);
11       $card_number = $_POST['card_number'];
12       $card_cvv = $_POST['card_cvv'];
13       $card_expires = $_POST['card_expires'];
14       if (!is_present($card_type)) {
15         member_error('Card type is required.');
16       } elseif (!is_valid_card_type($card_type)) {
17         member_error('Card type ' . $card_type . ' is invalid.');
18       }
19       if (!is_present($card_number)) {
20         member_error('Card number is required.');
21       } elseif (!is_valid_card_number($card_number, $card_type)) {
22         member_error('Card number ending in ' . substr($card_number, -4) . ' is invalid.');
23       }
24       if (!is_present($card_cvv)) {
25         member_error('Card CVV is required.');
26       } elseif (!is_valid_card_cvv($card_cvv, $card_type)) {
27         member_error('Card CVV is invalid.');
28       }
29       if (!is_present($card_expires)) {
30         member_error('Card expiration date is required.');
31       }
32       elseif (!is_valid_card_expires($card_expires)) {
33         member_error('Card is either expired or the date entered is invalid.');
34       }
35       $order_id = add_order($card_type, $card_number, $card_cvv, $card_expires);
36       foreach($cart as $product_id => $item) {
37         $item_price = $item['list_price'];
38         $discount = $item['discount_amount'];
39         $quantity = $item['quantity'];
40         add_order_item($order_id, $product_id, $item_price, $discount, $quantity);
41       }
42       clear_cart();
43       redirect('../member?action=view_order&order_id=' . $order_id);
44       break;
     ...
```

Explanation

The previous listing posts the form with a hidden value 'process' that is evaluated from line 1 to 3 here. After receiving control, the controller executes the 'process' case (line # 5). Once again, the cart is checked for product existence. If there are no products, flow is redirected to cart directory, else, code from line # 9-13 is executed to store credit card information in different variables.

Code from line # 14 to 34 validates credit card data. All functions used here exist in Validation.php file.

The first IF block (line 14-18) checks whether the member has selected a value from the provided four card types. It calls couple of functions to validate user input. The remaining IF blocks validate credit card number, CVV number, and date of expiration. All these functions used for validation are discussed next.

After data validation, the controller calls add_order() function to insert provided information in master database table - Orders (line # 35). Here, the available four parameters (card type, number, cvv, and expiry) are passed to the function. The remaining information, customer id and addresses required in the Orders table, is fetched from the user session.

Line # 36 to 41 uses a loop to insert line items in the OrderItems table from the cart session. The code calls add_order_item() function to perform the insert operation.

Line # 42 calls clear_cart() function from Cart.php to clear the cart.

After successfully completing the whole process, the controller redirects flow (line # 43) to Member directory by passing an action 'view_order' together with current order id. In return, the controller in the Member directory displays a page that show the last placed order.

List T15-6A [Validation.php - Utility]

```
1    function is_present($value) {
2      if (isset($value) && strlen($value) > 0) {
3        return true;
4      } else {
5        return false;
6      }
7    }
```

Explanation

This function checks the existence and length of the received argument ($value). Previously, this function was called in *Add Product to Shopping Cart*. This time it is called multiple times to validate credit card information. For example, the initial call (line # 14) in the previous list passes $card_type parameter to this function. The IF statement checks whether the provided parameter exist - *isset($value)* - and (&&) that its length is greater than zero. The strlen() function returns length of the given string on success, and 0 if the string is empty. In the current scenario, for instance, if the member selects Visa as card type, a string value '2' is passed in $value. Since it's a single character, the value returned by strlen() would be 1 which is greater than zero. If both conditions are found true, the is_present() function returns true; otherwise false is returned to the calling script.

List T15-6B [Validation.php - Utility]

```
1    function is_valid_card_type($card_type) {
2      if (!is_int($card_type)) return false;
3      if ( $card_type < 1 || $card_type > 4 ) return false;
4      return true;
5    }
```

Explanation

This function checks whether the member selected a card type from the provided list. Recall that this list was created in Checkout_Payment.php and each card option was assigned a value. That value is received here as an argument. The first condition in this function returns false if the provided value is not an integer. The second statement also returns false if the value is either less than 1 or (||) is greater than 4. In contrast, if the provided value is an integer and also falls within the range (1-4), the value true is returned to the calling script, validating the card type.

List T15-6C [Validation.php - Utility]

```
1   function is_valid_card_number($card_number, $card_type) {
2     switch ($card_type) {
3       case 4:
4         $pattern = '/^\d{15}$/';
5         break;
6       default:
7         $pattern = '/^\d{16}$/';
8         break;
9     }
10    return preg_match($pattern, $card_number);
11  }
```

Explanation

As shown, two parameters are received by this function to validate credit card number. The first parameter, $card_number, holds the card number whereas the second one, $card_type, holds a value ranging from 1 to 4 to represent each card type. As mentioned earlier, the American Express card (given the value 4) accepts 15 digits as card number while the rest three types take 16 digits. To receive valid input, we used the SWITCH statement and evaluated card type value on line # 3. If the value is 4, the selected card is American Express. Next, on line # 4 we defined a pattern to validate the input. Pattern strings are defined inside a pair of forward slashes. The '^' pattern marks the beginning of the string while the '$' pattern signifies the end. The '\d' pattern represents any digit. The {n} pattern must repeat exactly n times. Thus the expression, '/^\d{15}$/', checks for 15 digits for American Express card and 16 digits for others (line # 7).

The Preg_Match() PHP function on line # 10 is used to search a string, and return a 1 or 0. If the search was successful a 1 will be returned, and if it was not found a 0 will be returned. In this code, it searches the specified pattern in the card number string.

List T15-6D [Validation.php - Utility]

```
1   function is_valid_card_cvv($card_cvv, $card_type) {
2     switch ($card_type) {
3       case 4:                    // American Express
4         $pattern = '/^\d{4}$/';
5         break;
6       default:
7         $pattern = '/^\d{3}$/';
8         break;
9     }
10    return preg_match($pattern, $card_cvv);
11  }
```

Explanation

This function is similar to the previous one and validates card CVV number according to the selected option.

List T15-6E [Validation.php - Utility]

```php
1     function is_valid_card_expires($card_expires) {
2         $pattern = '/^\d{1,2}\/\d{4}$/';
3         if (!preg_match($pattern, $card_expires)) return false;
4         $date_parts = explode('/', $card_expires);
5         if (intval($date_parts[0]) <= 0 || intval($date_parts[0]) > 12) return false;
6         $now = new DateTime();
7         $expires = new DateTime();
8         $expires->setDate($date_parts[1], $date_parts[0], 1);
9         $expires->add(new DateInterval("P1M"));   // $expires->modify('+1 month');
10        $expires->sub(new DateInterval("P1D"));   // $expires->modify('-1 day');
11        $expires->setTime(23,59,59);
12        return ($now < $expires);
13    }
```

Explanation

Let's go through each line of code individually to understand what is happening here. Assume that the member enter 02/2016 (February, 2016) as card expiration date which is received by this function through the variable $card_expires on line # 1.

Line # 2 generates a pattern for validation. The pattern incorporates month and year values in digits separated by a forward slash. Members can either enter 1 or 01 for January.

Line # 3 returns false if the card expiry value doesn't match the defined pattern expression.

Line # 4 stores values from $card_expires something like this:

Name	Type	Value
$date_parts	array[2]	
[0]	string	"02"
[1]	string	"2016"

The explode() function breaks a string into an array. Here, the value of variable $card_expires is broken at the symbol "/".

Line # 5 returns false if the month value ($date_parts[0]) is not between 1 and 12.

Line # 6 stores current system date in a date object $now. For example, January 10, 2013 will be stored as: "2013-01-10 10:25:29". The second part of this string '10:25:29' represents current system time.

Line # 7 repeats the same process and stores current system date in another date object: $expires.

Line # 8 uses the setDate() function which resets the current date of the DateTime object to a different date. This code uses the two values from $date_parts array. Where the first value, [1], holds 2016 and the second one, [0], carries 02. The third argument (1) is passed for day one. This combination sets $expires to "2016-02-01 10:25:29".

Line # 9 uses a DateInterval object that represents a span of time, or a period of time specified under the parentheses - ("P1M"). The letter P begins the interval code. nM specifies the number of months. The add() method adds the amount of time specified by the DateInterval object. Note that this code requires PHP version 5.3.0 or higher. If the version is lower, use the alternate code provided next to it as a comment. After adding the duration of one month, the value of $expires becomes: "2016-03-01 10:25:29".

Line # 10 uses the same technique to subtract 1 day ("P1D") from $expires. This time the sub() method is used to subtract the specified amount of time. After subtraction, the value of $expires becomes: "2016-02-29 10:25:29".

Line # 11 sets the time portion in $expires using 24 hours format. It makes the timestamp in $expires to: "2016-02-29 23:59:59" and this is the value that we wished to obtain through this function. It is the last day and time when the card expires.

Line # 12 compares current date with the expiry date and returns the result. If current date is less than expiry, the card is accepted.

After providing all valid information, the member clicks the Place Order button. This action records order details in relevant master and detail tables (Orders and OrderItems) and calls a page that displays the last placed order. This is the same Order Information page that you saw in section 6.14.2 in the Admin module.

With the completion of this task, the development phase of our website project concludes. After completion, the site is ready for deployment on a hosting server and that is what the next task deals with.

6.25 Task 16 - Website Deployment

After completing the website and giving it a thorough test run, you're ready to deploy it on a hosting server from where the world could access it. The following steps need to be completed in order to accomplish this task.

1. Host the website
2. Install FileZilla FTP Client and upload files
3. Access control panel
4. Create a blank database and a database user. Grant database access privileges to the new user.
5. Call phpMyAdmin tool to create database tables using the Import option.
6. Install PEAR core and PEAR Mail packages

Step-1 Hosting the Website

To make your Web site visible to the world, it has to be hosted on a Web server. Every website on the Internet needs to be stored somewhere, and that's what referred to as "web hosting". A website host is just a computer that is on all the time and connected to the Internet. When you visit a website, you download some files from the machine that stores that particular website. Any computer can be used to host a website, even the one you are using now – but the computers used by professional hosting companies are incredibly powerful with lots of hard disks and memory, highly optimized to deliver the website files to thousands of readers simultaneously.

The two basic ways of hosting a website are: self and commercial.

Self Hosting

If you want to go the DIY free route, then it is in fact entirely possible to host your own website at home, on your own Internet connection. With advances that allowed Internet access to move away from dial-up services and into a realm of faster and more robust use of Internet resources, the possibility of self-hosting became more viable. As is true with many forms of electronic equipment, the hardware necessary to create and manage a hosting network became more affordable. At the same time, software packages that could help configure and operate the networks also became more cost-effective. Coupled with the fact that more people began to make use of the Internet for both personal and commercial purposes, and also became more familiar with how to design sites and understand bandwidth, the idea of self-hosting is now well worth consideration.

While self-hosting is certainly more viable than in years past, the process still requires securing the right equipment, using software to manage the resources, and protect the host from all the threats that could filter into the hosting process via the Internet connection. This means that users who are not comfortable with these types of management processes are likely to find that working with a hosting company rather than trying to handle the processes alone may still be the best bet. For others who feel competent to engage in self-hosting, the strategy can mean greater ease in managing resources and even allowing the entire project to be much more cost effective.

There are a lot of security issues that can come up when self-hosting. Configuration issues can take a bit of doing to get the right software installed, and set up to behave correctly. Also, a commercial host will usually have some monitoring set up, so they know if the site goes down. They'll also normally have redundancy set up, so that even if a hard drive or one of their internet connections goes down, your site doesn't lose connectivity or otherwise stop working.

Unless you are an extremely tech savvy individual and have some strong need to run everything from your home, hosting your own website is not going to be a good option for most people.

Just to give you an idea, here are some of the things you'd need to host your own site:

- A computer that is powerful enough to keep up with the server requests when your site receives traffic
- A copy of the Linux operating system
- Make sure your ISP will even allow this. Some may, but will charge you an additional fee
- Cable and DSL are not good enough. You should probably have a dedicated T1 line

It's also important to remember that the computer you use must be dedicated for this task. It is not recommended you use your personal computer to double as a web host because it could interrupt your website's performance levels. So as you can see the costs for hosting your own site will start piling up. First you'll need a second computer, then you'll have to pay your ISP additional money so they will allow you to even host your site. Plus you'll have to buy an additional T1 line and that may cost you several hundred dollars per month. Not to mention you'll spend a lot of time setting this up unless you know a great deal about computers, servers, etc.

Commercial Hosting

Here you have three flavors: shared, virtual private server and dedicated server.

Shared Hosting: So called because you share a hosting server with other websites that are also stored on the same computer. Shared hosting is the budget option where prices and packages vary. Shared hosting is a very cost effective solution to host your website. With shared hosting, your web site gets its own domain name, and is hosted on a powerful server along with other web sites. Shared solutions often offer multiple software solutions like e-mail, database, and different editing options with good technical support.

VPS and Dedicated Servers: These are the top 2 levels of website hosting, and mean you get the whole server to yourself. The difference between Virtual Private Server (VPS) and Dedicated Server is that a Dedicated Server is a single, physical system which you essentially "rent" inside of a data center. A virtual private server (VPS) is a virtual machine provided by an Internet hosting service. Although a VPS runs in software on the same physical computer as other customers' virtual machines, it is in many respects functionally equivalent to a separate physical computer. A VPS is dedicated to the individual customer's needs, has the privacy of a separate physical computer, and can be configured to run server software.

Initially I'd suggest heading straight to a shared hosting plan. Besides cost effectiveness, it saves you so many headaches down the line. When the time comes to upgrade, you can easily migrate to a more professional solution.

Step-2 Install FileZilla FTP Client and Upload Files

After purchasing a hosting plan, the next step is to upload your website files to the hosting server using some FTP client software.

FileZilla client is a cross-platform graphical FTP, FTPS and SFTP software with lot of features, supporting Windows, Linux, Mac OS X and more. It is used to transfer files between computers. It is open source software distributed free of charge under the terms of the GNU General Public License and can be downloaded from http://filezilla-project.org/. In order to use FileZilla client on your client PC, you must disable FTP Access Filter if you're behind a firewall such as Microsoft ISA Server.

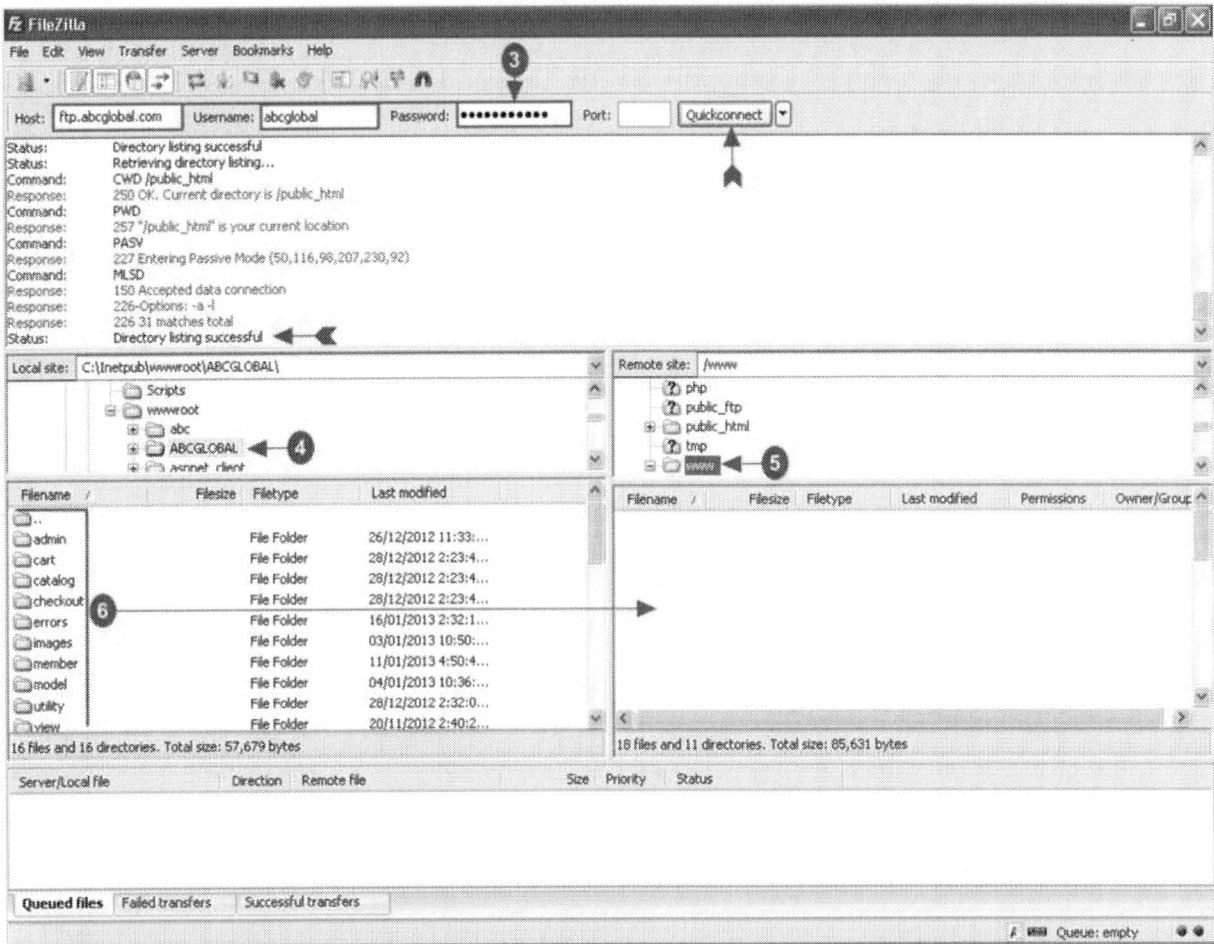

Figure 6-30

1. Launch the downloaded FileZilla_x.x.x.x_win32-setup.exe file on your PC and follow the wizard to complete the setup.
2. Run FileZilla client either from your desktop or from the program group
3. Enter the information (Host, Username, and Password) provided by your hosting company and click the Quickconnect button. After a while you will see a message *'Directory listing Successful'* in the upper pane which indicates that you're ready to upload your website files to the hosting server. Prior to uploading the files, make sure you've made necessary changes (especially to modules developed to send e-mails) described earlier.
4. From the Local site pane to the left, expand wwwroot directory and select ABCGLOBAL folder from your PC. This would list all the files being held in this directory as shown above.
5. Similarly, select www folder from the Remote site to your right which is the target directory on the hosting server where you'd transfer your website files.
6. From the lower Local site pane, select all files and drag them to the lower pane under the Remote site. This will start file transfer process which you can observe in the bottom pane.

After completion, a message *File transfer successful* will appear indicating that the hosting server is now ready to deliver your website. Your work is not over yet. Besides static pages that the world can access at this stage, you also have dynamic content being held in your database and that is what you are going to configure next. But first, you'll have to access the control panel to create your database on the hosting server.

Step-3   Access Web Hosting Control Panel

In web hosting, a control panel is a web-based graphical interface provided by the hosting company that allows customers to manage their various hosted services in a single place.

Some of the commonly available modules in most control panels are:

- Web-based file manager
- Configure and manage e-mail accounts
- Manage database
- Access to server logs
- Web log analysis software to provide traffic statistics
- Details of available and used web space and bandwidth
- Maintaining FTP users' accounts

It allows you to control all aspects of your site. You can upload files, create sub domains for your blogs like yourblog.yoursite.com, setup disk partition and bandwidth partition if you are hosting multiple sites, limit the use of MySQL database, install PayPal for your e-commerce site, and much more.

There are many kinds of control panels out in the web hosting market but the following three control panels are recommended and are widely used by many hosting companies.

C panel: http://cpanel.net - If you are new to web hosting control panel, c panel would be your best choice because it provides video tutorials which are very informative for new webmasters.

Plesk control panel: www.parallels.com - Plesk panel is best suited with MS based applications which make it unique. Plesk is very tough for both crackers and hackers to perform any malicious task on the server.

H-Sphere: www.parallels.com/products/hsphere - H-sphere is known for its compatibility with windows, UNIX and Linux and offers a special support ticketing system to keep you in touch with your hosting providers.

A Web hosting control panel plays a vital role when selecting a web host for your website. With many kinds of control panels and many web hosting companies out there - each with their own standard and resources - you need to understand your own specific web hosting requirements like which control panel you actually require and then only you can make a mature decision to go after a particular web hosting company.

In this exercise you will use cpanel interface to create your database and install couple of PHP packages.

1. In your browser type the url provided by your hosting company to access the control panel such as http://cpanel2.hostingserver.net:1234/.
2. Enter the username and password, also provided with the above information. After providing valid credentials, the following page appears. Note the four marked utilities under three different sections. In the upcoming exercises you'll be asked to select these utilities to perform some specific tasks according to the number displayed on top of them.

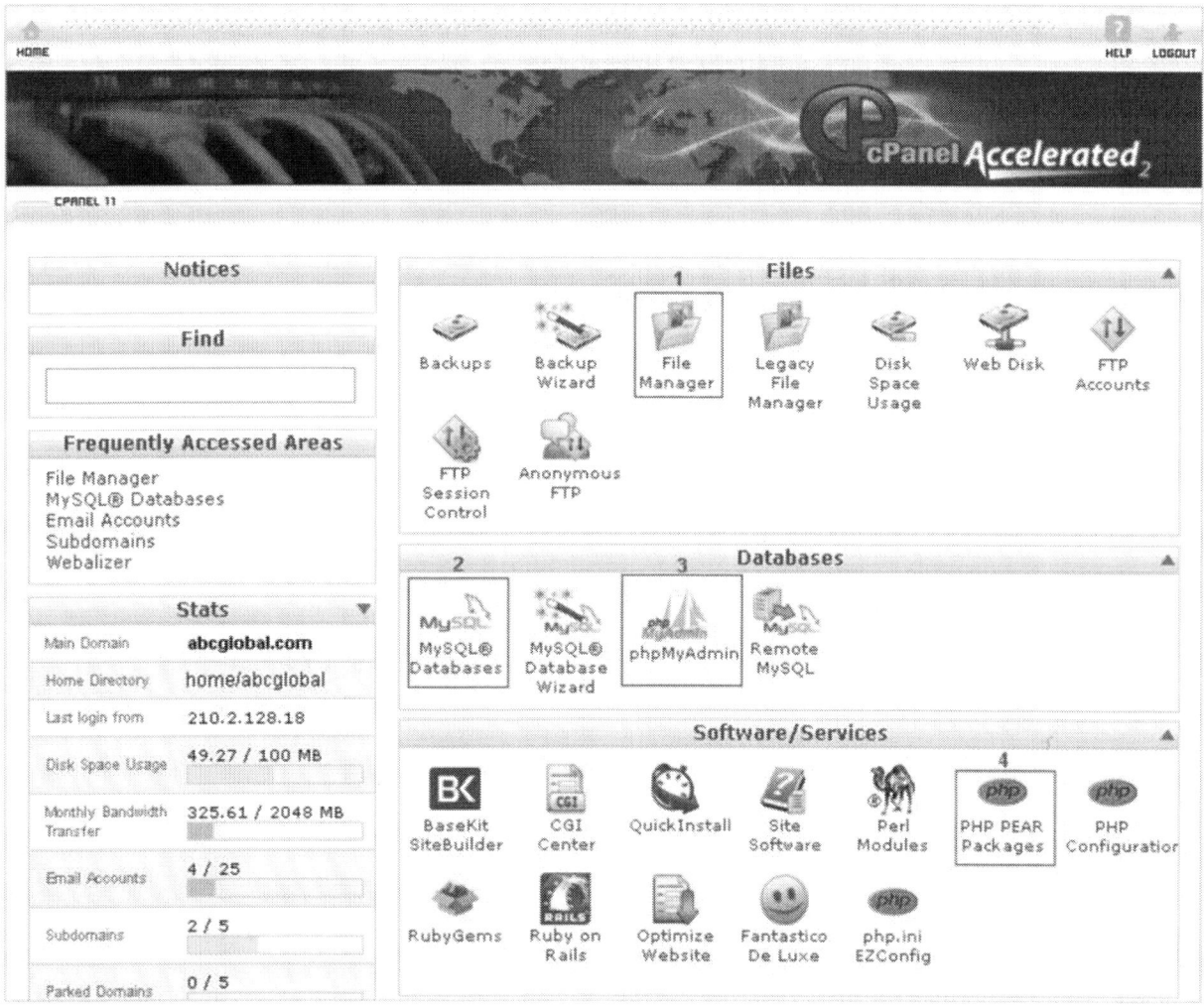

Figure 6-31

Check uploaded files from control panel

1. In the Files section click File Manager (marked as 1 in figure 6-31).
2. In Directory Selection, select *Document Root for* (fourth option), select *abcglobal.com* from the provided list and click *Go*. The File Manager page comes up with a list of files you uploaded in step 2. Some common functions that you can perform on this page are: Upload/Download files, rename a file or folder, and modify your code using the Edit button.

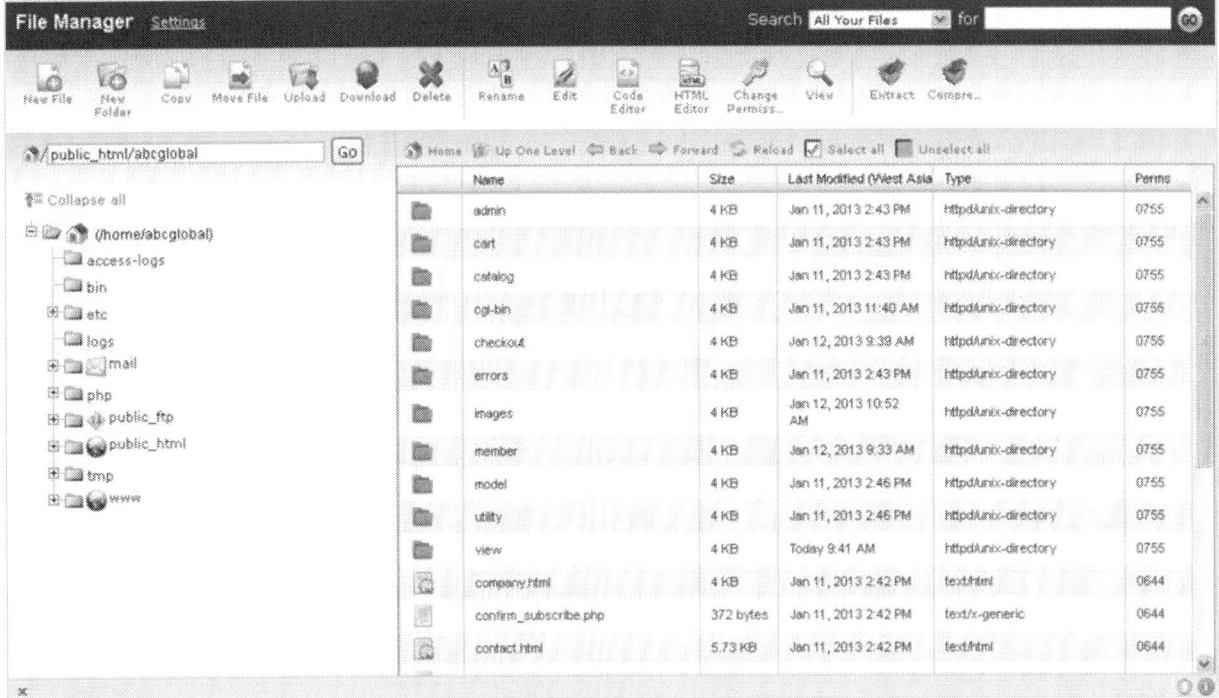

Figure 6-32

Step-4 Create Database & User

In this step you'll create a blank database and an internal database user who will be authorized to access and manipulate the database. Database access and manipulation consists of four actions: Select, Insert, Update, and Delete. These privileges will also be granted to the database user in this exercise.

1. On the cpanel home page click *MySQL Databases* utility (marked as 2). This will bring up the MySQL Database page.
2. In the New Database box type *db* and click the *Create Database* button. A confirmation page with the message *Added the Database abcglobal_db* appears.
3. Click the *Go Back* link.

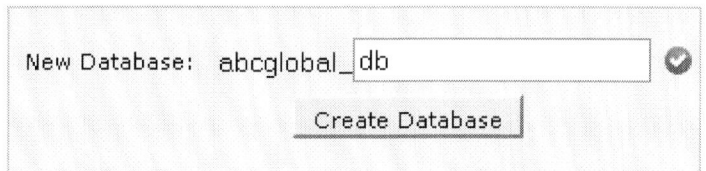

Figure 6-33

Many web hosting environments, including cPanel, use a database prefix (DB Prefixing) to designate which database resources belong to which account. cPanel uses the account name followed by an underscore. For example, if an account named 'myacct' were to create a database with the name 'somedb', the resulting database would actually be 'myacct_somedb.' Database users created and administered by the account would also have the prefix.

Add a new database user from the Add New Users section as illustrated below

1. In the Username box, type *admin*. Note that just like the database name; the user is also prefixed with the domain name.

2. To create a strong password for this user, click the *Password Generator* button which will return a password. Note down this password and keep it in a secure place.

3. Click the *Create User* button which will add a new user.

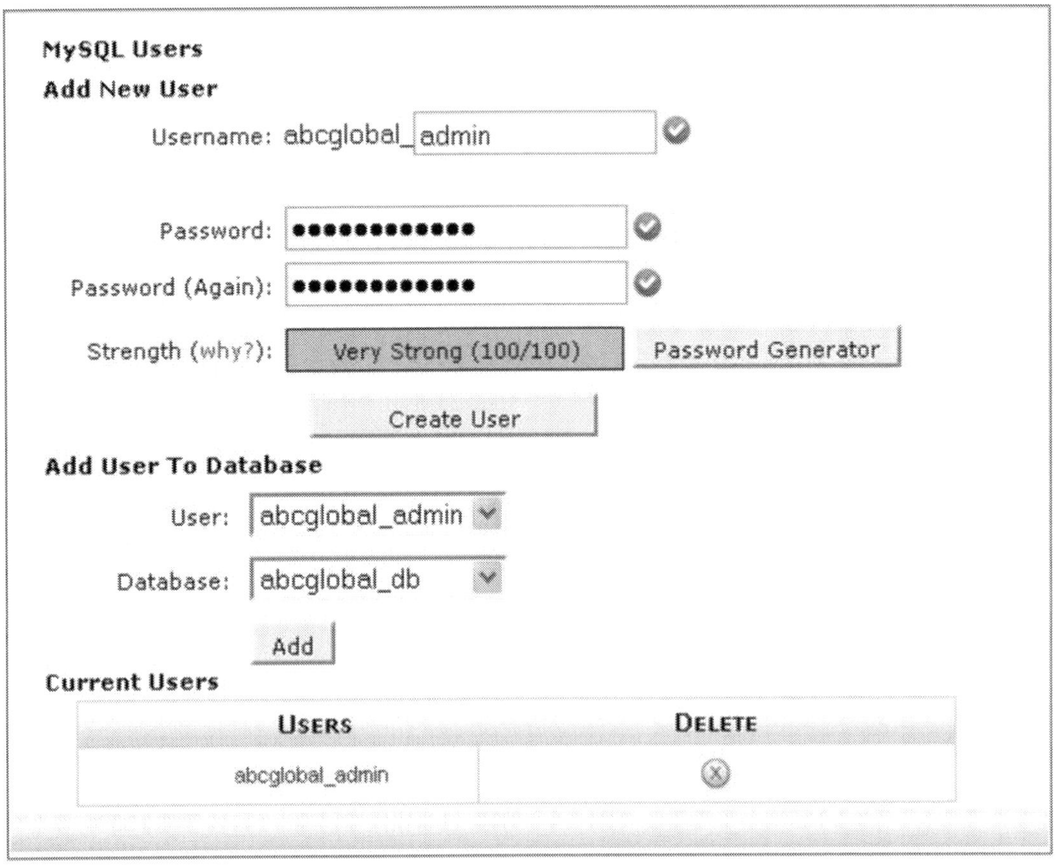

Figure 6-34

Note that while developing the website on your PC, you used the combination of root and gemini in your php files (such as db.php under the Model directory) to connect to the testdb database. To connect successfully in the hosting environment, that information needs to be updated with the current database name (abcglobal_db), username (abcglobal_admin), and password (provided by the Password Generator).

Grant database access privileges to the new user

1. Click the *Add* button under Add User To Database section in the above screen shot. MySQL Account Maintenance page comes up.
2. Click the *ALL PRIVILEGES* check box to grant all the listed rights to the new user and click the *Make Changes* button. A confirmation message *User "abcglobal_admin" was added to the database "abcglobal_db"* should appear. Click the *Go* Back link.

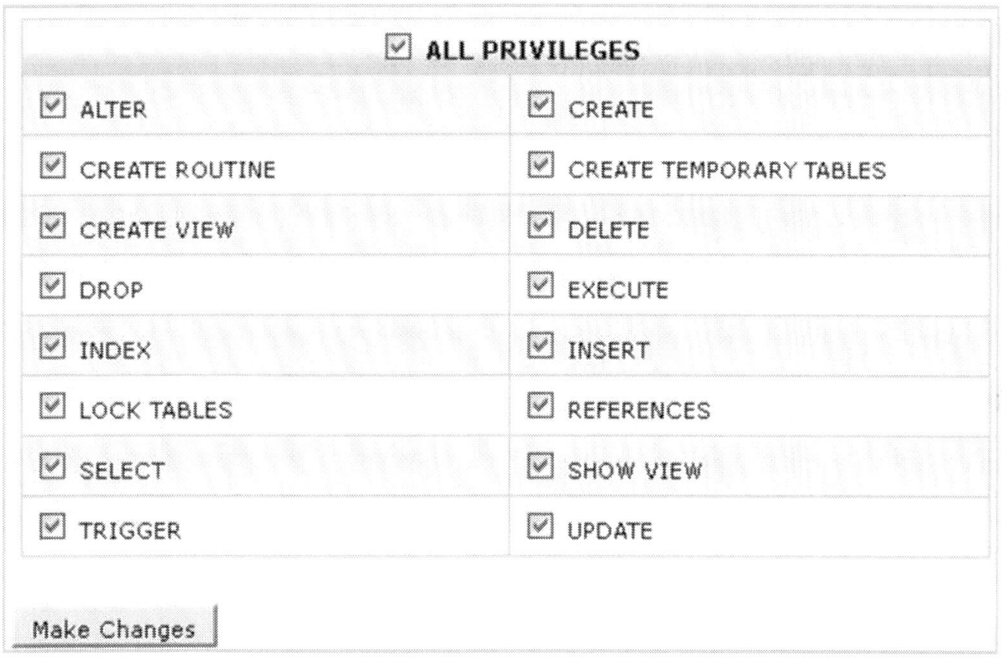

Figure 6-35

The above two steps would allow the new user to perform all operations on the abcglobal_db database tables that you are going to create next. The file db.php under the Model directory and subscribe.php file under the root folder provide authentication data (dbname, username, and password) to connect to the database. You need to alter those credentials with the information you defined here. For example, you need to replace dbname "testdb" with abcglobal_db, username "root" with abcglobal_admin, and password "gemini" with the newly generated password. Note that the user, you just created, would act as a super administrator of the site with all privileges. In the real world scenario, however, you have to create separate users with different rights. For example, a site member should not be allowed either to ALTER or DROP a database table, so, these two priviliges should be revoked from him.

Step-5 Create Database Tables

In step 4 you created a blank database with the name abcglobal_db. In this step you'll populate it with some tables along with dummy data through a script - abcDB.txt. The file abcDB.txt, provided with this book code, generates all the nine tables that you've been working with throughout this book. See section 6.7.4 - Database Structure for more details.

1. Click *phpMyAdmin* (point 3) on cpanel home page. This will call phpMyAdmin page.
2. Click the _db link being displayed in the left pane.
3. Click the Import tab - 📥 **Import**. Before clicking this tab, make sure the drop down list to your left is showing _db which is the database the script will run in. The next page will also confirm this with the text: Importing into the database "abcglobal_db".
4. Click the *Browse* button, select the file *abcDB.txt* from the source folder on your PC , and click the *Go* button appearing at the bottom of the page. A message "Import has been successfully finished, 16 queries executed. (abcDB.txt)" will appear with all nine files appearing in the left pane.

While developing the website, you were taught couple of MySQL tools (Command Line Utility and MySQL Workbench) to handle the testdb database. phpMyAdmin is a free and open source tool written in PHP intended to handle the administration of MySQL on your web host with the use of a Web browser. It can perform various tasks such as creating, modifying or deleting databases, tables, fields or rows; executing SQL statements; or managing users and permissions.

Step-6 Install PEAR Package

Recall that during the website development phase you downloaded and installed couple of PEAR packages that assisted in sending e-mails to subscribers and to the members who lost their passwords. See section 5.16 Send Mail from PHP for further details. In the hosted environment too, you need to install these two packages for the same purpose.

1. In cpanel home page, click *PHP PEAR Packages* (point 4) under Software/Services section. PHP Extensions and Applications Package Installer page comes up.
2. Type *PEAR* in the Search box and click the *Go* button. After a while the control panel returns with a list of modules. On top of this list is the PEAR Base System (PEAR x.x.x) that you need to install. Click the *Install* button next to it. Within a minute or two, you'll see a statistical page mentioning successful installation of the core package.
3. Return to the main PHP Extensions and Applications Package Installer page, type *Mail* in the search box and click *Go*. Once again the mail package you're looking for appears on top of the list. Click the *Install* button next to the mail module - Mail (x.x.x) Class that provides multiple interfaces for sending emails. As usual, the control panel will inform you about the installation status of this module.
4. After installation, the main page will have another section named *Installed PHP Extension(s) and Application(s)* that will show the two packages along with dependent modules similar to the one illustrated on the next page.

Installed PHP Extension(s) and Application(s)

MODULE NAME	VERSION	ACTIONS			
Archive_Tar	1.3.10	Update	Reinstall	Uninstall	Show Docs
Auth_SASL	1.0.6	Update	Reinstall	Uninstall	Show Docs
Console_Getopt	1.3.1	Update	Reinstall	Uninstall	Show Docs
Mail	1.2.0	Update	Reinstall	Uninstall	Show Docs
Net_SMTP	1.6.1	Update	Reinstall	Uninstall	Show Docs
Net_Socket	1.0.10	Update	Reinstall	Uninstall	Show Docs
PEAR	1.9.4	Update	Reinstall	Uninstall	Show Docs
Structures_Graph	1.0.4	Update	Reinstall	Uninstall	Show Docs
XML_Util	1.2.1	Update	Reinstall	Uninstall	Show Docs

Figure 6-36

Conclusion

After fitting in all the blocks at their proper locations, you should run this project on your hosting server to see how it works on the web. Refer to all the stuff provided in this book as you review this website project and explore new ways to improve it.

You have been introduced to the huge website development topic and taken to a position from where you can learn more about it on your own. This book served as a crucial starting point. The concepts covered herein provided invaluable information for your future projects. Specifically you learned about the various components that make up what we know as a tiered architecture model in that you have a client, the Web server, and a data store. You learned about the role client-side technologies such as HTML, CSS, and JavaScript play in the architecture model. You also saw how server-side technologies such as PHP and MySQL database fit into the model.

Aside from the theoretical material provided in this book, you also learned how to install and configure all the required software such as Microsoft's Web server IIS, PHP with its packages and MySQL database.

You also went through how to build static and dynamic web pages. Created a prototype on your development machine and were guided on how to deploy a website on a hosting server with all necessary base information.

While this book introduced what seems like a ton of concepts, terminology, and so on, it's merely a stepping stone to move you forward to explore the enormous world of web development.

Riaz Ahmed is an IT professional with over twenty years of hard-earned experience. He started his career as a programmer in early 90's and is currently working as the head of IT with a reputed group of companies. His areas of interest are web-based development technologies. Prior to this book, he wrote "Create Rapid Web Applications Using Oracle Application Express" (which is listed on Oracle Corporation's web site) and Implement Oracle Business Intelligence. You can reach him at:

E-mail: *realtech@cyber.net.pk*
Blog - The Web Book: *http://the-web-book.blogspot.com/*
Blog - Oracle APEX and BI: *http://Oracle-Tutorial-Books.blogspot.com*

Create Rapid Web Applications Using
Oracle Application Express – Second Edition

**A practical guide to rapidly develop
professional web & mobile applications**

Implement Oracle
Business Intelligence

**Analyze the Past
Streamline the Present
Control the Future**

http://www.amazon.com/Create-Applications-Oracle-Application-Express/dp/1492314188

http://www.amazon.com/Implement-Oracle-Business-Intelligence-Volume/dp/1475122012

Download Book Code → http://www.creating-website.com/TheWebBookCode.rar
URL → http://www.creating-website.com

D

F